Web Style Guide
4th edition

Web Style Guide

Foundations of User Experience Design

4th edition

Patrick J. Lynch
Sarah Horton

Foreword by Ethan Marcotte

Yale UNIVERSITY PRESS

New Haven & London

First edition 1999. Fourth edition 2016. Earlier editions were published as
Web Style Guide: Basic Design Principles for Creating Web Sites.

Yale University Press books may be purchased in quantity for educational, business,
or promotional use. For information, please e-mail sales.press@yale.edu (U.S.
office) or sales@yaleup.co.uk (U.K. office).

Interior designed by Sarah Horton.
Illustrations by Patrick J. Lynch.
Set in Goudy and Myriad type by Sarah Horton.
Printed in China through World Print Ltd.

Library of Congress Control Number: 2015952373
ISBN 978-0-300-21165-8 (paper : alk. paper)
A catalogue record for this book is available from the British Library.

This paper meets the requirements of ANSI/NISO Z39.48-1992 (Permanence of
Paper).

10 9 8 7 6 5 4 3 2 1

For Susan, Alex, Devorah, and Tyler
PL

For my son (sun), Nico
SH

Contents

Foreword

My favorite high school English teacher had this little ritual: in the early days of autumn, at the start of each of his classes, he'd lean against the chalkboard at the front of the room, his chalk-covered hands stuffed in his pockets. And as he stood there, he'd start telling a story about the syllabus before us—the authors whose works we'd be reading throughout the year, the themes we'd explore, the discussions we'd have.

Toward the end of the introduction, he'd remind us that while we'd be spending an entire year together, one class wasn't quite enough time to explore a topic *fully*. Instead, he'd say, "this course is like a tour through a foreign country. We'll spend the next few months exploring this new territory, and discussing some wonderful books together. Like all tours, however, we'll only have a little time together…but if I've done my job right, I'll have shown you just enough sights so that when you're ready, you'll come back. And you'll have seen enough landmarks so that you can find your own way, and perhaps explore a bit further."

Now I'll tell you a little secret: this isn't a book you're reading. It's a map.

The web is a sprawling, strange place, filled with disciplines and languages aplenty. And truthfully, it can be a daunting place to explore. But thankfully, you hold a copy of *Web Style Guide*. Drawn up by Patrick Lynch and Sarah Horton—two talented educators and writers, yes, but also *cartographers*—this is a chart of the web's borders. Patrick and Sarah understand the intricacies of page layout, how to scope a design project, the fundamentals of web typography, and so much more.

Whether you're a new traveler or a well-seasoned one, *Web Style Guide* will provide you with a path through your next project, and introduce you to ideas, concepts, and landmarks you'll want to revisit.

So let's start exploring.

—Ethan Marcotte

Discipline is remembering what you want.
– David Campbell

Preface

Ser experience is an overarching consideration that involves a wide range of activities by anyone who makes decisions and takes actions that affect how people experience a web site. Every person on the web development team has a role to play. On many sites, users are active contributors, which means that they also influence whether a web site offers an enjoyable and accessible user experience. And providing a good user experience is a critical factor in the success of any enterprise. Nothing is better for building a loyal following than providing a good experience, where people are successful in accessing and using content and features that they value.

When we posted the first version of *Web Style Guide* on the web in 1993, "user experience" wasn't a thing. The web offered only rudimentary design options and basic interaction through hyperlinks. Our guidance focused on basic best practices within the constrained available options: how to title a page to support scanning in a list of bookmarks, how to structure text to accommodate the reading habits of online readers. Over time and with subsequent editions, we were able to offer guidance on more attributes, such as page design and graphic design, as web technologies became more powerful and robust. Our early editions focused on the craft of web design, teaching how to use the available tools and materials to best effect. These editions had lots of code examples and coverage of technical concerns, like image and video compression algorithms, because building a web site meant knowing how to trick a rudimentary hypertext markup language into performing feats of graphic design, and how to deliver data-intensive images and media to people on slow modems. There was much more science than art in the early web.

Things have changed, and so has *Web Style Guide*. Now, more than twenty years later, the technology platform is more mature. Users are more demanding—less willing to compromise—and they expect to encounter accessible and usable sites. Organizations are realizing the importance of design and are adopting a more strategic approach to designing and delivering quality experiences.

This fourth edition of *Web Style Guide* reflects a more serious and mature environment—one focused on users, not technology. It has fewer code samples. Knowledge of HTML and CSS is no longer required to be an effective web professional (although knowing what's happening under the hood remains a distinct advantage). A new strategy chapter acknowledges that good user experience and effective de-

sign require vision and understanding. The next chapter, on research, demonstrates that understanding cannot happen in a team meeting room, on a whiteboard, but requires engagement with people—in all their diversity—who will use the site. And throughout the book there is a strong emphasis on quality content and interaction for meeting users' needs and preferences. Previous editions bore the subtitle *Basic Design Principles for Creating Web Sites*. The fourth edition subtitle is *Foundations of User Experience Design*.

With a shift in focus to user experience design, we mapped our chapters to the five planes of user experience described by Jesse James Garret in his book *The Elements of User Experience*. His classic diagram (which you can find at wsg4.link/ ux-elements) is both an exposition of the dimensions of user experience design and a road map for user experience in the design and development process.

The process of mapping the long-standing and new chapters of *Web Style Guide* was revealing. We have over time given more attention to providing guidance for activities at the base of the framework—the strategy and scope planes. Good user experiences require clear purpose and a close understanding of user needs and prefer-

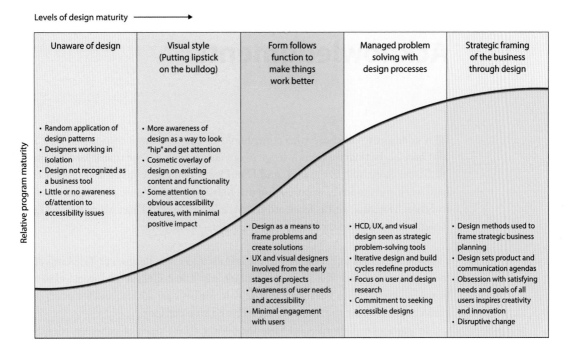

Levels of design maturity ⟶

Unaware of design	Visual style (Putting lipstick on the bulldog)	Form follows function to make things work better	Managed problem solving with design processes	Strategic framing of the business through design
• Random application of design patterns • Designers working in isolation • Design not recognized as a business tool • Little or no awareness of/attention to accessibility issues	• More awareness of design as a way to look "hip" and get attention • Cosmetic overlay of design on existing content and functionality • Some attention to obvious accessibility features, with minimal positive impact	• Design as a means to frame problems and create solutions • UX and visual designers involved from the early stages of projects • Awareness of user needs and accessibility • Minimal engagement with users	• HCD, UX, and visual design seen as strategic problem-solving tools • Iterative design and build cycles redefine products • Focus on user and design research • Commitment to seeking accessible designs	• Design methods used to frame strategic business planning • Design sets product and communication agendas • Obsession with satisfying needs and goals of all users inspires creativity and innovation • Disruptive change

Relative program maturity (y-axis label)

ences, and successful projects require planning. And we have added a new and critically important plane, which we call Substance. The Substance plane is at the top of the framework, and includes text, images, and video. The past years have seen a growing understanding that "content is king," and no amount of eye candy or fancy widgets can have more impact than content that appeals to users.

Another refreshing change we've seen since we began the *Web Style Guide* project twenty-three years ago is the broad, deep recognition of the value of design of all kinds: user experience design, interface design, content design, and visual communications design. Today business thought leaders like Apple, Google, Amazon, Facebook, and Adobe are not just technology leaders—in each instance what people admire most in these companies is superb design. In function, in the user experiences they create, and in the look and feel of their products and services, design is a critical strategic process integrated into every level of the business. We've seen the best enterprises steadily climb the design maturity curve, and derive tremendous business value as a result. Designing for people, in all their diversity, has become recognized as a distinct advantage. A company that holds accessible user experience design as a core value, supported by a user-centered practice of design, reaps the benefits of successful, satisfied, and loyal customers.

FIGURE 2
Recognition of the strategic value of design and a thorough integration of design, user experience, and universal usability are hallmarks of enterprise maturity.

Acknowledgments

In addition to all those who contributed to the first three editions of *Web Style Guide* and whom we acknowledge in our earlier prefaces, we thank Jean Thomson Black, Samantha Ostrowski, and Dan Heaton at Yale University Press for their hard work and guidance in producing this fourth edition. We are particularly grateful to Ethan Marcotte for his foreword to this edition, and to Peter Morville and Louis Rosenfeld for their forewords to earlier editions of the guide.

I EXTEND HEARTFELT THANKS to my friends and my colleagues at Yale University for their counsel over the years, particularly my Yale colleague and world-class web front-end engineer and designer Victor Velt, for his wise advice, and for many great conversations about the future of the web and web content.

In particular, I thank Carl Jaffe for almost thirty years of generous friendship and wise counsel since our work together at Yale Center for Advanced Instructional Media. Much of Carl's wisdom and insight appears on these pages. I also thank my coauthor and dear friend Sarah Horton for her enduring commitment to this enterprise, and for her efforts in making the web more accessible to everyone.

Without family, none of this would have meaning. For her unfailing love, support, and generosity of spirit, I thank the wisest woman I know, Susan Grajek. For their love, support, and no small amount of advice now that they know much of coding and the Interwebs better than I do: Devorah Lynch, Alex Wack, and Tyler Wack.

—PL

WITH THIS FOURTH EDITION of *Web Style Guide* I have a lot to celebrate and be grateful for.

I celebrate more than twenty years of partnership with my dear friend and coauthor, Pat Lynch. Our collaboration and friendship began in 1991, when he took me under his wing and taught me so much, about Photoshop and design, scripting and interaction, friendship and collaboration, music and life. Pat is the most talented and multidimensional person I know, and he has a huge heart. Fate looked kindly on me when she put me in Pat's way.

I also celebrate more than twenty years working in higher education, at Yale, Dartmouth, and Harvard. There is no better place to learn and grow, and I am grateful to my mentors and friends who have guided me along the way. Since the previous edition I spent time at Harvard as web strategy project lead, and in that position I learned a great deal about how to advance a user experience strategy in a decentralized and largely autonomous organization. I am grateful to Perry Hewitt and everyone at HPAC, HUIT, and HWP (Harvard-speak for Harvard Public Affairs and Communications, Harvard University Information Technology, and Harvard Web Publishing) for support, encouragement, and opportunities to grow.

In 2014 I left higher ed to join The Paciello Group, helping to build a user experience practice focused on accessibility. I am immeasurably grateful to my UX colleagues, David Sloan and Henny Swan, who are right beside me, cutting a path toward accessible user experience. Their insights are woven into mine so completely that their words are echoed throughout these pages, along with those of the team of accessibility experts who fill my head each day with new knowledge: Mat Atkinson, Ashley Bischoff, Graeme Coleman, Steve Faulkner, Bill Gregory, Karl Groves, Hans Hillen, Patrick Lauke, Gez Lemon, Mark Novak, Ian Pouncey, Cédric Trévisan, and Léonie Watson. I am grateful to TPG leadership, Mike Paciello, Charlie Pike, and Deb Rapsis, for having the vision to pursue user experience as a path toward ensuring that everyone can participate online.

I am grateful to Malcolm Brown for his support, wise counsel, and creative problem solving.

I am grateful to my mother and father, and my large and wondrous family, who wait patiently while I chase deadlines.

Nico is, as ever, my son (sun), and I follow him like a flower. He grew up alongside *Web Style Guide* and is its biggest fan. I am grateful for his commitment to this enterprise and his support and patience all these years, even when writing kept me from playing.

The writing's done. Let's play!

—SH

Web Style Guide
4th edition

Simple clear purpose and principles give rise to intelligent behavior.
Complex rules give rise to simple stupid behavior.
– Dee Hock

To live outside the law, you must be honest.
– Bob Dylan

CHAPTER 1

Strategy

<p style="margin-left:auto; width:25%;">

We use the word "strategy" so widely and casually that it is worthwhile to step back and ask what exactly having a strategy for your web site project means, and why having one is so important.

Strategy is the art of sensible planning to marshal your resources toward their most efficient and effective use, over a significant period of time. A good strategy is flexible, and shows proper humility in the face of challenges. It does not pretend that miracles are possible or even desirable. It favors step-by-step progress toward your goals. A serious strategy does not depend on a lone "strategic thinker." It acknowledges the major roles that chance and culture play in determining success. Great strategies are born from the efforts of small cohesive groups of people who are willing to be adaptive while never losing sight their primary goal.

A strategic approach takes time and effort, and the benefits are not immediately evident. Project success indicators, such as increased sales and subscriptions and happy customers, do not always map directly to elements found in a project strategy. The return on investment for project strategy becomes clear over time, through a well-executed project that produces a successful product, and is further evidenced by an ongoing attention and care to sustain that project and produce success over time.

You keep using that word, I do not think it means what you think it means.

—Inigo Montoya, The Princess Bride

STRATEGIC PLANNING

Strategic planning is not a bag of tips, tricks, or special techniques. It's not about predicting the future—we create strategies precisely because we can't predict the future. Strategic planning is not a way to eliminate risk. At best, strategy is an attempt to identify and take the right risks at the right times.

CREATING A STRATEGIC PLAN

In his book *Good Strategy/Bad Strategy* management expert Richard Rumelt lays out a three-step process for creating a coherent strategy:

- Diagnose your situation
- Create guiding principles
- Design a set of coherent actions

FIGURE 1.1
Strategy is a cyclical
process that doesn't
end with the launch
of the site. Well-
maintained and
useful web sites
reflect a continuing
process of analysis,
refinement, and
rebuilding.

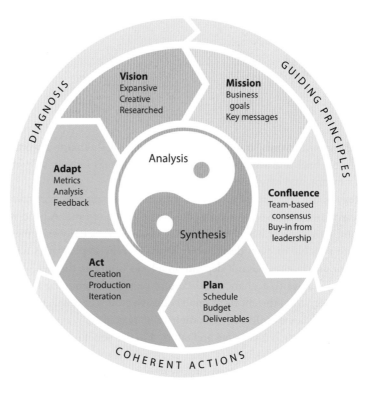

Diagnose your situation

Identify your business goals, and let go of past practices and commitments. Strategy always starts with a vision of how to reach your business goals, and asks, "What do we have to do now to attain our objectives tomorrow?" Strategy starts with the facts as you establish them through research, diagnose the top few problems and needs to address immediately, and then form an overall plan of action.

- **Be forward-looking:** Strategy is inherently about the future. Don't let planning discussions get bogged down in history and decisions that were made in the past. Keep the discussion focused on the future, defining what resources and tactics you will need to attain your goals.
- **Stay focused on priorities:** A good strategy doesn't just create new things. It actively plans for decommissioning the old and outmoded, and pares away mediocre ideas and marginal priorities. If you can't firmly articulate what business problem or user need your project will address, you can't create a coherent strategy. Prioritizing is essential here, so don't try to "boil the ocean" with an ambitious list of problems and needs. Your project can't solve every known problem or user request. Prioritizing is hard. Too many projects fail

because participants could not face the process of throwing out ten good ideas to focus on the top three or four great ideas or problems to solve.

Create guiding principles

Make every decision align with your road map. Every project plan is basically an answer to a series of questions: What do we need to do and when do we need to do it to step closer to our goals? There are no "short-term tactics." Every decision and tactical work action today is a strategic move. Successful long-term projects are always built one strategic decision at a time, incrementally and iteratively moving the team forward toward purposeful work in support of business goals.

Design coherent actions

Consider your strategy a portfolio of options. Nobody has a crystal ball, so rationality demands flexibility. Insisting that business goals and deliverables must not change during a project is as absurd as insisting that we can perfectly predict the future. A good strategy is not a predetermined set of choices. It is a set of options that do not limit your tactical flexibility to respond to changing conditions. These options are often generated in advance by working through scenarios for how your project will respond to particular challenges that might arise and potentially change the budget, schedule, or deliverables of the project.

The truest test of any plan is whether it results in useful work on the correct tasks. Your strategy will succeed if it is rational, flexible and based on solid data and research, and if it takes advantage of the working knowledge of the team. But knowledge and a solid plan are not the goals—the successful product is the goal, and only smart work well executed with get you there.

SHAPING THE STRATEGIC PLAN

All too often, strategic planning activities never get any farther than a high-level vision statement. To put a plan into action, you first need to identify the people involved and their roles, then create a map to follow, through these processes:

- Define roles and responsibilities with project governance
- Adopt a user-centered approach
- Draw a strategic road map with a project charter

Define roles and responsibilities with project governance

Structure your team for a successful outcome. Most projects require collaboration within a project team and across the organization. You must clearly define goals from the start, and each person involved in the project must understand where she has authority to make decisions, and her accountability for the decisions she makes.

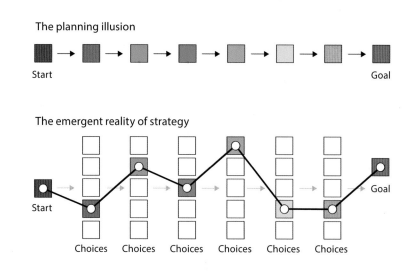

The planning illusion

Start   Goal

The emergent reality of strategy

Start   Goal

Choices   Choices   Choices   Choices   Choices   Choices

Participants must also understand their responsibilities with respect to project activities. Additionally, they must understand roles and responsibilities of everyone on the project team, as well as those of the project sponsors. We can't stress enough the importance of clearly defined project governance. Without it, projects can get bogged down, with team members working at cross-purposes, on activities that run counter to expectations from leadership.

To determine which governance model best suits your project, determine who has authority, responsibility, and accountability for different aspects of the project. Some aspects may involve multiple people; always identify one person who has primary responsibility. Some possible questions include:

- Who has the authority to initiate the project?
- Who has the authority to approve the design?
- Who is responsible for defining strategic direction for the project?
- Who is responsible for specifying the technology architecture?
- Who is responsible for assuring that the project is executed according to schedule?
- Who is responsible for the quality of the content?
- Who is responsible for coordinating site content?
- Who is responsible for creating content?
- Who is responsible for the day-to-day maintenance?
- Who is accountable if the project fails to meet stakeholder needs?
- Who is accountable if the project does not meet quality standards?
- Who is accountable for errors and misinformation?

EVIDENCE OF CLEAR PRIORITIES (OR LACK THEREOF)

Often you can see an organization's confusion about priorities simply by glancing at its home page or its product line.

When Steve Jobs returned to Apple in 1997, Apple was selling sixteen to eighteen models of Macintosh computer. Jobs told an interviewer that even he couldn't give clear advice to a friend on which Mac model she should buy for her home. Jobs's first major strategic project was to cut the number of Macintosh models to four: two desktop computers and two laptops. Today the Macintosh product line still reflects this strategic focus on real user needs and a meaningful differentiation of products, and Apple is now the world's most valuable company.

In contrast, designers of the National Oceanic and Atmospheric Administration's site seem to throw everything they can think of at their home page, and the resulting clutter and confusion reflects poorly on the excellent work that NOAA does in researching and monitoring the natural environment.

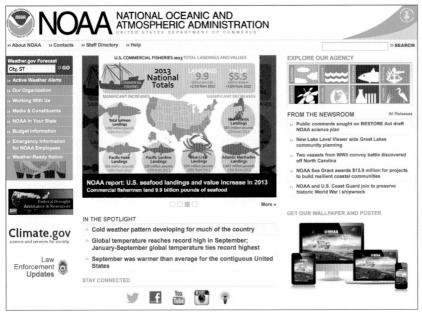

FIGURE 1.3 The National Oceanic and Atmospheric Administration (NOAA) does vital work in researching and analyzing the earth's environment, but by throwing as many topics as possible onto its home page, it fails to communicate those fine efforts effectively.

Answers to questions such as these will help define who has decision-making roles, such as project sponsor, project lead, and product owner. The answers will clarify who is in development and production roles, such as technology lead and content editor. We cover these roles in more detail in Chapter 3, Process. The key in the strategic planning phase is to construct a solid governance model, and communicate roles and responsibilities to everyone who has a hand in the success of the project. Lisa Welchman's book *Managing Chaos* is an excellent primer on strategy and governance in web and information technology.

Adopt a user-centered approach

Focus on user needs and perspectives. Web sites are developed by groups of people to meet the needs of other groups of people. Unfortunately, web projects are often approached as "technology problems," and projects can get colored from the beginning by enthusiasms for particular web techniques (particular content management systems, responsive or adaptive designs, mobile-first design, web layout frameworks) rather than by human or business needs that emerge from engaging users in the development process. People are the key to successful web projects at every stage of development. Although the people who will visit and use your site will determine whether your project is a success, those users are the people least likely to be present and involved when your site is being designed and built. Remember that the site development team should always function as an active, committed advocate for the users and their needs.

Experienced committee warriors may be skeptical here: These are fine sentiments, but can you really do this in the face of management pressures, budget limitations, and divergent stakeholder interests? Well, yes, you can—because you have no other choice if your web project is to succeed. If you listen only to management directives, keep the process sealed tightly within your development team, and dictate to supposed users what the team imagines is best for them, be prepared for failure. Involve real users, listen and respond to what they say, test your designs with a spectrum of users of different ages, abilities, and interests, and be prepared to see your cherished ideas change and evolve in response to user feedback.

Draw a strategic road map with a project charter

Establish a common understanding of the path to desired outcomes. Successful projects begin with a high-level, shared understanding of goals and intent. The most critical requirement of this initial planning activity is to ensure all project participants are on the same page and working toward the same goals. A project charter document provides a conceptual framework and serves as a basis for decision making throughout the project life cycle. It consists of a project definition and high-level strategies for achieving project goals.

A project charter includes the following sections:

- **Purpose:** What purpose does the product serve?
- **Goals:** What outcomes does it need to achieve?
- **Target audience:** Whom must the product appeal to and work for?
- **Success indicators:** How will you know you have achieved project goals?
- **Strategies:** What approaches will help to realize the goals?
- **Tactics:** What activities might help to realize the strategies?

One of the best ways to ascertain the goals and objectives for a project is to envision what changes will occur if the project is successful. We often begin projects with a brainstorming exercise around indicators of success, asking the question "What changes will there be in the world if this project is successful?" The key in the exercise is not to get bogged down with questions like "Is that success indicator really measurable?" or "Can we really ascribe that change to this project?" By allowing free-flowing ideation and imagining you might come up with indicators like, for example, "happy customers" for a retail web site, or "better learning" for an open educational resource, or "healthier kids" for a game about children's health. Stay with those, even though they are difficult to measure and correlate, because they tell you a great deal about purpose, objectives, and target audience.

The strategies and tactics section is where you begin to map out how you will go about realizing the project. A strategy is a general approach you might take to help you reach your goals. Each strategy has associated possible tactics—specific activities to support the strategy. The proposed tactics are tangible ideas for how you might implement content and functionality on your web site. For example, to produce the result of happy customers on a retail web site, one strategy should be to provide a user experience that is accessible and enjoyable for all visitors. Tactics for supporting that strategy would include following conventions for design and interaction, providing clear and consistent navigation, and testing usability with a wide range of users, including people with disabilities and older adults.

Share early drafts of the charter document with project stakeholders and the project team and invite changes and comments. Allow several editing cycles and be receptive about incorporating changes, remembering the importance of acceptance and support of the overall approach. Stay true to the format of the charter—make sure proposed tactics always support a strategy, which in turn serves a goal and supports the overall purpose.

Finalize the project charter before moving to the next phase of the project, with the understanding that the charter is a living document that may change over the project life cycle.

A SAMPLE PROJECT CHARTER

The project charter is a concise statement of goals, values, and intent, and it drives the direction for everything that comes after. When you're up to your neck in the daily challenges of building a site, it can be easy to forget why you are doing what you are doing and to lose sight of your original priorities, not knowing whether the decisions you are making firmly support the overall objectives. A well-written project charter is a powerful daily tool for judging the effectiveness of a development effort. It becomes a compass to keep the team firmly pointed at the goals established when you started the journey. A good project charter becomes a daily reference point for settling disputes, avoiding "scope creep," judging the potential utility of new ideas as they arise, measuring progress, and keeping the development team focused on the end result. At the conclusion of a project, revisiting the charter can serve as confirmation that the design decisions made along the way were guided by strategy, and that the development team successfully met the project objectives.

Here we present the project definition portion of a project charter for a fictional app called Walk with Me, created by an outdoors equipment retailer that we will call Get Outdoors Equipment, or GOE. The app uses geolocation to track the route you are walking and collect photos and video, tagged with location details. The editor allows you to compile the route, media, and descriptive details into a trail guide to share with other Walk with Me users.

The **purpose** of the app is to create and share maps of favorite walks.

Get Outdoors Equipment provides the app for free. GOE is a retail company, but part of its core mission is to encourage outdoor activities for the purpose of promoting health and well-being. The company sees these activities as interdependent—a healthy customer base is more likely to purchase goods, and providing high-quality, affordable goods results in active and engaged customers.

GOE's **goals and objectives** in creating Walk with Me are to:

- Sell outdoors equipment
- Create a community of people who value walking and nature
- Increase awareness of walks
- Add to general knowledge of available walks
- Get people outside and walking

GEO has a loyal customer base. That said, there are other outdoors equipment retailers that have strong offerings, and GEO must continually raise its efforts to keep its customers from changing brands. GEO knows that current customers are key to their continued success, since loyal customers repurchase and recommend—two key loyalty behaviors.

The **target audience** for Walk with Me is, in priority order:

- Current GEO customers
- Prospective GEO customers
- Walking and nature enthusiasts—who may become future customers

Measuring the success of the app is relatively straightforward, through downloads, account sign-ups, and contributions to the knowledge base. Indirect support makes it difficult to directly correlate the app with increased sales. However, it's still worth monitoring, and certainly any direct links from the app to retail features should be closely tracked.

GEO can measure and monitor the following to use as **indicators of success** for the Walk with Me app:

- Downloads of the Walk with Me app
- Sign-ups for Walk with Me accounts
- Contributions to the Walk with Me knowledge base
- Sales, particularly for outdoors equipment related to walking

The next step is to build from the project definition strategies and tactics to support the project. For example, to support the goal of selling outdoors equipment, one strategy might be to provide an integrated experience between the Walk with Me app and the GEO retail web site. Tactics would include ensuring that the GEO retail web site experience is exceptional, then adding explicit links between the app and the web site.

ACCESSIBLE USER EXPERIENCE

User experience, or ᴜx, is a lens through which to view the whole range of site production tasks, from the earliest strategic planning and research to finished graphics. User experience incorporates all these things (at least in part), but the term really centers around core questions like How easy is a site to use? How memorable (even delightful) is a site? Is the site efficient? Most of all, did I get what I came to find? In short, the quality of user experience is measured by how usable and enjoyable a site is for people to use.

Core attributes of good ᴜx include:

- **Learnability:** How quickly can first-time users learn what they need to know to find the information, services, or products they need from your site?
- **Ease of orientation:** Can users confidently and correctly judge their locations within your site's navigation system?
- **Efficiency:** How quickly can users perform their browsing, searching, or other interactions to complete their tasks?
- **Memorability:** Can a user who has not visited for a long time quickly reestablish proficiency?
- **Accessibility:** Can users with physical or sensory challenges use the majority of your site's content or services efficiently?
- **Error forgiveness:** Is your site forgiving of common user errors, and how often do users make errors in using your site?
- **Delight:** Do users typically enjoy using your site, or is it a chore?

The core user experience concepts of learnability, orientation, efficiency, and accessibility should influence every stage of site development, from the earliest concept sketches to site maintenance and continuous improvement.

Cultural context changes constantly: today there are few Internet "newbies" beyond preschool age, and there are now millions of adults who can't remember a world before the web. Even in an age where smartphones, tablets, ultraportable laptops, and even smart watches and other digital "wearables" have vastly expanded the reach and use cases for web-based information, there is a timelessness about web user experience challenges. The range of devices we use to access the web has exploded, but neither the human nervous system nor the fundamental paradigms of browsing the web have changed that much in twenty-five years, and even lifelong users of the web will face challenges if your site is not well designed.

Today responding to the usability challenges of the web is more important than ever. Twenty years ago the web was a fascinating new toy, growing in usefulness, but mostly peripheral to our everyday life experiences. Ten years ago the web was optional: you might drop your newspaper subscription in favor of news sites, or shop on Amazon rather than do a tedious run to the shopping mall. Today the web is vital in everyday life: you may not be able to get health insurance, stay in contact with distant children, find medicines at an affordable price, or find your way home from an unfamiliar town without using the web.

Usability is a measure of quality and effectiveness. It describes how well tools and information sources help us accomplish tasks. The more usable the tool, the better able we are to achieve our goals. Many tools help us overcome physical limitations by making us stronger, faster, and more sharp-sighted. But tools can be frustrating or even disabling. When we encounter a tool that we cannot work with, either because it is poorly designed or because its design does not take into account our needs, we are limited in what we can accomplish.

In designing web sites our job is to reduce functional limitations through design. When we aim for universal usability, we improve the quality of life for more people more of the time. On the web, we can work toward universal usability by adopting a universal design approach to usability.

Human-computer interaction (HCI) pioneer Ben Shneiderman defines universal usability as "having more than 90% of all households as successful users of information and communications services at least once a week." Note that Shneiderman is not just calling for any use of technology but is specifying successful use. He goes on to explain that, to achieve universal usability, designers need to "support a wide range of technologies, to accommodate diverse users, and to help users bridge the gap between what they know and what they need to know."

Accessible user experience is informed by several initiatives, primarily accessibility, usability, and universal design.

Web accessibility Since the World Wide Web Consortium established the Web Accessibility Initiative in 1999, the imperative of web accessibility has gained the attention of individuals, organizations, and governments worldwide. WAI promotes best practices and tools that make the web accessible to people with disabilities. They also safeguard universal web access by providing expert input for development initiatives to ensure that accessible designs can be accomplished using current and future web technologies.

Web accessibility is a critical element of universal usability. The guidelines produced by WAI and other accessibility initiatives provide us with techniques and specifications for how to create universally usable designs. They ensure that designers have the tools and technologies needed to create designs that work in different contexts. They provide a framework for evaluating digital products for accessibility, and identifying potential barriers.

Usability and user-centered design Usability is both a qualitative measure of the experience of using a tool and a phenomenon that can be quantified as a concrete means to judge a design's effectiveness. Quantitative usability metrics include how quickly we complete tasks and how many errors we make in the process. But usability can also be gauged by qualitative measures, such as how much satisfaction we derive in using a tool. "Learnability" is another important measure: how quickly we learn to use a tool and how well we remember how to use it the next time. Usability has an impact not only on our effectiveness but also on more fundamental qualities, such as loyalty. The more usable the tool, the better we feel about using it and, in the case of web sites, the more likely it is that we will return to the site.

The most common method for achieving usability is user-centered design (UCD). UCD includes user-oriented tools such as task analysis, focus groups, and usability testing to understand user needs and refine designs based on user feedback. UCD involves determining what functionality users want in a product and how they will use it. Through iterative cycles of design, testing, and refinement, UCD practitioners continuously check in to make sure they are on track—that users like the design and will be successful using it.

Universal usability arises from user-centered design, but with a broad and inclusive view of the user. UCD is applied to the task of designing web sites that are easy to learn and use by a diversity of users, platforms, and usage contexts.

Universal design Universal design incorporates access requirements into a design, rather than providing alternate designs to meet specific needs, such as large print or Braille editions for vision-impaired readers. A common example of universal design in the built environment is the ramped entryway, which can be used by everyone and eliminates the need for a separate accessible entrance. Universal design has many benefits. A single design that meets broad needs is often less costly than multiple designs. And designs that anticipate a diverse user population often have unanticipated benefits. For example, curb cuts in sidewalks are intended to help mobility- and vision-impaired users, but many others benefit, including people making deliveries, pushing a stroller, or riding a bike.

CREATING ACCESSIBLE UX STRATEGY

The first step toward the goal of universal usability is to discard the notion that we are designing for a "typical" user. Universal usability accounts for users of all ages, experience levels, and physical or sensory limitations. Users also vary widely in their technical circumstances: in screen size, network speed, browser versions, and specialized software, such as screen readers for the visually impaired. Each of us inhabits multiple points on the spectrum, points that are constantly shifting as our needs and contexts change. For example, virtually all adults over fifty have some form of mild to moderate visual impairment. And within that context our needs change as we move from viewing web pages from the back of an auditorium to sitting in front of a large desktop display monitor to walking down the street peering at a small mobile display. A broad user definition that includes the full range of user needs and contexts is the first step in producing universally usable designs.

Next we need a design approach that will accommodate the diversity of our user base, and here we turn to the principle of adaptation. On the web, universal usability is achieved through adaptive design, where documents transform to accommodate different user needs and contexts. Adaptive design is the means by which we support a wide range of technologies and diverse users. The following guidelines support adaptation.

Flexibility Universal usability is difficult to achieve in a physical environment, where certain parameters are necessarily "locked in." It would be difficult to make a book, and a chair to read it in, that fit the needs and preferences of every reader. The digital environment is another story. Digital documents can adapt to different access devices and user needs based on the requirements of the context.

A web page contains text, with pointers to other types of documents, such as images and video. Software reads the page and acts on it by, for example, displaying the page visually in the browser. But because of the nature of the web, the same page can be accessed on a smartphone, using a screen reader, or printed on paper. The success of this adaptation depends on whether the design supports flexibility. Pages designed exclusively for large displays will not display well on the small screens of cell phones.

The web environment is flexible, with source documents that adapt to different contexts. When considering universal usability, we need to anticipate diversity and build flexible pages that adapt gracefully to a wide variety of displays and user needs.

User control In many design fields, designers make choices that give shape to a thing, and these choices, particularly in a fixed environment, are bound to exclude some users. No one text size will be readable by all readers, but the book designer must make a decision about what size to set text, and that decision is likely to produce text that is too small for some readers. In the web environment, users have control over their environment. For example, users can manipulate browser settings to display text at a size that they find comfortable for reading.

Flexibility paired with user control allows users to shape their web experience into a form that works within their use context.

Keyboard functionality Universal usability is not just about access to information. Another crucial component is interaction, which allows users to navigate and interact with links, forms, and other elements of the web interface. For universal usability, these actionable elements must be workable from the keyboard. Many users cannot work with a mouse, and many devices do not support point-and-click interaction. For example, nonvisual users cannot see the screen. Some users employ software or other input devices that work only by activating keyboard commands. For these users, elements that can be activated only with a mouse are inaccessible.

Make actionable elements workable via the keyboard to ensure that the interactivity of the web is accessible to the broadest spectrum of users.

Text equivalents Text is universally accessible. (Whether text is universally comprehensible is another discussion!) Unlike images and media, text is readable by software and can be rendered in different formats and acted upon by software. When information is presented in a format other than text, such as visually using images or video or audibly using speech, the information can be lost on users who cannot see or hear. Web technology anticipates format-related access issues and supplies methods for providing equivalent text. With equivalent text, the information contained in the media is also available as text, such as a text transcript or captions along with spoken audio.

Text equivalents allow universal usability to exist in a media-rich environment by carrying information to users who cannot access information in a given format.

CONTENT STRATEGY

Content strategy governs and defines how the content you develop will meet your business goals. To experienced writers and editors, most of "content strategy" will seem the "same as it ever was" for complex publications. Editorial work has always been concerned with the purpose, form, development, and integration of all kinds of content assets: text, illustrations, and, for the past few decades, interactive and audiovisual materials that are integrated into electronic publications.

However, content development today has to contend with additional layers of complexity. Presentation media for content range from traditional paper and web publications to mobile applications that appear on an increasingly wide spectrum of screen sizes and different contexts for use. This flexibility in the various ways content might be deployed requires much more structure, modularity, and metadata than print-only publications.

It might be best to think of modern content as the elements of a database, in which sections, chapters, descriptions, and even individual paragraphs of text might be remixed and displayed in myriad ways for print, web, applications and apps, and social media. Content strategy seeks the flexibility to move beyond a single medium and a single fixed presentation narrative so that your content can work effectively across the breadth of your communications channels. Today content also needs to be as visible as possible to search engines, and also accessible to all audiences.

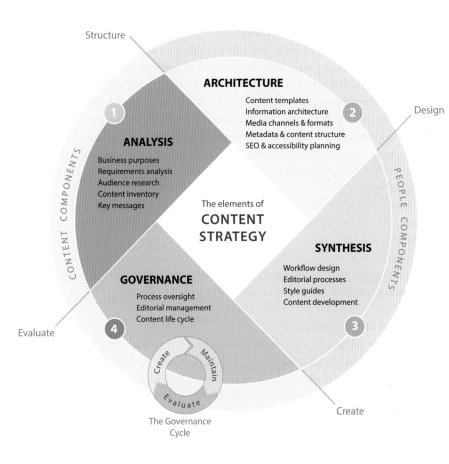

Structure

ARCHITECTURE

Content templates
Information architecture
Media channels & formats
Metadata & content structure
SEO & accessibility planning

Design

1

2

ANALYSIS

Business purposes
Requirements analysis
Audience research
Content inventory
Key messages

CONTENT COMPONENTS

PEOPLE COMPONENTS

The elements of

CONTENT STRATEGY

SYNTHESIS

Workflow design
Editorial processes
Style guides
Content development

GOVERNANCE

Process oversight
Editorial management
Content life cycle

Evaluate

4

3

Create

Create

Maintain

Evaluate

The Governance
Cycle

FIGURE 1.4
Content strategy
is another cyclical
strategic process
(also see fig. 1.1), in
which continuing
cycles of analysis,
planning, building,
and examining the
results assure that
the web site stays
up to date and
optimized over time.

In this new multichannel media universe a comprehensive content strategy produces a road map to guide the whole content life cycle, from needs assessments and business strategy alignment to development, deployment, and revision or deletion. Content development is not a project, it's an ongoing process, and it is never "done" until the site goes offline and is archived. A good content strategy explicitly acknowledges that today's shiny new site or app will one day seem painfully dated, and that content begins to drift out of date from the moment it goes "live" online. As content strategist Karen McGrane says, "It's not a strategy if you can't maintain it."

A good content strategy also looks both backward and forward, working with site managers to create and measure benchmarks and performance metrics—gauging the success of your content and assessing its current strengths and weaknesses at meeting the needs of your audience—and uses those metrics to establish priorities for fixing, revising, or updating areas of content.

CREATING A CONTENT STRATEGY

The goal of a content strategy is not editorial work or content creation, although in many cases the same people will be involved in both creating a content strategy and implementing the strategy recommendations. The key result, or "deliverable," is a content strategy document that details all of the elements described below, with recommendations for resources, workflows, and editorial team members and their roles and responsibilities, while incorporating guidance or style documents that describe the voice and tone, content structure, content templates, and other guides for content contributors like writers, photographers, graphics artists, and audiovisual media creators.

Content strategy is more broad in scope than most conventional web editorial processes; it includes business goals and branding processes, and covers the whole content life cycle, not just the creation and deployment of content. It also deals with the more technical aspects of digital content, such as content structure, metadata, file formats, search engine optimization (seo), and the accessibility of content across various delivery media.

Define your target audience

It is impossible to develop a coherent content strategy without clear ideas about whom you are speaking to, what their needs and interests are, and how those needs might be met by your content. Audiences are rarely homogeneous, and you'll need to identify primary audiences as well as possible subgroups within your audience that might need slightly different information and marketing messages, or a different voice and tone in your presentations.

- **Prioritize audiences:** Not all possible audiences are equally important to your business goals. One of the key processes in identifying your audiences is to prioritize the various groups of readers and users so that your messaging strategy and mix of media (web, apps, social, print) are carefully targeted at your most important audience. This is not to say that secondary audiences are not important. If your site's primary audience is prospective customers, you must also support existing customers, even if your primary business goal is increased sales, because poor support will eventually damage your sales and reputation.
- **Develop personas:** User interface professionals often develop detailed audience *personas*—individualized portraits of representative audience members (see Chapter 2, Research), usually fashioned around some particular interest or audience demographic. For content strategy, it helps to understand the major characteristics and interests of each audience group as a reference for prioritizing your messaging, so that your writers and designers thoroughly understand whom they are speaking to when creating content.

A MOBILE-FIRST APPROACH TO CONTENT STRATEGY

The rapid and widespread development of mobile computing may be the best thing that ever happened to desktop computing, because once companies understood how many mobile-first and "mobile-often" customers there are out there—more every day—they realized that foisting a stripped-down, dumbed-down version of their content on mobile users just wouldn't work. It's far too expensive and complicated to maintain several versions of your large site or e-commerce store. Yet mobile screens are so small. What to do?

Cut, cut, cut. Cut all the bloated, irrelevant verbiage, "features" your user data say that no one ever touches, giant photos and graphics nobody bothered to optimize for fast download, useless wads of CSS code from three versions ago that everyone is afraid to touch (is it still live somewhere?). In short, the severe restrictions on what will work well in the mobile context, as well as the concise content approach required for mobile content, are also wonderful in desktop situations. A well-executed mobile content strategy can result in lean, focused, high-priority content across all of your mobile and desktop audiences.

There's no such thing as "mobile content." What all your readers and users need is *good* content, available wherever and whenever they need it, on any device. If some of your current content looks superfluous on a mobile device, it's certainly superfluous for desktop users as well. Get rid of the useless fluff—it makes everyone's day harder, and it's expensive to maintain. Prioritizing your content is essential, but don't dumb down your content for mobile users. Make all of your content concise and highly informative. Both desktop and mobile users will thank you for it.

Simplicity is a must. In content strategy and user experience the "mobile-first" design philosophy makes a great heuristic for cutting away the crap and getting down to essential content and features—for all users, across all devices.

Articulate key messages and business value

Messaging is the process of prioritizing and matching your key business strategy messages with particular audience segments. This is impossible without a clear understanding of your business goals, and every piece of content you develop should have a direct relationship to business goals, or a key message to your audience. If you are lucky, your enterprise may already have a clearly articulated business strategy and well-established marketing or communications messages, and your project should support those goals. If not, one of the most important aspects of content strategy will be to develop a concise statement of business purposes and key desired outcomes for each audience type, so that each key message has a clear "job" to do to support your overall goals.

The concept of "messaging" might seem nebulous on a relatively small department site, but the same principles apply whether you are developing the web site for a large enterprise or a help desk site for the enterprise's IT department. For a help desk your key messages might be that your site provides fast, accurate, and user-friendly access to the technical information your users need to get their jobs done. Each piece of content should reflect these high-level goals for effective and usable support information and services. Technically obtuse, bloated, or inaccurate content is not compatible with your key messaging. Whoever is developing your content needs to keep the high-level goals in mind for each sentence and paragraph, as the overall "message" of your site is built from the aggregate impressions given by every piece of content your audience encounters.

Choose your distribution media

One of the principal advantages of digital content is the ability to deploy the same material over a wide variety of communications channels, but this potential flexibility is available only if you plan for it carefully and ensure that your content is well suited in messaging, tone, and technical structure for each potential use. In the parlance of marketing, each communication medium is a "channel," and each medium could have multiple channels. For example, your internal enterprise intranet and your latest marketing campaign site may both be web-based, but they are different channels with different audiences and goals.

Corporate web sites, blogs, the various social media that your company uses, mobile applications, online video sites like YouTube, podcasts, magazine and newspaper advertising, marketing publications in print and PDF, and television advertisements are all potential "channels" for matching your key messages to your target audiences. Not every medium is equally suitable to your business purposes, and unless you are working for a large enterprise, you may be able to support content in only a few of the available media channels. Content strategy for distribution is the process of identifying and prioritizing the most effective channels for your messages, and creating a plan that specifies the content character, structure, and tone for each medium.

Specify the content structure

Once you know which communications channels you will support, you need to be sure that the content that you create, curate, or license is structured to meet your needs for each channel. "Content structure" in this case is only partly related to conventional editorial structures like titles, chapters, subheads, paragraphs, and figure references. The goal for strategic content structuring is to anticipate the unique

The flexible advantages of highly structured content

Simple text listing of a recipe:

Rustic Cherry-Apple Galette
For the tart crust:
- 1.25 cups all-purpose flour
- .25 cup crushed toasted almonds
- 10 tablespoons of frozen unsalted butter
- 3 tablespoons of frozen vegetable shortening
- .75 teaspoon salt
- About .5 cup ice water

1– Add all ingredients into a food processor and spin until they form crumbly, coarse balls of dough
2– Dump the dough onto a sheet of plastic wrap and press the dough by hand into a roughly flat circle about 7-8 inches in diameter
3– Wrap the dough in plastic and put it in the freezer for 10 minutes to cool the dough before rolling
4– (Make the pie filling while you wait for the dough to cool)
5– After cooling, roll the dough out to about 10-11 inches in diameter. Put the dough into the refrigerator if you are not assembling the tart immediately
etc....

Divide the recipe into structural components

- Title
- Brief description
- Long description
- Tweet text
- Difficulty category
- Photo of prepared dish (high-res)
- Thumbnail photo of prepared dish
- Other photos of preparation
- General meal categories: (dessert, pie)
- Other keywords: (apple, cherry, gallete)
- Number of portions
- Time required
- Preheat temperature
- Ingredients listing
- Process listing
- Cooking or baking time
- Other notes

Content structure allows great flexibility in how components can be deployed

Structure: Tweet with image

Title		Tweet text
Tweet text		
Thumbnail photo		

Structure: Facebook post

| Title |
| Brief description |
| Larger photo of prepared dish |

Structure: Web or mobile content page

| Title |
| Larger photo of prepared dish |
| Long description of recipe |
| Keywords |
| Number of portions |
| Time required | Preheat temperature |
| Ingredients listing |
| Process listing |

etc.

needs of each known communication channel, and to be sure that the content you develop or repurpose is organized in an optimal way for many different potential uses.

Detailed specifications for content structure also bring consistency and modularity to the development of large amounts of content, which often combines the work of many writers and designers.

FIGURE 1.5
Content is most useful and flexible when it is properly structured.

Provide voice, tone, and editorial guidance

In daily life we all adjust our tone of voice and manner of speaking to the context we're in: informal and matter-of-fact among friends, still informal but more careful in routine emails with office mates, and more formal when writing a company white paper on an aspect of business strategy. Although most enterprises have established editorial and graphics guides for general corporate identity, they rarely are up to date enough to include guidance on social media and other newer communications channels. What sounds perfectly appropriate for business-to-business communication or a LinkedIn article might sound oddly stilted in a tweet or a Facebook post.

Content strategy looks at each communication channel and provides general guidance on the voice and tone of communications for that channel and its audience. Guidelines for each medium and each audience will help your writers and other contributors develop content that "sounds right" for the intended communications channel (see Chapter 10, Editorial Style).

A good content strategy will include at least general recommendations for editorial style, particularly if organizational standards, identity guidelines, and language style guides do not already exist.

Create an editorial workflow

A good content strategy looks at available editorial resources and existing content in light of stated business goals for your project, and develops specific recommendations and workflows for the staff, media, and editorial resources need to successfully meet your goals and production schedule.

Many editorial tasks are predictable, and a good strategy will spell out roles and responsibilities for each task, how handoff and approvals will occur, typical workflows for each type of content (text, photos, graphics, etc.), and who has the final authority to publish the finished content. Common editorial tasks include:

- Planning
- Creating content inventories (see Chapter 10, Editorial Style)
- Maintaining the editorial calendar
- Creating or sourcing content
- Editing and revising content and the expected workflow
- Adding metadata and checking for accessibility issues
- Testing the content as it is integrated into a working version of the web site
- Getting final approvals from editors, stakeholders and marketing staff, and legal
- Getting technical approvals for highly programmed or interactive content
- Getting clarity on who has the authority to publish content, and how that final workflow will occur
- Reviewing current "live" content for editorial quality and proper functioning
- Receiving and responding to reader feedback, requests for information, or reports of problems
- Determining how error reports will be handled, ideally in a ticketing system to track and prioritize known problems
- Removing outdated or incorrect content, with clarity on who has the authority to remove content from the "live" site, and how that workflow will occur

Most content strategies recommend the development (or continued use of) an editorial calendar. If the project is new and doesn't have an established calendar, it's good to be clear on exactly what you hope to accomplish with an editorial calendar, and how it will be used to record key dates for product announcements, events, recurring annual events, product rollouts. It should be clear who maintains the editorial calendar, and whose responsibility it is to develop and post content for each event.

Stipulate governance and the content life cycle

Many web sites are considered to be projects that are "finished" at site launch, and then often languish with increasingly outdated content, broken links, and eroding interactive functionality, principally because the site never had a clear governance structure beyond the launch date. Content strategy and web governance are tightly related because only through governance can the content life cycle be maintained with high quality and functionality (see "Define roles and responsibilities with project governance," above).

Governance for content strategy specifies roles and responsibilities related to content, from conception, creation, and launch to eventual revision or removal. Ongoing support is usually the most crucial element, as it is only with continued support that content will be maintained. A content governance model assures:

- Clear communication among the site editorial staff, site stakeholders, and management.
- Established roles, responsibilities, and ongoing support for editorial staff, clarifying who supplies subject matter expertise for each content area as technologies and circumstances change over time.
- Communication between major stakeholders and the editorial staff on the overall business success of the site: Is the content supporting the original or evolving business goals, and at what point will substantial changes need to be planned?

SOCIAL MEDIA STRATEGY

As the infrastructure of the web has become bigger, more complex, and richer with communications possibilities, the web is now much more than the content of individual web sites and blogs. For most individuals—and a growing list of major enterprises—their presence on various social media channels has at least as much impact on audiences as their corporate sites or enterprise blogs.

Social media are often reviled as playgrounds for the trivial, but they finally accomplished what no previous Internet technology had successfully done before: they brought masses of ordinary people onto the web, with all their foolishness, trolls, flame wars, wisdom, connection, and deep humanity.

CREATING A SOCIAL MEDIA STRATEGY

After an initial few years of diffidence, businesses and other enterprises have long since adopted social media technology because of the unprecedented forum it provides for easy, fast interactive communication, bringing with it far more opportunity than the older one-way media channels of television, print, and static web sites.

However, social media channels also pose new challenges to marketing, branding, and communications professionals. Strategy and tactics in social media need to be flexible, ready to change quickly as conditions, practices, and expectations change. New functionality—and even whole new social media channels—emerge almost weekly, and channels like Facebook and Twitter change their policies and technology frequently. One thing doesn't change, though: a quality enterprise social media presence is expensive and requires careful attention from both experienced communications professionals and senior management. Without clear goals and solid business objectives your social media efforts will wander, and may reflect poorly on your reputation.

Define business objectives

Do you have clear understanding and agreement on what are you trying to accomplish through using social media? What key performance indicators (KPIs) are most important to you and your overall enterprise business strategy? A good social media strategy should always begin with your enterprise-wide goals, and clearly work to support those goals.

Social media can help:

- Develop new customers, clients, or community members
- Increase sales or other forms of engagement with your current customer community
- Broaden and deepen your brand's reputation
- Provide customer support and useful product information

Define your audience

Are you clear on who your most important social media audiences are, what you have to say to them, and what information or services are most important to audience members? Social media interactions play out in real time: do you know what most interests your potential audiences, and at what times of day are your audiences most active and engaged?

Learn about your target audience, including:

- Gender, age group, or interests
- Level of education or professional interests
- Geographic locations, time zones, and languages spoken
- Social media channels preferred

Most large enterprises have one "main" account for each major social medium like Facebook or Twitter but also maintain other accounts targeted at more specific audiences. For example, Yale University maintains a primary institutional Twitter account but also maintains dozens of other Twitter accounts from more specialized sources, like academic departments and programs, as well as Twitter accounts aimed primarily (but not exclusively) at on-campus audiences. A coordinated approach to enterprise social media is an ideal way to extend the reach of more specialized content (through retweets to the general audience), but the general audience for the main enterprise feed also benefits from a wide variety of content of more specialized topical posts.

Project—and protect—your brand and enterprise identity

Social media can be powerful tools for projecting your business brand or enterprise identity, but only if you plan carefully, and provide enough of the right resources to solidify and enlarge your reputation through daily interactions with your audience members. Your social media efforts should always be consistent in tone and design with your existing enterprise identity guidelines and policies.

Expand your branding guidelines to include provisions for social media, including:

- **Visual branding:** Each social medium has its unique graphic formats and pixel dimensions for themes, background images, header and profile images, and ideal image formats for visual posts. You'll need to consult (and probably update) your standard enterprise identity guidelines for each social media channel to be sure you have the best-quality brand images.
- **Video titling standards:** The most effective online videos are short—ideally no more than two to three minutes long—and relatively lengthy "cinema style" beginning and ending video graphics are counterproductive for channels like Facebook, YouTube, or Vimeo. Online audiences won't sit through fifteen seconds of fancy titles to see whether your video is interesting. You'll need to give your video "fast-start" titles that appear over content that starts to play immediately (see Chapter 12, Video).
- **Voice and tone:** Traditional print or broadcast branding guidelines rarely provide useful counsel for deeply interactive social media channels, where the usually conservative editorial guidelines may prove to be too neutral in tone for the relatively informal conversational style of social media channels like Facebook and Twitter. Developing the right editorial "voice" will depend heavily on the characteristics of your particular audience demographics, and which channels you are using. Facebook tends to be relatively informal, whereas the more business-oriented LinkedIn audience will expect a more neutral "corporate" voice.

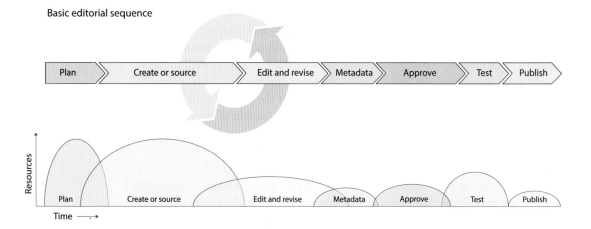

Basic editorial sequence

Plan ⟩ Create or source ⟩ Edit and revise ⟩ Metadata ⟩ Approve ⟩ Test ⟩ Publish ⟩

Resources

Plan | Create or source | Edit and revise | Metadata | Approve | Test | Publish

Time →

FIGURE 1.6
A generalized overview of the editorial development process.

- **Integration with existing online branding:** Most enterprises have long since developed policies for web site and blog identities and graphics, but may neglect to thoroughly integrate social media into existing web sites, blogs, and mobile content efforts such as smartphone or tablet apps. Linking your social media efforts to your existing web communications through "like" and "share" buttons is a crucial piece of a mature social media strategy, and cross-linking your web site by embedding your latest social media posts can help boost audience traffic to both your web site and your social media efforts.

- **Response policy:** Participating on social media channels opens enterprises to possible reputational risk. For example, enabling a commenting feature on articles invites contributions from readers, and those comments may not always be complimentary. Some implementations may invite more risk than others—for example, allowing anonymous posts may lead to more "trolls" using the comments feature to shout contrary viewpoints. Any social media strategy must have a plan for how to respond to negative and potentially harmful engagement on social media channels. The policy should take into account the risks of moderation as well—how will your brand stand up to claims of censorship? Create a "code of conduct" that encapsulates your enterprise's core values, post the code on your social media channels, and ensure that all staff who engage in social media channels know how to respond to violations.

Produce compelling content

What information will you share with social media audience members? If you sell goods, you might share information about your products and how they are used, as well as success stories from customers. Local governments and universities might share information on local events and programs, interesting people, current research, and publications. Social media are also ideal for projecting a sense of place, and for giving distant audiences (prospective students or potential new businesses, for example) a taste of what it is like to live, work, or study in your local environment. Each social media channel requires a tailored mix of media best suited to that audience's expectations, but in general highly visual content like photos and video does best, and content that provokes positive discussion and reader feedback will both increase your engagement with individual readers and boost the overall visibility of your social media content.

Content curation—selecting and sharing social content produced outside your enterprise—has become a crucial component of most enterprise social media strategies, as it helps provide a rich mix of content well beyond the content you produce yourselves. Your audience members are not interested just in your home-grown communications; they usually want to know what you find interesting enough to retweet or repost among relevant industry news, graphics and videos, or comments produced by others.

Whom to "follow" on Twitter or Facebook has become a subbranch of content curation, as a "follow" list from your Twitter account is a powerful statement of which corporate sources, news outlets, and individuals you find interesting and relevant enough to pay attention to.

Determine optimal timing and frequency of posts

Two general characteristics of social media channels can be useful in creating your strategy: the ideal posting frequency of the medium, and the general level of posting "noise" typical of each medium. For example, it is rare for large enterprises to post more than four or five times per day on Facebook, and posts on LinkedIn are even less frequent. Audiences will quickly come to resent too many posts from a business, as both Facebook and LinkedIn are communities of individuals who have chosen to associate with one another. Too many commercial posts mixed in with their usual news from friends and family will cause users to "unfriend" or "unfollow" a business.

In contrast, Twitter is a completely open social medium, where almost all tweets are inherently public, and where many tweets from a wide variety of sources may swamp your message amid the general noise of the typical user's Twitter feed. Twitter postings ("tweets") are ephemeral, so most organizations post multiple times per day to assure that the average follower sees some piece of content per day. Studies show that the "half-life" of a tweet (50 percent of all retweets) occurs within eighteen minutes. Still, an enterprise should normally post no more than once an hour (and usually much less), as even Twitter users will quickly resent a company that seems to be monopolizing their feed with too many tweets.

A LIST OF REMINDERS
—With apologies to E. B. White

Place yourself in the background Start and end with the users' interests in mind. If your site doesn't provide useful things to the audience, nothing else matters. Design your web site using universal usability principles.

Work from a suitable design Avoid the perils of the "ready, fire, aim" syndrome. The crucial part of the project is the planning. Know what you're doing, why you're doing it, and for whom you're doing it before anyone touches HTML or CSS.

Do not overwrite Small is good. A concise, high-quality site is much better than a big contraption full of broken links. Produce the minimum necessary to achieve an excellent result.

Prefer the standard to the offbeat Web conventions are your friends. Always favor the tried and true, and save your creativity for the hard stuff: interesting content and features.

Be clear Craft your page titles and content carefully, and make sure that the page title is consistent with your major headings.

Do the visuals last Early visual design discussions can ruin any chance of a rational planning process. Louis Sullivan was right: form follows function.

Revise and rewrite Design iteration in the early stages of the project is good. In planning, keep the team open to new ideas, feedback from existing and potential users, and the interests of your project stakeholders. However, development iteration—where you tear down and revise things late in the process—can ruin quality control, budgets, and schedules.

Be consistent Consistency is the golden rule of interface design. Be consistent with the general conventions of the web, of your home institution if you have one, and within your site.

Do not affect a breezy manner Avoid gimmicky technology fads. "We should use Sass" is not a technology strategy, unless you know exactly why and how Sass with CSS might help you to achieve your strategic goals. Never use pointless CSS or GIF animations to "make the site more interesting." To make your site more interesting, add substantive content or features.

Degrade gracefully Apply universal usability principles in your site development and careful quality controls in your web applications. Provide a carefully designed "404" error page with helpful search and links in case the user hits a broken link on your site.

Do not explain too much Be concise, and be generous with headers, subheads, and lists, so that the user can scan your content easily.

Make sure the user knows who is speaking Good communication is always a person-to-person transaction. Use the active voice at all times, so the user knows who is speaking. Make it easy to find your mailing address and other contact information.

All social posts have relatively short lifespans, ranging from as brief as the eighteen-minute half-life of a Twitter post to several hours for most Facebook posts, and perhaps days for less frequently visited sites such as LinkedIn.

Many studies have looked at the optimal times to post in the major social media channels, but only one rule ultimately matters for your situation: Use data from your audience to tailor the timing of your posts. Use the metrics available in Facebook and Twitter, make careful notes on which of your posts get the most engagement and when they get it, and tailor your posting schedule to your particular audience. If you have a nationwide U.S. audience, you'll need to account for the various time zones in the country, and also determine the best times to post for international readers in Europe or Asian markets.

That said, there are consistent trends in the way people typically interact with the major social media channels. In general, for Facebook and Twitter (more than 90 percent of current social media traffic), weekday midafternoons and early evenings (measured in Eastern Standard Time, EST) are best for engagement on Facebook postings, and Twitter users are most likely to engage with a tweet in a broader range of the day, from late morning through early evening. The late-day EST bias for Facebook and Twitter engagement is probably influenced by the various U.S. time zones, because it is still early afternoon for midwestern and West Coast readers while East Coast readers are in late afternoon or early evening.

Both Facebook and Twitter show more engagement early in the workweek. Weekends tend to be quiet times for business uses of Facebook and Twitter, but business posts aimed at personal users may see higher levels of engagement on Sunday, mostly because so few businesses post on weekends, so the few that appear on Sunday are more prominent.

Organize and schedule social media activities

Social media are inherently immediate, but that does not mean that it is a good idea—or even practical—to produce all of your social media posts in real time. Popular social media organizing and scheduling tools like Hootsuite, Buffer, and Sprout Social allow you to schedule sets of social media posts for all the major social media channels at various dates and times, often far in advance. Multiple users can see, edit, and coordinate content campaigns across a variety of media and a variety of individual accounts in a single place, which makes for much more coherent and strategic social media content.

REACHING YOUR AUDIENCE THROUGH SOCIAL MEDIA CHANNELS

What social media channels will you use—Facebook, Twitter, Instagram, Tumblr, Google+, YouTube, blogs? Each of the major social media channels has unique characteristics. With limited resources you'll want to choose just a few channels that best suit your business objectives, and determine what level of engagement best suits your resources and strategy. Facebook (more than 80 percent of users) and Twitter (roughly 20 percent of users) account for more than 90 percent of adult time spent on social media in the United States. While we concentrate on Facebook and Twitter in this chapter, the strategy, design, and staffing considerations also apply to other widely used social media channels like LinkedIn, YouTube, Tumblr, and Instagram.

Facebook is a business whose primary product is access to the enormous international community of Facebook users. More than a billion worldwide users, or about one in thirteen people on earth. In the United States more than 80 percent of time spent on social media sites is on Facebook.

If you are a business or personal user of Facebook, then every content posting you make on the medium will appear on your Facebook Timeline page. However, 90 percent of Facebook users who "like" or "follow" your Timeline page on Facebook will never revisit your Timeline page, and will see your content only on their personal Facebook News Feed. Facebook's News Feed filtering algorithms (previously called the EdgeRank algorithm—see "Facebook Ranking Algorithms" sidebar) determine how often users see the content you post to Facebook.

New users of Facebook are often unpleasantly surprised to discover that relatively few posts they make on Facebook make it into the News Feed of every person who has "friended," "liked," or "followed" a commercial or personal Facebook page. Facebook has long used a variety of techniques to filter the sheer volume of daily posts, both to better tailor content for individual Facebook users and to help steer commercial users of Facebook toward the company's paid services to boost viewership of postings. The result is that only about 6–16 percent of posts reach the News Feeds of people who have liked their pages, and some industry experts find that organic reach has fallen to as little as 2–3 percent for some commercial Facebook users. Facebook says that average "organic reach" of about 6–16 percent is typical of both individual Facebook users and commercial or brand pages. If you want to reach more of the audience that has liked or followed your page, you must use one or both of these basic Facebook content strategies:

- Create compelling content tailored to the specific characteristics of Facebook as a social medium.
- Pay Facebook to "sponsor" or "boost" the percentage of users who see your posts.

Through careful Facebook-specific design of your content, it is possible to increase the ranking your posts receive, thereby increasing the total organic reach of your posts and the visibility of your content.

- **Engaging content:** Posts with photos, illustrations, or videos get more reader engagement. Carefully determine your target audiences, and create highly visual content with concise text captions of no more than about 150 characters. Try to provide unique content in your Facebook feed, with Facebook-first news and information, sneak-peek information on upcoming announcements and sales, or useful product tips.
- **Posting frequency:** In previous years most experts advised commercial companies not to post more than once or twice per day to avoid annoying their audience. The current News Feed system severely limits the organic reach of your posts, so many organizations have begun to send two or three posts per day, with the assumption that most Facebook users may see only one or two of those posts in their News Feeds. Many brands post no more than once a day (five or six times per week).
- **Post timing and maintaining a calendar:** There are general rules for the timing of social media posts, but the only metric that really matters is the best timing for your particular audience. Use your page metrics to pay close attention to the timing of your most successful posts, and adjust your timing accordingly. Use a detailed calendar to plan your social media campaigns, both to assure that your lessons learned are applied systematically and to be sure that everyone on the social media team understands the daily and weekly strategy for content and post timing.

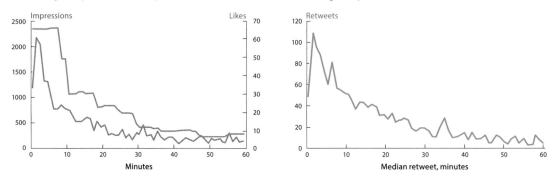

Average lifespan of a Facebook post

Average lifespan of a Twitter tweet

Minutes

Median retweet, minutes

FIGURE 1.7

The useful lifespan of a Facebook or Twitter post is only about twenty minutes. This argues for carefully scheduling repeated posts of the same content in different time windows, to try to reach your audience members in the brief moments where they are online and paying attention to the continuous streams of social media content.

- **Interactions with fans:** Your overall News Feed scores and your organic reach will rise with the degree to which you engage with readers who comment on your Facebook posts. Two-way conversations help build customer loyalty and assure your audience that there is somebody listening to and thinking about comments, suggestions, and complaints.

Most of us already use Facebook in our personal lives, and it may appear odd to discuss the components of something that seems so familiar, but professional uses of Facebook are costly and far from casual, and you'll want to be sure to create the most effective posts you can to increase your audience reach and engagement.

- **Length:** Keep the copy in your Facebook posts short, ideally no more than 100 characters. Facebook does not carry the strict 140-character limit of Twitter, but that doesn't mean that you can ramble. Only the first two or three sentences are visible in a Facebook post anyway before Facebook cuts off the rest of the text with a "See More" link. Be concise: Facebook posts of 80 characters or fewer receive 66 percent higher engagement from readers.
- **Photography and graphics:** This is simple: If you want people to pay attention to what you say on Facebook, always include a graphic in your posts. Facebook is a highly visual medium, and posts with graphics consistently outperform text-only posts. A recent study found that graphic posts generate 53 percent more reader engagement than text posts. The graphics do not need to be large. Facebook typically displays News Feed graphics in a 4:3 horizontal rectangle in JPEG format, and the graphic needs to be no larger than 504 pixels wide to fill the full width of the News Feed or the timeline. If you have photos or graphics that will benefit from the extra resolution when a reader clicks on the photo, do use a larger JPEG, but there is little point in uploading graphics larger than about 1,300 pixels in width, as Facebook will scale down large graphics,

FACEBOOK RANKING ALGORITHMS

Facebook users aged eighteen to forty-nine have on average about 250 friends, are connected to an average of 80 commercial, organization, or event pages, and create about 90 pieces of content a month. With such a heavy potential volume of posts on a user's News Feed, Facebook has long used a proprietary set of algorithms to determine what posts from friends and brand pages appear on a given user's News Feed. Originally Facebook called the algorithms EdgeRank, and although the company no longer uses the term internally, it is still widespread in the social media communications industry. Recently the social media community simply refers to the News Feed, or to News Feed algorithms, in describing Facebook's filtering of what appears in the user's News Feed.

In Facebook parlance an "edge" is any interaction with a piece of content within the Facebook universe. The original EdgeRank algorithm weighed three major factors to determine the likely relevance of a given post for a particular Facebook user:

Affinity A numerical scoring of the user's relationship to the source of a piece of content. If the user frequently "likes" posts, comments on posts, or shares posts from a given source, the higher the affinity score, and the more likely that the user will see more posts from the same source.

Weight A ranking of common interaction types on Facebook. "Liking" a post takes little effort and gets a low "weight" score, but commenting on a post or sharing a post takes more user effort, and creates a higher weight score.

Time decay A simple measure of the time a given post has existed. The older a post is, the lower it scores in time decay, because the vast majority of user engagement with a post (likes, comments, shares) occurs within the first half hour of the post's existence.

Since 2013 Facebook has moved away from the term "EdgeRank" in its internal communications, and now claims to weight as many as 100,000 factors in its News Feed algorithms determining the relevance of content to a particular Facebook user, although the original three weighting factors above still account for most of the algorithm's results.

FIGURE 1.8

Generalized temporal patterns of social media engagement for Twitter and Facebook.

TWITTER — Best times (U.S., EST) to post links in tweets for the most clicks

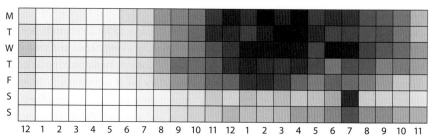

FACEBOOK — Best times (U.S., EST) to post links in Facebook posts for the most clicks

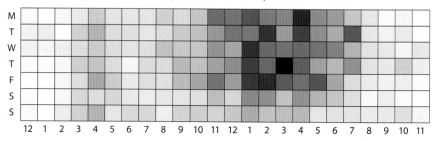

and most users won't have enough screen real estate to view very large photos within the Facebook page framework anyway.

- **Hashtags:** Hashtags are a relatively new feature of Facebook, but although they are not yet widely used, they function the same way they do in Twitter, providing a searchable tag that allows readers to see collections of posts that all reference the same hashtag. Facebook hashtags are now used mostly by television companies to identify posts about sports and news events, but it is likely that usage will grow as Facebook users become more familiar with them.

Twitter has more than 271 million active monthly users and is often reported to be the fastest-growing social network. For the average user Twitter is a very cluttered and fast-changing medium, where dozens of tweets per hour flow through the feed. Given such a volume of information, few users attempt to "drink from the fire hose"—try to pay attention to every tweet. Twitter is a noisy medium where older tweets are quickly forgotten by most users, if they are ever seen at all. The average active Twitter user follows 102 accounts, resulting in an average active lifespan per tweet of less than half an hour before retweets and comments fall to near zero.

The immediacy of Twitter lends itself to commenting "real time" on news and entertainment events as they unfold. Twitter is commonly used by journalists and

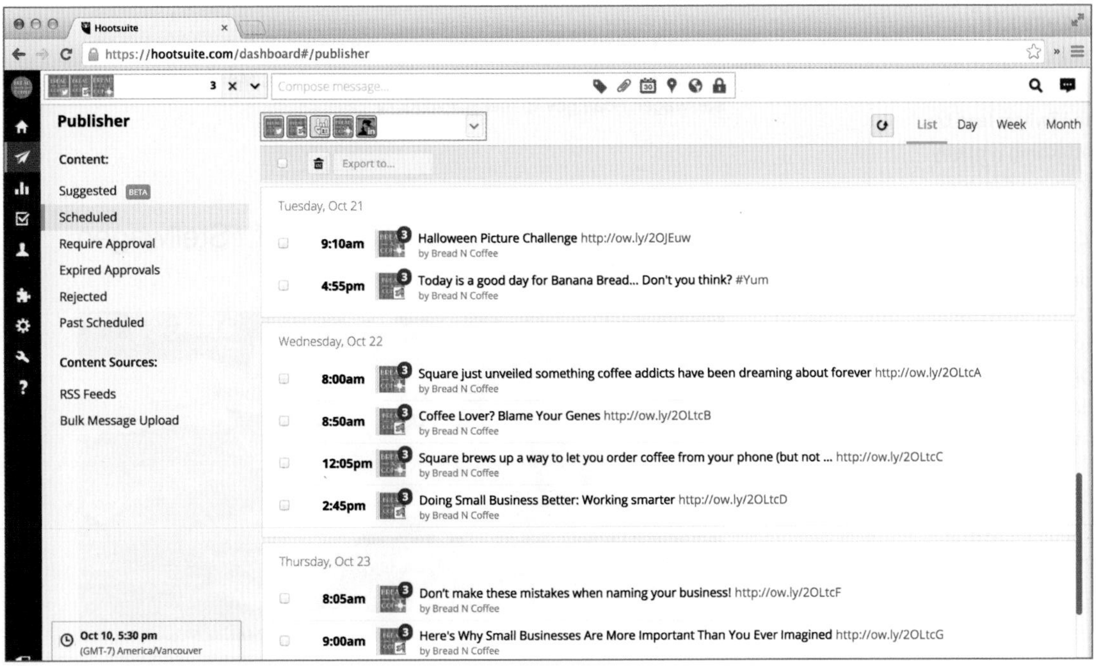

FIGURE 1.9
Most business
users of social
media channels use
management and
scheduling software
such as Hootsuite to
distribute their social
content.

news organizations to break and follow news, and is often the first (if not the most reliable) source for major news events.

Twitter recommends that commercial accounts tweet three to five times per day. Twitter postings ("tweets") are famously brief, at no more than 140 characters. However, there are best practices for writing, forming, tagging, and adding media links to tweets.

- **Length:** Data show that tweets of 70–100 characters or fewer are ideal, as they are more informative than a very short tweet, are quickly scanned, and leave room in the message for retweets that add comments, @username additions, and added metadata hashtags. Tweets in the recommended size range average 17 percent more engagement than very long or very short tweets.
- **Linked media:** Tweets with graphics get more engagement and retweets than plain-text tweets, but not all graphics are equally effective. You can link graphics as large as 1,024 × 512 pixels to your tweet, but linking large graphics is a bit pointless, as large graphics simply appear as links in a tweet—the user sees only a plain-text tweet and has to click on the link to see your large graphic. It's a much better practice to limit your twitter graphics to what will fit within the Twitter stream, no larger than 440 × 220 pixels, so that your post now benefits from the eye-catching effect of the graphic in the Twitter stream.

FIGURE 1.10
You can optimize your visibility within the Twitter feed by attaching properly formatted images. Images that are too large or not properly proportioned will still be attached to your tweet, but probably only as a link to the photo, not as the photo itself.

- **Hashtags:** Twitter hashtags are a great way to call out your tweet to particular audiences or user communities. Many users habitually search for favorite hashtags as a way of cutting through the general Twitter noise to find relevant content. However, excessive hashtag use looks amateurish and calculated to game the system. Use no more than two hashtags on a tweet, and if you use two, make sure you keep within the 100-character guideline.

Because the average tweet lifespan is so ephemeral, most enterprises tweet at about twice the rate that they post to Facebook, or about three to six posts per day, and often more for news organizations, particularly when major stories are breaking. The ultimate metric here is your number of followers. Experiment with more frequent tweets, but if you tweet too often, people will begin to "unfollow" your account and your number of followers will drop accordingly.

The short lifespan of a tweet also presents opportunities to reuse good or important content, as most tweets have an engagement rate of less than 5 percent, often because most users simply didn't see the tweet flow by at a time when they were not looking at Twitter.

The majority of very active individual Twitter users, including most enterprises, use some kind of scheduling service (Hootsuite, Buffer, Sprout Social) to at least partially automate their flow of tweets. Scheduling software like Hootsuite can be useful for "preprogramming" this evergreen curated content over several weeks or months, repeating good material at different times of day or days of the week, assuming that a reader who missed your original tweet on a busy Tuesday morning might happen upon it on a quiet Sunday afternoon.

STAFFING YOUR SOCIAL MEDIA TEAM

Most organizations already have individuals or whole social media teams on staff and have an existing track record in representing the brand or enterprise. More often than not these teams are run as part of broader marketing and communications efforts, as those existing writing, strategy, and media skills are the most relevant to the newer channels of social media. If you have the resources to expand your team and social media efforts, consider media professionals with expertise in online graphics, photography, and short videos, as graphic media are often the key to higher engagement from readers.

If you are not already using stock photography agencies for visual material and simple illustrations, work with designers to establish reliable, high-quality sources of photography, as you will need new visual material almost every day. If you are not in a core media relations or communications department, try to establish good relationships with the media people in your company, as most larger enterprises produce a steady flow of news releases, product photography, and other material that you can repurpose to feed your social media channels.

Start small, and if your resources are stretched, then stay small. No law says you need to address every new social medium that comes along, as every new channel is a significant maintenance commitment. It's much better to maintain a few high-quality feeds to Facebook or Twitter than to strain to produce mediocre content for half a dozen social media channels.

RECOMMENDED READING

Halvorson, K., and M. Rach. *Content Strategy for the Web*. 2nd ed. Berkeley, CA: New Riders, 2012.

Kissane, E. *The Elements of Content Strategy*. New York: A Book Apart, 2011.

Redish, G. *Letting Go of the Words: Writing Web Content That Works*. 2nd ed. Waltham, MA: Morgan Kaufmann, 2012.

Rumelt. R. *Good Strategy/Bad Strategy*. New York: Crown Business, 2011.

Shneiderman, B. *Leonardo's Laptop: Human Needs and the New Computing Technologies*. Cambridge: MIT Press, 2003.

Wachter-Boettcher, S. *Content Everywhere: Strategy and Structure for Future-Ready Content*. Brooklyn, NY: Rosenfeld Media, 2012.

Welchman, L. *Managing Chaos: Digital Governance by Design*. Brooklyn, NY: Rosenfeld Media, 2015.

If you can't explain it simply,
you don't understand it well enough.
– Albert Einstein

Design needs to be plugged into
human behaviour. Design dissolves
in behaviour.
– Naoto Fukasawa

CHAPTER 2

Research

I n designing web pages we often base initial plans on widely used page layout and navigation patterns, and use best practices such as consistency, modularity, and simplicity in creating our web interfaces. However, the best method for making design decisions is to expose these design best practices and familiar web layout conventions to a regimen of close consultation with users at each stage of the design process. Involving users in the development process helps us understand user requirements, which allows us to make informed design decisions and produce more effective designs.

In this chapter we cover research methods that support a research-directed approach to web site development. Every aspect of user experience design benefits from engaging with people, through activities such as brainstorming, observation, inquiry, and usability testing. We also discuss the use of web analytics as a way to gain insights into how users work with digital products. Analytics can provide a useful perspective but are insufficient on their own in providing a window into understanding user needs and preferences.

Research goes beyond asking questions and delivering solutions based on what people ask for. As a quotation attributed to Henry Ford goes, "If I had asked people what they wanted, they would have said faster horses." Research is about identifying opportunities to meet even unexpressed needs, and to devise innovative solutions that provide improved ease of use for everyone.

One never knows, do one?

—Thomas "Fats" Waller

BRAINSTORMING

One of the most important parts of the process of developing an innovative and highly functional site is ideation and brainstorming, and the research and exploration of user needs that should always precede ideas about how to create or improve the user experience of your online content. Although open-format free-for-all brainstorming sessions work well in some instances, it is a good idea to set ground rules to guide expectations about how the results of ideation will influence prototyping and later site development. It's also good to have a process framework for developing new ideas that is based solidly on user-centered design principles and research.

USING "DESIGN THINKING" FOR BRAINSTORMING

Charles Eames, asked in a 1972 interview, "Does the creation of design admit constraint?" answered, "Design depends largely on constraints." This tension between creativity and constraints is at the core of "design thinking," a creative approach to problem solving popularized by the design firm IDEO. A design thinking approach encourages the use of creative, human-centered methods to identify real needs and to build solutions that can be successful within environmental constraints.

- **Inspiration:** Defining the problem that needs solving.
- **Ideation:** Engaging in a process of generating and trying out solutions.
- **Implementation:** Taking a solution from concept to product.

IDEO's human-centered design process is not specific to the web, and was developed primarily to help nongovernmental organizations (NGOs) in their support and charitable work with poor communities. Nonetheless, the design thinking approach is applicable to any ideation, design, and prototyping process, helping to provide structure at each step along the way and, perhaps just as important, establishing a filtering process by which to judge which ideas are truly worthy of development into prototypes and working products.

H-C-D framework

IDEO's H-C-D framework (Hear, Create, Deliver) is particularly appropriate for fast-paced and iterative development of user observations, potential solutions, and design deliverables. The process starts with a substantial period of exploration, research, and simple old-fashioned listening to what real users would find helpful or interesting. These exploration sessions are by far the most trustworthy way to generate ideas that not only are interesting and helpful to users but also help the development team to understand the audience's perspective on different aspects of the project, such as desktop versus mobile uses of your site. Web developers who sit at desks all day in front of double-monitor rigs often severely underestimate the needs and ambitions of mobile users.

- **Hear:** In this phase the design team collects user stories, looks at both general and specific use cases for any existing web sites (or similar or competing sites), collects feedback and suggestions from users, and gets to know representative members of the audience that will use the final designs. The goal in this phase is to collect as much information as possible from real users and project stakeholders, and as many ideas as possible about how to serve their needs. This is the time to engage in user research activities, to put people first and learn about real end-user needs and preferences rather than make assumptions.

Ideating for human-centered design: H-C-D

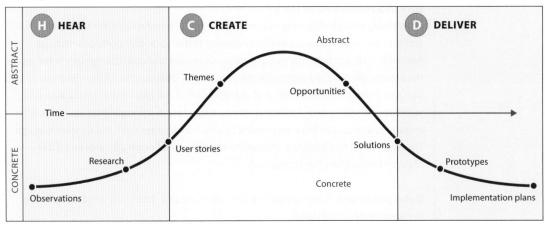

- **Create:** The design team works together in informal workshop sessions to examine and prioritize user stories, look for general themes that might underlie or unite some user stories into broader ideas and solutions, and brainstorm about how this better understanding of user needs might translate into concrete prototypes and finished designs.
- **Deliver:** In this phase, working detailed plans and working prototypes are first developed and then translated into detailed production plans for specific content, features, and code to support the highest-priority user stories and develop finished site elements.

Generating ideas and making choices

Good ideation processes will generate far more ideas than will be practical or wise to act upon. The final stages of a properly run ideation process winnow the mass of ideas into the small percentage that are worth the time and resources to develop into working prototypes of final project deliverables. How do you decide which stories, problems, and solutions are most practical, given the real-world constraints of time, resources, and budgets? In the design thinking process each potential solution must pass through three filters:

- **Desirability:** How much do people want this?
- **Feasibility:** Can we actually create this successfully?
- **Viability:** Do we have the financial resources and stakeholder support to make this happen?

FIGURE 2.1

The IDEO design firm worked with the Gates Foundation to produce a general framework for ideation in all kinds of circumstances, from community action in nongovernmental organizations to more conventional design and technology brainstorming (wsg4.link/h-c-d).

This filtering can be crucial to project success: as we'll show in the next chapter, the vast majority of software project "features" are seldom or never used; every mediocre idea or unneeded feature that survives the filtering process wastes time and money, and will clutter and complicate your final product (see "filtering failure" in fig. 2.2). This rigorous prioritization is especially important in projects run with agile methods, as the core idea of an agile process is always to focus sprints on the most important features or goals.

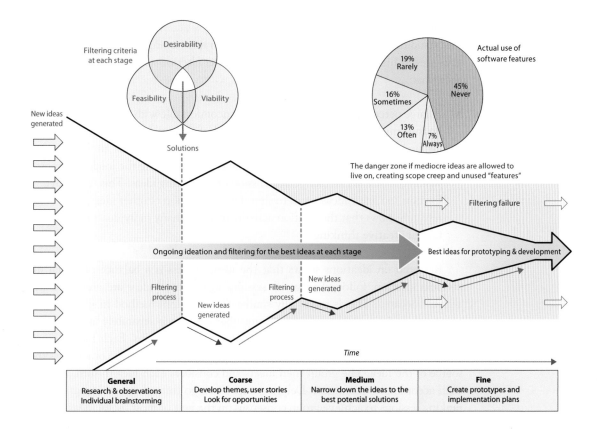

The danger zone if mediocre ideas are allowed to live on, creating scope creep and unused "features"

Filtering criteria at each stage

Desirability

Feasibility   Viability

Solutions

New ideas generated

Actual use of software features

45% Never
19% Rarely
16% Sometimes
13% Often
7% Always

Ongoing ideation and filtering for the best ideas at each stage

Filtering failure

Best ideas for prototyping & development

Filtering process

New ideas generated

Filtering process

New ideas generated

New ideas generated

Time

General	Coarse	Medium	Fine
Research & observations Individual brainstorming	Develop themes, user stories Look for opportunities	Narrow down the ideas to the best potential solutions	Create prototypes and implementation plans

This business of filtering might be the most important—and socially awkward—phase of the whole design process. We tend to concentrate on the fun and positive aspects of ideation, where "all ideas are welcome, and there are no bad ideas." This wide-open "divergent thinking" start to ideation is crucial for real innovations to emerge. However, also important is "convergent thinking," where ideas are eliminated and choices are made. As each idea is held up against the filters of desirability, feasibility, and viability, many good ideas are set aside in favor of great ideas. But all ideas contribute to the strength and depth of the ideas that remain. It's crucial that all participants understand that good group ideation is a team process, and that the final great ideas are a team product. The whole team loses every time a mediocre idea survives the filtering process.

FIGURE 2.2
A healthy brainstorming or ideation process will always produce more good ideas than you can actually act on. What's crucial is to use the desirability-feasibility-viability filtering process to identify the really great ideas, in which you might usefully invest further time and money.

Group versus individual ideation

The standing presumption about ideation and brainstorming is that these are group activities. While group activities are useful at later filtering stages of ideation, studies show that:

- A large percentage of the population is uncomfortable with group brainstorming techniques, and individual ideation produces more unique ideas.
- Group ideation sessions tend to home in quickly on a few ideas, to the exclusion of others. Some of this is social dynamics, where the loudest or most passionate voices can dampen discussion of competing ideas. This "cognitive fixation" on a few ideas tends to shut down discussion of other ideas, and research shows that the fixation actually hampers many individuals from further creative thinking.

Research on ideations shows that the ideal process is a balance of initial individual ideation, followed by group sessions in which all ideas are presented and actively debated. This is essentially similar to the Delphi method in ideation and group consensus building, where each member of a group separately and privately records his or her best ideas or answers to particular problems. Each idea is given to a group facilitator, who anonymizes each contribution, so that no one knows the source of the idea. The group then meets and considers each idea in turn, ranking each according to usefulness. Delphi groups often go through several ideation and ranking sessions to achieve group consensus on the best or most useful ideas.

The H-C-D process also supports individual and group ideation phases. The early "hearing" and research period is well suited to individual ideation. The later "deliver" phases are best for group sessions and vigorous discussions about which ideas are best to pursue, and the Delphi method is ideal for this. Appoint a neutral moderator for brainstorming groups to act as timekeeper, run Delphi ranking sessions, and monitor against the cognitive fixation phenomenon that can too quickly shut down discussion of competing ideas.

USER RESEARCH

The first step in any web site design process is to gather information about users—who they are, what their goals are—and identify their requirements for working with the site. The research phase is normally the most time-consuming phase of any design project, but the time spent on research makes the design and evaluation phase move more rapidly. With good user research, the decisions that drive the design are based on a solid understanding of users' goals and requirements and therefore are far more likely to hit the mark without many cycles of iteration.

DEFINING SCOPE

Engaging with users is critical in the design process, particularly at the beginning phases, where the team is engaged in defining the need and devising the solution. As much as members of a web development team may feel they understand the problem domain, other points of view are essential. The problem may seem obvious and the solution straightforward—until you learn the constraints from stakeholder interviews and the unexpected user behaviors from field studies.

Several techniques exist for collecting feedback directly from users about their goals and behaviors. The information gathered from these collection techniques is subjective; it represents what users say they do, which is not necessarily the same as what they actually do and care about.

Surveys

Surveys are helpful for collecting a broad range of responses about demographics and goals. Web site surveys typically ask initial questions to help define the user: age, gender, audience type (customer, potential customer, buyer, seller). Then there might be questions related to frequency of use: first-time visitor, sometimes visitor, frequent visitor. The meat of the survey is likely to be determining which elements of the site are most used, along with some assessment of the effectiveness and enjoyment derived from using them. This question might be represented as a list of site sections, each with a sliding scale measuring the success of use. Finally, an open-ended question inviting general feedback is always a good idea. Although the information is difficult to analyze, a simple read of the responses will yield common themes that may be useful for planning.

Interviews

In-person techniques open the door to more accurate and detailed information gathering because of the opportunity for interaction and exchange. In an interview, you inquire into user goals, interests, needs, and behaviors. One effective method for understanding user behaviors is to ask users to give a verbal walkthrough that describes their typical interaction and task flow when accomplishing a goal. For example, in designing a new dating web site, you might ask users from your target audience to describe their current process when interacting with a similar web site and how they make connections without the help of the web. The key is to get the user talking and keep him or her talking. Ask clarifying questions, pursue important details, and periodically sum up the important elements of the conversation. Don't be too quick to speak when the conversation lags; pause, and give the user the opportunity to continue the discussion thread. Also, don't be too rigid in sticking to the script; digressions may lead to valuable insights.

PROFILE OF A DESIGN THINKER

One shortcoming of "design thinking" is in its name—the word "design." Most people do not consider themselves designers, and this can be particularly true on technology projects. As Tim Brown notes in his *Harvard Business Review* article "Design Thinking," to be a design thinker you don't need to wear "weird shoes or a black turtleneck." He presents the following characteristics, suggesting that the right development and experiences can bring these out in many people, who can then use design thinking to build innovative solutions (wsg4.link/hbr-designthinking).

Empathy Taking a "people first" approach and getting into the shoes of potential users means you can arrive at solutions that are based on real needs and address real concerns. Without empathy, solutions are often based on factors that are not relevant to users, such as organizational priorities or assumptions of user needs made by project team members.

Integrative thinking Being able to see issues across multiple data points and even contradictory research findings means you can analyze complex needs and constraints and devise solutions that are better suited to the reality of the problem area.

Optimism Having the conviction that there is a solution, and holding fast to that optimism, gives you the persistence and endurance to stay the course, seeking out the best alternative.

Experimentalism Creativity requires trial and error. You must be willing to try new ideas, and ready to discard ideas that don't measure up and aren't worth pursuing.

Collaboration Dialog and exchange of ideas and insights with people who have other areas of expertise build synergy and yield creative approaches.

Focus groups

Focus groups have a very different dynamic. Whereas the interview is all about the individual, the focus group is about the collective—a group of users who share common concerns. Focus groups have a number of benefits, not the least of which is economy; they offer an opportunity to hear many different perspectives at once. Also, the collaborative nature of focus groups helps people contribute insights that they may not have been aware of on their own. One user raises an issue that resonates with another, and the second user picks up the issue and takes it farther, and the next farther still.

Field studies

Observing users in their natural setting yields valuable insights and objective information about user behaviors and the efficacy of designs. With observational methods, we move beyond self-reported goals and behaviors to observed goals and behaviors. In a field study, you observe users working with a system, typically in their own context. For example, in designing a library catalog system, observation of library patrons as they navigate the library is an excellent way to understand how they work with online catalog systems and how such systems help or hinder them in achieving their goals. Field studies are particularly helpful at the beginning of a project. For a redesign, observe users working with your current system to identify points of conflict between the design and user goals. For a new web site project, observe users working with a similar web site.

GUIDING DESIGN DECISIONS

Design is a process of making decisions. When user research is part of the design process, those decisions are guided by user perspectives and insights gleaned from observation. The following methods ensure that those insights and perspectives remain part of the decision-making process.

Personas

Personas are fictional representative users placed in narratives to stand in for real users during the design process. Personas arise from the research phase and are informed by surveys, interviews, focus groups, and other research methods. A persona typically includes a name, demographic information, level of expertise, and such details about the fictional user's platform as connection speed, operating system, and browser software. Personas also include detailed information about user goals and motivations.

For universal usability, personas should push the boundaries of the fictional "average user" to include a range of use contexts and user motivations. Personas should represent the full range of age groups, computer expertise, and access technologies, including mobile devices, the wide but short screens of typical laptop computers, and screen reader software for nonvisual access.

Goal analysis

A person uses a system in response to specific goals he or she is trying to achieve. When we roll out of bed and into the shower in the morning, our goal is not turning on the water; our goal is to get clean and wake up. It's the tasks we undertake to accomplish this goal that involve water, faucets, and soap. In design, it's important to focus on goals rather than tasks in making design decisions. A focus on goals helps us think outside the box and create better designs. Instead of designing a shower from

FIGURE 2.3
Complex data displays can easily overwhelm the reader. Travelocity's generous use of white space and the carefully honed interface of its search results pages help make a complex list manageable and unintimidating.

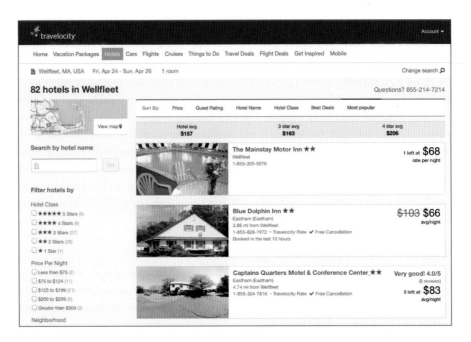

the perspective of the tasks it needs to support, we can focus on the goal of getting clean and waking up, which opens the door to new approaches.

For example, let's say our goal when interacting with a travel web site is to get from Boston to Barbados without spending too much time or money. To accomplish our goal, our tasks are to compare flight schedules and prices. The designer who designs for our goal will understand that time spent in transit and cost are the primary factors and will design an interface that shows information in a way that permits easy comparisons. Other information related to the trip, such as meals served or type of aircraft, is secondary and available on request.

Goals come in many shapes and sizes and emerge from different perspectives. Users have both personal and professional goals: being more productive, having fun, saving time and money. Organizational goals also vary: increasing revenue, recruiting more and better employees, offering more services. With any web site project, user goals should be the driving factor behind design decisions and the compass to steer by throughout the design process.

Scenarios

Scenarios, or use cases, are brief narratives that tell the story of a particular user's path in accomplishing his or her goals. To construct a scenario, we use personas representing our users and walk them through the various tasks necessary with the web site in order to accomplish their goals. In composing a scenario, we can play out

different approaches to design and functionality and in the process identify possible problems with each approach.

EVALUATING DESIGNS

The design phase is an iterative one in which we conceptualize designs to create mock-ups, which we then evaluate and refine, often repeatedly, before arriving at a final design and finished web site. Consulting with users during the design phase allows us to home in on a design that presents content and functionality in a shape that maps to user goals and behaviors, and leads to successful and enjoyable user experiences.

Wireframes

Wireframes provide low-cost and highly effective support for iterative design. Wireframes are easy to create and, most important, easy to change—far easier than a coded web site or web application. The wireframe phase should provide a conceptual screen design and task flow and, through testing, evolve into a solid interface and task flow to hand off to programmers.

Spend ample time creating and testing wireframes. By virtue of their malleability, they are your best defense against poorly conceived, ineffective designs. Once you move your web site or application into development, changes to the user interface and task flows become more costly and are therefore less likely to be implemented.

Your initial wireframes might be simple sketches on paper or a whiteboard, to help conceptualize the user interface and task flow. Paper prototypes provide an inexpensive method for collecting user feedback on an evolving design. A paper prototype typically illustrates the location of page elements, such as site navigation, search, and content, and includes the labeling that will be used for these elements. These low-resolution mock-ups can be used in user research to determine whether the organization of the page and the navigation labels are easy to use and understand. For small projects, these may be sufficient to move a project from concept to development. Most projects, however, will move from sketches to diagrams created using software such as Adobe Illustrator, Visio, or OmniGraffle. These wireframes are best for complex projects with many design cycles because they are easier to modify and easier to share and distribute among the design team (see fig. 4.23).

Prototypes

A prototype is a set of wireframes used to simulate a functioning application. The prototype models the purpose of the application, its flow, and its patterns for interaction. With this model, you create an environment for walking a user through a task and identifying points of confusion or difficulty. You can then produce new wireframes to address any problems and test the prototype again (and again and again).

Paper prototypes consist of a set of wireframes, each on its own page (or index card), and can be used to conceptualize the flow of an application. Paper prototypes can be used for usability testing early in the design process, before any screens are built or code is written. To test a paper prototype, place the first screen of an application—say, the login screen—in front of the user and ask for feedback—what action would you take? Then replace the first screen with the one that would result from the user's action, and continue working through the various stages of the interaction. Ask for feedback all along the way, and spend time after the session collecting additional feedback and suggestions.

A "functional" prototype provides an intermediate step between a rough sketch and a fully designed web application and can furnish a framework for moving from the conceptual to the design phase of a project. HTML wireframes form the basis of this high-fidelity prototype, with the essential elements of the application represented on separate web pages. The "functional" features of the application are simulated using basic links among and between pages, allowing users to experience and respond to the flow of the application. The HTML prototype can be refined in response to user feedback and then retested and further refined. Once the functionality and back-end systems are fully developed and tested, the visual design and web site interface can be "poured" into the wireframe to produce a finished design.

Functional wireframes use the same minimalist design as paper prototypes, but on a functional web site. They take more time to develop than paper prototypes but are well worth the effort, particularly for sites that are built on complex information architectures and for web applications that contain high levels of interaction. For a functional wireframe, several layers of the web site are established to model the site's architecture, navigation, and functionality. For interactive sites, such as web applications, the wireframe should include a basic user interface in order to play out and test the flow of the application with users.

Include content in your user research activities. For example, use real content on your wireframes and prototypes rather than "lorem ipsum" dummy text. When you are seeking feedback on wireframes or prototypes, ask users questions about content, such as "What are the writer's goals for this content? Who do you think is the target audience for this content? What would you expect a user to do after reading this content?"

Usability testing

Usability testing is a controlled and directed observation of user behaviors when working with a design. Usability testing is used throughout the design process to evaluate different design approaches by observing how well, or how poorly, they work in helping users accomplish tasks.

A typical usability testing session has a tester and a participant who represents the target audience. The user is assigned a set of tasks intended to put specific elements of a design to the test and reveal any shortcomings of the approach. During the session, the user is asked to think aloud so that the tester can understand the rationale behind his or her choices. The session normally ends with an open-ended interview in which the user is given the opportunity to discuss his or her experience with the system more broadly and provide insights and suggestions on how the system might be improved.

Usability testing is valuable throughout the design process for identifying usability problems. The lessons learned from usability testing can be used in refining the design, improving usability, and ensuring that people can find and make use of the content.

Like accessibility, many development teams leave usability testing to the end of the project or, worse, do not budget in time and resources for usability testing, much less usability testing that involves people with disabilities. The inertia around usability testing appears to be due to a misconception that "real" usability testing must be complex and time-consuming, and must involve a usability lab, expensive equipment, lots of participants, and a bulletproof test design. While a lab and resources and trained researchers certainly are advantageous, the lack of these is no reason not to do usability testing. The gains from informal usability testing with one participant are exponentially greater than doing no usability testing at all.

In his book *Don't Make Me Think*, Steve Krug promotes do-it-yourself usability testing, in which you "do your own testing when you have no time and no money," and his book *Rocket Surgery Made Easy* describes in detail how to do it. His approach encourages short but frequent sessions with few people—one morning a month with three participants, followed by a debriefing session to decide what to fix.

INVOLVING PEOPLE WITH DISABILITIES IN RESEARCH ACTIVITIES

In *Change by Design*, Tim Brown suggests that innovative products are the outcome of observation, and suggests that we can learn a great deal by moving away from the mainstream and observing people who have what might appear to be singular needs and preferences. He explains, "By concentrating solely on the bulge at the center of the bell curve...we are more likely to confirm what we already know than learn something new and surprising."

Including people with disabilities in user research and usability testing is a great way to gain insights into issues that may seem unique but can have wide-ranging influence on the quality of user experience. Many examples of design that have arisen out of accommodating the needs of people with disabilities have improved quality of life for everyone: entry ramps, automatic door openers, lever handles, high-contrast colors. By including people with disabilities in your research activities, you will learn how to make your web site more accessible and usable for people with disabilities. You may also identify opportunities to provide accessibility features that will improve the user experience for everyone in your audience.

Beyond opportunities for innovation, there are many practical benefits to involving people with disabilities in user research. In some cases, there are standards that require or encourage consultation with people with disabilities, including, in the United States, the 21st Century Communications and Video Accessibility Act (CVAA), and, in the United Kingdom, the British Standards Institute Standard BS 8878. User research activities that involve people with disabilities will help meet obligations as well as highlight accessibility issues. The development team can work to resolve these issues. Any unresolved issues should be recorded according to the process standards, and be the focus of a defined plan for remediation and resolution.

With accessibility, adhering to defined standards and guidelines, such as the Web Content Accessibility Guidelines (WCAG) 2.0, can help meet legal obligations and improve usability for people with disabilities. However, user research can uncover additional issues that are not addressed by standard compliance, and that can be improved through design. Observation and inquiry can help identify solutions that go beyond standards compliance to create accessible and enjoyable user experience.

For many designers and developers, accessibility is a set of guidelines and checklist rather than something direct and experiential that provokes feelings of connection and empathy. Most people on web development teams don't know how a person who is blind uses, for example, a touchscreen, or how someone who doesn't use a mouse works the controls on a web page. This reflects not a lack of concern but simply a lack of exposure. By involving people with disabilities in user research activities, designers, developers, strategists, and writers can see firsthand how people use digital products and services, the issues they encounter, what works well, and what doesn't. Most designers and developers love solving problems, and will be eager to resolve problem features once they know their impact.

ANALYTICS

Web technology collects metrics about users: what operating system and browser they use, their screen resolution, what page they visited just before their arrival at your site. And although it's certainly useful to know these attributes, they are not necessarily helpful in defining the audience for your web site. Web metrics will not tell you precisely why users visit your site, what they hope to find from your site, or whether they are visually impaired, expert or novice, young or old.

In the end, even with the best web analytics, many things about your audience's hopes, motivations, and expectations will remain a mystery if you rely solely on web metrics to understand your users.

In contrast, a target audience is a group of users that you have identified as critical to the success of your site. For instance, you may be designing for a certain age group, such as grade school children, teens, or retirees. Or you may be designing for a specific technology, such as mobile devices. Bear in mind that members of your target audience may share common interests, but they are not likely to share access requirements. Some may be experts and others first-time users. Some may have impaired or no vision, and others may have mobility or dexterity issues. The same person may access your site on a laptop, table, or smartphone. And although you may target a certain audience, others will come. For example, an investment service for retirees will also draw visits from investors, competitors, family members, and those lucky enough to enjoy early retirement. It would be a mistake to design such a site to meet only the needs of older users.

And there is much at stake when you exclude users. Even if your web logs show that only 2 percent of your users use a specific brand of browser, don't make the mistake of using technology that excludes those users. It's bad business to exclude anyone from access to your information and services, and there is no way to place a value on those users who you have excluded. Who knows? Your next major donor might be one of the 2 percent you turned away at the door!

USING ANALYTICS AS A TOOL FOR DECISION MAKING

With each page served, web servers collect basic information about the user and save the information in a server log file. Web analytics involves using the data in the server logs to study user behaviors. More advanced web analytics make use of additional tracking techniques that usually involve embedding something on the client—a "bug" on the page or a session cookie—that enables collection of additional information. With web analytics, it's possible to reconstruct elements of a web site session, such as:

- Where the user was before arriving at your site
- Whether the user used a search engine, and if so, which keywords were used
- The sequence of pages the user visited while on your site
- Attributes of the user's configuration, including browser, operating system, and screen dimensions and color settings
- Whether the user was a new or repeat visitor
- The last page in the session before the user left your site

These and other site-specific metrics (the number of page requests helps determine which pages are most used; the number of distinct hosts helps determine how many site visitors there are) offer important insights into how users are working with your site, which is essential to any redesign process. But bear in mind that although web analytics appear to measure what is happening on your site, the reality is far more complicated. Many factors skew the data, such as browser caching, in which pages are stored locally on the client machine. When a user visits a cached page, that visit will not be logged in the server log file, since the server was not asked for the page. Use web analytics, but don't treat them as the last word on user behaviors. Use them to complement the other user-centered techniques described in this chapter.

A/B Testing

There is no "silver bullet" in web site design—no single solution that works for all users. Often design teams are faced with several approaches and must make a decision on where to focus energy and resources. In these cases it can be helpful to use

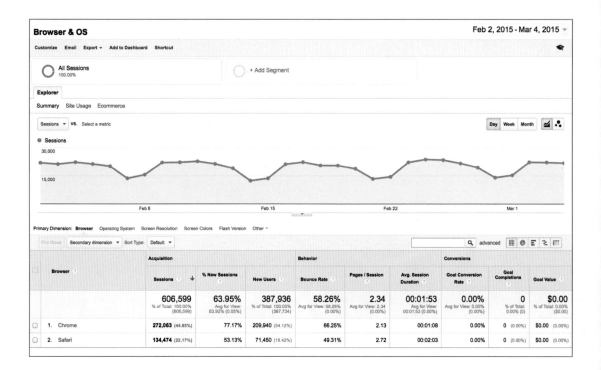

A/B testing, in which different versions of content and features are launched and evaluated for effectiveness.

The key to successful A/B testing is a clear set of measures that the team and stakeholders agree represents success in achieving project goals. These are typically derived from an increase in engagement, such as when more people sign up for a newsletter, click an advertisement, or purchase a product. They can also be based on user journeys, where each design affords a different path through the site. Through analytics, the team can assess which path is more direct in getting users to their destination.

RECOMMENDED READING

Brown, T. *Change by Design*. New York: HarperCollins, 2009.

Cooper, A., R. Reimann, D. Cronin, and C. Noessel. *About Face: The Essentials of Interaction Design*. Hoboken, NJ: Wiley. 2014.

Krug, S. *Don't Make Me Think, Revisited*. Berkeley, CA: New Riders, 2014.

———. *Rocket Surgery Made Easy*. Berkeley, CA: New Riders, 2010.

Martin, B., and B. Hanington. *Universal Methods of Design*. Beverly, MA: Rockport, 2012.

Shaffer, D. *Designing for Interaction: Creating Smart Applications and Clever Devices*. Berkeley, CA: New Riders, 2009.

FIGURE 2.4
Web analytics tools like Google Analytics are crucial for making informed decisions about the current usage patterns of your site. It is extremely important to collect good analytics data before planning a major site redesign, or you'll never have the baseline data you need to judge whether your new design is an improvement.

People think focus means saying yes to the thing you've got to focus on.
But that's not what it means at all. It means saying no to
the hundred other good ideas that there are. You have to
pick carefully. I'm actually as proud of the things we
haven't done as the things I have done.
Innovation is saying no to 1,000 things.
– Steve Jobs

EASTERN
AIR LINES

344

Start

Desireability

Feasability

Viability

12

Emerging solutions that are
desireable, feasible, and viable

CHAPTER 3

Process

Planning a web site is a two-part process: first you gather your development team, analyze your needs and goals, and work through the development process outlined here to refine your plans. Next you build on the strategy in the project charter with implementation details—what you intend to do and why, what technology and content you'll need, how long the process will take, what you will spend to do it, and how you will assess the results of your efforts. In this way, the project charter becomes both the blueprint for your process and the touchstone you'll use to keep the project focused on the agreed-on priorities and deliverables.

In theory there is no difference between theory and practice. But in practice, there is.

—Yogi Berra

PROJECT RESOURCES

The strategic importance and project budget for your web efforts will largely determine the size and skill depth of your development team. Even for a smaller project, however, you'll need to cover the core team disciplines. In most small to medium projects one person may handle multiple tasks, or someone with specialized expertise (graphic design, for instance) may be hired for specific assignments. Many managers who are assigned the responsibility of creating a web site don't have the luxury of picking specialist team members. Inventory the skills and aptitudes in the team you assemble, and consider careful outsourcing to supply any expertise your team lacks.

The core skill sets needed in a web development team are:

- Strategy and planning
- Project management
- Information architecture and content development
- Visual and interaction design
- Web coding for themes and templates, the content management system, and server-side engineering
- Site production

In larger web projects each role may be filled by one or several people, although in more specialized skill areas those contributors are not likely to be full-time team members for the duration of the project.

ASSEMBLING A WEB DEVELOPMENT TEAM

We describe the responsibilities and activities for each domain below. Here we organize core team responsibilities by domain, establishing the domain lead role and secondary roles. We strongly recommend cross-disciplinary teams over a more phased approach, in which each domain completes its activities and hands over responsibility to another team to complete the next phase of development. With the traditional "throw it over the wall" approach, every stage of the development process is carried out independently. While this approach provides more control over the overall process and is easier to track from a project management perspective (see "Project Management," below), it has many shortcomings. Communications suffer, and projects take more time as different domains work to resolve differences that arise from not working from a shared vision. Cross-disciplinary teams are more complex to manage, but the benefits outweigh the limitations. We all grow when exposed to views and knowledge that differ from our own, and the synergy powered by diverse viewpoints, the interdependencies that arise from collaboration, and the opportunities to build capacity for individuals and as a team more than compensate for the project management overhead.

- Project sponsor
  - Account executive
  - Steering committee
- Project lead
  - Product owner
  - Project manager
- User experience lead
  - Strategist
  - User researcher
  - Information architect
- Design lead
  - Graphic designer
  - Interaction designer
- Technology lead
  - Web application programmer
  - Content management system (CMS) development and template development expert
  - Web engineer (HTML, CSS, JavaScript)
  - Database administrator or systems integration expert
  - Web server specialist or systems engineer
  - Quality assurance specialist

- Production lead
  - HTML/CSS page coder and CMS expert user
  - Media specialist (photography, illustration, audiovisual)
  - Content subject matter expert (SME)
  - Writer
  - Site editor

Project sponsor

The project sponsor is the person who has authority to initiate the project and approve the final outcome. In most instances the sponsor is the client or customer for the web site development work, but in smaller in-house department projects the sponsoring manager and the project lead may be the same person. The sponsor provides the overall strategic vision and purpose for the site development project, approves the contract or work plan, and provides the resources to support the work of the site development team.

The sponsor is the client the team works to please, but sponsors have important work to perform as part of the overall site development team. Sponsors act as liaisons to the rest of the sponsoring organization, coordinating with the larger goals of the sponsoring organization and communicating project progress to leadership and the steering committee. They also provide critical domain expertise to the project and contribute to the site content. As such, it is crucial that sponsors and other stakeholders understand their responsibilities to the web team: late delivery of web site content is the most common cause of blown schedules in web development projects. Sponsors also are typically responsible for third-party or external content contracts, other media licensing negotiations, and coordination with other marketing, information technology, and communications efforts at the sponsoring organization or company. The sponsor is accountable to organizational leadership for budget, schedule, and project success.

Project lead

The project lead is the person responsible for overall project success. Activities related to leading and managing projects differ in that leading focuses on project success, while managing relates to process-related aspects of the project. Teams that use "scrum" or other "agile" frameworks divide these responsibilities between the roles of product owner and scrum master (see "Agile project management," below). On some teams, the same person has both responsibilities.

From a strategic perspective, the project lead steers project activities toward serving the goals and objectives outlined in the project charter, keeping the web team on course. The project lead makes the tough decisions related to direction and prioritization, and manages the communication channel between the team and the project sponsor. On a tactical level, the project lead coordinates and communicates the day-to-day implementation of the web site project, acting within the constraints of the project charter, project budget, development schedule, and quality objectives laid out in the strategy and planning stages. The project lead is the team member ultimately responsible for keeping the overall team activities focused on the site strategic objectives and agreed-upon deliverables, and he or she continually monitors the scope of the project activities to ensure that the team stays "on time and on budget." The project lead acts as the primary contact between the web team and the sponsor and manages the overall communication among creative, technical, and production elements of the web team. In larger web projects the project lead is not normally part of the hands-on production team, but in smaller in-house projects the sponsor, user experience lead, or technical lead may also act as the project lead for the site team. Project leads create and maintain the project planning and strategy documents, budget spreadsheets, project schedules, kanban boards and Gantt charts (see "Project Management," below), meeting notes, billing records, and other project documentation that details the team's activities (fig. 3.1).

User experience lead

The user experience lead is the primary user advocate on the web team, responsible for providing a quality experience to people who use the web site. User research and usability activities all fall within the domain of user experience, or UX. Information architecture, because it influences how users experience a site, is also typically part of UX. While several individuals may make up the UX team, in smaller teams the same individual often performs all user experience activities. User experience activities, particularly those related to user research and usability, are critical throughout the product development life cycle.

User research is the cornerstone of all successful product development, using observation and inquiry to understand user needs and preferences. In the initial stages of design, the user researcher is responsible for running interviews, field studies, and usability studies and for producing personas and scenarios to inform project requirements. Once designs are conceptualized in the form of diagrams, wireframes, and prototypes, the user researcher tests the designs with users and gathers feedback for the site designers and developers. In the final stages of a project, the user researcher evaluates the effectiveness of designs through additional field studies and usability testing, and ensures that universal usability goals are met. The user researcher is also responsible for evaluating the success of the project (Does the site accomplish the goals? Are users successful and satisfied with the design? Is the site usable and enjoyable for all users, including people with disabilities?) and for measuring project outcomes that correlate to good UX (Are more users visiting the site? Is the site producing more revenue? Are users responding to calls to action?).

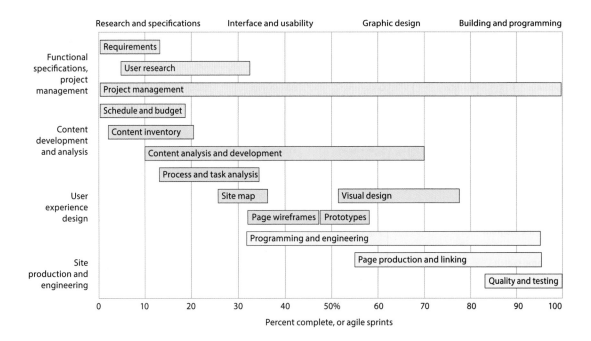

	Research and specifications	Interface and usability	Graphic design	Building and programming

Functional specifications, project management

- Requirements
- User research
- Project management
- Schedule and budget

Content development and analysis

- Content inventory
- Content analysis and development
- Process and task analysis

User experience design

- Site map
- Visual design
- Page wireframes | Prototypes
- Programming and engineering

Site production and engineering

- Page production and linking
- Quality and testing

| 0 | 10 | 20 | 30 | 40 | 50% | 60 | 70 | 80 | 90 | 100 |

Percent complete, or agile sprints

Information architecture is the process of organizing and categorizing web site structure and content. The information architect is most active early in the design and planning phases of the project, developing content categorization schemes, consistent site terminology, content structure across the site, taxonomies to support categories and tags, and site architecture diagrams that explain the overall site planning to both the sponsor and the team members. Information architects often have a background in library science, using controlled vocabularies, carefully designed content and navigation nomenclature, and search techniques to help users find relevant content. Information architects work closely with the site designers to craft page wireframes, the diagrammatic page grids that show how various areas of the page will be used to support site identity, navigation, and page content. Page wireframes form the crucial connection between the overall site architecture and what the user sees on each page of the site, determining how easily a user can find content and features, and shaping the user's overall experience. These visual representations are crucial to communicating site structure and user experience, particularly for the back-end technical developers who support the interactive elements of the site, and for use in testing concepts with users.

The information architecture strategy for a site also includes the content structure as implemented in content management systems (CMS) like Drupal, WordPress, or commercial CMS products. The content strategist and the information architect

FIGURE 3.1
Gantt charts represent one of the most widely used methods of communicating project work breakdowns, schedules, and current status.

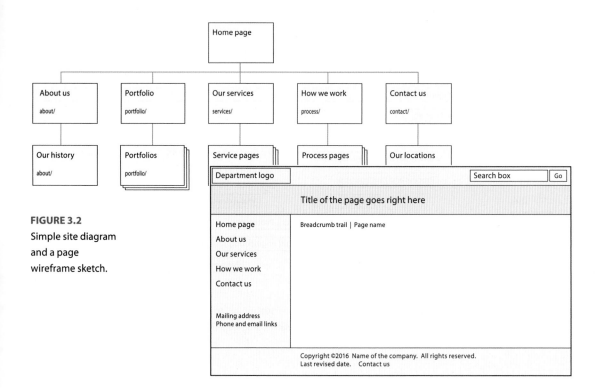

FIGURE 3.2

Simple site diagram and a page wireframe sketch.

will look at CMS content block and data entry architecture, modules for implementing content and navigation menu structure, and site themes and page templates. With the increasing importance of mobile content views, user experience activities must include creating a strategy for delivering content to the smaller viewports of smartphones, tablets, and even smart watches. Mobile computing has become so important that many organizations have adopted a "mobile-first" approach to creating sites, in which the foundation planning is done for the mobile views and content, and tablet and desktop views are handled as later iterations of the core mobile design.

Design lead

The design lead is responsible for the overall look and feel for the web site, establishing the site typography, visual interface design, color palette standards, page layout details, and the particulars of how the graphics, photography, other illustrations, and audiovisual media elements of the site come together to form an integrated whole. Many graphic design professionals specialize in designing for interactive media and are well versed in user interface design, web navigation, and site architecture. In smaller projects an experienced design lead sometimes assumes at least partial responsibility for the information architecture and user experience roles in addition to directing the visual design of a site. In larger organizations the design lead is usually the person responsible for assuring that the new web design work is consistent with any established corporate identity and user interface standards.

In the site development and planning stages the design lead creates or supervises the creation of increasingly complex design sketches to illustrate the evolving design proposals to the project sponsor and web team. As designs are approved, the design lead supervises the conversion of design sketches into detailed specifications of graphics and typography that engineers will need to create themes and templates.

Technology lead

The technology lead is the person responsible for the soundness and stability of the technology architecture. He or she must have a broad grasp of web publishing environments, including content management systems, development languages and frameworks, web database options, and network technology. The technology lead acts as the bridge, translator, and plain-English communicator between the technologists and the creative and project management elements of the team.

The technology lead creates, as part of the site planning process, the general blueprints for the collection of technologies that will support the chosen technology framework, including content management systems, database integration and support, integration with social media platforms like Facebook and Twitter, custom programming, cms theme and template development, and integration with other applications or databases that supply content or interactive features to the web site. The technology lead provides the primary data processing architecture for the project, determining the technical specifications for the overall web server and database server hardware architecture or web hosting services, shaping development frameworks, assessing the developing strategy and goals, and matching those needs to appropriate technology solutions. In larger projects the web technology lead typically manages teams of programmers, network and server engineers, database administrators, software quality assurance testers, and other information technology professionals who support the production and design teams.

Production lead

The production lead is responsible for the cohesiveness of the site and for the quality of the site over time. Site producers are usually experienced generalists. "Producer" is a title borrowed from audiovisual media, where a producer combines a project managerial role with extensive experience in integrating various creative elements (writing, hands-on web development, audiovisual or graphic production). The activities of the production lead change over the project life cycle.

Early in the design stage the production lead focuses on content development and production. Once the site has been planned and the design and information architecture plans have been completed, the production lead manages the work of building the site's pages, typically in a CMS, assembling the work of the information architects and site graphic designers into finished pages.

A key role within the production team is the site editor, who has overall responsibility for the written content and editorial quality of the finished site. The editor establishes the editorial tone for the web site, determines editorial style guidelines, and works with clients and subject matter experts (SMEs) to collect, organize, and deliver finished text to the production team. In smaller teams the editor creates site copy, interviews SMEs to create content, and may be responsible for creating news and feature material for the site. Experienced editors also play an increasingly important role in the technical and production aspects of site content, ensuring that written content from the sponsoring organization is provided on time, in the specified editorial and technical markup format, and with sufficient quality to meet site goals. This technical aspect of content structure and formatting is particularly important in content management systems.

In addition to ensuring editorial quality, a site editor must also make certain that the content of the site reflects the policies of the enterprise, is consistent with local appropriate use policies, and does not contain material that violates copyright laws. Many people who post on their own sites pictures, cartoons, audiovisual files, or written material copied from other sites do not understand copyright and the legal risks in using copyrighted materials inappropriately. A site editor is often an institution's first line of defense against an expensive lawsuit over the misuse of protected material.

Because most search engine optimization (SEO) efforts are based on careful, consistent use of keyword language and heading markup, the web editor is also the team member most likely to lead the day-to-day efforts to make the site as search-friendly as possible. Keeping the site optimized for both local search engine visibility (using local search tools built into the CMS) and keeping public sites maximally visible to general Internet search engines like Google and Bing are crucial strategic components of making the new content accessible and findable for your audience.

Unlike the other site development roles described above, the site editor's role is a long-term job, bridging the transition from a site development project into an ongoing web publication process that maintains the web site after launch and keeps the content fresh and relevant to your audience. If the project manager is the focal point of the early stages of creating your site, then the site editor should gradually assume the leadership role in the stages just before, during, and after the site launch. This transition of responsibilities ensures that the site won't become an orphan after the project team leaves the launch party and moves on to new assignments.

PROJECT PLANNING

CREATING A PROJECT IMPLEMENTATION PLAN

The project charter discussed in Chapter 1, Strategy, is the development team's concise statement of core goals, values, and intent in order to provide the ultimate policy direction for everything that comes next. Designing a substantial web site is costly and time-consuming. When you're up to your neck in the daily challenges of building the site, it can be easy to forget why you are doing what you are doing and to lose sight of your original priorities, not knowing whether the decisions you are making firmly support the overall objectives. A well-written project charter is a powerful daily tool for judging the effectiveness of a development effort. It becomes a compass to keep the team firmly pointed at the goals established when you started the journey. A good project charter becomes a daily reference point for settling disputes, avoiding "scope creep," judging the potential utility of new ideas as they arise, measuring progress, and keeping the development team focused on the end result.

The next step is to create a project implementation plan, defining the content scope, budget, schedule, and technical aspects of the web site. The best project plans are short and to the point, often outlines or bulleted lists of the major design or technical features planned.

A good project plan contains the following sections, with specifications for implementation details for the project.

Project overview

The project plan should begin with a concise narrative description of the content, features, and services that the new site will provide. This section answers the "why" of your project. It should be a short description of the sales, marketing, communications, or other goals that will be accomplished by creating the new web site, along with a rationale and general metrics for determining the success and return on investment (ROI) for the proposed web site. Think of it as a written version of your "elevator speech" to senior managers who must approve the project: your most concise, to-the-point rendition of your top three reasons why the new or redesigned web site should exist. This section should end with a short strategic statement that places the site project within the context of the sponsoring organization's missions and existing web presence.

Success metrics

Most web site projects have measurable goals: to increase traffic, boost sales, improve client relations, reduce support emails, and so on. Many of these measures rely on preexisting data to enable before-and-after comparisons of the site's success. Review the "success indicators" in your project charter to identify which to include in your

WEB TEAMS

The well-known information architect and web user interface expert Jesse James Garrett created "The Nine Pillars of Successful Web Teams," a concise graphic description of the core roles in site development (wsg4.link/jjg-9pillars). The disciplines and site development stages proceed from left to right in a logical progression from strategic planning to implementation and visual design.

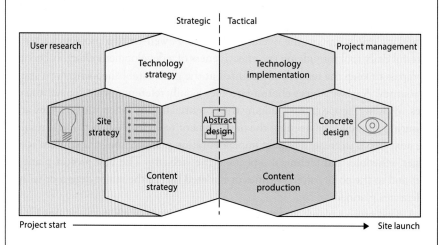

We've modified Garrett's pillars and added a more explicit time dimension and emphasis on the early and continuing role of project management throughout the process of web site development. We also emphasize the importance of getting broad participation and input in the user research and strategic planning stages of your project. The more you hear from stakeholders and potential users, the better your planning and design will be. Early in the process your designs and plans ought to change almost daily, as the iterative tasks of design, user research, and stakeholder input help you refine and improve your ideas. Design iteration is essential in developing the ordered complexity of a large web site.

Later in the process, however, the team should pare down to those core specialists who are building the site. Otherwise, continuing major design changes can lead to production churning, wasted effort, and blown schedules. Get broad input early on, make the best site design and project plan possible, and then focus the team on implementing the plan.

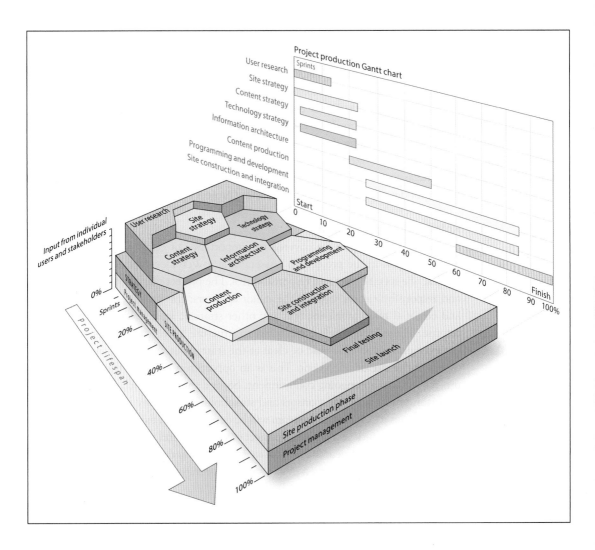

project plan as true success metrics. It is important to establish success metrics before you begin because you may need to be proactive about collecting "before" data before launching the site.

Project scope

Here you detail the "what" of the proposed site. In as much detail as possible for each stage of the project, describe the web site to be created, drawing on the strategies and tactics described in the project charter. Early in the planning process this statement will have to be general and should concentrate on the core "must-have" features, content, and purposes of the site. Avoid stipulating the use of specific technologies

("We're using JQuery for everything"), a decision that really should be determined after the web site team has made a thorough assessment. Ironically, it is often useful (and sometimes easier) to make a careful statement of what your project is not. This form of "is/is not" scope statement is particularly useful where your new site may have aspects that are similar to existing organizational sites or where your project sponsors may not immediately grasp your intent in creating the web site.

The project scope should be flexible in the planning stages of the project but should become a fixed specification before hard budget numbers or schedule deadlines are assigned to the project. See the section on "Site Definition and Planning," below, for details on specifying and refining project scope.

Roles and responsibilities

In the Strategy chapter we covered the importance of establishing project governance early on in the project. In "Assembling a Web Development Team," above, we describe specific roles and responsibilities. The project plan should formalize roles and responsibilities by naming the major sponsors; the project, design, technical, and editorial team members; and any other strategic stakeholders within the enterprise. There is no single correct way to structure a web site development effort, but everyone involved should be clear at the start about who is responsible for each aspect of the site development. This is an opportunity to make the point that the project requires an ongoing commitment, beyond the site launch. It is also another opportunity to clarify for sponsors and stakeholders that they have responsibilities and deadlines too, and that the team will be dependent on everyone's contributions. You should also outline a proposed project governance and approvals process, so that everyone involved is clear about how each major project milestone will be communicated and formally approved by the sponsors or major stakeholders.

Project budget and timeline

Your project budget should account for all of the expense categories and activities outlined in "Project Development Life Cycle," below. Make your best calculations on your people, hardware, software, content, and technology development expenses, and then add a hefty contingency budget. Web projects always grow, often by as much as 10 percent or more, even in tightly managed projects. It happens to everyone, and it will happen to you, too. Plan for it rationally, or deal with the pain later.

Here we emphasize often-overlooked considerations that must be accounted for when budgeting time and resources.

- **Accessibility:** Many web sites and other digital products are required to comply with standards for accessibility, such as Section 508 of the Rehabilitation Act in the United States and the Web Content Accessibility Guidelines

(WCAG) 2.0 from the Worldwide Web Consortium. The standards specify what accessibility features must be present so that people with disabilities are able to participate as fully as possible online. All projects should include accessibility as a requirement, regardless of legal obligation—access to the digital environment is a fundamental human right, and we benefit from a society that is fully able to participate in such a crucial aspect of modern life. The best way to ensure that your web site is accessible is to address accessibility requirements throughout the development process. That said, accessibility is often neglected until the end of the project, at which time someone on the project team raises the concern, the web site is evaluated, and more often than not there are issues that must be addressed. Budget for accessibility attention throughout your project, and budget time at the end to perform a thorough evaluation, and to remediate any problems that exist.

- **Security audits and managing security risk:** Databases and applications that deal with e-commerce or with sensitive personal, financial, or health-related information should be scrupulously maintained and periodically audited for data security threats. Even a minor security leak or unchecked programming error could allow a hacker to access your database records, cause malicious damage, or take over your server to support email spamming or other illegal Internet schemes. The data security environment changes daily, and what was perfectly secure six months ago might be hopelessly vulnerable today if your servers, databases, and applications are not under active management and maintenance. Any web-based application or web database must operate with a plan for periodic security audits, as well as the normal timely application and web server patching and maintenance that you'd expect in any well-managed data center or commercial web hosting service.

- **Ongoing technical support for hosting, databases, applications:** Nontechnical managers are often unpleasantly surprised by the expenses of hosting and maintaining web sites that require substantial database or programming support. Although basic hosting of "static" web sites is an inexpensive commodity, web sites that depend on databases and the complex interactive features of web applications must usually be hosted on two or more tightly interrelated servers for security and technical reasons. The multiple servers must be maintained and updated, regularly backed up to prevent data loss, and housed in a secure networked data center environment for maximum reliability and "up time." Make sure that your technical team lead has accounted for these ongoing system maintenance costs as well as the initial development and start-up costs.

- **Editorial maintenance:** Your brand-new web site starts aging the day you launch it into the world. If you don't maintain the site, technical changes,

FIGURE 3.3 (next page spread) A more detailed look at a typical web site development project. Note that although many people and disciplines contribute to building a site, not everyone is equally busy at the same time. Project management is essential to bring the right resources to bear when they are needed.

	10	20	30	40

Goals, strategies, business case

Requirements

Budget, schedule, team logistics — Project kickoff | Budget, schedule

Content inventories — Catalog existing content resources

Content analysis and development — Create or obtain new text and graphic content

Editorial management for content — Set standards, review existing content | Assign new content, supervise creation

Content placement into site

Task analysis for interactivity — User interviews, focus groups, personas | Explore use cases

Site map, wireframes — Map and final wireframe

Interface, page graphic design — Interface design, accessibility

Engineering use cases — Why, how, where interactive elements will be used, explore use cases, accessibility

Programming and site engineering

Page engineering (XHTML, CSS) — Wireframes to template

Page production, content assembly

QA testing of programming

QA review of links and functionality

Staging server; final server prep

Launch logistics

Percent completion, or sprints if using agile processes

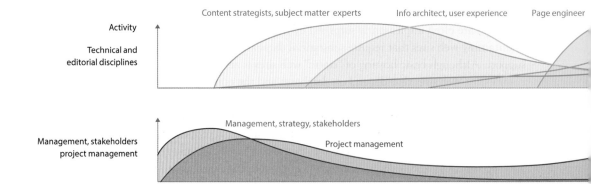

Activity

Technical and
editorial disciplines

Content strategists, subject matter experts · Info architect, user experience · Page engineer

Management, stakeholders
project management

Management, strategy, stakeholders

Project management

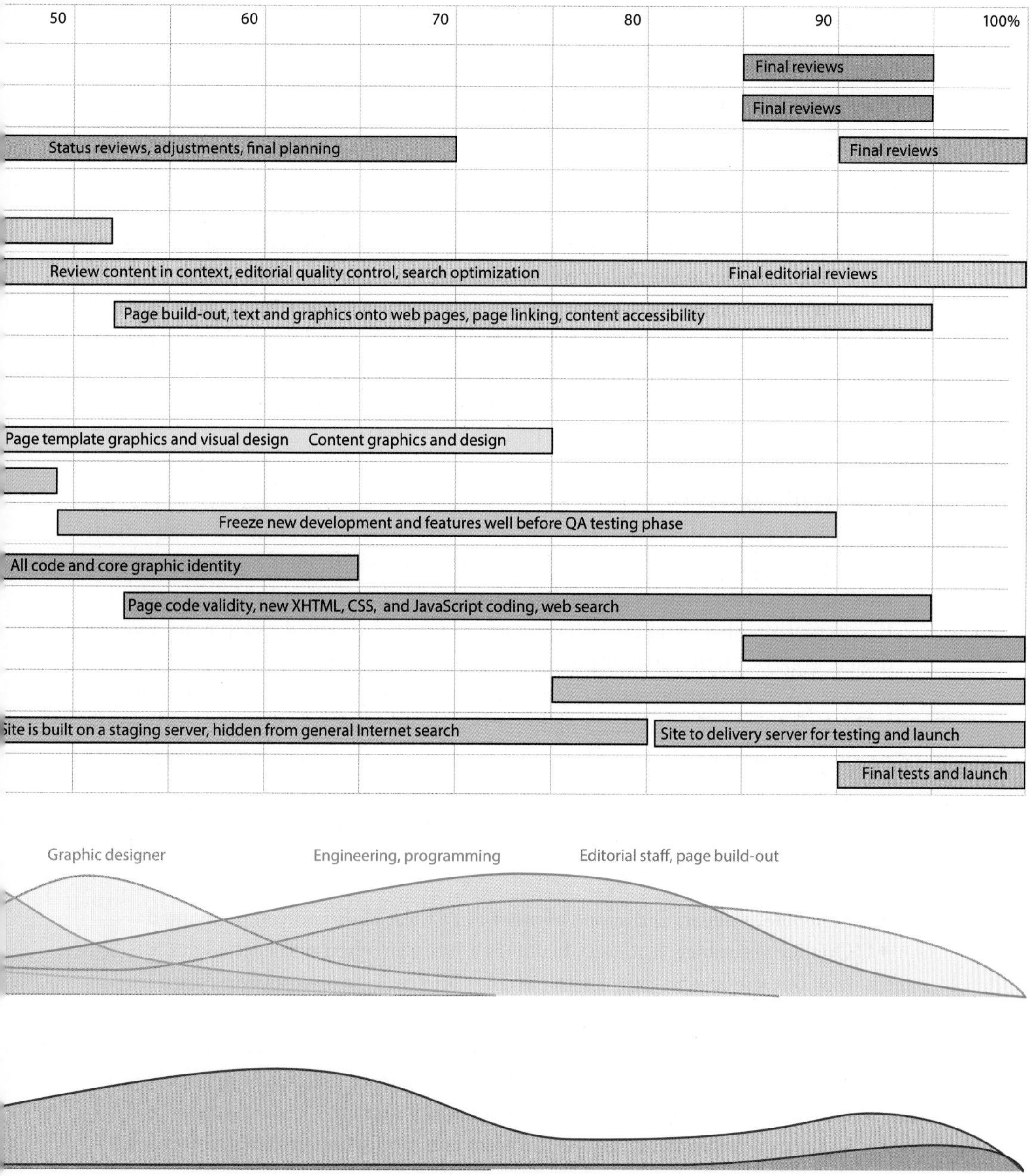

50	60	70	80	90	100%

Final reviews

Final reviews

Status reviews, adjustments, final planning

Final reviews

Review content in context, editorial quality control, search optimization

Final editorial reviews

Page build-out, text and graphics onto web pages, page linking, content accessibility

Page template graphics and visual design   Content graphics and design

Freeze new development and features well before QA testing phase

All code and core graphic identity

Page code validity, new XHTML, CSS, and JavaScript coding, web search

Site is built on a staging server, hidden from general Internet search

Site to delivery server for testing and launch

Final tests and launch

Graphic designer   Engineering, programming   Editorial staff, page build-out

FIGURE 3.4

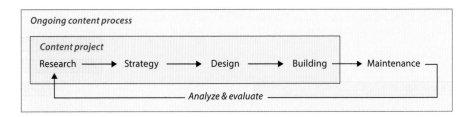

content changes, and the inevitable entropic "link rot" will degrade your site over time. Even a simple site with relatively stable content will deteriorate over time without basic maintenance, and business environment changes that affect your content will certainly happen. Plan for it, make sure you can clearly identify who is responsible for which content on the site, and make ongoing maintenance part of the original site planning. Great online content is always a live and continuing *process*, not a one-time project.

Project risk assessment

Every good project plan should outline the risks of failure in major components of the project. Although your whole project is unlikely to melt down, take a hard look at the various make-or-break components of the plan and think about "Plan B" alternatives. For example, what happens if your content development and site design work out well but your programmers don't meet expectations on interactive features? Will the site be viable? What happens to the project team if your designers and technologists do everything right but the client fails to produce the site content on time? What financial, schedule, quality assurance, or other contingencies could be written into the contract and project charter to mitigate those risks? Your project plan's risk-assessment section should detail plans for minimizing or mitigating risks. Common risk points in web projects include:

- **Schedule, budget, and scope of work:** Let these drift and you're doomed.
- **Quality assurance (QA):** QA becomes a problem when other schedules run long but the launch date doesn't change and QA testing is squeezed into the last few days before the site goes live.
- **Accessibility:** When accessibility is approached as a component of quality assurance, issues that arise late in the process can be difficult or impossible to mitigate, which can mean the product cannot launch.
- **Content development:** This is the most commonly underestimated factor in web publishing—ask any editor.
- **Application development:** Web projects rarely fail because an application does not function properly. Instead, they fail because the intended audience hates to use it or doesn't find its features useful.

SATISFICING IN DESIGN

The economist Herbert Simon coined the term "to satisfice" by combining "satisfy" and "suffice." Satisficing is consciously choosing not to try to find one perfect design solution but instead aiming at a balanced approach that roughly satisfies ("satisfices") all major design requirements. Complex or lengthy design iteration is expensive and necessarily involves the combinations of many unknown factors with no clear promise of a single optimum design solution. Although satisficing may sound like settling for mediocrity, satisfice strategies have produced some of the most successful designs of the past century.

The Douglas DC-3 was not the best competitor in any single performance class: each of its competitors could better it in some category of speed, engine power, range, or carrying capacity. Yet the DC-3 was such a successful satisfice of all design factors that today, eighty-three years after it was designed, more than a thousand DC-3 airframes are in daily use.

Don't allow contention over single points of your site design to paralyze the design process or to plunge your team into endless rounds of "Would it be better if . . . ?" All projects are in some measure satisfices, because there's no practical way to know whether a single best solution to every problem exists for every user. Don't let the perfect become the enemy of the very good.

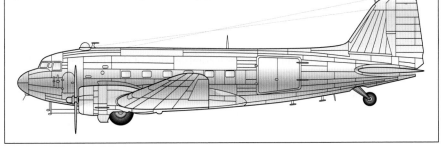

AVOIDING SCOPE CREEP

Scope creep is the most prevalent cause of web project failures. In badly planned projects, scope creep is the gradual but inexorable process by which previously unplanned features are added, content and features are padded to mollify each stakeholder group, major changes in content or site structure are made, and more content or interactive functionality than you originally agreed to create is stuffed in. No single overcommitment is fatal, but the slow, steady accumulation of additions and changes is often enough to blow budgets, ruin schedules, and bury an elegant original plan under megabytes of muddle.

FIGURE 3.5

The classic project management triangle of costs, scope, and schedule. Real-world projects are rarely a perfect balance of all three factors.

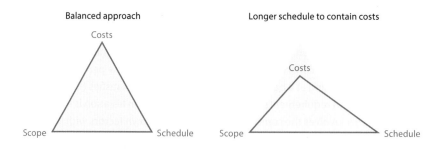

Changes and refinements can be a good thing, as long as everyone is realistic about the impact of potential changes on the budget and schedule of a project. Any substantial change to the planned content, design, or technical aspects of a site must be tightly coupled with a revision of the budget and schedule of the project. People are often reluctant to discuss budgets or deadlines frankly and will often agree to substantial changes or additions to a development plan rather than face an awkward conversation with a client or fellow team member. But this acquiescence merely postpones the inevitable damage of not dealing with scope changes rationally.

The firm integration of schedule, budget, and scope is the only way to keep a web project from becoming unhinged from the real constraints of time, money, and the ultimate quality of the result. A little bravery and honesty up front can save you much grief later. Make the plan carefully, and then stick to it.

PROJECT MANAGEMENT

All project management methods are in some measure balancing acts to accommodate the three core factors that govern all projects: scope, costs, and schedule. In web projects you might understand "scope" as a combination of the size, depth, and total functionality of the interactive features and content of web sites. Each of the three factors is intimately linked to the other two, and emphasizing one or two factors always affects the third. For example, a project might balance a small initial budget by allowing a small team to work over a longer period of time, or a very high-priority project might tolerate the high cost of a large team to finish the project more quickly. Inevitably, you make hard choices. The oldest joke in project management is: "How do you want your project? Good, fast, or cheap? Pick any two."

A full discussion of the discipline of project management is beyond the scope of this book, and many U.S. web professionals who seek careers in management now acquire formal certification as project management professionals (PMPs) from the Project Management Institute. In Britain and Europe the most popular project management certification is PRINCE2 (Projects in Controlled Environments). Either PRINCE2 or PMP professional-level certification usually takes several years to complete, and is essentially the equivalent of a master's degree in project management

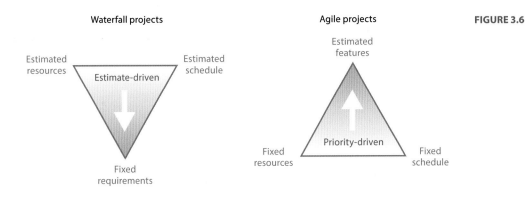

FIGURE 3.6

Waterfall projects

Agile projects

techniques. However, it is not necessary to study and practice for years to understand the basics of managing the development of web sites and online content projects.

CHOOSING A PROJECT MANAGEMENT METHOD

All project management techniques are attempts to manage risk. The two most popular current approaches to software and web project management—traditional "waterfall" handling of project stages versus the iterations or "sprints" of the newer "agile" development techniques—are both meant to supply reliable information on the current status of a project, an overall sense of priorities, tracking of who is supposed to be doing what at each stage, and information on how close the project is to meeting its three-part goals of agreed functionality, budget, and schedule.

Waterfall and agile techniques are fundamentally different in the way they generate and prioritize tasks to be completed and features to be delivered. Both techniques require careful research on user needs. Waterfall techniques rely on team estimates of the time and money that will be needed to produce what is ultimately a (theoretically) fixed set of deliverables. In the agile framework the team and product owner don't try to guess exactly which features the final product will contain. Instead, they emphasize user and product owner priorities: what are the most important user needs to work on at this time?

In this section we summarize the strengths and weaknesses of these two approaches to project management, and present a third hybrid option that combines the best of both.

Waterfall project management

In 1970 computer scientist Winston Royce wrote an influential article on software project management that laid out the process as a series of steps, each of which should be substantially complete before the next step is begun. That's the core idea in waterfall projects—you complete one phase before you move on to the next

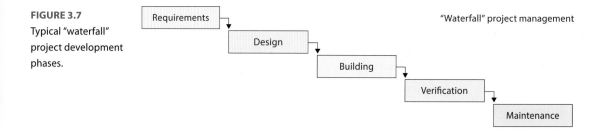

FIGURE 3.7
Typical "waterfall"
project development
phases.

"Waterfall" project management

phase, and the project work "flows" down a series of steps. Royce never used the term "waterfall" to describe the sequential completion of project stages, but the waterfall metaphor quickly caught on in software development.

Waterfall project management has since become the most widely used process for developing complex software and many other kinds of projects, as it offers a logical, easily understood, and predictable method that fits well within more broadly used practices in project and financial management. Although everyone (including Royce) acknowledges the potential drawbacks of a rigid waterfall process, it offers a powerfully intuitive step-by-step road map for handling very complex projects. Its simple but firm logic underlies the continuing popularity of the waterfall method.

Waterfall project management can be well suited to projects such as content-intensive web projects, in which extensive research and user requirements analysis must be done well before any active site building or coding of functionality. If you look at the details of how most web design firms handle their proposals for creating or modifying large sites, you'll see processes and project phases far more like traditional waterfall project management than the more "agile" techniques described below. Partly this is the reality of running service businesses that work with large enterprises where most of their internal projects and vendor contracting people expect waterfall approaches. But design and technology firms also use waterfall work sequences because many projects require complex or extensive requirements, design, and content creation phases before substantial programming or web site development can logically proceed. These days most waterfall projects are far more flexible in design, allowing for multiple concurrent (instead of sequential) project threads, and iterative design-build-analyze-improve cycles borrowed from the more recent agile techniques.

Although waterfall project management was created by programmers to deal with complex software projects, it is ironic that software development—and web site development—might be some of the least suitable uses for strict waterfall methods, primarily because creating software and complex content is such a plastic process that the details almost always wander from the plans laid out in the requirements and design phases. Nothing is immune to change, and there's never been a waterfall

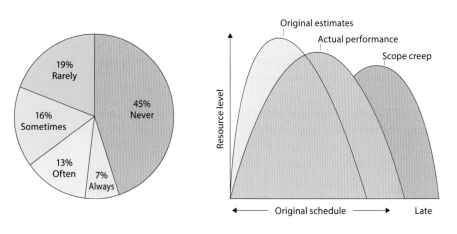

Actual use of software features

- 19% Rarely
- 16% Sometimes
- 13% Often
- 7% Always
- 45% Never

Scope creep in software projects

Original estimates

Actual performance

Scope creep

Resource level

Original schedule — Late

FIGURE 3.8

The bitter irony of scope creep and software project failures is that so much work often goes into "features" that users never asked for, and never use.

project that didn't evolve over time. Thus requirements documents created early in a project gradually (sometimes rapidly) become obsolete and irrelevant. There will always be problems that were overlooked, processes that were poorly documented, designs that were poorly conceived, and this becomes obvious in later phases of projects, when the problems are better understood. And every complex project is also a learning process, with new ideas emerging almost daily to influence the software design. The business and technical environment around a long-term software project is also a powerful influence on project success, as generally used hardware, operating systems, other applications, and leadership, sponsor, and user business objectives are constantly changing, making the original requirements and design documents potentially obsolete almost as soon as they are written and approved.

Classic waterfall project management techniques have also suffered from "analysis paralysis," in which excessively long and detailed documentation and requirements phases result in mountains of paperwork, elaborate visual design renderings, and hyperdetailed requirements and process charts that quickly become a smothering straitjacket once the building phase of the project begins. Or would, if anyone on the project actually read the documentation—which they often don't. Businesses don't create complex design documents because they are foolish. The extensive documentation requirements often seen in classic waterfall management reflect an attempt to do two important things: First, to reduce project risk through a thorough and documented research and requirements phase; and second, to communicate to large project teams with many managers and stakeholders. Unfortunately, a giant pile of paperwork rarely accomplishes either goal.

PROJECT MANAGEMENT "FAILS"

In their 2011 survey of U.S. IT projects, the Standish Group reported a failure rate of 29 percent, with an additional 57 percent of projects reported as "challenged" with significant problems; in 2013 the group reported a 38 percent failure rate of large IT projects within six- to eighteen-month time frames.

The 2013 survey reported a lower outright project failure rate (18 percent), largely attributed to the increasing use of agile project management techniques.

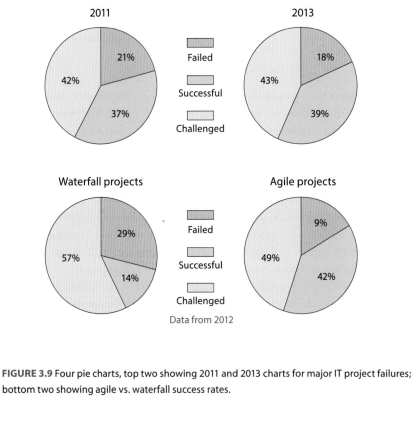

Resolutions for major software projects

FIGURE 3.9 Four pie charts, top two showing 2011 and 2013 charts for major IT project failures; bottom two showing agile vs. waterfall success rates.

From the site developer's perspective strict requirements and design phases are ways to deal with the bad side of changing ideas about what your project should accomplish: the dreaded "scope creep" or "feature bloat," in which an ever-expanding list of new requirements is added to the project deliverables, usually without matching changes to the budget and schedule. Even if the project has the time and money to accommodate many added tasks, many projects fail because all the added "features" result in complex and unnecessary code that is difficult to maintain and does not solve real user problems. Research has shown that a staggering two-thirds of software "features" are never or rarely used.

Agile project management

The tension between two factors that emerge in every project—the fluidity of software development realities versus the rigidity of a preplanned set of design requirements—gradually forced the development of more flexible, iterative project management approaches that acknowledge that while logical planning steps are necessary, a robust process must be flexible enough to accommodate changing requirements.

In 2001 a group of software developers met at the Snowbird resort in Utah to formally develop and promote a flexible—"agile"—method to develop complex software projects. The resulting Agile Manifesto has become the basis for the major alternative to traditional waterfall project management that addresses two fundamental challenges: creating a flexible process that acknowledges and welcomes changing requirements, but that also emphasizes a strict hierarchy of functional priorities to contain the "scope creep" of less important software "features."

Agile was born in reaction to the perceived rigidity of waterfall methods, which if poorly executed too often resulted in inflexible goals, a wandering set of daily and weekly priorities, excessive documentation requirements, and a shocking rate of failure in major information technology projects. The Agile Manifesto is a philosophical statement, not a working plan for the day-to-day development of software or web sites. It reads as follows:

We are uncovering better ways of developing software by doing it and helping others do it. Through this work we have come to value:

- Individuals and interactions over processes and tools
- Working software over comprehensive documentation
- Customer collaboration over contract negotiation
- Responding to change over following a plan

That is, while there is value in the items on the right, we value the items on the left more. (agilemanifesto.org)

Agile project management techniques emphasize:

- Iterative and incremental methods, with tight daily or weekly plan-act-review-implement cycles.
- A relentless focus on the most important, high-priority features and user problems.
- Constant face-to-face contact and communications with small groups of developers and clients or project sponsors.
- Smaller-scale, faster projects with rapid delivery of working software.
- Software that solves real, immediate user problems.
- Continuous software improvement through constant adaptive planning and a continuing evolution of requirements based primarily on user requests, needs, or reported problems.
- Deemphasis of formal project reporting, extensive software documentation, detailed graphic planning and communication reports and visuals, highly detailed screen wireframes, or very detailed user interface specifications.

The rapid timelines and modest scales of agile projects are deliberately planned. Dividing ambitious web or software plans into smaller chunks with relatively short schedules is an attempt to avoid the high failure rate associated with other project planning methodologies.

Several project management frameworks have emerged in the past decade to implement the agile philosophy in projects, the most popular of which is called "scrum." The term "scrum" is from the sport of rugby, in which a team moves forward incrementally in a series of short individual plays, or "scrums." Scrum project frameworks are built around relatively small teams—typically five to nine individuals who work in close physical proximity and tight collaboration on software or online content projects. Good scrum teams focus on "inspect and adapt" cycles that work toward continuous improvement of both the product and the development process. During short daily "standup" meetings, team members report what they have accomplished over the past day, and what they will be doing that day.

Team structures are simple and allow for only three project roles:

- **Product owner**: Supplies the overall vision and business case for the product, represents the interests of management, and owns the overall responsibility for the success of the product. Prioritizes the work to be done, and manages the backlog of items or features to be addressed.
- **Scrum master**: A unique "servant leadership" role, under which an experienced scrum framework user acts as a neutral and knowledgeable third party in meetings, and a process and approval facilitator for the team. A scrum

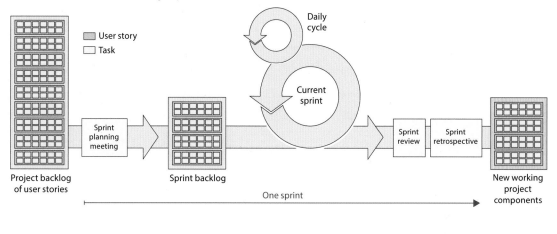

Overview of a single sprint

User story
Task

Project backlog of user stories

Sprint planning meeting

Sprint backlog

Daily cycle

Current sprint

Sprint review

Sprint retrospective

New working project components

One sprint

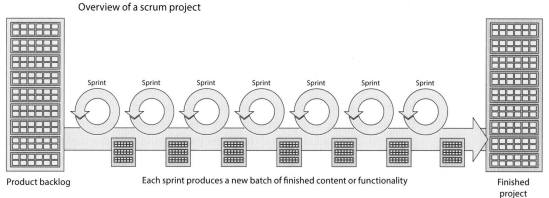

Overview of a scrum project

Product backlog

Sprint Sprint Sprint Sprint Sprint Sprint Sprint

Each sprint produces a new batch of finished content or functionality

Finished project

master acts as coach, helping the team stay focused on the highest current priorities, and in correctly applying scrum techniques.

- **Team member**: Scrum teams are small and highly collaborative, and typically organize the details of their work routines in daily morning "standup meetings" of around fifteen minutes. While the team roles may be specialized, each team member is individually responsible for the success of the whole team and the quality of the finished product. In web projects the roles may be specialized as page engineer, programmer, graphic designer, writer, editor, and so on, but everyone on the team is functionally coequal, with shared responsibility for the overall success of the project.

FIGURE 3.10

FIGURE 3.11

User story card

Title:	
As:	(User role, user persona)
I want to:	What action to take
So that:	What benefit from the action

| Priority | Author | Estimate |

Title:	Create calendar item, all-day event
As:	Calendar site user
I want to:	Create an all-day event that doesn't block the view of other shorter events
So that:	I can create the event but not complicate the view of other shorter events on the same day

| 2 | Pat | 6 hrs |
| Priority | Author | Estimate |

The scrum framework uses some unique terminology to describe the various elements of scrum processes. With the recent popularity of scrum and agile, these terms are leaking out into the general world of software development and web design, so it's good to have a general understanding of scrum terminology:

- **Sprint**: The fundamental scheduling unit of the scrum process, a period of from one to several weeks during which a defined set of tasks is to be accomplished by the team. Sprints can be as long as about a month, but once the sprint begins, the agreed-upon sprint duration is not variable.
- **Product backlog**: This is the cumulative list of product features or items to be delivered. The backlog covers the entire project, and related sets of individual tasks are broken down into several "sprints." Each sprint draws a new set of tasks to accomplish from the product backlog. The team leader sets priorities for items in the backlog.
- **Sprint backlog**: The list of tasks or the feature item to be accomplished during a sprint.
- **Kanban or task board**: Typically a large wall-mounted whiteboard in the team work area, where it is easily visible to be consulted by team members at any time. This type of display board originated at Toyota as a visual project management tool, and is often referred to as a "kanban" (Japanese for "visual signal"). Task boards typically have four columns, where the status of individual tasks in the current sprint are represented by colored stick-on notes that are gradually moved to the right as tasks are accomplished. On some teams the kanban-like functions may be handled with project management software like JIRA or Basecamp.
- **Burndown chart**: Another graphic way to display the current status of a sprint. The total estimated hours required for all tasks within the sprint are on the vertical axis, and the horizontal axis shows the total days in the sprint. The

Example schedule for a one-week sprint

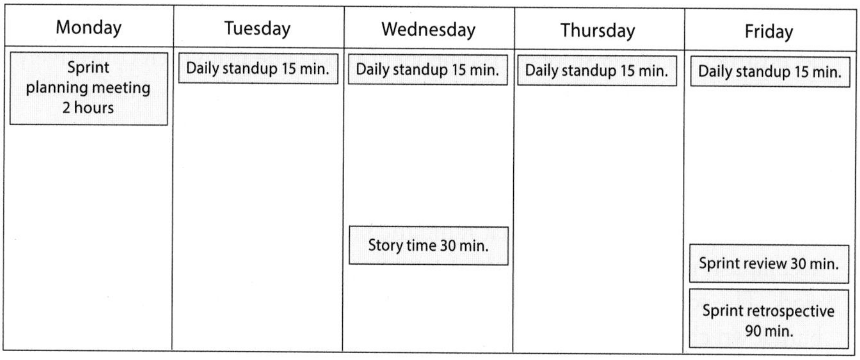

FIGURE 3.12

Monday	Tuesday	Wednesday	Thursday	Friday
Sprint planning meeting 2 hours	Daily standup 15 min.	Daily standup 15 min.	Daily standup 15 min.	Daily standup 15 min.
		Story time 30 min.		Sprint review 30 min.
				Sprint retrospective 90 min.

charts usually represent the estimated rate of completion and the actual state of finished tasks each day.

- **Story or user story**: Agile and scrum are focused on solving very concrete, real-world problems, and thus the definition of tasks centers around a "user story," often called a "use case scenario" in programming and user interface techniques. User stories are typically represented as 3×5 cards or sticky notes on which are written the task title, the user's role, the user's desired action, and the user's hoped-for result from the process. User stories usually break down into a number of tasks, which might require different team members with specialized skills to collaborate (user interface design, graphic design, page engineering, programming). The team collaboratively "sizes" each user story, deconstructing the overall functionality needed into component tasks to be done, and estimating the time required to accomplish each task.

- **Task**: A sprint task is a unit of work generally expected to be completed in four to sixteen hours. Team members typically volunteer for specific tasks, based on their specialized skills. They update the estimated number of hours remaining for each task on a daily basis, and this contributes to the daily status point on the sprint burndown chart.

The fundamental cyclical rhythm of scrum projects is based on the sprint, a fixed period of time over which a subset of the overall project backlog is addressed by team members. There is no fixed duration in the definition of a sprint. Most scrum projects work with sprints of one to four weeks, with sprints of one or two weeks being most common. Once a sprint has begun, the duration is fixed, and sprints are never extended beyond the planned deadline.

- **Sprint planning meeting**: This meeting has two purposes: The team leader proposes user stories to be addressed in the next sprint, and then team members deconstruct each user story into component tasks. The team then collectively makes a final commitment to a manageable number of stories and tasks to be completed within the new sprint. These planning meetings last no more than four hours.
- **Daily scrum meeting**: A short (fifteen-minute) daily early-morning meeting in which each team reports what it did the previous day, what it plans to accomplish today, and whether it foresees any obstacles to completing the work. The scrum master compiles the staff reports and updates the sprint burndown chart and task board. This meeting is often held with all participants standing—it is, in fact, sometimes called the "daily standup"—as a reminder to everyone to be concise in reporting and to keep the meeting brief.
- **Sprint review**: Typically an hourlong meeting on the last day of a sprint period, in which the results of the sprint are presented to project sponsors and stakeholders. The sprint review centers on new features, on sponsor and stakeholder reactions and concerns, and on how the current state of the project affects the next sprint.
- **Story time**: A meeting to review the scope and tasks related to user stories to be considered in future sprints. This is typically a midweek one-hour planning meeting to discuss what the team has learned so far, and how that might influence the way it handles future user stories and sprints.
- **Sprint retrospective**: A meeting with the team and scrum master (but usually not the product owner) that focuses on what processes and work estimates went well, with the goal of constant improvement of internal team processes and communication. These "inspect and adapt" meetings typically occur on the last day of the sprint, and last no more than two hours.

Smaller projects and ongoing maintenance and editorial activities can often be run entirely from a kanban board, augmented with frequent team meetings or short morning standup meetings. The kanban system is simple, highly visible, and often ideal for teams that work in a common area. Teams that are not in the same location can use project software like JIRA or Basecamp to create "virtual" kanban boards online.

All project management frameworks (waterfall or agile/scrum) are dependent on how well the component processes are understood and executed. With its emphasis on flexibility, scrum can lead to projects that bog down if the team and leadership are not accurate in their estimates for tasks, and are not ruthless enough in paring down potential user stories and tasks to only the most important elements, which in turn can practically fit within a planned sprint. With inaccurate estimates and too

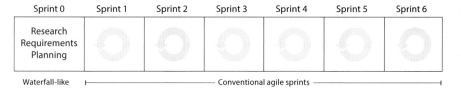

Sprint 0	Sprint 1	Sprint 2	Sprint 3	Sprint 4	Sprint 5	Sprint 6
Research Requirements Planning						

Waterfall-like ⊢——————— Conventional agile sprints ———————⊣

FIGURE 3.13

much flexibility in user story and task changes, scrum-based projects may be just as vulnerable to budget and schedule problems as waterfall-driven projects. However, research has repeatedly shown that scrum techniques are well suited to software and web projects, and have a much higher overall success rate than projects managed with traditional waterfall techniques.

Scrum's emphasis on relatively small teams and projects of short duration may be less suitable for managing large, long-duration projects with correspondingly large teams. The intense team communications techniques of small short daily and weekly meetings do not scale easily to much larger teams (twenty or more people), although it is often possible to adapt scrum processes to some components of a larger project, or to subdivide large projects into smaller sequences managed through the scrum framework.

Agile projects can suffer from a lack of cohesion. Every user story is a tree, every task becomes just another leaf, and the team can lose sight of how the forest is shaping up. The emphasis on fast delivery of working software developed in rapid bursts can also lead to a "ready-fire-aim" syndrome, in which holistic elements like user and business process research, user interface consistency, and site content and messaging strategies can get short shrift in the beginning sprints of an agile project. It is crucial for both content editors and designers to be on the development team and in every meeting to assure content and messaging continuity. User research, interface development and wireframes, and core visual design approaches are the foundational architecture of successful sites, and don't always lend themselves to short sprints, although the design and usability communities are quickly changing to accommodate the accelerated timelines of agile development.

The emphasis on building functional code and pages as soon as possible can lead to a bias toward lightweight, easily solved problems at the expense of bigger "wicked problems" with lots of ambiguous or poorly understood details and functional requirements. There's always the temptation to do the small, easy stuff simply because it fits well within the sprint framework, not because it's the most important thing to do at the moment. Agile teams may suffer from the "horizon effect" (also known as "kicking the can down the road"), in which difficult issues are continually moved into later sprints. You haven't solved a problem by pushing it back to sprint .

LEAN UX

Lean user experience is a way of integrating user experience design in a meaningful and effective way into the product development life cycle. It focuses activities on designing what people really want and value, and encourages big thinking and creativity in decision making and problem solving. A lean UX approach works well with agile project management, with its emphasis on flexibility and collaboration, through methods like design studios to develop "light" prototypes.

The Lean UX Manifesto is as follows:

> We are developing a way to create digital experiences that are valued by our end users. Through this work, we hold in high regard the following:
>
> **Early customer validation** over releasing products with unknown end-user value
>
> **Collaborative design** over designing on an island
>
> **Solving user problems** over designing the next "cool" feature
>
> **Measuring key performance indicators** over undefined success metrics
>
> **Applying appropriate tools** over following a rigid plan
>
> **Nimble design** over heavy wireframes, comps, or specs (wsg4.link/lean-ux-manifesto)

Hybrid waterfall/agile project management

Many organizations employ a hybrid of waterfall and agile project management, often using the early requirements and design planning aspects of waterfall techniques, then using scrum techniques to manage the building and quality control of the software or web site. There is one lesson from agile that is broadly accepted across all project management techniques: that software and web development projects must allow for flexibility and an iterative approach to continual improvements in the development process, and that subdividing massive projects into more manageable chunks yields much higher rates of success, especially when the smaller projects are managed with agile techniques. Hybrid systems also allow more concurrent project development threads, where content research and strategy, functional requirements, and technology planning occur simultaneously in early project phases, as shown in the Gantt charts in this chapter.

Many scrum projects institute a "sprint zero" period during which foundational project process, business, and research issues are addressed before the team moves into active code writing and site construction. Sprint zero periods are sometimes criticized as "waterfalls in disguise," but the strengths of the waterfall methods of early requirements gathering, user research, and the development of basic interface and wireframe approaches can be successfully married to the scrum process in the later building phases of a project. The key to a successful hybrid approach is to avoid lengthy requirements and design periods, and the excessive documentation deliverables that often plague the early phases of waterfall projects.

PROJECT DEVELOPMENT LIFE CYCLE

Every significant web project poses unique challenges, but the overall process of developing a complex web site generally follows seven major stages that you should think through before crafting your final project planning and proposal documents:

- Site definition and planning
- Content inventory
- Information architecture
- Site design
- Site construction
- Site marketing
- Tracking, evaluation, and maintenance

Most development projects have far-reaching budgetary, personnel, and public relations consequences for an organization, both during the development of the site and long after its deployment. Too many web sites begin life as ad hoc efforts, created by small interest groups working in isolation from their peers elsewhere in the organization and without fully considering the site's goals within the context of the organization's overall mission. The result of poorly planned, hasty development efforts often is an "orphan site," starved of resources and attention.

As you consider the development process outlined below, note that the construction of the pages that make up the web site is one of the last things that takes place in a well-designed project. Consider each step in the process and its impact on your project planning. Think before you act, and make sure you have the organizational backing, budget, and personnel resources you'll need to make the project a success.

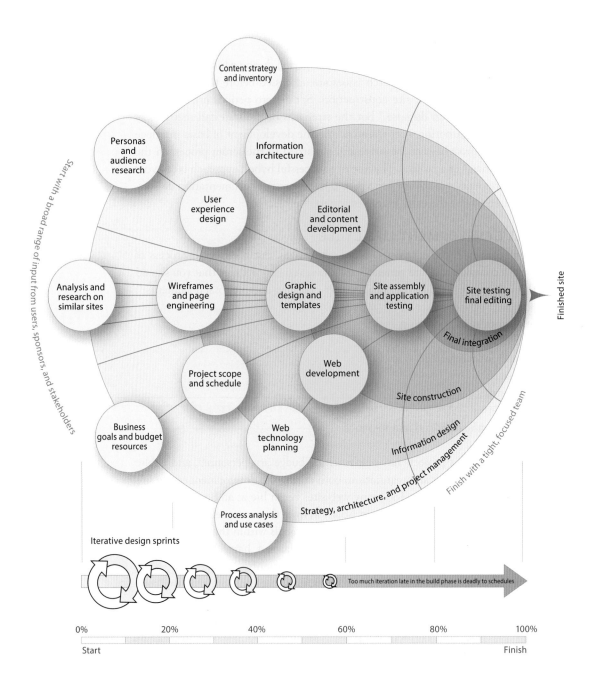

Start with a broad range of input from users, sponsors, and stakeholders

Content strategy and inventory

Personas and audience research

Information architecture

User experience design

Editorial and content development

Analysis and research on similar sites

Wireframes and page engineering

Graphic design and templates

Site assembly and application testing

Site testing final editing

Finished site

Final integration

Project scope and schedule

Web development

Site construction

Business goals and budget resources

Web technology planning

Information design

Finish with a tight, focused team

Strategy, architecture, and project management

Process analysis and use cases

Iterative design sprints

Too much iteration late in the build phase is deadly to schedules

| 0% | 20% | 40% | 60% | 80% | 100% |

Start

Finish

SITE DEFINITION AND PLANNING

This initial stage is where you define your goals and objectives for the web site and begin to collect and analyze the information you'll need to justify the budget and resources required. This is also the time to define the scope of the site content, the interactive functionality and technology support required, and the depth and breadth of information resources that you will need to fill out the site and meet your users' expectations. If you are contracting out the production of the web site, you will also need to interview and select a site design firm. Ideally, your site designers should be involved as soon as possible in the planning discussions.

CONTENT DEVELOPMENT

Once you have an idea of your web site's mission and general structure, you can begin to assess the content you will need to realize your plans. Building an inventory or database of existing and needed content will force you to take a hard look at your existing content resources and to make a detailed outline of your needs. Once you know where you are short on content, you can concentrate on those deficits and avoid wasting time on areas with existing resources that are ready to use. A clear grasp of your needs will also help you develop a realistic schedule and budget.

Content inventory

A good starting point for content development is to inventory existing content and identify new content development needs. Content inventory activities work well when structured, using a spreadsheet containing long listings of every page in the site, along with such essential characteristics as the page title, URL, people responsible for the content, and so on (see Chapter 4, Information Architecture, for details on creating a content inventory).

Content production

Content development is the hardest, most time-consuming, and most consistently underestimated part of any web site development project. In many instances your team will be looking to the sponsor to provide content or subject matter experts (SMEs). Be sure your sponsor or client understands the responsibilities and takes the content delivery deadlines seriously. Starting early with a firm content production plan will help ensure that you won't be caught later with a well-structured but empty web site—or worse, a site full of "lorem ipsum" dummy text.

Do not make the mistake of holding off on content production activities until the site is fully specified and constructed. Begin writing and revising content immediately, and integrate content into the site as soon as it's available. Use real content in designs and prototypes, in the user interface and for content pages. Push hard on

FIGURE 3.14

(facing page) Another concept of web development projects, here emphasizing the necessary tightening of focus from broad input and participation in the beginning, to a more narrowly focused team at the end. Tight focus assures that the project gets done on time and on budget.

THE SITE DESIGN AND DEVELOPMENT LIFE CYCLE

All development processes go through a series of stages that together form the classic "design cycle," here related particularly to web site design.

Requirements In larger projects the requirements phase may involve formal market and user research, web analytics research, focus groups of current or prospective
users, and formal usability testing. In smaller projects the requirements phase often
takes the form of team meetings with users, project stakeholders, and project sponsors to develop lists of functional requirements.

Design Design transforms lists of requirements into concrete form, first as rough
layouts and page wireframes, navigation interfaces, and site diagrams. Concentrate
on fundamental structure and function, and save detailed graphic design for later.

Development Development is the actual building of pages and coding of any associated web applications. Even if you use an iterative design process (most web teams
do), don't get too far into development until all major issues of design are settled.

Testing All site designs require both functional and usability testing and editorial
quality control. Too often web teams dominated by technologists shortchange the
editorial considerations, forgetting that content also requires an extensive quality
assurance process to produce a good product.

Classic design cycle

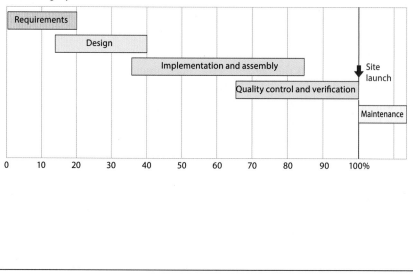

Linear or "waterfall" development Classic linear design projects march through each phase one at a time, completing each before moving on to the next. Linear development works best where tried and true methods exist and where the detailed specifications have been used successfully in the past. In less certain circumstances, linear development can seem brittle and plodding.

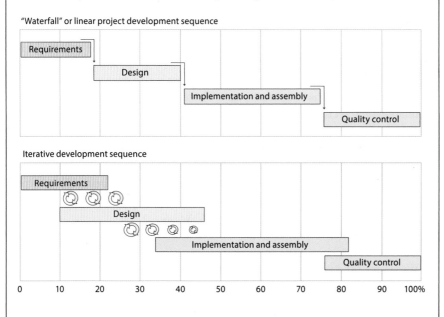

"Waterfall" or linear project development sequence

Iterative development sequence

Iterative model of design Most projects deal with complex sets of unknowns by moving through a series of partial analyze-design or design-build stages, progressively building complexity and design consensus into the developing system, especially in the early planning and design phases of the cycle. The iteration model begins to break down when cycles of design-build-redesign continue too far into the development phase. These development iterations can result in production churning and much wasted time and effort.

A hybrid approach Good project management uses the strengths of both iterative and linear models, where many design iterations are encouraged early in the process but are strongly discouraged later in the development and testing phases, when efficient development effort and control of the overall project scope and schedule become paramount.

the content production work, and don't let up until the items in your content inventory are done.

INFORMATION ARCHITECTURE

At this stage you need to detail the content and organization of the web site. The team should inventory all existing content, describe what new content is required, and define the organizational structure of the site. Once a content architecture has been sketched out, you should build small prototypes of parts of the site to test what it feels like to move around within the design. Site prototypes are useful for two reasons. First, they are the best way to test site navigation and develop the user interface. The prototypes should incorporate enough pages to assess accurately what it's like to move from menus to content pages. These prototypes can be used to test the information architecture with users. Second, creating a prototype allows the graphic designers to develop relations between how the site looks and how the navigation interface supports the information design. The key to good prototyping is flexibility early on: the site prototypes should not be so complex or elaborate that the team becomes too invested in one design at the expense of exploring better alternatives.

Typical results or contract deliverables at the end of this stage include:

- Detailed site design specification
- Detailed description of site content
- Wireframes and prototypes demonstrating site architecture—validated through user research and usability testing
- Taxonomies representing categories and tags
- Multiple graphic design and interface design sketches
- Detailed technical support specification
- Plans to create programming or technology to support specific features of the site
- A schedule for implementing the site design and construction

SITE DESIGN

At this stage the project acquires its look and feel, as the page grid, page design, and overall graphic design standards are created and approved. Now the illustrations, photography, and other graphic or audiovisual content for the site need to be commissioned and created. Research, writing, organizing, assembling, and editing the site's text content is also performed at this stage. Any programming, database design and data entry, and search engine design should be well under way by now. The goal is to produce all the content components and functional programming and have them ready for the final production stage: the construction of the actual web site pages.

Typical products or deliverables at the end of this stage include:

- Content components, detailed organization and assembly
- Text, edited and proofread
- Graphic design specifications for all page types
- Finished interface graphics for page templates
- Header and footer graphics, logos, buttons, backgrounds
- Detailed page comps or finished examples of key pages
- Site graphic standards manual for large, complex sites
- Interface design and master page grid templates completed
- Finished HTML template pages
- Illustrations
- Photography
- CMS templates for Drupal, WordPress, or whatever content management system you have chosen
- Content structures for the CMS
- JavaScript scripts, Java applets designed
- Database tables and programming, interaction prototypes completed
- Search engine designed and tested

SITE CONSTRUCTION

Only at this mature stage of the project are the bulk of the site's web pages constructed and filled with content. By waiting until you have a detailed site architecture, mature content components, fully tested wireframes and prototypes, and a polished page design specification, you will minimize the content churning, redundant development efforts, and wasted energy that inevitably result from rushing to create pages too soon. Of course, you will always learn new things about your overall design as the prototype matures into the fully functional web site. Be prepared to refine your designs as you and your users navigate through the growing web site and discover both weak spots and opportunities to improve navigation or content.

Once the site has been constructed, with all pages completed and all database and programming components linked, it is ready for user testing. Testing should be done primarily by people outside your site development team who are willing to supply informed criticism and report programming bugs, note typographical errors, and critique the overall design and effectiveness of the site. Fresh users will inevitably notice things that you and your development team have overlooked. Only after the site has been thoroughly tested and refined should you begin to publicize the URL of the site to a larger audience.

Typical products or deliverables at the end of this stage should include:

- Finished HTML/CSS for all web pages, all page content in place
- Finished navigation link structure
- All programming in place and linked to pages, ready for usability testing
- All database components in place and linked to site pages
- All graphic design, illustration, and photography in place
- Final proofreading of all site content
- Detailed testing of database and programming functionality
- Testing and verification of database reporting features
- Testing of site user support procedures, email response, etc.
- Archives of all site content components, HTML code, programming code, and any other site development materials

TRACKING, EVALUATION, AND MAINTENANCE

Your web server software can record an abundance of information about visitors to your site. Even the simplest site logs track how many people (unique visitors) saw your site over a given time, how many pages were requested for viewing, and many other variables. By analyzing the server logs for your web site, you can develop quantitative data on the success of your site. The logs will tell you which pages were the most popular and what brands and versions of web browser people used to view your site. Server logs can also give you information on the geographic location of your site users. Detailed logs provide the key to quantifying the success of a web site. Your webmaster should archive all site logs for long-term analysis and should be prepared to adjust the information categories being logged as your needs and interests change.

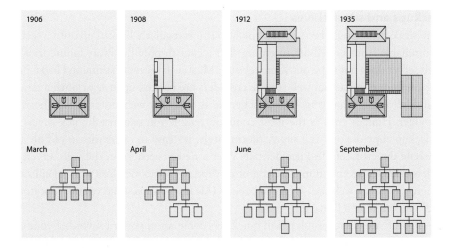

FIGURE 3.16
Much as old buildings grow through additions and adaptation over time, sites grow and change in response to changing needs and ideas.

Google Analytics (GA) is the most popular and widely used web analytics software, and not just because it is free. Google Analytics has evolved significantly from a fairly basic "client side" tool—analytics events are triggered when a reader's browser opens a page with an embedded GA tracking script—into a complex web tracking and reporting suite. Applying GA tracking scripts to page code does not require deep HTML skills, and many content management systems offer built-in access to GA, so all you have to do is supply your GA account information to begin tracking your site. However, you may also want to augment the reporting you get from GA with "server-side" web analytics tools that track requests directly from your web server. If your site is hosted by your company's IT department, or by a commercial web hosting service, you may already have access to server-side analytics reports. Server-side and client-side analytics supply complementary streams of information that produce a more complete picture of how your site is used, and how server performance might affect the way users interact with your site.

Maintaining the site

Don't abandon your site once the production "goes live" and the launch parties are over. The aesthetic and functional aspects of a large web site need constant attention and grooming, particularly if a group of individuals shares responsibility for updating content. Your site editor will need to be responsible for coordinating and vetting the new content stream, maintaining the graphic and editorial standards, and ensuring that the programming and linkages of all pages remain intact and functional. Links on the web are perishable, and you'll need to check periodically that links to pages outside your immediate site are still working. Don't let your site go stale by starving it of resources just as you begin to develop an audience—if you disappoint users by not following through, it will be doubly difficult to attract your audience back to the site.

Backups and site archives

The site editor should be sure that the web site is regularly backed up onto a secure and reliable storage medium to ensure that a catastrophic hardware failure in your web server does not wipe out your web site. Most web servers maintained by IT professionals or commercial web service providers are backed up at least once a day. If you don't know what your backup schedule is, ask your webmaster or web hosting provider. Human error is the most common reason you may need quick access to a backup copy of your web site. Unfortunately, it's easy to overwrite an old file (or a whole directory of files) accidentally over a newer version on the web server, to delete something important in error, or to wipe out someone else's work by mistake when updating a web site. A recent backup (ideally no more than twenty-four hours old) can often be a lifesaver.

If your site is successful, it will quickly become an important record of your enterprise's work, your accomplishments, and the "state of things" as the site evolves over time. Unfortunately, too little attention is paid to this aspect of web sites, and we are collectively losing huge pieces of our history because no one thinks about preserving permanent records of a web site. Unless your web site is prohibitively large, your web site editor should arrange to collect and store the files of the site periodically or contract with your web service provider to set aside a backup version at regular intervals as a long-term archive. We take for granted the "paper trail" of history left by conventional business and work practices. Without a plan for preserving our digital works, our collective online history may vanish without a trace.

COMMON PROJECT DEVELOPMENT MISHAPS

There are many choices between you and a successful project outcome—one that meets the objectives in your project charter and does not place too much burden on your budget and resources, and one that will keep its value and integrity over time. Here we describe common pitfalls and recommend ways to avoid them.

Ready, fire, aim

The prospect of creating a new or revised web site is exciting, and many teams (especially agile-based teams) will find it irresistible to jump in and start "sketching" or prototyping site designs long before anyone on the team knows:

- Exactly whom you're designing the site for and what those users want (not what you imagine they want).
- Your business goals and messaging strategies.
- Essential content structures, and navigation and interactive features.

Don't let the process get hijacked by eager beavers who "just want to make some pages." Decide the big strategic things first, and make pages only when you have all the important answers in place to guide the rest of the design process intelligently.

Form before function

The fastest way to run a web project off the rails is to start your planning process by discussing the home page visuals or what the overall graphic design of the site should look like. Pour the foundation and build the walls before you let anyone fuss over the color of the drapes. The visual form of your site should flow from careful and informed decisions about site structure, navigation, content and interactivity requirements, and your overall business goals. Detailed visual design should always come later in site planning: premature graphic design decisions will confound you at every turn. This isn't to say that designers should not be involved throughout the project, just that the major visual forms of the site should be based on the business and content strategy, not the other way around.

Too many meetings

Meetings are generally reviled because so often they are poorly conceived and unorganized. Too frequently you find yourself sitting in a conference room only because it's "the weekly meeting": there's no formal agenda, and you end up spending an hour on someone's random problem-of-the-moment, not on what's most important to the current project.

The fact that many meetings are boring time wasters is almost beside the point. *Meetings are very expensive.* Multiply the length of the meeting by the average hourly rate of the people in the room and you quickly come up with impressive total costs. Then consider the preparation time, travel time, and the task "switch time" of disrupting each participant's normal work, and an average one-hour meeting of six web professionals could easily be worth $600-800 or more. At those rates, whatever transpires in that hour had better be well planned and worth the cost.

- Have a clear agenda, distributed beforehand.
- Assign a time limit to each major agenda item.
- Time the meeting thoughtfully. Not every meeting has to last an hour. Short meetings keep people focused.
- Assign a timekeeper to keep the meeting on schedule.
- Keep the meeting as small as is practical.
- Always assign a participant to document the meeting results, and distribute the meeting log to the broader team (and relevant stakeholders if needed) so that other members of the project know what transpired in the meeting.

FIGURE 3.17
Elegant sites are
never more complex
than they need to be.

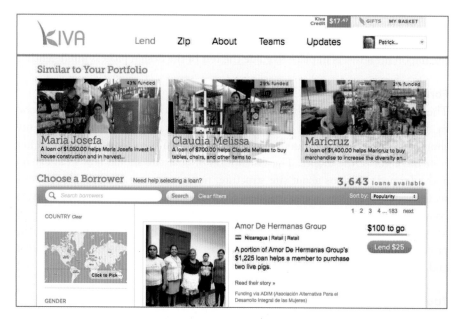

Content and feature bloat

Often the easiest way to "manage" a site project is by adding content or features to avoid contention on the team or with stakeholders, particularly if you look only at the initial programming or design costs. Large web sites are expensive to maintain, and it's easy to bite off more than you can chew. Every new page, link, or application feature requires a long-term maintenance commitment. Stay small if you can, and stay focused. A small, high-quality site is infinitely better than a giant contraption with outdated content and broken links. The Kiva site is a model of straightforward design and functionality—staying small while accomplishing enormous good.

Neglect

These days, for the vast majority of your public audiences, *you are your web site*. You would never leave the front door of the company or your primary customer service phone lines unattended, and you can't leave your site unattended either. It makes far more long-term sense to treat your site as an ongoing customer engagement process, making constant small improvements in the site, while building up a large pool of relevant user data that can drive key decisions about where to invest in new or updated content and features.

Giant redesigns

These days 90 percent of web design projects are actually web *redesign* projects, done for clients who have had a web presence for many years. In spite of the web's domina-

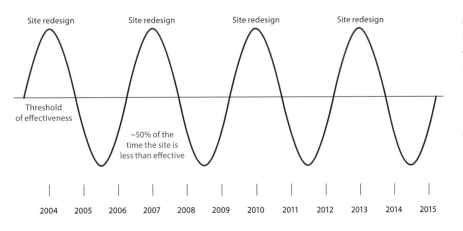

Site redesign   Site redesign   Site redesign   Site redesign

Threshold
of effectiveness

~50% of the
time the site is
less than effective

2004   2005   2006   2007   2008   2009   2010   2011   2012   2013   2014   2015

FIGURE 3.18

If you redesign every few years and don't maintain your site, most of the site's lifespan will be spent in a suboptimal condition.

tion of business communications for at least a decade, many senior enterprise decision makers are still stuck in print-era paradigms, where the high cost and inflexibility of print production governed all assumptions about managing communications. This is owing to:

- An obsession to get every detail right before launch—a concern driven by the extreme cost of correcting mistakes in print communications.
- The print-based assumption that large presentations (like printed sales materials) are projects that require only periodic attention and can easily be outsourced.
- The notion that communications projects end at publication.
- The idea that revised publications must change most or all of the content, often for mere novelty.
- Ignorance of the fact that there are already active users of the site who might not appreciate a new way of doing things.

As Paul Boag points out in his book *Digital Adaptations*, this kind of "boom-and-bust" thinking about web projects ignores the iterative flexibility of the web, and also ignores the fundamental change in communications from one-way marketing "messages" to active, ongoing conversations in interactive media. He points out these key differences:

- Changing things on the web is fast and usually easy.
- Conversations and interactions with readers and users are constant processes that are now fundamental to all enterprise communications.
- Online communication is now a 24-7-365 process that does not end.

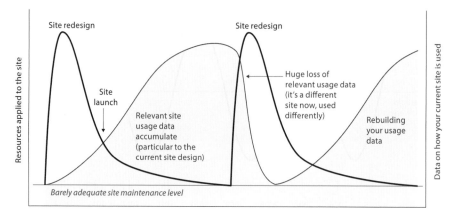

FIGURE 3.19

Every time you do a major redesign you effectively throw away your usage data history and must start afresh to build data on how users interact with your site.

Resources applied to the site

Site redesign

Site launch

Relevant site usage data accumulate (particular to the current site design)

Site redesign

Huge loss of relevant usage data (it's a different site now, used differently)

Rebuilding your usage data

Data on how your current site is used

Barely adequate site maintenance level

If you treat your web presence as a periodic project, your web presence is doomed to be suboptimal for about 50 percent of its lifespan between major redesign projects, with all the attendant damage to your customer relations and business reputation.

When you suddenly make massive functional and stylistic changes in your web presence after years of design stasis, you also lose a huge amount of data about how your audiences uses (or *used to use*) your web site, and at the launch of the newly re-designed site you are almost back to zero for the user experience data that ought to be driving a process of continuing improvement. Some enterprises make major changes in their sites so often that they have no idea what kind of return on investment they are getting because they have so little useful data on how people use their sites.

Your current site is also the best prototype for any new site, as it was designed to solve very similar business problems. Even if the site was not totally successful, there are important lessons to be learned from your current site before replacing it with a new site. You want to be sure that you understand which content and features are heavily used, that the new site covers similar content and features, and that you don't alienate existing users with the new design. Even if you have not been actively collecting and analyzing data from your current site, you should initiate a user research and analysis campaign before replacing the old site, to be sure that you have gleaned as much information as possible from the old site before launching the redesigned site. In addition to usability tests on your existing site, it's good to ask users to evaluate competing or similar sites to see which content or features are most appealing, and how you might incorporate that learning into the new site (see Chapter 2, Research).

Information architect Louis Rosenfeld points out another irony of massive site redesigns, which is that only a small fraction of the content of your site is seen by most users. Data on what users search for generally follow a Zipf distribution,

Foundations & roles in the user experience

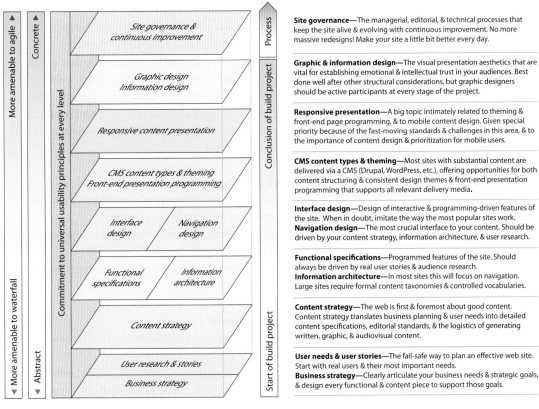

Site governance—The managerial, editorial, & technical processes that keep the site alive & evolving with continuous improvement. No more massive redesigns! Make your site a little bit better every day.

Graphic & information design—The visual presentation aesthetics that are vital for establishing emotional & intellectual trust in your audiences. Best done well after other structural considerations, but graphic designers should be active participants at every stage of the project.

Responsive presentation—A big topic intimately related to theming & front-end page programming, & to mobile content design. Given special priority because of the fast-moving standards & challenges in this area, & to the importance of content design & prioritization for mobile users.

CMS content types & theming—Most sites with substantial content are delivered via a CMS (Drupal, WordPress, etc.), offering opportunities for both content structuring & consistent design themes & front-end presentation programming that supports all relevant delivery media.

Interface design—Design of interactive & programming-driven features of the site. When in doubt, imitate the way the most popular sites work.
Navigation design—The most crucial interface to your content. Should be driven by your content strategy, information architecture, & user research.

Functional specifications—Programmed features of the site. Should always be driven by real user stories & audience research.
Information architecture—In most sites this will focus on navigation. Large sites require formal content taxonomies & controlled vocabularies.

Content strategy—The web is first & foremost about good content. Content strategy translates business planning & user needs into detailed content specifications, editorial standards, & the logistics of generating written, graphic, & audiovisual content.

User needs & user stories—The fail-safe way to plan an effective web site. Start with real users & their most important needs.
Business strategy—Clearly articulate your business needs & strategic goals, & design every functional & content piece to support those goals.

in which a few queries and content topics dominate, and most site content falls somewhere out on the "long tail" of seldom-used, seldom visited material. Check the search logs and usage data of most sites and you'll see that revising just a small percentage of pages will have a huge impact on what the average user sees.

When was the last time you heard Amazon, Facebook, Apple, or Google announce a "site redesign"? The smart players on the web don't announce redesigns because *they are redesigning their sites all the time, every day*, in small, incremental ways that continually improve the customer experience. These small, fast, agile-driven site improvements happen all the time, to quickly fix or improve the site. If A/B testing or other site data show that the new processes don't result in better usability, these small changes can be undone or fixed almost immediately.

FIGURE 3.20
Attention to user experience starts at the earliest strategy and sketching stages, and doesn't end until the last graphic is loaded onto the server for site launch.

TEN PROJECT STRATEGY AND PROCESS BEST PRACTICES

All digital projects and online services have common elements and challenges, and all can benefit from the lessons learned by successful teams over the past thirty years of online publishing. The following general principles were inspired in part by two major government sources: the U.S. Digital Playbook (playbook.cio.gov), which emerged from the successful redesign of the healthcare.gov site in support of the U.S. Affordable Care Act of 2010, and the widely admired U.K. Government Service Design Manual (gov.uk/service-manual), which specifies design standards and best practices for U.K. government online services.

1. Understand what people need from you

- When planning your project, spend time with current or prospective users of your site, to thoroughly understand their needs and concerns.
- Use a range of qualitative and quantitative research methods to understand people's goals, needs, and concerns.
- Document your research concisely in the form of brief data reports, common use cases, and short quantitative reports.

2. Consider the whole user experience

- Understand that whole range of your user's experience, from initial contact to satisfactory conclusion.
- Don't get obsessed with one particular medium. Users may interact with your enterprise through many media (web, print, social media, mobile applications, telephones, audiovisual media). Be consistent and integrated across all media. Use common design standards throughout so that people recognize your various voices as one entity.
- Use a consistent enterprise identity and user interface throughout large web sites. Departments that try to individualize their little pieces of the enterprise web presence just create a collective Tower of Babble for readers who must use many of your enterprise's sites every day.
- Identify your current pain points and broken processes, and use an issue or ticket tracking process to log known problems.
- There is no "typical user." Be sure to use universal usability principles to make your site as accessible as possible to all users.

3. Favor simple, familiar designs

- Simple is fast, simple is cost-effective, and simple is almost always easier to use and maintain.

- Create or use an existing simple and flexible design, and use it consistently throughout your communications with your customers, readers, or users.
- Adopt familiar, commonly used web design standards and interaction patterns. Example: In an online store, don't stray far from Amazon's patterns for web purchasing, checkout, and customer service.
- Provide clear feedback to users on where they are within a multistep process.
- For long processes and forms, always provide a way for users to save their work and return later.
- Provide clear and immediate feedback. If the user has missed some required form field, highlight the field and provide a note on what information is missing.
- Never force users to reenter data just because they didn't notice a detail in your form process.
- Use consistent language and terms throughout your customer experience.

4. Never let content or function follow form

- When "function follows form," projects fail because features and content are simply crammed into a predetermined site design, usually very late in the project. Craft your messages, craft your content, then design the site.
- Content is not the gray wordy stuff that gets poured into your page designs. Content form, structure, style, and key messages should always be at the heart of an online publication process.
- Elegant technical frameworks and beautiful pages are pointless without useful, elegant, and beautiful content.

5. Build using agile and iterative practices

- Use an incremental, iterative, fast-paced style of design and technology development wherever appropriate, such as agile and scrum processes.
- Ship a "minimum viable product" (MVP) as soon as possible.
- Beware of any technology project that lasts longer than three months. The world and the web move quickly, and longer projects will probably need to be revised as the environment changes around them.
- Reduce the risk of failure by developing small initial components that solve real user problems immediately, and build on user feedback to adjust your project plans accordingly.
- Ensure good communication with daily "standup" meetings with team members and key business process owners, designers, developers, and content creators.
- Keep a prioritized list of key features and known bugs, and use an issue or ticket tracking process to log known problems.

6. Ensure that contracts and budgets support strategic best practices

- Budget for research, discovery, and prototyping work.
- Contract for relatively small, frequent deliverables and milestones, with the flexibility needed to support agile development practices and deliverables.
- Ensure that open-source frameworks and software (think Drupal, WordPress, JQuery) are fairly compared with proprietary, closed software systems. It is far easier to find qualified staff and contractors if you stick with a widely used and open technology.
- Ensure that all enterprise data and custom code generated by all software systems used within your online publishing are the property of your enterprise, and can be extracted from the system in usable form.

7. Assign a single leader for the project

- A single, accountable, widely agreed-upon leader is critical to project success.
- The project leader is responsible for creating a work plan, budget, and production, and assuring funding sources for all phases of the project.
- All stakeholders and senior managers must agree that the project leader has the managerial and budget authority needed to assign tasks, adjust short-term schedules, and change the details of deliverables within an agile development process.

8. Choose your technology thoughtfully

- Use widely known and supported technology stacks and frameworks to support your site. Use valid HTML and CSS, Apache web servers, Drupal or WordPress content management systems, and JQuery or other widely supported code libraries.
- Create your site to run on standard hardware and servers, managed by your hosting company. Focus on standard Unix/Linux or Windows servers and hardware widely used by cloud computing vendors.
- Your hosting service should be able to rapidly provision and deploy additional generic servers as needed to meet unusual demand spikes, and to decommission unneeded servers quickly once demand falls.

9. Use data to drive decisions

- Use current data to back up all key decisions and project evaluations.
- Good data provide the perfect antidote to HIPPO syndrome (highest paid person's opinion). Never argue on the basis of personal authority. Convince people with data.

- Know your key metrics for user behavior, and run constant A/B testing to generate data on the successes or failures of your site's features and systems.
- Monitor as many key metrics as possible in real time, or at least daily, particularly in the early stages of testing and deployment.

10. Appoint a managing editor, and actively manage your content
- The most common reason online publishing ventures fail to meet their objectives is that the initial development project did not transition into an active publishing and maintenance process.
- Every publishing project must create a viable plan for long-term content maintenance.
- Appoint a single managing editor for your site, and hold that person responsible for updating and maintaining the content of your site.
- Appoint subject matter experts (SMEs) for sections of your site containing detailed business process, technical content, or product information. The SMEs may create draft content themselves, or work with writers or the managing editor to produce final content.
- Small is good. Keep your content as concise as possible, and aggressively prune unneeded or outdated content.

RECOMMENDED READING

Boag, P. *Digital Adaptation*. Freiberg, Germany: Smashing Magazine, 2014.

Byron, A., A. Berry, N. Haug, and B. De Bondt. *Using Drupal*. Sebastopol, CA: O'Reilly, 2012.

Garrett, J. *The Elements of User Experience: User-Centered Design for the Web*. Berkeley, CA: New Riders, 2000.

Knowlton, B. *A Practical Guide to Managing Web Projects*. Penarth, UK: Five Simple Steps, 2012.

Layton, M. *Agile Project Management for Dummies*. Hoboken, NJ: Wiley, 2012.

MacDonald, M. *WordPress: The Missing Manual*. Sebastopol, CA: O'Reilly, 2014.

Redish, G. *Letting Go of the Words: Writing Web Content That Works*, 2nd ed. Waltham, MA: Morgan Kaufmann, 2012.

Rosenfeld, L. "Stop Redesigning and Start Tuning Your Site Instead." *Smashing Magazine*, May 16, 2012, wsg4.link/stop-designing.

Sims, C., and H. L. Johnson. *The Elements of Scrum*. Foster City, CA: Dymaxicon, 2011.

———. *Scrum: A Breathtakingly Brief and Agile Introduction*. Foster City, CA: Dymaxicon, 2012.

I have always imagined that Paradise will be a kind of library.
– Jorge Luis Borges

GRANDE	LA GRANDE	LA GRANDE	LA GRANDE	LA GRANDE	LA GRANDE	LA GRANDE	LA GRANDE			LA GRANDE	LA GRANDE
LOPÉDIE	ENCYCLOPÉDIE	ENCYCLOPÉDIE	ENCYCLOPÉDIE	ENCYCLOPÉDIE	ENCYCLOPÉDIE	ENCYCLOPÉDIE	ENCYCLOPÉDIE			ENCYCLOPÉDIE	ENCYCLOPÉDIE
–DUÈGNE	UEL–EŒTVŒS	ÉOLE–FANUCCI	ANUM–FRANCO	FRANCO–GONON	GONSALVE–HÉRON	HÉRONAS–JANICK	JAN–LAMOT	LAMOT–MANZONI		MÃO–MOISSON	MOISSONNEUSE
14	15	16	17	18	19	20		22		23	24

CHAPTER 4

Information Architecture

In the context of web site design, information architecture (often referred to in web parlance as IA) describes the overall conceptual models and general designs used to plan, structure, and assemble a site. Every web site has an information architecture, but information architecture techniques are particularly important to large, complex web sites, where the primary aims of IA are to:

A garden is finished when there is nothing left to remove.

—Zen aphorism

- Organize the site content into taxonomies and hierarchies, systems of classification that proceed from the general to the specific. Often this hierarchy becomes the basis for both browse navigation and search systems.
- Create controlled vocabularies for the major categories of content, so that similar things are labeled consistently throughout the site.
- Communicate conceptual overviews and the overall content and site organization to the design team and clients.
- Research and design the core site navigation systems.
- Test proposed site organization and navigation concepts with representative users, often using techniques like card sorting.
- Set standards and specifications for the handling and structure of content in content management systems and databases.
- Define appropriate metadata standards for content (for example, controlled descriptions and keywords that describe the content).
- Define standards for accessibility-related metadata ("alt" HTML tags for images, captioning standards for video, alternate navigation standards).
- Design and implement search engine optimization (SEO) standards and strategies.

The information architecture of a site is much more than the details of how the content is organized and subdivided. A good information architecture process looks holistically at the total user experience, how business and cultural context affects information seeking, and what the users want the site to deliver to them. In this larger view the site content is just one aspect of a good information architecture process.

FIGURE 4.1

The overall context
of how we use
information.

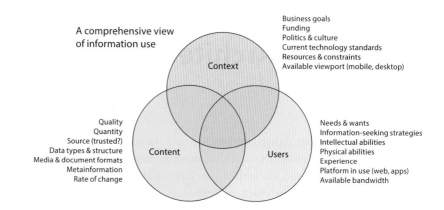

A comprehensive view
of information use

Context

Business goals
Funding
Politics & culture
Current technology standards
Resources & constraints
Available viewport (mobile, desktop)

Quality
Quantity
Source (trusted?)
Data types & structure
Media & document formats
Metainformation
Rate of change

Content

Users

Needs & wants
Information-seeking strategies
Intellectual abilities
Physical abilities
Experience
Platform in use (web, apps)
Available bandwidth

INFORMATION ARCHITECTURE IN SITE DEVELOPMENT

Information architecture is one of a broad range of design and planning disciplines, and the boundaries across information architecture, technical design, user interface, and graphic design are necessarily blurred by the need for all of these communities of practice to cooperate to produce a cohesive, coherent, and consistent experience for the site user. Information architecture probably overlaps the most with content strategy, as both are concerned with planning for the proper structure and deployment of content. The core of content strategy, however, concerns the creation of useful and appropriate content that supports the overall goals and messages of the site, whereas information architecture is primarily concerned with how that body of content is structured and categorized with the site to support successful navigation and search.

What's important to remember about closely related professional fields like content strategy and information architecture is that these are not just job titles. Information architecture and content strategy are tasks that need to be performed for all site designs, regardless of the job title of the person doing the work. We estimate that about 95 percent of web projects are small and straightforward enough that content strategy and information architecture will be done by the same team member, and these days that person will probably be called a "content strategist." A site with a huge body of content to organize, however, will need an experienced information architect, probably with a library science background, because of the complex organizational and structural challenges of such large pools of information.

Architecture is an appropriate metaphor for the assembling of complex multidimensional information spaces shared by many different users and readers, where the underlying structure of information must first be framed out before more specific disciplines such as interface and graphic design can operate effectively. The user interface and visual design of the site may be much more visible to the user initially,

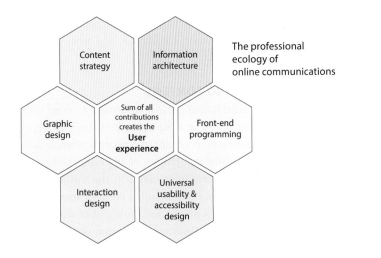

The professional ecology of online communications

Content strategy

Information architecture

Graphic design

Sum of all contributions creates the **User experience**

Front-end programming

Interaction design

Universal usability & accessibility design

but if the underlying organization of the site and its content is poorly constructed, visual or interactive design cannot fix the structural and conceptual problems.

Many of the most prominent information architects have backgrounds in library science, a discipline built upon centuries of knowledge on how to categorize large bodies of information. However, in many projects the information architecture of the site will become a joint project among the design, editorial, and technical teams. Regardless of how the role is filled, the information architecture tasks form the crucial planning bridge between your general discussions of site goals and audiences and the specific design, user interface, and technical solutions you'll use in the finished site designs.

METHODS FOR INFORMATION ARCHITECTURE

Our day-to-day professional and social lives rarely demand that we create detailed architectures of what we know and how those structures of information are linked. Yet without a solid and logical organizational foundation, your web site will not function well even if your basic content is accurate, attractive, and well written.

There are five basic steps in organizing your information:

1. **Inventory your content:** What do you have already? What do you need?
2. Establish a **hierarchical outline** of your content and create a controlled vocabulary so the major content, site structure, and navigation elements are always identified consistently.
3. **Chunking:** Divide your content into logical units with a modular structure.
4. Draw **diagrams** that show the site structure and rough outlines of pages with a list of core navigation links.

5. **Analyze your system** by testing the organization interactively with real users, through card-sorting exercises, paper prototyping, and other user research techniques; revise as needed.

INVENTORYING AND AUDITING CONTENT

A content inventory is a detailed listing of basic information about all the content that exists in a site to be redesigned or, in some cases, a site to be newly created from existing content resources. Although a content inventory is often tedious and time-consuming to create, it is an essential component of any rational scope planning for a web project. Content inventories are most useful in the initial project planning and information architecture phases, but a detailed content inventory will be useful throughout the project for both planning and build-out of the site. The work of moving through an existing site and recording information on each page is detailed, but it's also easy to divide among team members who work through different subsections or directories of the site. The team members making the site inventory must both have access to the site pages in a web browser and be able to view the site structure within the CMS or on the server to ensure that all sections of content are inventoried.

Web content inventories of existing sites commonly take the form of a spreadsheet file with multiple worksheets, containing long listings of every page in the site, along with such essential characteristics as the page title, URL, people responsible for the content, and so on. Each page typically gets a row on the spreadsheet, with columns listing such basic information as:

- Unique ID number for project purposes
- Page name
- Page template or type
- Section name
- URL
- Short description
- Date of last update
- Content owner

An inventory is an important starting point. However, a strategic approach means focusing efforts on content that meets project goals and is relevant to the target audience. To aid in decision making and support moving content forward, include action-oriented columns in the content inventory document, such as:

- Action (create, edit, move, delete)
- Priority (high, medium, low)

Page ID num	Navigation title	Page title	Link - current URL	Meta description	What is this page about?	Type of page	Files and i	Last updated	Expiry or 'review	Conte
0.0	Home	The European Commission Represen	http://ec.europa.eu/unite	The website for th	Mix of news and links to l	Dynamic with	Links to full	29.06.12	Weekly	
1.0	About us	What we do	http://ec.europa.eu/unite	The European Cor	What the office does	Text	Links to ear	08.04.11		
1.1	Office in London	Office in London	http://ec.europa.eu/unite	The European Cor	London office contacts	Text and photos		12.06.12	27.6.12	
1.2	Office in Northern Ireland	Office in Northern Ireland	http://ec.europa.eu/unite	European Commis	Latest NI news	Dynamic		09.02.12		
1.2.1	About us	About us	http://ec.europa.eu/unite		NI office contacts	Text and photos		09.01.12		
1.2.2	EC Info-Point	EC Info-Point	http://ec.europa.eu/unite		The Belfast info point	Text		31.10.10		
1.2.3	Northern Ireland Task	Northern Ireland Task Force	http://ec.europa.eu/unite		About the task force	Text		30.03.11		
1.2.4	Reporting Europe	Reporting Europe 21 June 2012	http://ec.europa.eu/unite		The latest newsletter	Text		27.06.12		
1.2.5	Reporting Europe - Ind	Reporting Europe - Index	http://ec.europa.eu/unite		Past issues of newsletter	Links		27.06.12		
1.3	Office in Scotland	Office in Scotland	http://ec.europa.eu/unite	The European Cor	Contact details and some news					
1.3.1	Neil Mitchison (not in r	Neil Mitchison	http://ec.europa.eu/unite		Biography of Neil	Text and photo				
1.4	Office in Wales	Office in Wales	http://ec.europa.eu/unite	European Commis	History and contacts	Text and photos				
1.5	History (not in nav)	History	http://ec.europa.eu/unitedkingdom/about	History of the UK and the	EU					
1.5	Contact	Contact	http://ec.europa.eu/unite		List of offices and their c	Text				
2.0	Press Room	Press Room	http://ec.europa.eu/unite							

FIGURE 4.3

Content inventories are usually done in spreadsheet software like Microsoft Excel.

- Person responsible
- Date due
- Status (to be done, in process, published)

Site analysis applications like seo Spider can crawl existing sites and automatically produce a spreadsheet-based listing of page headings and urls for each page of the site. It also reports on broken links, suboptimal heading and markup issues, and (as you might guess) an analysis of page content as it relates to search engine optimization (seo). This kind of report is not a substitute for a content inventory, but it can be a way to speed the process of gathering information.

Hierarchies and taxonomies

Hierarchical organization is a virtual necessity on the web. Most sites depend on hierarchies to create their high-level navigation categories, moving from the broadest overview of the site (the home page), down through increasingly specific submenus and content pages. In information architecture you create categories for your information and rank the importance of each piece of information by how general or specific that piece is relative to the whole. General categories become high-ranking elements of the hierarchy of information; specific chunks of information are positioned lower in the hierarchy. Chunks of information are ranked in importance and organized by relevance to one of the major categories. Once you have determined a logical set of priorities and relations in your content outlines, you can build a hierarchy from the most important or general concepts down to the most specific or detailed topics.

Taxonomies and controlled vocabularies

Taxonomy is the science and practice of classification. In information architecture, a taxonomy is a hierarchical organization of content categories, using a specific, carefully designed set of descriptive terms and labels. As any experienced editor or librarian can tell you, one of the biggest challenges of organizing large amounts of information is developing a system for consistently referring to the same things the same way: a controlled vocabulary, in library science parlance. One of the most important jobs of the information architect is producing a consistent set of names and terms to describe the chief site content categories, the key navigation site links, and major terms to describe the interactive features of the site. This controlled vocabulary becomes a foundational element of the content organization, the user interface, the standard navigation links seen on every page of the site, and the file and directory structure of the site itself.

ORGANIZING CONTENT

When designing a new web site or extensively overhauling an existing one, it can be useful to step back from the details of the content inventory and take a fresh look at both how your information is organized and the underlying paradigms that drive conversations about content and site organization.

Some common underlying paradigms for site organization are:

- **Identity sites:** Dominated by projected organizational identity and marketing. Most general corporate sites fall into this category.
- **Navigation sites:** Dominated by navigation and links, usually for sites with very large bodies of information, like news or reference sites.
- **Novelty or entertainment sites:** Dominated by news and "what's new," like Buzzfeed or the Onion.
- **The org chart site:** Designed around the organization of the enterprise. Department sites are often organized this way, and as long as they are not heavily used service sites this may make sense. Often the basis of confused or poor site organization (see below).
- **Service sites:** Organized around service, content, or products categories. Fast access to services should always dominate here, as in IT help desk sites, or enterprise human resources sites.
- **Visual identity sites:** Use interaction and visual flash to define the identity of a brand and draw an audience mostly through visual sensation. Many restaurant and luxury consumer brand sites fall into this category.
- **Tool-oriented sites:** Organized around a tool or service technology. Google or Bing search engines are obvious examples, but popular online software services like Basecamp, Dropbox, and Evernote are other tool-oriented sites.

In a given context some paradigms or site themes are clearly better than others: it's rarely wise to fall in love with a particular site organization before you have a clear rationale for using it, or for projecting your identity to the extent that you subordinate the motivations and concerns of your potential readers and users. Good sites balance meeting your users' needs with delivering your message to the world. There is no formula for finding the right organizational paradigm, but in the early planning you should always examine your standing prejudices and explicitly justify them.

Clumsy "org chart sites" arranged solely by how the organization is managed are a standing joke among web designers, but are much less amusing to users who can't find what they're looking for because they don't understand—or care—how your management is organized. The vast majority of users want products, information, or services from your web site, but many management structures don't follow this service-oriented organization.

In some special situations users really do want to know how you are organized and will find contact information and content more easily with navigation based on business units. For example, in business-to-business (B2B) relationships a buyer or salesperson might really want an understanding of who manages what parts of an organization. But more often than not "org charts sites" reflect a poor understanding of what your readers and users need from you.

If you see these underlying mindsets and management silos driving or distorting early site organization discussions, put them on the table for discussion and brainstorming. Everyone has mental models, favorite paradigms, and blind spots. Be sure you've acknowledged and examined your underlying assumptions and biases and have chosen the best organizing theme for your site.

Content mapping

Even if the major categories of your content organization are clear to the design team, it still may be hard to sort through where each piece of content belongs or what organization scheme will seem most intuitive and predictable to your users. User research can be crucial in building controlled vocabularies for labeling and navigation.

For example, in large biomedical research hospitals there are many varieties of "doctors" (people with doctoral degrees), so in professional language medical doctors are often distinguished as "physicians." But most laypeople seeking medical help are not looking for "physicians"; they want a doctor. Both "physician" and "doctor" are appropriate terms, but how and where you use each term will depend on what your audience will expect and understand.

Card sorting—also called content mapping—is a common technique for creating and evaluating content organization and web site structures, and for clarifying and refining controlled vocabularies. In classic card-sorting techniques, index cards are labeled with the names of major and secondary content categories, and indi-

FIVE HAT RACKS: THEMES TO ORGANIZE INFORMATION

In his book *Information Anxiety* Richard Saul Wurman posits that there are five fundamental ways to organize information: the "five hat racks" on which you can hang information.

Category Organization by the similarity of characteristics or relatedness of the items. This is a particularly useful approach when all the things being organized are of equal or unpredictable importance. Examples include topics of books in a bookstore or library and items in a department or grocery store.

Time Organization by timeline or history, where elements are presented in a sequential, step-by-step manner. This approach is commonly used in training. Other examples include television listings, a history of specific events, and measuring the response times of different systems.

Location Organization by spatial or geographic location, most often used for orientation and direction. This most graphic of the categories obviously lends itself to maps but is also used extensively in training, repair, and user manual illustrations and other instances where information is tied to a place.

Alphabetic Organization based on the initial letter of the names of items. Obvious examples are telephone and other name-oriented directories, dictionaries, and thesauri, whose users know the word or name they are seeking. Alphabetic systems are simple to grasp and familiar in everyday life. This method of organization is less effective for short lists of unrelated things but is powerful for long lists.

Continuum Organization by the quantity of a measured variable over a range, such as price, score, size, or weight. Continuum organization is most effective when organizing many things that are all measured or scored the same way. Examples include rankings and reviews of all kinds, such as the U.S. News and World Report ranking of colleges and universities, the best movies in a given year, darkest or lightest items, and other instances for which a clear weight or value can be assigned to each item.

vidual team members or potential site users are then asked to sort through the cards and organize them in a way that seems intuitive and logical. Users may also be asked to suggest new or better names for categories. The resulting content outline from each participant is recorded, usually in a spreadsheet, and all the individual content schemes are compared for commonalities and areas of major disagreement. The

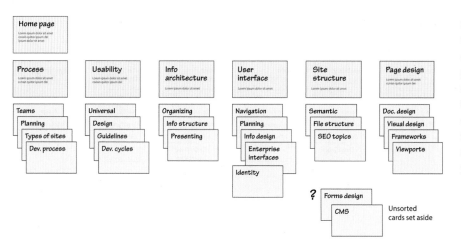

FIGURE 4.4
Card-sorting exercises provide a great way to make sure that your terminology and site organization match the mental models and vocabulary of your audience.

best card-sorting data come from individual sessions with representative current or potential users of your site. If you have enough participants, combining the results of each card-sorting session produces a powerful "wisdom of crowds" aggregation of many individual judgments about what content organization makes sense. These user-derived (or user-informed) category taxonomies are sometimes called "folksonomies," a neologism coined by information architect Thomas Vander Wal that combines "folk" and "taxonomy."

Card-sorting exercises come in a few varieties, and the exercises may be done with groups of participants working together, or with individual participants each working on his or her own. In open card sorting, subjects are asked to create their own names for major categories and subcategories of the site. The subjects typically start with blank index cards and a written description of the site and what its purpose and likely content will be, but are encouraged to name major categories as they see fit, and to group subcategories using their own logic about where things belong within each major category. The information architect running the card-sorting research then combines the most popular category names to form a taxonomy. This is often helpful when you suspect that your internal team might not use the same vocabulary used by your target audiences.

The more common closed card sorting uses preprinted index cards, and a full set of major and subcategory cards is given to each participant. The participant is then asked to select a few major categories—or create her or his own names for major categories if the existing names don't seem right—and to place the remaining cards logically within each category to form a site taxonomy that makes sense to that participant. The cards should be carefully printed by hand for maximum legibility, or you could use Avery index card sheets compatible with laser printers to make the

FIGURE 4.5
Reverse card sorts
are often done
later in the research
process, to test
how well your
organization scheme
holds up when users
search through it to
find specific items.

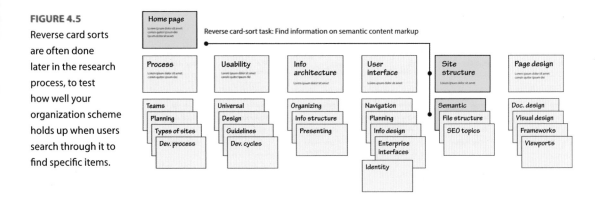

cards from your computer. This is often the best option when you need to create large groups of cards for testing.

The resulting taxonomies—one from each participant—are then compared both statistically and informally to the taxonomy that was created by the site designers or the information architect. More often than not the summary of the research participants' taxonomies will be similar to the design team's taxonomy, but the primary value of card sorting is to find those instances where the design team's logic differs from the target audience's about where to find a particular category within the site's navigation.

In a reverse card sort, a taxonomy of major categories and subcategories is laid out in front of the participant, and the participant is given a sample task to perform by finding the category card that most closely represents the place in the taxonomy where the participant can complete the task. Reverse card sorts are usually done late in the research phase, as the primary value of reverse card sorts is to evaluate the effectiveness of a proposed taxonomy, not to generate a new one.

For smaller or less formal site projects, you can have group whiteboard sessions with techniques similar to card sorting. Participants are asked to sort through cards or sticky notes labeled with the names of major content elements, which are then posted on a whiteboard and sorted by the group until there is consensus about what overall organization or taxonomy makes the most sense. In most cases you'll achieve quick consensus on the major categories of content and navigation, and the whiteboard organization becomes a useful first look at the site org chart that can help the group resolve the more problematic questions of what content belongs in which category. Use your phone to take snapshots of the various steps along the way, and of the finished whiteboard. Post-it has a smartphone app that can be useful in recording and sharing whiteboard Post-it sessions.

Some practical tips for card sorting:

- Name the major categories as clearly as possible, without duplications or redundancies in terminology.
- If category names are not obvious or are ambiguous, try using an "open" card sort early in your research, to allow the users to create their own names for categories.
- Have a complete inventory of all your major categories and subcategories of content, with each category on its own card.
- Limit the total number of cards to about forty. If your site is large and complex, divide the content into more manageable chunks of no more than forty category cards each.
- Use real card stock, not cut-up paper. Paper "cards" won't last more than a session or two.
- Prepare thorough instructions for individual card-sorting sessions.
- Assure all participants that there are no "wrong" answers, and that they have complete freedom to arrange things and rename things as they see fit.
- Not every card will find a place in the organization. Tell participants that if they can't find a logical place for a particular card, they should just set the card aside and move on.
- Refrain from prompting or coaching participants.
- Never discourage an idea from a user—even if you think it is a mistaken one—and allow free brainstorming.
- Have plenty of supplies for new categories and improved terminology.
- Bring a good digital camera with enough resolution to record the proposed card-sort organizations and whiteboard layouts. Make sure to check your photos for the legibility of all labels and notes.

While small projects with a few dozen categories and subcategories might not require software tools, larger projects with extensive content and/or many research participants to record and analyze may benefit from card-sorting software. xSort (Macintosh only) and uxSort (Windows only) are free but quite capable applications for designing and conducting card-sorting exercises. OptimalSort is a professional web-based card-sorting application well suited to complex bodies of information and large numbers of research participants, particularly where the research participants are scattered geographically. OptimalSort allows you to build a preliminary information architecture and controlled vocabulary, design card-sorting exercises, and coordinate communication with test participants via the web and email. The main value of tools like OptimalSort is probably in the analysis and reporting

FIGURE 4.6

Applications-based or web-based card-sorting software can be invaluable when you have complex content organizations and are testing larger numbers of users.

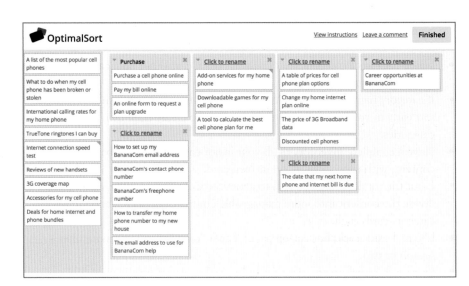

phase, where it can process the data and produce finished charts that summarize the results of all of your card-sorting sessions.

Regardless of the exact methods that you use, card sorting can be an inexpensive but valuable means to test your ideas on representative members of your potential audience. You don't need huge numbers of research participants to get useful data. Methods research has shown that you can get about 80 percent of the value of user testing from as few as five test participants, and virtually 100 percent of the value of research with as few as fifteen test users. Card-sorting techniques have been used for many years, and if you carefully choose representative or potential users of your site, they offer "real-world" validation of ideas from your sponsors, stakeholders, and team members.

SEGMENTING INFORMATION

Most information on the web is gathered in short reference documents that are intended to be read nonsequentially. This is particularly true of sites where the contents are mostly technical or administrative documents. Long before the web was invented, technical writers discovered that readers appreciate short chunks of information on pages that can be quickly scanned for titles, subtitles, and bulleted lists. This method of presenting information translates well to the web for several reasons:

- Few web readers who are hunting for information will read long unstructured passages of text onscreen. Visual scanning aids like lots of titles and subtitles, lists, and tables help readers to quickly home in on relevant information.

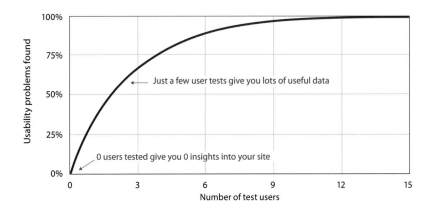

FIGURE 4.7
Research from the Nielsen-Norman Group shows that you need only a few participants to get great benefits from user testing.

- Discrete chunks of information lend themselves to web links. The user of a web link typically expects the link to provide a specific unit of relevant information, not a book's worth of general content.
- Chunking can help organize and present information in a modular layout that is consistent throughout the site. This allows users not only to apply past experience with a site to future searches and explorations but to predict how an unfamiliar section of a web site will be organized.
- Concise chunks of information are better suited to the computer screen, which provides a limited view of long documents. The limited viewports of mobile devices like tablets and smartphones make it even more important to keep your content concise and carefully designed to highlight major topics and keywords.

Content chunks

In linked hypertext systems like the web, content is often organized in modular, consistently organized "chunks" (also called "rhetorical clusters" by some authors) of information on specific topics. When you click on a web link about a particular topic, you expect the link to take you to a specific piece of content and not to the home page of Wikipedia. For example, you'd expect a web link for "chicken saltimbocca" to take you to a recipe or a short article on the dish, not to the first page of a whole book on Italian cooking. In print volumes such specific linking or footnoting is done using the basic unit of print, a numbered page. On the web a "page" can be of any arbitrary length, but if a web link on saltimbocca brings you to the top of a five thousand–word web page that (somewhere) includes the term "chicken saltimbocca," you would feel misled. Why didn't the link bring you to specific information on chicken saltimbocca? To meet these user expectations for specific blocks of information, neither too large nor cluttered with irrelevancies, your content must ideally

Content types ➕ Add content type   Home ▸ Administration ▸ Structure

NAME		OPERATIONS		
Basic page (Machine name: page) Use *basic pages* for your static content, such as an 'About us' page.	edit	manage fields	manage display	delete
Blog entry (Machine name: blog) Use *blog entries* for a site-wide or multi-user blog.	edit	manage fields	manage display	
Customer (Machine name: customer) Use *customer* content to display a profile of one of your site's customers.	edit	manage fields	manage display	delete
FAQ item (Machine name: faq_item) Use a *FAQ item* to provide a question and answer about your site.	edit	manage fields	manage display	delete
Forum topic (Machine name: forum) A *forum topic* starts a new discussion thread within a forum.	edit	manage fields	manage display	
Gallery (Machine name: media_gallery) A flexible gallery of media.	edit	manage fields	manage display	
News item (Machine name: article) Use *news items* for time-specific content like press releases or announcements.	edit	manage fields	manage display	delete
Poll (Machine name: poll) A *poll* is a question with a set of possible responses. A *poll*, once created, automatically provides a simple running count of the number of votes received for each response.	edit	manage fields	manage display	
Testimonial (Machine name: testimonial) Use a *testimonial* to display a customer's quote about your site.	edit	manage fields	manage display	delete

FIGURE 4.8

Content management systems like Drupal offer many tools to subdivide and structure types of text content.

be "chunked" into modular units structured and organized to meet the expectations of web users.

The concept of a chunk of information must be flexible and consistent with common sense, logically organized in the context of your topics, and convenient to use. Let the nature of the content suggest how it should be subdivided and organized. Although short carefully structured web pages are in general better than long rambling pages, it sometimes makes little sense to divide a long document arbitrarily into multiple short pages, particularly if you want users to be able to print easily or save the document in one step.

Your content management system (CMS) may also be structured to allow a set of content "chunks." For example, a longer article or blog post often has both a main article field and a separate field for short or abstract versions of the article, as well as keywords and links to illustrations. CMS software like Drupal also allows you to create custom article structures and controlled vocabularies of keywords if your content needs more structure than the typical title–short version–full article–keywords default configurations for CMS content. Content is much more powerful and adaptable when it is consistently organized in modular formats that can be deployed flexibly across web sites, mobile apps, and social media platforms, all from the same core database.

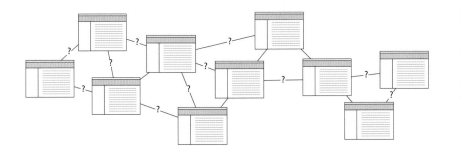

FIGURE 4.9
Don't create a
confusing web of
links. Designers
aren't the only ones
who create mental
models of web
sites. Users also try
to imagine the site
structure as well,
and a successful
information
architecture will
help the user build a
firm and predictable
mental model of
your site.

INFORMATION ARCHITECTURE DESIGN

When confronted with a new and complex information system, users build mental models. They use these models to assess relations among topics and to guess where to find things they haven't seen before. The success of the organization of your web site will be determined largely by how well your site's information architecture matches your users' expectations. A logical, consistently named site organization allows users to make successful predictions about where to find things. Consistent methods of organizing and displaying information permit users to extend their knowledge from familiar pages to unfamiliar ones. If you mislead users with a structure that is neither logical nor predictable, or if you use inconsistent or ambiguous terms to describe site features, users will be frustrated by the difficulties of getting around and understanding what you have to offer. You don't want your user's mental model of your web site to look like Figure 4.9.

SUPPORTING BROWSE AND SEARCH

Once you have created your site in outline form, analyze its ability to support browsing by testing it interactively, both within the site development team and with small groups of real users. Efficient web site design is largely a matter of balancing the relation of major menu or home pages with individual content pages. The goal is to build a hierarchy of menus and content pages that feels natural to users and doesn't mislead them or interfere with their use of the site.

Web sites with too shallow an information hierarchy depend on massive menu pages that can degenerate into a confusing laundry list of unrelated information. Menu schemes can also be too deep, burying information beneath too many layers of menus, requiring too many "clicks" on links. Having to navigate through layers of nested menus before reaching real content is frustrating.

Although it is always tempting to limit your top-level content categories to as few as possible, beware of creating too deep a site hierarchy. Deep hierarchies tend to confuse users, who prefer a broad range of choices to survey over just a few necessary vague or generic categories at the top of a deep hierarchy. A deep hierarchy with

FIGURE 4.10
The "long tail" of web
search. Large sites
are just too large to
depend solely on
browsing. Heavily
used pages are likely
to appear on site
menus, but obscure
pages buried deep
within a site will be
found and read only
through web search
technologies.

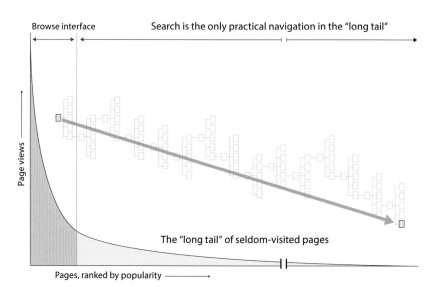

many nested categories also forces the user to remember more as she clicks down through the layers. A wide range of content categories also provides more "scent of information," the ability to quickly survey many organizational categories and accurately guess where the desired information or product might be located.

If your web site is actively growing, the proper balance of menus and content pages is a moving target. Feedback from users (and analyzing your own use of the site) can help you decide whether your menu scheme has outlived its usefulness or has weak areas. Complex document structures require deeper menu hierarchies, but users should never be forced into page after page of menus if direct access is possible. With a well-balanced, functional hierarchy you can offer users menus that provide quick access to information and reflect the organization of your site.

If your site has more than a few dozen pages, your users will expect web search options to find content in the site. In a larger site, with maybe hundreds or thousands of pages of content, web search is the only efficient means to locate particular content pages or to find all pages that mention a keyword or search phrase. Browse interfaces composed of major site and content landmarks are essential in the initial phases of a user's visit to your site. However, once the user has decided that your site may offer the sought-after information, he or she crosses a threshold of specificity that only a search engine can help with.

No browse interface of links can assure the user that he or she has found all instances of a given keyword or search phrase.

Search is the most efficient means to reach specific content, particularly if that content is not heavily visited by other users and is therefore unlikely to appear as a link in a major navigation page.

As with popular books at the library or the hit songs on iTunes, content usage on large web sites is a classic "long-tail" phenomenon: a few items get 80 percent of the attention, and the rest get dramatically less traffic. As the user's needs get more specific than a browser interface can handle, the search engine is the means to find content out there in the long tail, where it might otherwise remain undiscovered.

CHOOSING A SITE STRUCTURE

Web sites are built around basic structural themes that both form and reinforce a user's mental model of how you have organized your content. These fundamental architectures govern the navigational interface of the web site and mold the user's mental models of how the information is organized. Three essential structures can be used to build a web site: sequences, hierarchies, and webs.

Sequences

The simplest and most familiar way to organize information is to place it in a sequence. This is the structure of books, magazines, and all other print matter. Sequential ordering may be chronological, a logical series of topics progressing from the general to the specific, or alphabetical, as in indexes, encyclopedias, and glossaries. Straight sequences are the most appropriate organization for training or edu-

FIGURE 4.11
A sequential training site on laboratory safety.

a. Straight linear sequence

b. Linear sequences with supporting digressions

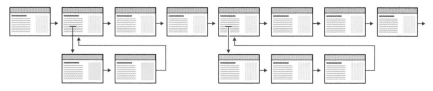

FIGURE 4.12
Hierarchies are
inevitable in web
design. Most
content works
well in hierarchical
structures, and users
find them easy to
understand.

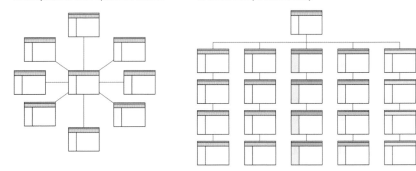

a. Simple hub-and-spoke structure   b. More complex hierarchy

cation sites, for example, in which the user is expected to progress through a fixed set of material and the only links are those that support the linear navigation path.

More complex web sites may still be organized as a logical sequence, but each page in the sequence may have links to one or more pages of digressions, parenthetical information, or information on other web sites.

Hierarchies

Information hierarchies are the best way to organize most complex bodies of information. Because web sites are usually organized around a single home page, which then links to subtopic menu pages, hierarchical architectures are particularly suited to web site organization. Hierarchical diagrams are familiar in corporate and institutional life, so most users find this structure easy to understand. A hierarchical organization also imposes a useful discipline on your own analytical approach to your content, because hierarchies are practical only with well-organized material.

The simplest form of hierarchical site structure is a star, or hub-and-spoke, set of pages arrayed off a central home page. The site is essentially a single-tier hierarchy. Navigation tends to be a simple list of subpages, plus a link on each back to the home page.

Most web sites adopt some form of multitiered hierarchical or tree architecture. This arrangement of major categories and subcategories has a powerful advantage for complex site organization in that most people are familiar with hierarchical organizations, and can readily form mental models of the site structure.

Note that although hierarchical sites organize their content and pages in a tree of site menus and submenus off the home page, this hierarchy of content subdivisions should not become a navigational straitjacket for the user who wants to jump from one area of the site to another. Most site navigation interfaces provide global navigation links that allow users to jump from one major site area to another without being forced to back up to a central home page or submenu. In Figure 4.13, primary

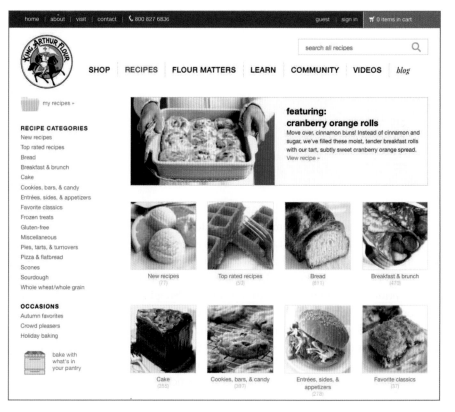

FIGURE 4.13
The King Arthur site organizes its recipes, products, and learning resources in a straightforward hierarchical way that is easy to understand and navigate, with a persistent header of major categories, and category details in the left column.

categories in the header allow the user to move from one major content area to another, the left navigation menu provides local subcategories, and a search box allows the user to jump out of categorical navigation and find pages based on a web search engine.

Webs

Weblike organizational structures pose few restrictions on the pattern of information use. In this structure the goal is often to mimic associative thought and the free flow of ideas, allowing users to follow their interests in a unique, heuristic, idiosyncratic pattern. This organizational pattern develops with dense links both to information elsewhere in the site and to information at other sites. Although the goal of this organization is to exploit the web's power of linkage and association to the fullest, weblike structures can just as easily propagate confusion. Ironically, associative organizational schemes are often the most impractical structure for web sites because they are so hard for the user to understand and predict. Webs work best for sites dominated

FIGURE 4.14
A simple web of
associated pages.

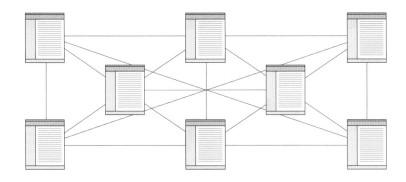

by lists of links and for sites aimed at highly educated or experienced users looking for further education or enrichment, and not for a basic understanding of a topic.

The academic site Arts & Letters Daily is a great (albeit complex) example of a web organization. This site is designed for a highly educated audience that needs little context or structure provided by the site organization, because users bring a high level of prior personal knowledge to the content. Simple lists based on a few major categories are all this audience needs for pointers to recent interesting content.

Most complex web sites share aspects of all three types of information structures. Site hierarchy is created largely with standard navigational links within the site, but topical links embedded within the content create a weblike mesh of associative links that transcends the usual navigation and site structure. Except in sites that rigor-

FIGURE 4.15
Arts & Letters Daily
is a site for experts,
who want a carefully
curated but not
heavily categorized
selection of the best
of what the day's
news and content
sites have to offer
a professional
academic audience.

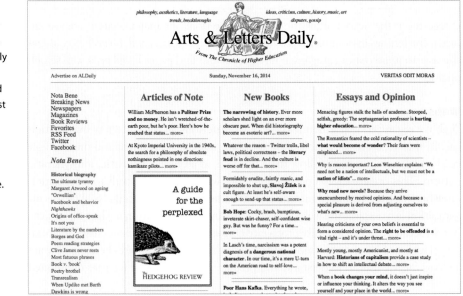

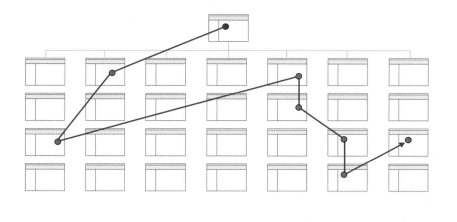

FIGURE 4.16
Users who are hunting for information rarely move through a site in a linear progression of pages in each category. A good intuitive browse navigation scheme allow users to move freely within a site without feeling lost.

ously enforce a sequence of pages, users are likely to traverse your site in a free-form weblike manner, jumping across regions in the information architecture, just as they would skip through chapters in a reference book. Ironically, the clearer and more concrete your site organization is, the easier it is for users to jump freely from place to place without feeling lost.

The nonlinear usage patterns typical of web users do not absolve you of the need to organize your thinking and present it within a clear, consistent structure that complements your overall design goals. Figure 4.17 summarizes the three basic organization patterns against the linearity of the narrative and the complexity of the content.

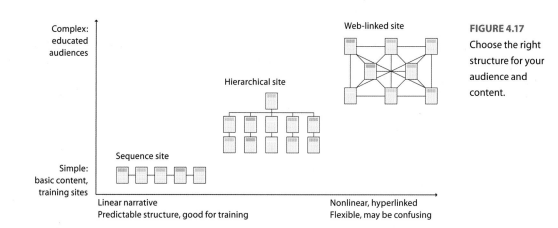

FIGURE 4.17
Choose the right structure for your audience and content.

Middle and corners

Rule of thirds

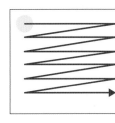
Gutenberg Z

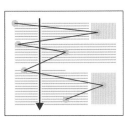
Reading gravity

FIGURE 4.18

Classic rules of composition and our reading habits combine to govern how we approach information displays.

ARCHITECTING THE PAGE

What governs how people scan pages of information, in print or on the screen? According to classical art composition theory, the corners and middle of a plane attract early attention from viewers. In a related compositional practice, the "rule of thirds" places centers of interest within a grid that divides both dimensions in thirds. These compositional rules are purely pictorial, however, and are probably most useful for displays or home pages composed almost entirely of graphics or photography. Most page composition is dominated by text, and there our reading habits are the primary forces that shape the way we scan pages. In Western languages we read from top to bottom, scanning left to right down the page in a "Gutenberg Z" pattern. This preference for attention flow down the page—and a reluctance to reverse the downward scanning—is called "reading gravity" and explains why it is rarely a good idea to place the primary headline anywhere except the top of a page. Readers who are scanning your work are unlikely to back up the page to "start again." Search engines also have a well-known bias toward items near the top of a page.

The Poynter Institute has studied eye-tracking by readers looking at web pages and has found that readers start their scanning with many fixations in the upper left of the page. Their gaze then follows a Gutenberg Z pattern down the page, and only later do typical readers lightly scan the right area of the page. Eye-tracking studies by Jakob Nielsen show that web pages dominated by text information are scanned in

FIGURE 4.19

Eye-tracking studies show that our page-scanning patterns are dominated by top-left scanning for the most important words and links on a page.

a. Poynter eye-tracking study

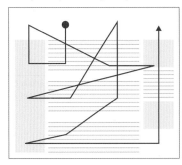

b. "F" pattern and the "golden triangle"

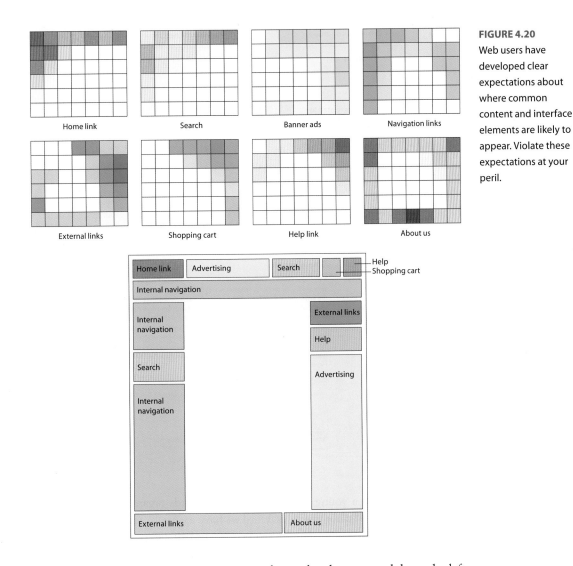

FIGURE 4.20
Web users have developed clear expectations about where common content and interface elements are likely to appear. Violate these expectations at your peril.

Home link

Search

Banner ads

Navigation links

External links

Shopping cart

Help link

About us

Home link | Advertising | Search | | Help / Shopping cart

Internal navigation

Internal navigation

External links

Search

Help

Internal navigation

Advertising

External links | About us

an "F" pattern of intense eye fixations across the top header area, and down the left edge of the text.

When readers scan web pages, they are clearly using a combination of classic Gutenberg Z page scanning and what they have learned from the emerging standards and practices of web designers. As the web nears its twenty-fifth anniversary, some common patterns form the basis for "best practice" recommendations in web page composition. Human interface researchers have done studies on where users expect to find standard web page components and have found clear sets of expectations about where some items are located on web pages.

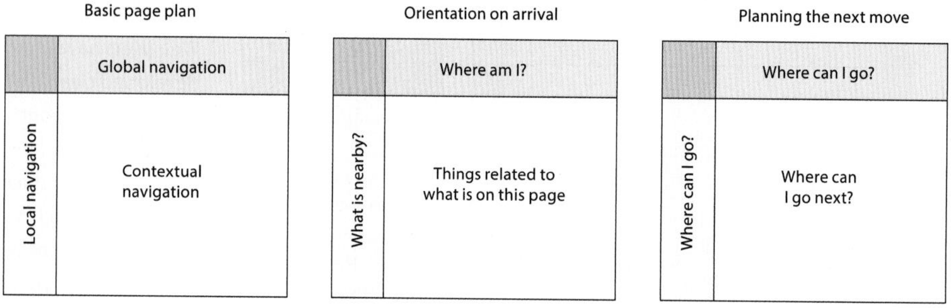
Basic page plan
Global navigation
Local navigation
Contextual navigation
Orientation on arrival
Where am I?
What is nearby?
Things related to what is on this page
Planning the next move
Where can I go?
Where can I go?
Where can I go next?

FIGURE 4.21
Typical patterns of web page organization in information-oriented sites, and a typical wireframe drawing.

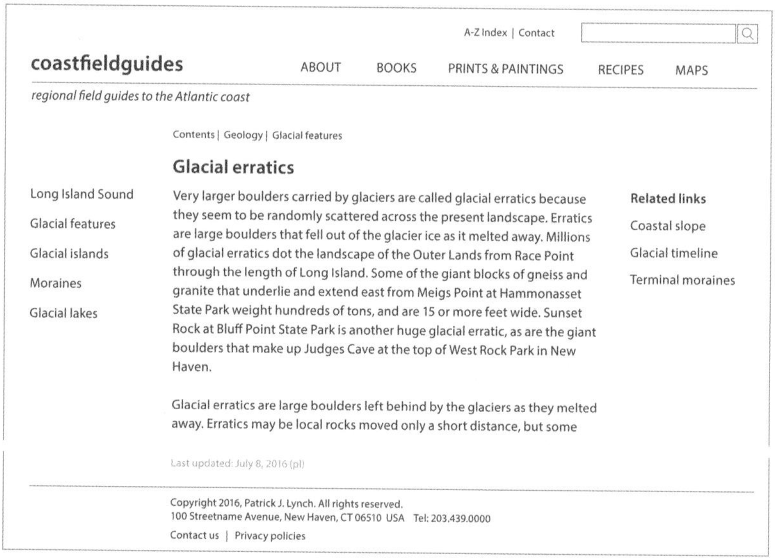
A-Z Index | Contact
coastfieldguides
ABOUT
BOOKS
PRINTS & PAINTINGS
RECIPES
MAPS
regional field guides to the Atlantic coast
Contents | Geology | Glacial features
Glacial erratics
Long Island Sound
Glacial features
Glacial islands
Moraines
Glacial lakes
Very larger boulders carried by glaciers are called glacial erratics because they seem to be randomly scattered across the present landscape. Erratics are large boulders that fell out of the glacier ice as it melted away. Millions of glacial erratics dot the landscape of the Outer Lands from Race Point through the length of Long Island. Some of the giant blocks of gneiss and granite that underlie and extend east from Meigs Point at Hammonasset State Park weight hundreds of tons, and are 15 or more feet wide. Sunset Rock at Bluff Point State Park is another huge glacial erratic, as are the giant boulders that make up Judges Cave at the top of West Rock Park in New Haven.
Glacial erratics are large boulders left behind by the glaciers as they melted away. Erratics may be local rocks moved only a short distance, but some
Related links
Coastal slope
Glacial timeline
Terminal moraines
Last updated: July 8, 2016 (pl)
Copyright 2016, Patrick J. Lynch. All rights reserved.
100 Streetname Avenue, New Haven, CT 06510 USA Tel: 203.439.0000
Contact us | Privacy policies

The web is still a young medium with no standards organizations to canonize existing typical page layout practices. Until we have a *Chicago Manual of Style* for the web, we can at least combine current mainstream web design practice, user interface research, and classic page composition to form recommendations for the location of identity, content, navigation, and other standard elements of pages in text-dominant, information-oriented web sites.

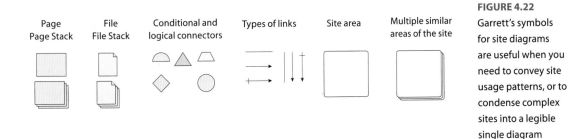

Page Page Stack	File File Stack	Conditional and logical connectors	Types of links	Site area	Multiple similar areas of the site

FIGURE 4.22

Garrett's symbols for site diagrams are useful when you need to convey site usage patterns, or to condense complex sites into a legible single diagram (wsg4.link/jjg-visualvocab).

PRESENTING INFORMATION ARCHITECTURE

Site planning with a team is often easier if you base your major structural planning and decisions on a shared master site diagram that all members of the group can work with. The site diagram or site map should evolve as the plan evolves and act as the core planning document as changes are proposed and made in the diagram. Site diagrams are excellent for planning both the broad scope of the site and the details of where each piece of content, navigation, or interactive functionality will appear.

For major planning meetings consider printing at least one large diagram of the site organization, so that everyone can see the big picture as it develops from meeting to meeting. The site diagram should dominate the conference table, becoming a tactile, malleable representation of the plan. Everyone should be free to make notes and suggest improvements on the printed plan, and the revised diagram becomes the official result of the meeting.

Site diagrams

As your team works out the information architecture and major categories of content, site diagrams visualize the developing information hierarchy and help communicate the organizational concepts to the team and to stakeholders and project sponsors. This communications role is crucial throughout the project, as the site diagram evolves in iterations from a brainstorming and planning document into a blueprint for the actual site as it will be developed.

Site diagrams can range from a simple hierarchical "org chart" diagram to a more complex and information-rich map that both shows the major divisions of the site as the user experiences them and acts as an overview of the site directory and file structure. The well-known information architect Jesse James Garrett developed a widely used visual vocabulary for site diagrams that has become the de facto standard, and the symbols are broadly useful for portraying site structure and interactive relationships and user decision points.

Major elements of a mature site diagram include:

- Content structure and organization: major site content divisions and subdivisions
- Logical functional groupings or structural relationships
- The "click depth" of each level of the site: how many clicks are required to reach a given page?
- Page type or template (menu page, internal page, major section entry point, and so on)
- Site directory and file structure
- Dynamic data elements like databases, RSS, or applications
- Major navigation terms and controlled vocabularies
- Link relationships, internal and external to the site
- Levels of user access, log-ins required, or other restricted areas

Site diagrams start simply and may evolve into two distinct variations: a conceptual site diagram that communicates at a general level the evolving site structure to clients and stakeholders, and a more complex blueprint diagram that is used by the technical, editorial, and graphic design teams as a guide to the structure of both the user interface and the directories and files.

Figure 4.23 depicts a simple site diagram for use in presentations and general overviews and the same site shown in greater detail for use by the site development team. These site diagrams can be developed with drawing software such as Adobe Illustrator but are usually developed with specialized diagrammatic software such as Microsoft Visio, ConceptDraw, or OmniGraffle.

Wireframes

The information architecture process is fundamentally one of avoiding the particular while insisting on the general. At various points in this conceptual phase, stakeholders, clients, and even members of your design team may find it irresistible to launch into specific proposals for the visual design of pages. In particular, concern about the possible look and feel of the home page is notorious for driving planning processes off the rails and into detailed discussions of what colors, graphics, photos, or general character the home page should have, long before anyone has given serious thought to the strategic goals, functions, and structure of the site. Visually plain page wireframe diagrams force teams to stay focused on the information architecture and navigation vocabulary without getting sidetracked by the distraction of purely visual design.

If site diagrams provide the global overview of the developing web site, then wireframes are the "rough map" that will eventually be used by graphic and interface designers to create preliminary and final page designs for the site. Wireframes are rough two-dimensional guides to where the major navigation and content elements of your site might appear on the page. When carefully designed they bring a consistent modular structure to the various page forms of your site and provide the fundamental layout and navigation structure for the finished templates to come.

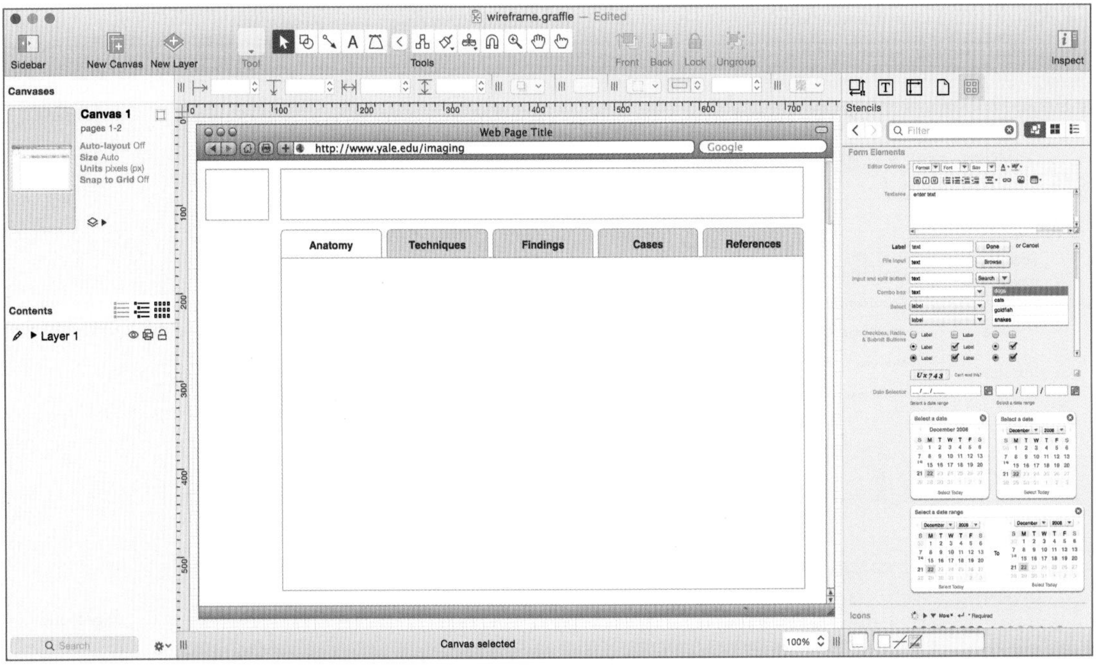

Things that might appear as standard elements of a web page wireframe include:

- Organizational logo
- Site identity or titles
- Page title headlines
- Breadcrumb trail navigation
- Search form
- Links to a larger organization of which yours is a part
- Global navigation links for the site
- Local content navigation
- Primary page content
- Mailing address and email information
- Copyright statements
- Contact information

FIGURE 4.23

Almost any drawing tool can be used to create wireframe sketches, but the OmniGraffle app (Mac OS) includes templates and features specifically designed for web page and application sketching.

Site identity or logo   Utility links   Local search

Tagline

Breadcrumb trail

Secondary navigation

Dateline or last update

Left scan column or left rail

Contact & legal information

Right scan column or right rail

A-Z Index | Contact

coastfieldguides   ABOUT   BOOKS   PRINTS & PAINTINGS   RECIPES   MAPS

regional field guides to the Atlantic coast

Contents | Geology | Glacial features   Primary navigation

Page header

Page title

Long Island Sound

Glacial features

Glacial islands

Moraines

Glacial lakes

Very larger boulders carried by glaciers are called glacial erratics because they seem to be randomly scattered across the present landscape. Erratics are large boulders that fell out of the glacier ice as it melted away. Millions of glacial erratics dot the landscape of the Outer Lands from Race Point through the length of Long Island. Some of the giant blocks of gneiss and granite that underlie and extend east from Meigs Point at Hammonasset State Park weight hundreds of tons, and are 15 or more feet wide. Sunset Rock at Bluff Point State Park is another huge glacial erratic, as are the giant boulders that make up Judges Cave at the top of West Rock Park in New Haven.

Glacial erratics are large boulders left behind by the glaciers as they melted away. Erratics may be local rocks moved only a short distance, but some

Related links

Coastal slope

Glacial timeline

Terminal moraines

Scan columns & content column

Last updated: July 8, 2017 (pl)

Copyright 2017, Patrick J. Lynch. All rights reserved.
100 Streetname Avenue, New Haven, CT 06510 USA   Tel: 203.439.0000
Contact us | Privacy policies

Page footer

To keep the discussion focused on information architecture and navigation, keep your wireframe diagrams simple and unadorned. Avoid distinctive typography, use a single generic font, and use gray tones if you must to distinguish functional areas, but avoid color or pictures. Usually the only graphic that appears in a mature wireframe will be the organization logo, but even there it may be better simply to indicate the general location of the logo. The page wireframe will acquire more complexity as your thinking about global and local navigation matures and you are more certain about the nature and organization of the primary site content.

The page presentation functions of content management systems link Drupal and WordPress are structured by general site themes and page templates that can be extensively customized by front-developers who know the necessary HTML, CSS, and PHP methods. Drupal's Zen 2 HTML5-based responsive "mobile-first" layout theme is a particularly flexible theme that can be used initially to wireframe a site and then can be used as a flexible basis for further visual development of the site. Regardless of which CMS you are using for your site, you might want to consider a plain, visually sparse "wireframe" version of your site templates for your planning and architecture phases, to concentrate on the interactive qualities of site navigation while deferring detailed visual designs until late in the process. Both Drupal and WordPress also allow you to change a site's theme quickly, and examining and using your preliminary site architecture under various kinds of display themes may help to point up navigation or organizational problems, or give you some good ideas for features you may want to include in the finished site theme.

RECOMMENDED READING

Brown, D. *Communicating Design: Developing Web Site Documentation for Design and Planning.* Berkeley, CA: Peachpit/New Riders, 2007.

Covert, A. *How to Make Sense of Any Mess.* Seattle: CreateSpace, 2014.

Halvorson, K., and M. Rach. *Content Strategy for the Web.* Berkeley, CA: New Riders, 2012.

Morville, P., and L. Rosenfeld. *Information Architecture for the World Wide Web.* Sebastopol, CA: O'Reilly, 2006.

Norman, D. *The Design of Everyday Things.* New York: Doubleday, 1990.

Wurman, R. S., *Information Anxiety.* New York: Bantam, 1990.

FIGURE 4.24 (facing page) A final wireframe of the desktop view of a site. In these days of responsive web design aimed at a host of different screen sizes, it is rarely worthwhile to do sketches beyond this level of detail. From this point the design process will proceed as quickly as possible into working HTML/CSS sketches to further refine the concepts for various screen sizes and then gradually introduce refined typography and graphic elements into the working site prototype.

Content management isn't a software problem at all.
It's a process problem.
– Jeffrey Veen

The single biggest problem in communication is the
illusion that it has taken place.
– George Bernard Shaw

Themes Regions Views

Visible
elements
on pages

Abstract
content
& system
architecture

Individuals Editorial roles Groups
& permissions

CHAPTER 5

Site Structure

Much as foundational concrete and piles define the stability and longevity of buildings, so the structural underpinnings of web sites affect their success in ways that, though not visible on the surface, are ultimately far more important than color and typography. Site structure determines how well sites work in the broader context of the web, and on all the various mobile and desktop screens we use today. The methods you use to mark up pages determine whether they can be read well by software and indexed well by search engines. The logic and stability of the underlying files and directories on which your web site rests affect its functionality, as well as its potential for growth and expansion.

The content management system you choose will affect your web design choices for years, but will also bring power and flexibility that you could never practically achieve with static HTML methods. Attention to these behind-the-scenes structural components from the start produces a web site that will hold up over time, work effectively within the larger web environment, and adapt and grow as needed.

I want to know what things are for, how they work, what they can or should be made of, before I even begin to think what they should look like.

— Jonathan Ive

COMPONENTS OF A WEB SITE

Here we describe the main technologies that make up the platform on which we structure web sites. We provide further details and best practice recommendations for specific site components in subsequent chapters.

Although most web sites are now built using a web content management system (CMS) that will insulate you from much of the code that makes up your site, it is still important to have a solid understanding of basic code and principles. It is possible to become a good musician without being able to read music, but the inability to read musical charts will be a lifelong impediment to becoming a great musician. So it is with web technologies: much of the foundational concepts and abilities of the web will remain a mystery to you if you don't understand at least basic HTML.

USING HYPERTEXT MARKUP LANGUAGE (HTML)

Creating web content used to be easier. All you had to do was check your HTML code against two or three major desktop web browsers and you were all set. Today web content is accessed using many kinds of desktop applications in addition to the major web browsers. Mobile computing devices of all kinds, including screen readers, many smaller "wearable" devices like fitness bands, Apple Watches, and other mobile devices, display web content. Many kinds of cameras, household appliances, televisions, medical devices, and other "smart" products now depend on web content and communications. Web content is also read by search engines and other computing systems that extract meaning and context from how the content is marked up in HTML. All of this makes it much more critical that you understand the core principles of what makes good HTML, and the most critical concept to understand is semantic markup.

The following section presents some of the core principles of HTML content markup, but presenting the full breadth of HTML markup is beyond the scope of this book, and we strongly urge you to consider one of the basic HTML books we recommend at the end of this chapter. The most current version of HTML at this writing is HTML5, and the examples we present here use HTML5 conventions.

Semantic markup

Proper use of HTML is the key to getting maximum flexibility and return on your investment in web content. From its earliest origins, HTML was designed to distinguish clearly between a document's hierarchical outline structure (Headline 1, Headline 2, paragraph, list, and so on) and the visual presentation of the document (boldface, italics, font, type size, color, and so on). HTML markup is considered semantic when standard HTML tags are used to convey meaning and content structure, not simply to make text look a certain way in a browser.

This semantic approach to web markup is a central concept underlying efficient web coding, information architecture, universal usability, search engine visibility, and maximum display flexibility. Consider this simple piece of HTML coding:

```
<h1>This is the most important headline</h1>
<p>This is ordinary paragraph text within the body of
   the document, where certain words and phrases may be
   <em>emphasized</em> to mark them as <strong>particularly
   important</strong>.</p>
<h2>This is a headline of secondary importance to the headline
   above</h2>
<p>Any time you list related things, the items should be
   marked up in the form of a list:</p>
<ul>
<li>A list signals that a group of items are conceptually
   related to one another</li>
<li>Lists may be ordered (numbered or alphabetic) or unordered
   (bulleted items)</li>
```

```
<li>Lists may also be menus or lists of links for navigation</
    li>
<li>Cascading style sheets can make lists look many different
    ways</li>
</ul>
```

Even in the simple example above, a search engine would be able to distinguish the importance and priority of the headlines, discover which keywords were salient, and identify conceptually related items in list form. A cascading style sheet (css) designed to respond to various screen sizes could display the headlines and text in fonts appropriate for small mobile screens, and a screen reader would know where and how to pause or change voice tone to convey the content structure to a blind listener. All of this flows from the semantic structure embedded in the HTML: the ranking of headlines by importance, the emphasis of certain keywords, and a list markup that signals a group of related items.

Document structure

Properly structured HTML documents may contain the following elements:

- HTML document structure (`<head>`, `<body>`, `<div>`, `<span>`)
- Text content
- Semantic markup to convey meaning and content structure (headlines, paragraph text, lists, quotations)
- Visual presentation using css to make content look a certain way
- Links to audiovisual content (.gif, .jpeg, or .png graphics, media files)
- Interactive behavior (JavaScript, PHP, or other programming techniques)

In properly formed HTML, all web page code is contained within two basic elements:

1 head (`<head>`...`</head>`)
2 body (`<body>`...`</body>`)

In the past these basic divisions in the structure of page code were there primarily for good form: strictly correct but functionally optional and invisible to the user. In today's much more complex and ambitious World Wide Web, in which intricate page code, many different display possibilities, elaborate style sheets, and interactive scripting are now the norm, it is crucial to structure the divisional elements properly.

The `<head>` area is where your web page declares its code standards and document type to the display device (web browser, mobile phone, tablet, and so on) and where the all-important page title resides. The page head area also can contain links to external style sheets and JavaScript code that may be shared by many pages in your site. Both JavaScript coding listings and CSS style code may be complex and lengthy these days, so often web designers and CMS programs keep long code listings in separate files that are linked to the HTML file. This shared code arrangement simplifies the code required in each HTML file, and (most important) allows a single CSS or JavaScript file to be shared across all the pages of your site.

The `<body>` area encompasses all page content and is important for CSS control of visual styles, programming, and semantic content markup. Areas within the body of the page are usually functionally segmented with division (`<div>`) or span (`<span>`) tags. For example, most web pages have header, footer, content, and navigation areas, all designated with named `<div>` tags that can be addressed and visually styled with CSS.

The HTML document type declares which version and standards the HTML document conforms to and is crucial in evaluating the quality and technical validity of the HTML markup and CSS. Your web development technical team should be able to tell you which version of HTML will be used for page coding (for example, XHTML or HTML5) and which document type declaration will be used in your web site. HTML5 is the current basic standard for web page markup. The older XHTML standard is similar to HTML5, but XHTML has more exacting markup requirements. Although XHTML is still common on the web, there are powerful advantages in using HTML5 as your standard for page markup, including:

- Compatibility with current document structure techniques, and the powerful new media capabilities of HTML5.
- Maximum compatibility with non-HTML web markup standards such as MathML for scientific documents and scalable vector graphics (SVG).
- Future compatibility with newer content markup and programming techniques, content management systems, and other evolving web technologies that will benefit from HTML5 markup standards.

Content structure

Semantic markup is a fancy term for commonsense HTML usage: if you write a headline, mark it with a headline tag (`<h1>`, `<h2>`). If you write basic paragraph text, place the text between paragraph tags (`<p>`, `</p>`). If you wish to emphasize an important phrase, mark it with strong emphasis (`<strong>`, `</strong>`). If you quote another writer, use the `<blockquote>` tag to signal that the text is a quotation. Never choose an HTML tag based on how it looks in a particular web browser. You can adjust the visual presentation of your content later with CSS to get the look you want for headlines, quotations, emphasized text, and other typography.

A few exclusively visual HTML tags such as `<b>` (boldface) and `<i>` (italics) persist in HTML because these visual styles are sometimes needed to support purely visual typographic conventions, such as italicizing a scientific name (for example, Homo sapiens). If you use semantically meaningless tags like `<b>` or `<i>`, ask yourself whether a properly styled emphasis (`<em>`) or strong emphasis (`<strong>`) tag would convey more meaning.

HTML also contains semantic elements that are not visible to the reader but can be enormously useful behind the scenes with a team of site developers. Elements such as classes, ids, divisions, spans, and meta tags can make it easier for team members to understand, use, visually style, and programmatically control page elements. Many style sheet and programming techniques require careful semantic naming of page elements in order to make your content more universally accessible and flexible.

Web page files don't contain graphics or audiovisual material directly but use image or other pointer links to incorporate graphics and media into the final assembly of the web page in the browser. These links, and the alternate text ("alt" text) or long description ("longdesc") links they contain, are critical for universal usability and search engine visibility. Web users don't just search for text. Search engines use the alternate text descriptions to label images with keywords, and visually impaired users depend on alternate text to describe the content of images. Proper semantic markup will ensure that your audiovisual media are maximally available to everyone in your audience and to search engines.

Set careful markup and editorial standards based on semantic markup techniques and standard HTML document types, and adhere to those standards throughout the development process. Today's web environment is a lot more than just Google Chrome or Firefox on a desktop computer—hundreds of kinds of mobile computing devices are now in use, and new ways of viewing and using web content are being invented every day. Following semantic web markup practices and using carefully validated page code and style sheets is your best strategy for ensuring that your web content will be broadly useful and visible into the future.

USING CASCADING STYLE SHEETS (CSS)

Cascading style sheets allow web publishers to retain the enormous benefits of using semantic HTML to convey logical document structure and meaning while giving graphic designers complete control over the visual display details of each HTML element. CSS works just like the style sheets in a word-processing program such as Microsoft Word. In Word, you can structure your document with ranked headlines and other styles and then globally change the visual look of each instance of a headline just by changing its style. CSS works the same way, particularly if you use linked external style sheets that every page in your web site shares. For example, if all of

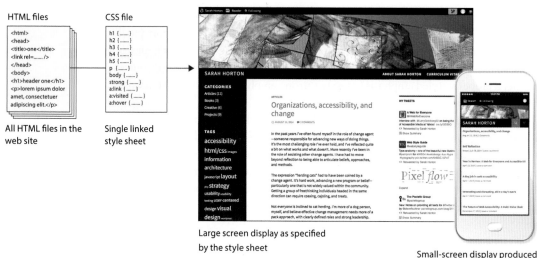

HTML files

```
<html>
<head>
<title>one</title>
<link rel=....... />
</head>
<body>
<h1>header one</h1>
<p>lorem ipsum dolor
amet, consectetuer
adipiscing elit.</p>
```

All HTML files in the
web site

CSS file

```
h1 { ....... }
h2 { ....... }
h3 { ....... }
h4 { ....... }
h5 { ....... }
p  { ....... }
body { ....... }
strong { ....... }
a:link { ....... }
a:visited { ....... }
a:hover { ....... }
```

Single linked
style sheet

Large screen display as specified
by the style sheet

Small-screen display produced
by the same style sheet

FIGURE 5.1
Style sheets
modify the visual
presentation of
HTML in the browser,
in this case for both
desktop and mobile
views.

your pages link to the same master css file, you could change the font, size, and color of every <h1> heading in your site just by changing the <h1> style in your master style sheet.

Many users of cascading style sheets know how to change the look of standard HTML components with css but don't pay much attention to the powerful cascade features of css. css is an extendable system, in which a related set of css instructions spread across multiple css files can cascade from very general style and layout instructions shared by all of your pages to extremely specific styles that only a handful of pages in your site may share.

CSS cascade hierarchy

css has multiple hierarchical levels that cascade in importance and priority, from general css code shared by all pages, to code that is contained in a particular page file, to code that is embedded in specific HTML tags. General page code overrides shared site code, and css code embedded in HTML tags overrides general page code. This hierarchical cascade of css priorities allows you to set very general styles for your whole site while also permitting you to override the styles where needed with specific section or page styles.

Shared CSS across many pages

Multiple css files can work together across a site. This concept of multiple css files working together in a modular way is the heart of the cascade system of pages that all

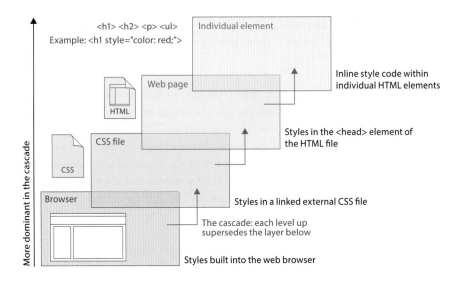

<h1> <h2> <p> <ul>
Example: <h1 style="color: red;">

Individual element

Web page

HTML

CSS file

CSS

Browser

More dominant in the cascade

Inline style code within
individual HTML elements

Styles in the <head> element of
the HTML file

Styles in a linked external CSS file

The cascade: each level up
supersedes the layer below

Styles built into the web browser

FIGURE 5.2
Each level of the style sheet "cascade" overrides the one below. Thus you can use very general styles, but also add CSS code to customize individual elements and pages where necessary.

share code via links to master css files that control styles throughout the site. This system has obvious advantages: if all your pages share the same master css file, you can change the style of any component in the master css file, and every page of your site will show the new style. For example, if you tweak the typographic style of your <h1> headings in the master file, every <h1> heading throughout the site will change to reflect the new look.

In a complex site, page designers often link groups of css files to style a site. Packaging multiple css files can have many practical advantages. In a complex site css code can run to hundreds of lines, and it's often more practical to subdivide such elements as the basic page layout css from the master site typography styles. It's easy to link to css files and let the master css layout and typography styles control all the pages in your site.

The powerful advantage of the "cascade" in css is built into the themes used by cms programs like WordPress and Drupal, but both programs also allow you to create custom variations on the theme styling by creating a master style sheet that tweaks the specific styling of the theme you are using. For example, you may be very happy with the overall look and feel of your WordPress theme, but might wish that all of the headlines used the Tahoma font instead of the theme's built-in Arial font for headlines. Most WordPress themes allow you to add your own css to customize various aspects of the theme. For example, in the WordPress Dashboard, see the menus Appearance > Customize > css to access the custom css listing. To change all the headers in your site to Tahoma you could just add this line to the custom css listing:

```
h1, h2, h3, h4, h5, h6 {
   font-family: Tahoma, sans-serif;
   }
```

Thanks to the "cascade" in style sheets, you do not have to specify every aspect of every header styling (font size, weight, color, spacing, and so on) in your custom sheet, because through the style cascade your custom Tahoma headers inherit all those other header properties from the master theme style sheet. So your headers all change to the Tahoma font, but all other aspects of the theme headers' size and styling remain the same. The Drupal CMS has a similar system that allows you to tweak the CSS of a Drupal theme through a CSS "Injector" module for custom CSS code.

Media style sheets and responsive CSS styling

Another advantage of CSS is the ability to provide context-appropriate designs using media style sheets that are specific for display screens or printing on paper. With media style sheets, it's possible to adapt a page layout specifically for printing on paper. Print style sheets often drop header and sidebar navigation elements and strip away the web page framing to emphasize page content. Print styling can also make the full URL of embedded links visible to the reader of the printed document, so that a reader who wants to follow a link has the URL as a reference.

Similarly, "responsive" CSS styling customizes the presentation of navigation and content based on the size of the user's screen, using CSS3 media queries to determine the maximum or minimum width of the user's display screen. In this simple example we use a media query statement (@media) to hide a left navigation sidebar on small mobile screens:

```
<style>
@media (max-width: 600px) {
   .left_sidebar {
   display: none;
   }
}
</style>
```

See the next chapter, Page Structure, for more information on responsive web design techniques.

INTERACTIVE SCRIPTING

JavaScript is a language commonly used to create interactive behaviors on web pages. JavaScript is also a key technology in web page content delivery strategies such as

AJAX, and widely used code libraries like JQuery. In most circumstances JavaScript code belongs in the "head" area of your web page, but if your code is complex and lengthy, your "real" page content will be pushed dozens of lines down below the code and may not be found by search engines. If you use page-level JavaScript scripting (also called client-side scripting), you should place all but the shortest bits of code in a linked JavaScript file. This way you can use lengthy, complex JavaScript without risking your search ranking.

OTHER DOCUMENT FORMATS

The web supports document formats other than HTML. PDF (portable document format) is a document format widely used to provide functionality and paper-oriented formatting that is not available using basic HTML. PDF files are often favored for documents that originated in word-processing and page layout programs, in order to retain the appearance of the original document. In general, the best approach is to offer documents as plain HTML because the markup offers greater flexibility and is designed to enable universal usability. At times, however, the additional features and functionality offered by these other formats is essential; in this case, be sure to use the software's accessibility features. Adobe in particular has made efforts to incorporate accessibility features into its web formats by supporting semantic markup, text equivalents, and keyboard accessibility. Major search engines like Bing and Google can "read" and index the content of PDF files, but many mobile devices don't display PDF files well on small screens.

BUILDING A SOLID STRUCTURE

Well-designed sites contain modular elements that are used repeatedly across many dozens or hundreds of pages. These elements may include the global navigation header links and graphics for the page header or the contact information and mailing address of your enterprise. It makes no sense to include the text and HTML code that make up standard page components in each file. Instead, use a single file containing the standardized element that repeats across hundreds of pages: when you change that one file, every page in your site containing that component automatically updates. HTML, CSS, and current web servers offer the power and flexibility of reusable modular components, and most large, sophisticated sites are built using dozens of reusable components.

Browser variations

Web browsers have become much more consistent in following web standards for HTML and CSS, but typography, forms, positioning, and alignment sometimes work slightly differently in each brand or operating system version of web browser, and the proliferation of various mobile web browsers has added complexity. The subtle variations between browsers often pass unnoticed or make little difference to the function or aesthetics of sites, but in precise or complex web page layouts the browser differences can lead to nasty surprises. Never trust the implementation of html5, css, JavaScript, Java, or any browser plug-in architecture such as Adobe Flash until you have seen your web pages displayed and working reliably with each major desktop and mobile web browser and both major operating systems (Microsoft Windows, Apple Macintosh, Apple's mobile ios, and Google's Android mobile os).

Check your web logs or use a service such as Google Analytics to be sure that you understand what browser brands, browser versions, and operating systems (Mac, Windows, mobile) are most common in your particular readership. If you encounter a discrepancy in how your pages render in different browsers, you can confirm that you are using valid html and css code by using a code validation service such as those from the w3c (for html, validator.w3.org; for css, jigsaw.w3.org/css-validator). Not every browser supports every feature of css3 (the most current version at this writing), particularly if that feature is seldom used or has recently been added to the official standards for CSS3 code. For example, although drop-shadowed text is a valid CSS3 option, not every browser supports it.

File names

Web pages are a constellation of files delivered to and assembled by the browser into the coherent page we see on our screens. Attention to file and directory names is essential to keeping track of the myriad pages and supporting files that make up a web site.

Never use technical or numeric gibberish to name a component when a plain-language name will do. In the early days of personal computing, clumsy systems like MS-DOS and old versions of Microsoft Windows imposed an "eight-dot-three" file name convention that forced users to make up cryptic codes for file and directory names (for example, "whtevr34.htm"). No word spaces and few nonalphanumeric characters were allowed in file names, so technologists often used characters like the underscore to add legibility to cryptic file names (for example, "cats_003.htm").

Habits developed over decades can be hard to break, and looking into the file structure of another team's web site can sometimes feel like cracking the German Enigma codes of World War II. Current file name conventions in Windows, Macintosh, and Linux systems are much more flexible, and there's no reason to impose cryptic names on your team members, site users, and colleagues who may one day have to figure out how you constructed your site.

Most CMS programs like WordPress or Drupal will allow you to use "friendly" URL naming conventions that have two advantages: they are easier for people to make sense of, and they contribute to the relevance rankings in search engines like Bing and Google.

It's pretty easy to figure out the page content of these "friendly" WordPress URLs:

patricklynch.net/recipes/beef/beef-tomato-chili-in-a-slow-cooker/
coastfieldguides.com/books/a-field-guide-to-north-atlantic-wildlife/

There's an old saying in programming that when you use plain-English labels and add explanatory comments to your code, the person you are probably doing the biggest favor for is yourself, three years from now. Three years from now, will you know what's in a site directory called "x83_0002"?

Use plain-language names for all of your files and directories, separating the words with "breaking" hyphen characters. This system is easy to read and understand, and since conventional word spaces are not allowed, the hyphens "break" the file name into individual words or number strings that can be analyzed by search engines and will contribute to the search rankings and content relevance of your

FIGURE 5.3
Mirror the major
interface and content
divisions when you
structure the pages
and directories of
your site.

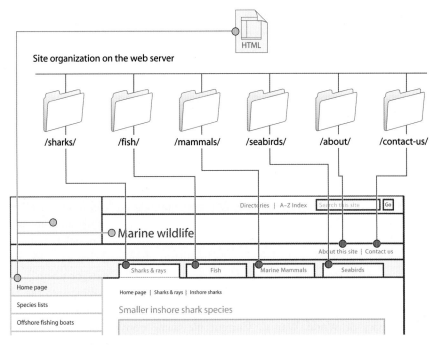

Site organization on the web server

/sharks/   /fish/   /mammals/   /seabirds/   /about/   /contact-us/

Page navigation wireframe

pages. We recommend this convention for directory names, too. And always try to mirror the visible structure of your site's content organization in the directory and file structure you set up on the web server.

CONTENT MANAGEMENT SYSTEMS

A web content management system (CMS) is server-based software that simplifies, structures, and manages the creation and delivery of web content, providing a graphic user interface that allows users to create web pages and other web information without having to learn HTML, CSS, or other kinds of web coding. Content management systems offer powerful advantages over old-style hand-coded static web pages. The key to understanding the advantages of a CMS is the separation of content from presentation code. This separation of content and form is much more flexible than static HTML web pages, where content is embedded in one fixed format of HTML markup and CSS page styling. In a CMS the content is drawn from a web database and can be presented in many different kinds of templates, in many different arrangements, and for many kinds of display devices, including desktop computers, laptops, tablets, and other mobile devices.

POPULAR CONTENT MANAGEMENT SYSTEMS

Virtually all large business, e-commerce, and other enterprise sites are now created and delivered using some form of CMS. Popular open-source content management systems like WordPress, Drupal, and Joomla are the most widely used CMS programs for individuals, governments, universities, and small to medium-sized businesses. Large business, government, news, and e-commerce sites typically use more complex commercial CMS programs like OpenText CMS (formerly Red Dot), Ingeniux CMS, or Ektron CMS. Commercial CMS products typically can handle much larger volumes of content, and offer sophisticated systems to support e-commerce, large-volume credit card transactions, and other business and financial functions.

Here we'll mostly use as examples two open-source products, WordPress and Drupal, for several reasons:

- Both of these widely used web content management systems are available to install free of charge. With moderate technical skills you can download and install either program in about half an hour, from WordPress (wordpress.org), or Drupal (drupal.org).
- Both Drupal and WordPress are also available as hosted products, through WordPress.com (wordpress.com) and Drupal Gardens (drupalgardens.com), and the basic feature set of both programs is available in free hosted accounts.
- WordPress and Drupal reflect different CMS approaches: Drupal is a powerful, highly extensible CMS well suited for complex bodies of content. WordPress is also packed with features, but is far easier to get started with, and much more approachable for nontechnical designers and writers.
- We strongly suggest that you spend a bit of time with both Drupal and WordPress in their hosted versions, which is the fastest way to get acquainted with the world of content management systems.

Users of a cms typically do not need to know any more than rudimentary html or css code, and can use the cms much the way they use a word-processing program. Editorial workflow, collaborations to create content, and permission to publish content are handled by the cms, facilitating the work of creating and maintaining content. cms-based content is also enormously more flexible than static web content, as elements of content are not in fixed web pages but can be assembled multiple ways, in various kinds of pages and formats, without having to duplicate content. The cms can also handle site administration tasks, such as taking the whole site offline for maintenance.

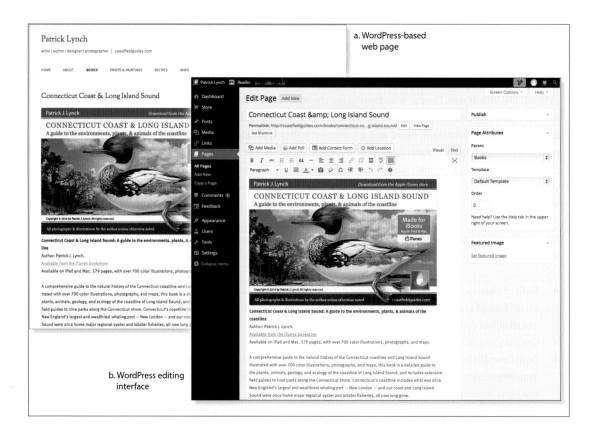

a. WordPress-based web page

b. WordPress editing interface

FIGURE 5.4

Web content management systems like WordPress and Drupal provide a graphic interface that allows you to quickly add text and graphics to pages without having to know much about the HTML markup language.

ESTABLISHING AN EDITORIAL WORKFLOW

One of the central features of a content management system is to formalize editorial roles and create an organized workflow for content creation and publication. If you are not already working within an experienced editorial department, these defined roles, responsibilities, access, and publication privileges may seem a bit alien and excessively complex. In many small businesses the person who manages the web site is chief cook, bottle washer, and all-around web task manager rolled into one. But even if you are the sole person managing a web site, the workflow features of a content management system can still help you manage your site, by referring draft web pages to colleagues and content experts for review before publication, and through scheduling features that allow you to choose exactly when a particular page becomes "live" on the site.

For collaborative content creation groups a CMS offers powerful advantages to carefully structure and formalize editorial work and publication procedures. In business and government sites the ability to post content is often more complex than just

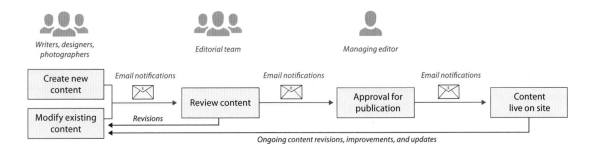

Writers, designers, photographers · Editorial team · Managing editor

Create new content / Modify existing content — Email notifications → Review content — Revisions — Email notifications → Approval for publication — Email notifications → Content live on site

Ongoing content revisions, improvements, and updates

meeting quality standards and stated business objectives—proposed content for the site may also need to pass formal reviews by the legal department, product managers, or senior managers before publication. Without workflow features these multiple cycles of approval can be a nightmare round-robin of emails, faxes with handwritten markup, and lots of telephone calls. Good workflow features can manage the process from initial content creation by a writer, through review by an editor, to review by other company executives, to final publication, with each step triggering emails or other CMS-based notifications to all participants along the way, so there are no nasty surprises when the new content goes online.

Writers, designers, photographers, and other media experts can create new content collaboratively with their peers, without deep technical knowledge of the web or HTML markup. Subject matter experts can review material and comment on the content, without being able to complicate the web site by accidentally publishing material that is not ready for public view. Editors can verify that the final versions of content are ready for public release, and immediately post the new content, or hold it for publication at a particular date and time in the future.

Roles and responsibilities

The ability to specify roles and levels of access to unpublished content is an important feature of content management systems. Some organizations have simple arrangements of writers, an editor, reviewers who check the accuracy of content, and a designated person—perhaps a senior editor or department manager—who has the formal authority to publish new content on the web site. Writers typically have the ability to add unpublished content to a CMS. The new content is available to other editorial team members but not visible on the public site until publication. Designated reviewers or content experts have the ability to see unpublished content, but may or may not have the ability to annotate or change the content. Editors can see and change the work of writers and reviewers, but may or may not have the authority to publish the new content to the live web site. Finally, publishers have the ability to see and change all unpublished content, and the ability to publish new

FIGURE 5.5

More sophisticated CMS software provides for various levels of editorial control over content creation, review, and approvals, and also helps facilitate editorial workflow.

content, remove older content, and administer other aspects of the site, such as taking the whole site offline for maintenance or major changes.

Workflow and notifications help avoid process "choke points," where publication is held up because one of the team members or reviewers didn't know he or she was supposed to do something at a particular time, or team members don't know what the exact status of a piece of content is (edited, reviewed, ready to publish?). The CMS helps manage the traffic problem in workflows by sending notifications to authors and editors at each stage of the process, so that everyone can see the current status of unpublished content. Workflow processes can also help by reminding everyone on the team to add metadata to content, such as keywords for search engine optimization (SEO), or alternate text for images that both aids visually impaired readers and improves the SEO of content by accurately describing the content of images.

CMS as part of content strategy

Advanced content management systems like Drupal give you so many options to structure and display your content that careful strategic planning is required to both assess your existing and required new content and design an efficient system to produce and accurately structure and label the content. "Content strategy" differs from more conventional editorial processes in that it looks well beyond the production of appropriate text, graphics, and photography, considering how best to organize the content within the information blocks, views, and taxonomies of a CMS, then structuring the requirements for content production so that writers and editors understand the eventual contexts within which their writing will appear, and how to categorize and label ("tag") the content for efficient entry into the CMS database.

Among the primary "deliverables" from a content strategy project are content production templates that not only describe the general intent for a new piece of content and its intended audiences and uses but also include instructions to the writers to generate the suggestions for the best categories, subcategories, and keywords that will be used within the CMS. See Chapter 1, Strategy, for an overview of content strategy.

CHOOSING A CMS

Choosing a web content management system is a consequential decision that should be made only after careful research on the features and advantages of various CMS products, as well as your own business goals and current and future needs. One immediate division in the CMS marketplace is price: open-source CMS products like WordPress, Drupal, and Joomla are free for downloading. Commercial proprietary content management products can cost thousands of dollars just for software licensing alone. Here are a few realities to consider in choosing a CMS.

Completed pages in browser
The finished pages are indistinguishable from "static" HTML pages, but are more flexible because your content can easily be re-purposed in many different display formats for desktop browsers, tablets, and smartphones.

User interface, editing views
All CMS programs give writers and editors a word processor–like interface for entering and formatting content. The better systems like Drupal are WYSIWYG editors with views that closely match the finished page.

▲

Visible elements on pages

Theme layouts, regions, views
Themes are the overall visual presentation of layout regions and graphics, usually with multiple templates for specific uses. Views allow you to create preset types of content displays, like slide shows, staff directories, or product descriptions.

Themes   Regions   Views

Abstract content & system architecture
▼

User permissions, rules for content, expirations
CMSs allow you to set up editorial workflows with different levels of editing permissions and access for the various roles (publisher, editor, writer, reviewer), and include notifications of new content, and the ability to create predetermined content publication or expiration dates.

Individuals   Editorial roles & permissions   Groups

Blocks, menus, taxonomies, other content organizations
Features like blocks (preset arrangements of content and function) and taxonomies (controlled vocabularies and information architecture) allow you to add highly flexible yet consistent structure to your content.

Modules, extended functionality
The core functionality of Drupal and WordPress and most other CMS programs is highly extensible through the addition of modules that add specific new or advanced capabilities to the CMS.

Extend the functionality of the core CMS code

Text   Numeric

Images   AV media

MySQL database

Content elements (nodes)
In a CMS the various elements of content (text, alphanumeric data) are held in a database. The database also holds pointer links to visual and AV media components. This is much more flexible than "static" content in HTML.

Core CMS code

P PHP, Perl, Python code

M MySQL database

A Apache web server

L Linux or other OS

Core CMS functionality and system components
CMS systems like WordPress and Drupal have a core set of features which is always present in the basic installation. Most open-source CMS systems are built on the so-called LAMP set of server configurations.

"Free" systems like WordPress and Drupal may become deceptively costly if you try to build a complex site with them. Most major CMS installations require extensive customizations, server hardware and software configurations, and custom programming and template development. Even if you choose a hosted solution like WordPress.com or Drupal Gardens, you'll still have a great deal of work to do in customizing your site, developing themes suitable for your needs, and setting up your content structures. If you have a small site, limited content, straightforward theme needs, and an experienced editorial crew, you can get a moderately sized WordPress site launched in a week or two, and a Drupal site almost as quickly. Since these tools are so widely used, there are numerous tutorials and how-to guides available.

But most business, government, and education web sites are more complex, and in a months-long process of bringing up a major new business site, the initial costs of the CMS software might be just a small line in the budget compared to the personnel time, hardware and services costs, custom code development, and content creation required for the site.

On the other hand, expensive commercial CMS products aren't automatically better than open-source products. Many major business and consumer sites use open-source CMS software. Products like Drupal, WordPress, or Joomla have improved tremendously over the past decade and now rival all but a few top commercial CMS products in range of features and performance. The open-source technical community is far larger than the support groups and specialists of particular commercial CMS products, and it is much easier to find server expertise for Drupal, WordPress, PHP, and Linux-Apache-MySQL-PHP (LAMP) than for unique proprietary CMS systems running on more exotic server configurations. WordPress alone powers about 23 percent of the top ten million web sites. Even the largest commercial CMS vendors have tiny installed bases (less than 0.5 percent of the top ten million web sites) and user groups compared with open-source products, so if you go with a commercial CMS product, you'll have to grow your own staff experts, or pay a significant premium for experienced people who already know your proprietary CMS.

Commercial CMS products may offer much deeper capabilities in workflow design, access management, e-commerce features, and integration with other corporate or enterprise systems, and they may include capable digital asset management systems (DAMs), which are critical for organizations that need to management huge collections of graphics or other media files.

WordPress

WordPress has by far the friendliest and most polished user interface of any of the major web content management systems. It is also the most widely used CMS on the web today, with more than forty-six million downloads of the software, powering about 46 percent of all web sites using a CMS. You can download and install

WordPress on your own server or personal computer from WordPress.org, and many web hosting services like Rackspace and Media Temple offer "one-click" installations of WordPress on your hosted server. The simplest way to start with WordPress is to use it in the hosted version from WordPress.com, which manages all server issues and you just use the software. Simple WordPress.com sites are free, and more complex sites with custom domain names, more advanced themes, and other features are modestly priced.

Both WordPress and Drupal were initially created to support web logs (blogs), but WordPress has remained closer to its blogging roots, particularly in the simplicity with which it handles content creation and workflow. WordPress is justly renowned for ease of use, and many smaller sites or web teams just don't require the complex content structuring capabilities or workflow features offered by Drupal. If your content needs are not complex, and you want to get up and running quickly with a site that easily mixes short pages of text and graphics, WordPress may be the perfect solution for you.

WordPress is extensible via plug-ins—add-on pieces of software that bring new features and capabilities to the core WordPress functionality—particularly for adding in more advanced CMS features. UltimateCMS and White Label CMS are two such plug-ins, but a word of caution: the core virtue of WordPress is simplicity. If you have tried WordPress and quickly hit its limits as a content organizing tool, you may be better off considering Drupal instead. Drupal is harder to get started with, but it will take you much farther if you have complex content needs.

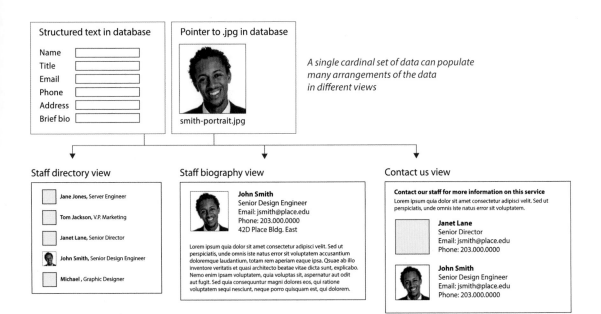

Structured text in database

Name
Title
Email
Phone
Address
Brief bio

Pointer to .jpg in database

smith-portrait.jpg

A single cardinal set of data can populate many arrangements of the data in different views

Staff directory view

Jane Jones, Server Engineer

Tom Jackson, V.P. Marketing

Janet Lane, Senior Director

John Smith, Senior Design Engineer

Michael , Graphic Designer

Staff biography view

John Smith
Senior Design Engineer
Email: jsmith@place.edu
Phone: 203.000.0000
42D Place Bldg. East

Lorem ipsum quia dolor sit amet consectetur adipisci velit. Sed ut perspiciatis, unde omnis iste natus error sit voluptatem accusantium doloremque laudantium, totam rem aperiam eaque ipsa. Qsuae ab illo inventore veritatis et quasi architecto beatae vitae dicta sunt, explicabo. Nemo enim ipsam voluptatem, quia voluptas sit, aspernatur aut odit aut fugit. Sed quia consequuntur magni dolores eos, qui ratione voluptatem sequi nesciunt, neque porro quisquam est, qui dolorem.

Contact us view

Contact our staff for more information on this service
Lorem ipsum quia dolor sit amet consectetur adipisci velit. Sed ut perspiciatis, unde omnis iste natus error sit voluptatem.

Janet Lane
Senior Director
Email: jsmith@place.edu
Phone: 203.000.0000

John Smith
Senior Design Engineer
Email: jsmith@place.edu
Phone: 203.000.0000

FIGURE 5.8
One powerful advantage of database-backed content management systems is the ability to present the same data in many different ways.

Drupal

Drupal is a powerful web content management framework that can support a wide range of sites, from simple blogs up to major institutional sites with thousands of pages of content and complex information architecture needs. All this power and flexibility comes at the price of initial ease of use. Drupal has a reputation for being considerably less "friendly" than WordPress, with a much less polished user interface. However, the latest version of Drupal (version 7 at this writing) has made giant strides toward a less intimidating interface for new users, and the coming Drupal 8 is also focused heavily on making Drupal easier to use. About 7–8 percent of sites using a CMS use Drupal, but this probably understates Drupal's core market of medium-sized institutional and commercial web sites. For example, Drupal is the dominant CMS in higher education, with about 27 percent of the market.

Drupal includes powerful tools for structuring content and creating taxonomies (controlled vocabularies for sorting and labeling content), and offers lots of flexibility in designing workflow roles and editing access privileges; moreover, Drupal has a huge and active user and developer community, far larger than that of any equivalent commercial CMS product. Modular structure makes Drupal attractive to experienced PHP developers, because the basic Drupal software core can be easily extended with code modules that add new functionality.

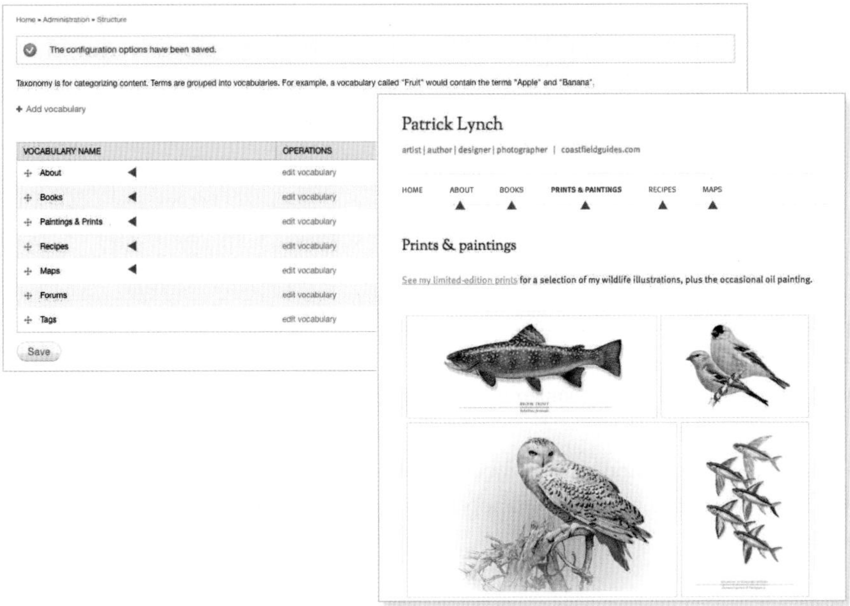

FIGURE 5.9
In a CMS the major content categories that you establish usually become the major navigation links for the site.

ORGANIZING CONTENT AND FUNCTIONALITY

Every web content management system has a unique internal structure, and many of the complex commercial cms products also have exacting server hardware and operating system requirements. However, all cms software is structured in layers of functionality, built from the base server operating system and configuration up to the graphic and presentational layers that users actually see on your web pages. Here we have used the open-source product Drupal as an example of a moderately complex and capable cms with a lot of built-in tools for organizing and structuring content, for organizing editorial workflow and access privileges, and for the visual display of your content and interactive functionality. While the exact details of cms structure and organizational details vary from system to system, Drupal makes a great (and free) introduction to cms concepts, even if you expect to later move on to a more complex commercial product for large enterprise needs.

Blocks

Blocks are areas of content or interactive functionality within page layout regions. Think of blocks as predesigned modular units or "building blocks" that can be placed into a page-layout template to add predefined bits of functionality to the page. For example, a user login area could be a block, as could a user poll, a search entry form, or a particular kind of navigation link layout. In Drupal blocks are often the visual interfaces of add-on modules that extend the basic capabilities of the cms. Blocks

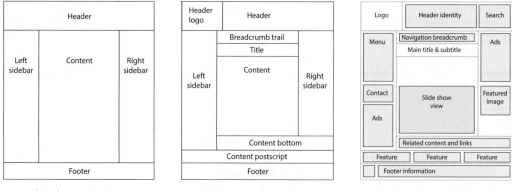

a. Simple page regions   b. More complex regions   c. Blocks or views within regions

FIGURE 5.10

Content management systems like Drupal allow you to populate regions of your page themes with blocks (specific types of content chunks) or views (preset arrangements of multiple blocks, such as a staff listing with photos).

can be configured to appear a number of different ways, and a CMS administrator can decide where the block should appear within a page region (header, left sidebar, footer).

Views

Views allow you to arrange specific kinds of text and visual content in a number of different ways. For example, one commonly seen "view" in Drupal business sites is a directory of people in a department. The directory draws specific bits of content from the CMS database to assemble a brief profile of each person, which might include a link to a photo, the person's name and title, contact information, email address, and so on. You establish a "view" that repeats this basic setup for everyone within your department, producing a department directory on a page. A related profile view might appear when you click on a particular person's name, linking to a view that shows a larger version of the same portrait photo, the person's basic contact information, and also perhaps additional information on his roles and current projects.

Each of the two views (directory, profile) draws information from the same database sources but displays the information in a different way: a compact listing for a directory, a much larger layout for a staff profile. In this way views allow you to reuse content flexibly. For example, a listing of company services view might include the photos of the people to contact about those services. The contact photos and information in the services view would be drawn from the same database listings as the company directory and staff profiles—three very different page views drawing upon the same sources of information.

Taxonomy

CMS taxonomy systems allow you to precisely structure and control information used to label your content—metainformation such as general and specific categories the

a.   b.   c.

content might fit into, and keywords and other descriptors about the content. The English language is enormous, often rich enough to allow several people to accurately describe a piece of content without using the same words. Without a shared and controlled vocabulary of terms, it is impossible to organize complex content. "Heart attack" and "myocardial infarction" both describe the same medical event, but unless there is general agreement about how to label heart attacks, you'll end up with multiple categories with redundant information—or even worse, with mislabeled information that is essentially lost to site users even though it is in the database.

Taxonomies allow you to create controlled lists of vocabulary terms for how your content will be labeled and categorized, and also to add additional keywords that provide detail beyond the controlled vocabulary terms. The categories and subcategories you create with your taxonomy system often then become the basis for your site navigation.

A successful taxonomy is flexible, both describing the current site content and anticipating future content. As you add new content to the site, revisit your taxonomies to ensure that they include all needed categories and tags.

CREATING THEMES AND TEMPLATES

Themes control most of the visual aspects of your CMS-based web site, including the overall page layout, the typography, the color scheme, graphics, and other visual details of your pages and page headers, and positioning of content organizational elements such as regions, blocks, and views. Most WordPress or Drupal themes come with several different "page types" or "page templates"—the terminology varies from one CMS to another but the basic concepts are the same. Page types like the home page, basic content web pages, blog-style posting pages, and image galleries are common page varieties within themes.

Theme regions divide the page into familiar layout conventions like headers, footers, and columns (see fig. 5.10a). More complex themes may provide many more subdivisions of the page regions (see fig. 5.10b and c). While you will rarely use all of

FIGURE 5.11
One powerful advantage of a CMS like WordPress is the complete separation of content (text, images) from the theme layout and graphics. Here three WordPress themes have been applied to the same content.

the regions and subregions of a complex theme on a single page, this network of potential regions gives you enormous flexibility in where you can place content, blocks, and views on the page, all without having to know or write HTML or CSS code.

Many of the basic types of pages on your site are created semiautomatically by the theme you choose. As you enter content, you determine what basic kind of initial presentation you want (conventional web page, blog post, and so on), and the template lays out the content for you within your chosen theme. You can easily change the formatting of content later if you choose to, or even change the whole theme of your site later if you find another theme that suits you better.

More sophisticated CMS programs like Drupal allow you to go much farther than basic page types. Through the use of content regions, blocks, and views you can develop a wide variety of page layouts. This flexibility requires you to know your CMS program pretty well, but in systems like WordPress or Drupal you can usually achieve great page layout flexibility without advanced HTML/CSS or programming skills.

Custom themes

Most themes for WordPress or Drupal allow you to add CSS code that supersedes the built-in theme CSS to customize various visual or typographic aspects of the theme. For example, with relatively modest CSS code additions you could change the background graphic of a theme, modify the colors of specific elements of the theme, or even change the typography of all of the headers in a theme.

If you are more ambitious or have exacting requirements for a site layout theme, there are several plastic and modifiable Drupal themes that have been created specifically for flexible customization without your having to create a custom theme entirely from scratch. For example, Drupal's "Zen" theme is a highly customizable theme framework designed to provide a rich visual and layout toolkit for more advanced Drupal users who are experienced with HTML and CSS.

Before tackling custom CMS theme development—or more likely, hiring a theme developer to create one for you—you should thoroughly investigate the secondary marketplace for Drupal, WordPress, Joomla, and commercial CMS themes. There are literally hundreds of sophisticated themes you can purchase for relatively modest costs, and many dozens more open-source themes that you can start with for free and then customize. When investigating themes, don't get too distracted by the superficial aspects of colors, graphics, and typography. These are certainly important, but particularly in a professionally developed commercial theme you should also be looking in detail at the theme's region layouts, prebuilt options for menu building, page types, and options to further customize the theme with your own custom CSS, blocks, and views. The theme should be adaptable to your particular content taxonomy, graphic and multimedia needs, and any e-commerce functions you plan for your site. Carefully review the support documentation that should accompany any

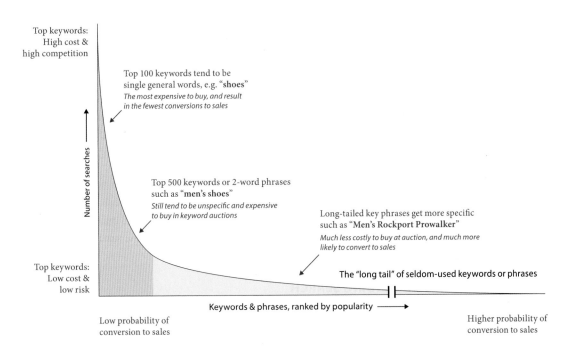

Top keywords:
High cost &
high competition

Top 100 keywords tend to be
single general words, e.g. "**shoes**"
*The most expensive to buy, and result
in the fewest conversions to sales*

Number of searches →

Top 500 keywords or 2-word phrases
such as "**men's shoes**"
*Still tend to be unspecific and expensive
to buy in keyword auctions*

Long-tailed key phrases get more specific
such as "**Men's Rockport Prowalker**"
*Much less costly to buy at auction, and much more
likely to convert to sales*

Top keywords:
Low cost &
low risk

The "long tail" of seldom-used keywords or phrases

Keywords & phrases, ranked by popularity →

Low probability of
conversion to sales

Higher probability of
conversion to sales

professionally developed theme, and if possible, ask the developer for examples of how the theme has been successfully applied in existing sites.

SEARCH ENGINE OPTIMIZATION

When the web first rose to popularity in the 1990s, people spoke of browsing or surfing the web, and users located interesting sites primarily by finding and clicking on links listed on major web directory sites like Yahoo! and Netscape. As the size of the web has exploded over the past decade (Google now indexes well over thirty trillion web pages), browsing through sites by following web links has become an increasingly inefficient means to initiate a search for new or specific information. You may still browse the home page of the New York Times or a personal portal page like MyYahoo!, but if you need anything more specific, you will probably go straight to a search engine such as Bing or Google.

The way your pages appear to the automated software that search engines use to "crawl" links between web pages and create search indexes has become the most important factor in whether users will find the information you publish on the web. SEO isn't difficult and will make your site better structured and more accessible. If your site uses proper HTML structural markup and all of your pages are linked together well, you've already done at least 80 percent of the work to make your site as visible as possible to search engines.

FIGURE 5.12
Search is essential to finding content in large sites.

Search optimization techniques are not the magic sauce that will automatically bring your site to the top of Google's page rankings, however. Nor is SEO a cure-all for an ineffective site—it can increase the traffic volume to your site and make things easier to find, but it can't improve the quality of your site content. SEO techniques ensure that your site is well formed and lessen the possibility that you have inadvertently hidden important information while constructing your site. Over the long run, though, only good content that is popular with readers and has many reference links from other highly ranked web sites will get you to the first page of Google or Bing's search results.

A note on language: In any discussion on SEO you'll hear a lot about "keywords," the words that users type into search engines to find relevant web sites. Keywords could literally be single words (for example, "Honda"), but more often they are actually multiword key phrases like "2015 Honda Accord." For the sake of brevity we'll refer to both keywords and key phrases as "keywords."

UNDERSTANDING SEARCH

Most patterns of web site use follow what are widely known as long-tail distributions. That is, a few items are overwhelmingly popular, and everything else gets relatively little attention. If you rank the popularity of every web page in your site, you will typically see a long-tailed curve, in which the home page and a few other popular pages get lots of views, and most other pages get much less traffic. This long-tailed distribution pattern in popularity is true for products in stores, books for sale at Amazon, songs to download on iTunes, or Blu-ray discs for sale at Walmart.

Although Wired magazine's Chris Anderson popularized the concept of the "long-tail" distribution for many things on the Internet, interface expert Jakob Nielsen first used Zipf curves (the formal mathematical term for long-tail phenomena) to describe the distribution patterns seen in web site usage. Long-tail usage patterns are fundamental to explaining why web search has become the most popular tool for finding information on the web, whether you are making a general Internet search or merely searching your company's internal web site. Once users get past the home page and major subdivisions of a large site, they are unlikely to browse their way through all the links that may be required to find a specific page, even if every link is well organized, intuitively labeled, and working properly.

Search engine components

Links and individual web pages are the primary elements of web search. Search engines find web pages by following web links from one page to another. Search engine companies use an automated process to find and follow web links and to analyze and index web page content for topical relevance. These automated search programs are collectively called web crawlers. This emphasis on links and pages is crucial to understanding how web search works: crawlers can find your pages only if links exist for them to follow, and search engines do not rank web sites—they rank the popularity and content relevance of individual web pages. Since the home page of a site is almost always the most popular page on a site, the home page is usually the first page listed on a search engine result page (SERP). Each page of your site needs to be optimized for search and well linked to other pages, because from a search engine's point of view, each web page stands alone.

Search engine crawlers

Search engine crawlers can only analyze the text, the web links, and some of the HTML markup code of your web page and then make inferences about the nature, quality, and topical relevance of your pages based on statistical analysis of the words on each page.

The following are not visible to most search engines:

- Display text within graphics, headers, banners, and company logos.
- The content of Flash or GIF animations, video content, and audio content.
- Pages with little text content and lots of unlabeled graphics.
- Older kinds of site navigation that uses graphics-based "rollovers" or other graphic links or HTML image maps.
- Navigation links that depend on JavaScript or other dynamic code (web crawlers do not usually execute JavaScript code).
- Content features such as RSS feeds and other text that depend on JavaScript to appear on the page.

The following may cause search crawlers to bypass a web page:

- Pages with very complex structure: deeply nested tables, or unusually complex HTML.
- Lengthy JavaScript or CSS code at the top of the page HTML code listing: crawlers give up on a page that seems to contain no content.
- Pages with many broken links: crawlers abandon or de-rank pages with many broken links, and they can't follow the broken links to find new pages.
- Content with keyword spamming (repeating keywords many times in hidden text, alternate image text, or meta tags): search engines now ignore these primitive relevance-biasing schemes, and your page may even be banned from the search index if you use these techniques.
- Long, complex URLs with special characters (&, ?, %, $) that are often generated by dynamic programming or databases. Use plain English in site directories, and always opt for "friendly" URLs if you are using a CMS to run

your site. Search engines look at URLs, and use the recognizable words they find in the URL to assess relevance.

- Slow-loading pages with inefficient dynamic links to content management systems or databases: if the page doesn't load in a few seconds, many crawlers give up and move on. Use a tool like Google's PageSpeed Insights (developers. google.com/speed/pagespeed/) to check the loading speed of your pages.
- Pages that use frames or iframes: crawlers often ignore pages with complex frame schemes because they can't make sense of the individual HTML files that make up each framed "page."
- Some dynamic pages that are assembled on request by a web application and database; be sure your developers know how you want to handle the search visibility of your content before they choose a development technology or content management tool for dynamic web sites. The URLs for these application-assembled pages are often full of programming gibberish. Ask your developers for more readable English URLs for better search engine visibility.

In addition to making your pages less searchable, these poor practices make your site less accessible, particularly to people who use screen reader software to access web content. SEO, valid HTML markup of content, and universal usability make a wonderful confluence of worthy objectives: by using the best web practices for content markup and organizing your content and links with care, your site will be both more visible to search and more accessible to all users. Commercial SEO products like Moz Pro Tools (moz.com/tools) can help you do detailed analysis of the state of your current site SEO, and can make detailed suggestions for improving your search rankings. A subscription to Moz Tools is not inexpensive, but you might consider using the service for a few months to give you good data while you create new content or overhaul your existing site for SEO. A thirty-day trial subscription to Moz Tools is free.

Search engine rankings

So what exactly are the rules for good search rankings? We can't tell you, and the search engine companies won't give you any exact formulas for high search rankings either. If search engines like Google and Yahoo! told everyone how they rank pages and how they detect and ban search-scamming techniques, unscrupulous web publishers would instantly start to game the system, and soon we'd all be back to the pre-Google 1990s, when general web search had become almost useless. What we can say is what the search engines themselves gladly tell web content developers: create compelling page content with proper structural markup and good linkages to other pages and sites. Don't hide your content with poor page development techniques, and your pages will rank well in any search engine.

Current search engines use a combination of two information sources to rank the relevance of a web page to any given search term:

1. **Internal factors:** Characteristics of the text and links within the page—the page title, content headings, the body text, the alternate text in image HTML tags, web links both internal to the site and external to other sites, and the frequency and distribution of topical keywords. Organized metainformation such as keyword and description HTML meta tags also factor in page ranking, although not as heavily as page titles, headings, and words within the page content. Even your domain name and the names of files and directories within the URL of your web page may count toward relevancy rankings, so always use plain-English file names, site directories, and URLs whenever possible.

2. **External factors:** The degree to which your page is linked with existing highly ranked pages on the same topic, how often people who get your page in their search results click on the link to your page, and other statistical factors that the search engines glean from their own data on the searches users perform and the link choices they make for a given topic or keyword. Links from popular pages that send readers to your pages are essentially votes that your site is relevant to the search topic. Links from other high-ranking pages constitute one of the most important factors in determining rank, but overall volume counts, too: the more links your page has from other pages and the more search users who click on your page link in search engine results, the higher your overall page ranking.

When web search services became popular in the 1990s, early search engines used internal content factors almost exclusively to rate the relevance and ranking of web pages. Search rankings were thus childishly easy to manipulate. By inserting dozens of hidden keywords on a page, for example, an aggressive web page author could make a page seem richer in popular topic relevance than other web pages ("sex, sex, sex, sex"). By the late 1990s even the largest search engines were considered only marginally useful in locating the best sources of information on a given topic, and the top-ranked sites were often those that used the most effective manipulation techniques to bias the early web search engines.

The innovation that transformed web search in the late 1990s was Google's heavy use of external page factors to weigh pages' relevance and usefulness. Google's algorithms balance external ranking factors with statistical analysis of the page text to determine relevance and search ranking. Google's fundamental idea is similar to peer citations in academic publications. Every year thousands of science papers are published, so how can you tell which articles are the best? You look for those that are most frequently cited ("linked") by other published papers. Important science papers get cited a lot. Useful web sites get linked to a lot, and every link is a popularity vote that increases the results ranking of a site.

USING KEYWORDS AND KEY PHRASES

People find your content by entering keywords or key phrases into search engines like Google or Bing. Keyword targeting is a key concept in both SEO and online search advertising, which are basically two sides of the same coin. The searcher wants to find your site, and you want to be found, so you might "buy" keywords in Google's Adwords auction to get more prominent listings on SERPS. In either case, you need a keen understanding of the words or phrases that best describe your site, its content, and any products you have for sale.

You start the process of optimizing your site for search by generating lists of keywords or key phrases that best describe your content or products. The Google Adwords Keyword Planner (see adwords.google.com/KeywordPlanner) is ideal for conducting research on keywords and phrases in your industry. Although the Planner is designed to help businesses that buy access to search terms in Google's Adwords keyword auctions, anyone can set up an account and use the Keyword Planner for free to analyze the results of search terms relevant to a particular site, business, or general industry, in a specific geographic region, city, or town. Most important, the Planner can help you identify the most common search terms that will bring a potential customer to your web site. With this information you can optimize your page content for those target keywords. As you evaluate your search rankings and keywords over time, it might be a good idea to occasionally buy keywords in Google's Adwords auction that you want to investigate, as this will give you even more detailed data on whether your primary keywords are actually driving sales or visits to your site.

As you evaluate possible keywords to emphasize on your pages, remember that you are not your audience. Avoid "insider" jargon and professional language for sites aimed at the general public. For example, in medicine it's common to refer to people with M.D.s as "physicians." In the real world people call M.D.s "doctors." If possible do some focus groups or user research with representative members of your audience to see how they might search for the information on your site. Also, once you have your keyword list for each page, look for logical synonyms or alternate language that means the same thing as your primary keywords. Having alternate language can help you guess other relevant words or phrases readers may search for, and will also help you avoid repeating the same words or phrases too many times in page content or headings.

Like the popularity of pages within a web site, keywords for a given topic typically follow a long-tail distribution pattern. A few words are searched thousands of times, but most terms appear much less frequently. Long-tail keywords tend to be much more specific and relevant. For example, if you start your web research to buy a new car with the term "auto sales" you are likely to get too general a listing on the SERP. The phrase "auto sales" is popular and widely used, but not terribly useful if you already know that you are interested in Honda models. It's much better to narrow your search term to something much more specific, like "new Honda Accord Connecticut." If you sell Honda autos, there is little point in optimizing your site content for nebulous but frequently used keywords like "auto sales." Even though the terms are used less frequently, you are much better off optimizing your site content for more specific keywords and phrases like particular models of Honda cars, listed on pages that prominently feature your address and other contact information.

General considerations

Once you have your lists of target keywords or phrases, you need to look at each page of your existing site and see how each of these elements either supports your keyword strategy or needs to be rewritten to include the most relevant keywords for the content on the page:

- **URL:** Yes, search engines look for recognizable words in URLs. Use keywords in the URL whenever possible.
- **Page title:** The HTML `<title>` element is the single most critical element in page SEO. Make sure your main keywords appear in the page title tag. The page title also forms the link text on SERPs.
- **Description:** The HTML meta description tag. This tag is not visible on the page but is in the HTML header code for the page. Meta tags do not contribute much to search engine rankings, but the text of the "description" meta tag on your home page is important, as search engines like Google often use that text just below your page title link on SERPs.
- **Headers:** Your first `<h1>` header should be at the top of your content area, and must include your major keywords or phrases. Use keywords in other headers as much as good prose style allows.
- **Body text:** Your keywords and phrases should appear here as well, but don't overdo this. Search engines will de-rank pages that seem to use far more repetitions of keywords than you would see in normal prose.
- **Images, embedded video:** Always use the `alt` and `title` attributes of link code to supply accurate descriptions of the contents of the picture or video. Never load these tags with irrelevant or repetitive keywords.
- **Title tags on other web links:** Most web authoring programs like Dreamweaver or CMS programs will prompt you for alternate descriptive text ("alt text") for images, or descriptive text for link "title" tags. Use language that accurately describes the linked material. Don't get lazy and use the same title text for

many links or images, as search engines are wary of seeing the same phrase repeated many times and may de-rank your page.

The language analysis software used by Google and Bing is sophisticated, using detailed statistical analysis to look at the normal patterns in language as seen in millions of example pages, and to assess how pages that are popular (lots of traffic, many clicks from search results pages) look when examined statistically. If your page falls significantly outside these normal statistical parameters for language related to your keywords, your content may be de-ranked for not being relevant to a user's search keywords. If your content contains an unusual pattern of repeated keywords, your page may be de-ranked for trying to game the search engine into a higher relevance ranking. The general rule for major keyword repetition is five to seven times in the equivalent of about a letter-sized page of text (roughly one thousand words). Repeating the same keyword or phrase more often than that could harm your search ranking, as the repeats produce abnormal language statistics, which suggest that you are trying to game the system by artificially loading the page with keywords (a practice called "keyword spamming").

Links

Selecting text on your web page and linking that text to other relevant web pages is a powerful semantic statement: it establishes that the linked text is important and highly relevant to the content on the page, and thus associates the page with other relevant content. On a typical web page there are two basic kinds of links:

- **Navigational links:** Typically in the header or side columns of the page, and repeated on most pages of the site.
- **Contextual links:** Links that bind together pages with related content.

Web crawlers use navigational links as a means to evaluate the general structure of your site and major content topics. When a crawler hits a link, it looks at the linked text for keyword relevance, but it also evaluates the page the link points to for relevance. Ideally both pages should share similar keywords, as this reinforces the relevance ranking, especially if you pointed the link to a page that is already ranked high by Google or Bing for similar keywords. Links like this are essentially a signal to the search crawler that your content is well matched to the keywords in your page title, headers, and other page elements. This also suggests that you should avoid linking to pages outside your site that are only parenthetically related to the content of your page. Seemingly gratuitous links to pages that seem unrelated will frustrate both your human readers and web search crawlers.

The fact that you have selected and linked a word or phrase signals to the search crawler that the linked text is important. This is why it is critical to avoid using uninformative phrases like "click here" or "link" in your page links. "Click here" does nothing to inform your readers or the search crawler about either the on-page content or the content you are pointing to. Always use descriptive keywords and phrases in your link text, and use the link title attribute to further inform the reader about where the link will bring her.

Schemas

Web search engines are pretty good at finding and interpreting information like addresses, but there are ways to add extra markup information to your web pages that make it easier for search engines to interpret your key business information. "Schemas" (see schema.org) are established sets of extra markup you can add to your page's HTML markup that label some of your page content in carefully structured arrangements that search engines can find and read. Schema information won't be visible to visitors to your site, but can be read by search engines and other kinds of Internet directories. Schemas can go well beyond your basic "NAP" information (name, address, phone), and there are existing schemas for places, restaurants, menus, local businesses, events, schools and other organizations, and many others.

Local search

You have probably noticed that SERPS are much more informative now about local businesses. Now you can enter "Whole Foods hours" and get not just the hours but the locations of the stores nearest to you. For "brick and mortar" local businesses, search engine optimization boils down to four major factors: relevance, distance, reputation, and mobile search.

- **Relevance:** Is your site well organized around your services and products, with all the likely search keywords and phrases covered? Ideally you should have an optimized page for each major service or product you offer, and use the on-page SEO techniques we've covered above.
- **Distance:** What geographic area does your business serve, and is your location and coverage information prominent on your home page and major service of product pages? Search engines use this basic NAP information to determine how relevant you are to customers in your city or region. Place your NAP contact information prominently on the home page, and in the footer of every page of your site, and frequently cite your coverage area in your page content. Think carefully about what geography keywords your customers might use, and how specific they might be (for example, New York City, Brooklyn, Bay Ridge, Fourth Ave. and 86th St.).
- **Reputation:** How locally prominent is your business? Do positive references to your business appear in local news sites, blogs, customer review sites like Yelp and FourSquare, or in social media sites like Facebook? The more often your business is positively mentioned on other sites, the higher it will rank in search results. Regularly search for references to your business, follow your Yelp and other review sites closely, and respond quickly and helpfully to any negative reviews.
- **The increasing prominence of mobile search:** The majority of web searches are now done on mobile devices (smartphones and tablets). How mobile-friendly is your business's web site? Many small local businesses have sites built with older web technologies, and are not well maintained and up-to-date. Today it is crucial to shift your site to a mobile-friendly template, as customers will quickly leave your site if it looks too hard to use on a small cell phone screen.

Code optimization

Beyond your content and keywords, there are a few technical issues to look at on both your web pages and your web server to be sure that your site is regularly crawled by search engines, and that technical problems with your code or your server hardware don't harm your search result rankings.

Search engines penalize sites with lots of poorly formed HTML code, broken links, and haphazard patterns of linking within the site. Broken links are especially important to fix, because web crawlers find pages only by following links. Be sure that your links work, and use the Google and Bing webmaster tools to see whether the search engine crawlers have flagged your site for broken links or poor HTML code.

- Google Webmaster Tools: www.google.com/webmasters/tools
- Bing Webmaster Tools: www.bing.com/toolbox/webmaster

The webmaster tool sets will help you evaluate how your whole site is crawled. If you have specific pages that need to be fixed or improved, you can also use the w3c's html code validator to be sure you have found and fixed your code issues:

- w3c Markup Validation Service: validator.w3.org

Server optimization

Web sites that are slow to respond frustrate both human readers and web search crawlers. Google's crawlers now index more than 30 trillion web pages and produce about 100 billion crawler sessions a month. With all that web hopping to do, neither search crawlers nor human readers are likely to linger over your slow-loading pages. If your pages seem to be loading very slowly, use a tool like Google's PageSpeed Insights (developers.google.com/speed/pagespeed/insights) to check load speed. Slow page loading can be a particular problem on modest servers that support a cms like Drupal or WordPress (or most other kinds of cmss) to deliver content. Most cms programs create pages by dynamically assembling the page each time a request for the page is made from a web server. All that assembly takes time and server cycles, and if your server is not up to the task, your pages will be slow to load.

There are potential fixes for slow-loading pages that do not involve getting a new server. Many cms-based sites use a server cache to help reduce the load on the cms. Each time a page is requested from the server, the server keeps a copy of the assembled page in a memory cache, and if the page is requested again, the server sends the cached version, reducing the load on the cms itself. This caching of popular pages can greatly increase the apparent loading speed of high-traffic pages like the home page. Most caching software has a time limit for sending cached pages—typically several minutes, sometimes longer. After the time limit expires, the server retrieves a new version of the requested page and places the updated version in the cache. This way pages that actively change will never be more than a few minutes out of date. Check with your webmaster or web server administrator to see whether you are using a caching scheme with your cms.

Overall server reliability also affects search engine rankings. If a crawler has previously indexed your site and revisits only to find the server down and the site dark, this will decrease your search rankings because it makes your site look unreliable. A professionally managed web server should be operating well over 99.5 percent of the time. While this may sound almost perfect, a 99.5 percent availability rate means that your server could be down almost forty-four hours a year—a major problem for e-commerce or other high-traffic sites. Get statistics from your IT department or web hosting service on down time rates over the past year.

SUBMITTING A SITE FOR INDEXING

For new sites by far the best way to get your site listed in the major search engines is to request links from other existing sites that point to your new site, via news releases, by contacting local business directory sites, or simply by asking other related but noncompetitive organizations if they might list your new site in a brief news piece, or along with other "Resources" or "Related sites." The largest search engines offer pages that allow you to submit the URL for a new web site, but there is no guarantee that the search crawlers will find your site immediately. It could take several weeks or more for web search crawlers to visit your new site and index it for the first time, but normally the process just takes a day or two.

Site maps

In the context of search optimization, the term "site map" has several meanings, depending on its context:

- **Site map pages:** Most web site maps are ordinary web pages with lists of links to the major elements of your web site. These master lists of the major pages in your site are excellent resources for search engine crawlers, and site map pages provide a great way to ensure that every important page of your site is linked in a way that search crawlers and users can easily find. Site map or "index" pages are common elements of web sites, and users who prefer to browse through lists of links know to look for site map or index pages in a well-organized site. In the earlier days of the web you'd see site maps that were laid out as diagrammatic charts or visual maps of the site, but the graphic site "map" metaphor has largely faded in favor of much more efficient and search-visible lists of links.
- **XML site maps for search engines:** The second common type of "site map" is a text file in XML format that sits at the level of your home page and informs web search crawlers about the major pages in your web site, how to find the pages, and how often the pages are likely to be updated (daily, weekly, monthly). These XML-based site maps are not visible to users of your site, but they provide an efficient means of conveying the structure of your site to search engines like Google and Bing. See the sitemaps.org site for details on how to construct XML site map files.

Creating an XML site map requires some technical steps, but if you've had a bit of experience with HTML markup, the process is straightforward and the instructions at sitemaps.org are thorough. An XML site map is just a carefully structured plain-text file that you can submit to Google or Bing using either of their webmaster tools sites.

RECOMMENDED READING

Byron, A., A. Berry, and B. Bondt. *Using Drupal,* 2nd ed. Sebastopol, CA: O'Reilly, 2012.

Cederholm, D. *CSS3 for Web Designers.* New York: A Book Apart, 2015.

Clifton, B. *Advanced Web Metrics with Google Analytics,* 3rd ed. Hoboken, NJ: Wiley-Sybex, 2012.

Enge, E., S. Spencer, J. Stricchiola, and R. Fishkin. *The Art of SEO: Managing Search Engine Optimization,* 2nd ed. Sebastopol, CA: O'Reilly, 2012.

Keith, J. *HTML5 for Web Designers.* New York: A Book Apart, 2010.

MacDonald, M. *HTML5: The Missing Manual,* 2nd ed. Sebastopol, CA: O'Reilly, 2013.

———. *WordPress: The Missing Manual.* Sebastopol, CA: O'Reilly, 2014.

McFarland, D. *CSS3: The Missing Manual,* 3rd ed. Sebastopol, CA: O'Reilly, 2013.

The visual power of design derives from the idea of contrast.
If you ask why something works and you push back far enough,
eventually everything seems to be based on contrast: the ability to
distinguish one thing from another.
– Chris Pullman

CHAPTER 6

Page Structure

Two major changes have influenced the profession of web design over the past decade, one evolutionary and one that has much more profoundly affected design thinking on the web. First, the latest versions of the web markup and styling languages—especially HTML5 and CSS3—were released, bringing new capabilities to "standards-based" web design. These changes to page markup finally reflected the real-world interests and behavior of web professionals, incorporating widespread coding practices into official W3C standards and making the web a much more friendly and capable place for web-based applications and complex interactivity. As interesting as they have been, the new markup languages reflect the steady evolution and growing maturity of the craft and tools of web publishing.

It's the burst of new hardware and usage situations for web-based content that has created the biggest paradigm change in the way we think about web-based delivery of information. Today mobile hardware like smartphones and tablets gets most of the attention in this second, much larger change in the web, but the explosion in the size ranges and sheer diversity of mobile hardware and screens just presages an even bigger change now just beginning. The combination of ever-cheaper smart devices, near-ubiquitous wireless networking, and even tinier—and larger—viewports will make today's "mobile-first" web design seem like the simple days of yore. When everything in your environment, from wall-sized environmental monitors to smart watches and other wearables, is a web-connected computer, you won't use the web—you'll live within it. Many of us already do.

A structure must exhibit the three qualities of solidity, usefulness, and beauty.

—Marcus Vitruvius Pollio

BASICS OF PAGE STRUCTURE

MARKING UP PAGE STRUCTURE

Let's look back for a moment at the way markup languages were headed in the mid-2000s. The state of the art then was a full embrace of carefully validated semantic XHTML markup, combined with CSS for page layout, typography, and basic page graphics. To use the capabilities of CSS for page layout, designers stuffed their HTML code with dozens of generic division `<div>` (and `<span>`) containers to hang their CSS markup upon, and the resulting explosion of `<div>` containers sometimes made even basic page layouts absurdly complex (fig. 6.1).

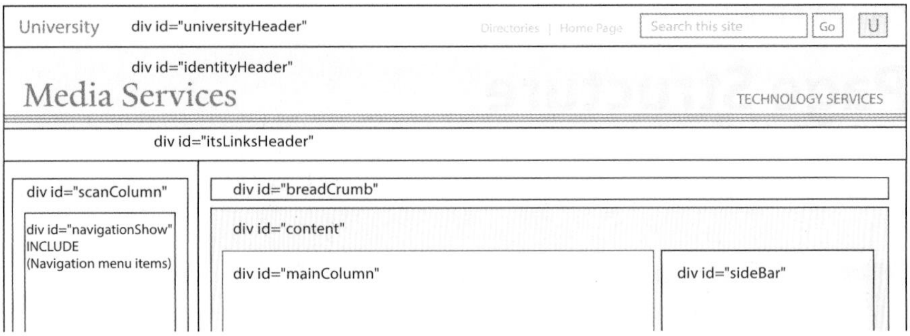

FIGURE 6.1

The complex nesting of HTML <div> elements allows page coders great flexibility in styling the visual elements of the page with CSS targeted to each unique <div> tag, at some cost in code complexity and page loading speed.

As these new page design practices became widespread, many designers noticed both the complexity and the redundancy of the new coding practices, and the implicit irony: page design with CSS was supposed to help simplify page markup. But because the new capabilities of CSS inspired designers to ever greater graphic complexity, markup code was becoming more complex than ever. In 2005 Google did a study that parsed the page code of more than a billion published web pages, specifically looking at how designers were using HTML class, <div>, and id names, and discovered common semantic patterns in page code. The dominant naming patterns were pretty logical, and centered on common page regions such as "header," "footer," "navigation," and "content" or "main content."

The explosion in the coding of <div> containers wasn't just related to styling with CSS: it was also clear that if HTML was to mature as a markup language, it would have to incorporate a richer set of semantics to describe common content containers like sections, articles, and asides or pull-quotes. Designers were increasingly using the generic <div> container to both visually style blocks of content and make specific blocks of content more amenable to content syndication schemes like RSS, in order to make up for the markup restrictions of early-2000s HTML 4.0 and XHTML. Thus it was common to see markup like <div class="article">, <div class="section">, <div class="pullquote"> as designers struggled with the semantic limitations of XHTML.

The new HTML5 that gradually emerged in the late 2000s was designed specifically to address the needs of real-world web design for more logical page structural tags, a richer set of semantic markup for content, and tools for developing web-based applications. Many of the new markup tags in HTML5 were specifically designed to "pave the cowpaths" of contemporary web practice, bringing the informal but logical improvisations of real-world coding methods into the formal specifications for HTML5. In HTML5 there are now new sets of semantic markup tags to describe page structure and provide a richer set of content semantic tags.

Page structure semantics

Page structure semantics designate common types of pages regions like headers, footers, and navigation areas. Instead of needing to create many unique `<div>` ids to contain these common page elements, coders can use the new elements and style them directly. This regularizing of long-standing practice in page region layout makes it much easier for automated systems like search engines and browsers for the blind to find, highlight, or skip past structural elements on the page.

In addition to longtime HTML page structural tags like `<head>` and `<body>`, in HTML5 we now have these new tags to enrich the description of page elements:

- **Header:** Defines the header area of a page, or the header of a section or article. Page headers often contain navigation elements (`<nav>`). Articles, sections, and asides can all contain their own header areas.
- **Navigation:** An element designed to contain the main navigation elements. These are often global navigation links to major site sections, or navigation to local subsection topics.
- **Main:** Designed to contain all of the main content elements of a page. This tag is useful in accessibility for screen reader web browsers, as it allows the reader to jump straight to page content. It's also useful in enabling search engines to flag the central content of the page.
- **Aside:** The `<aside>` element has two main uses: as a page layout container like a sidebar used for navigation, or for other content "aside" from the main page content. An `<aside>` element can also be used to designate parenthetically related content set aside from the main content narrative of the page, as in a "sidebar" article or explanatory note.
- **Footer:** `<footer>` elements generally mark the end of the page, and usually contain general information about the web site, copyright or other date information, and contact information. The `<footer>` element can also be used at the end of a section or article, to hold footnotes, bibliographies, or other material generally listed at the end of a section or article.

New content semantic elements in HTML5

This is a partial list of the new content semantic elements in HTML5. The new elements provide a much more detailed way to label content sections and components so that search engines and other automated page-scanning systems can "read" the pages with more intelligence. More detailed content markup also makes it easier to reuse defined blocks of content like sections and articles.

- **Article:** A self-contained or self-standing chunk of content. Designed as a means to designate a block of content that might be reused on a different page

FIGURE 6.2
(facing page) The
new semantic
page elements
of HTML5 such as
"header," "nav," and
"main" make HTML
code better for
accessibility and for
automated systems
like search engines,
and are also useful
for reusing content
within web content
management
systems.

or site and still be self-contained and understandable outside of its original context. Note that neither `<section>` nor `<article>` elements should be used just to visually style or lay out content on a page. Use the `<div>` element if you just need a container to apply css styling to a page area.

- **Aside:** Content that is parenthetically related to the main content, but set aside from the main content narrative. In print publications asides are often set apart as "sidebar" articles. An `<aside>` element could also be used to designate a sidebar column of a page layout.
- **Details:** A new element intended to designate explanatory content that can be disclosed or hidden, as in pop-up explanatory notes driven by JavaScript. Click to disclose the details; click again to hide the note. See the related `<summary>` element.
- **Figure:** A container for an individual figure or group of closely related graphics like illustrations, photos, diagrams, and the like.
- **Figcaption:** Designates the caption for a figure. The `<figcaption>` element should be nested within the related `<figure>` element.
- **Mark:** Defines marked or highlighted text, or text distinguished for other semantic purposes.
- **Section:** Defines a section of a document. This is a deliberately broad definition, left largely to the author to decide. A section could just be a paragraph or two, or a whole chapter.
- **Summary:** The visible text associated with a pop-up `<details>` element. `<summary>` and `<details>` elements are used for pop-up explanatory notes, usually controlled by JavaScript. The user clicks on a summary, a `<details>` element appears with explanatory text, and then when the user clicks again the details text disappears.
- **Time:** Defines a date (normally in yyyy-mm-dd format) or a time (24-hour clock). For example:
  ```
  <p>Curtain time for the play is <time>20:00</time>.</p>
  <p>The first performance of the play is on <time>2016-05-15,
     20:00</time>.</p>
  ```
- **Canvas:** The `<canvas>` element allows you to specify a rectangular area of a web page where—under script control via JavaScript or other logic programming—you can create highly interactive graphics and animations, including future possibilities for interactive 3D objects. Thus far the `<canvas>` element has been an interesting possibility with very little practical application beyond quirky graphics demos and crude animations. With the recent support for canvas interactivity in Adobe's Flash Professional cc, we may see more useful interactive content that takes useful advantage of the possibilities

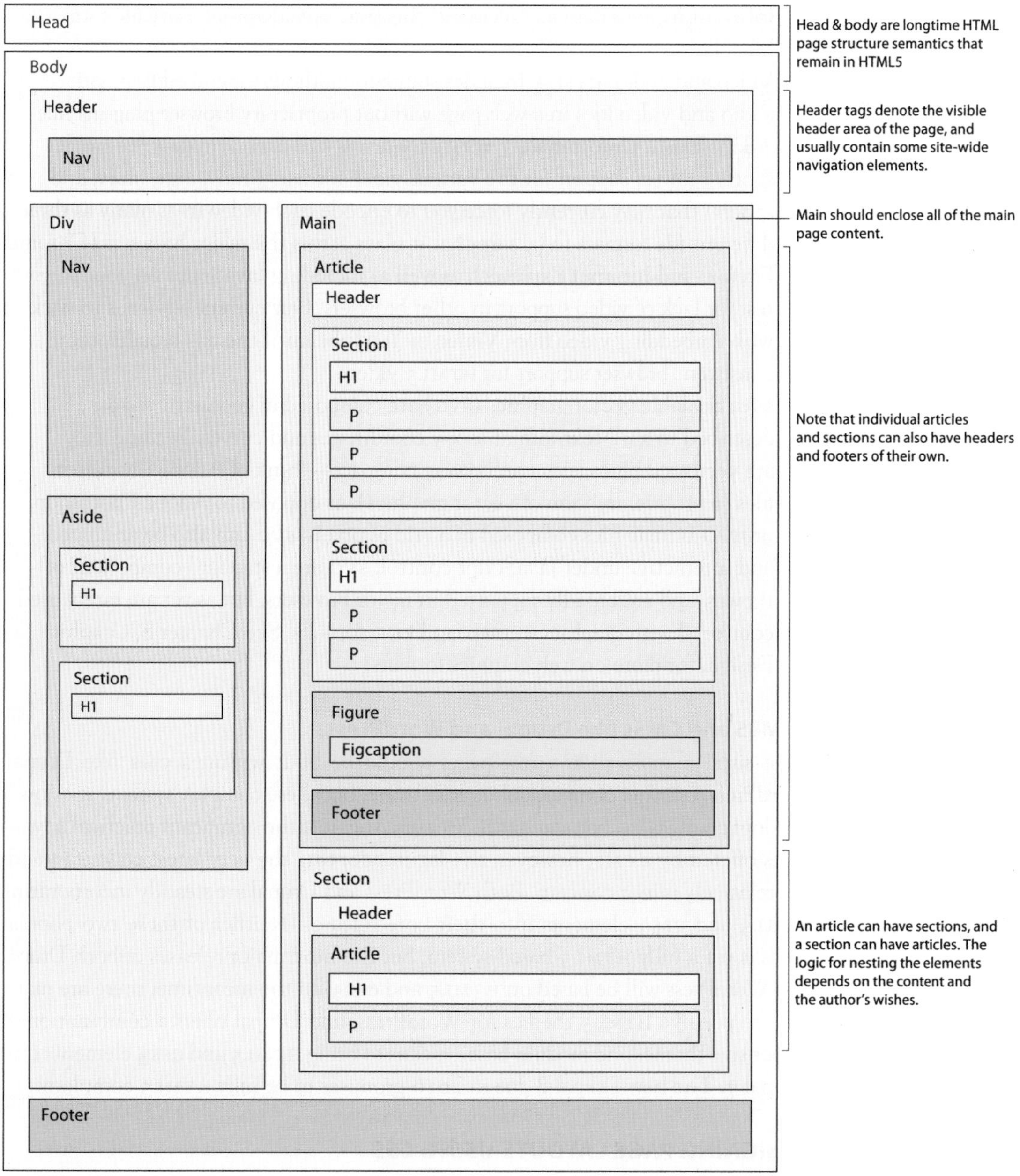

Head

Head & body are longtime HTML page structure semantics that remain in HTML5

Body

Header

Nav

Header tags denote the visible header area of the page, and usually contain some site-wide navigation elements.

Div

Main

Main should enclose all of the main page content.

Nav

Article

Header

Section

H1

P

P

P

Note that individual articles and sections can also have headers and footers of their own.

Aside

Section

H1

Section

H1

Section

H1

P

P

Figure

Figcaption

Footer

Section

Header

Article

H1

P

An article can have sections, and a section can have articles. The logic for nesting the elements depends on the content and the author's wishes.

Footer

inherent in the `<canvas>` element, this time outside proprietary file formats like Flash.

- Video and audio: HTML5 includes standard methods for embedding both audio and video files in a web page without proprietary browser plug-ins like Adobe Flash. Unfortunately, HTML5 video is still a work in progress, with spotty browser support for the various video formats (.mov, .ogv, .m4v, and others) that may currently force you to encode each video in as many as three different file formats to be sure that it plays across the major browsers (Chrome, Firefox, and Internet Explorer), as well as including JavaScript on your page to test for lack of video support in other browsers. Our current advice is to stick with embedding video from Vimeo or YouTube until there is broader, more consistent browser support for HTML5 video.
- SVG: Scalable vector graphics (SVG) are composed of geometric shapes described in XML text format as x-y coordinates and curves. Because they are vector graphics, SVG can be very compact—think of Adobe Illustrator files (a proprietary form of vector graphics), as opposed to Adobe Photoshop or JPEG bitmap files composed of a grid of pixels. SVG can also be animated and interactive under JavaScript control. SVG are a standard component of HTML5 and are broadly supported in major browsers, but as yet are rarely used compared with graphics in JPEG and PNG formats. See Chapter 8, Graphic Design, for more on web graphics formats.

HTML5 and CMSs like Drupal and WordPress

Most sites of more than a few pages should be built within a CMS like Drupal, WordPress, or other commercial CMS software, but these complex systems are slower to adopt changes in code standards. Measured against the significant practical advantages offered by a CMS, however, the lag in adopting the very latest code standards is a relatively minor concern. Both WordPress and Drupal are steadily incorporating HTML5 and CSS3 elements into their core releases. Neither of these two popular CMSs is yet a fully HTML5-based system, but the next major releases of both Drupal and WordPress will be based on HTML5 and CSS3. In the meantime, there are many fully responsive HTML5 themes for WordPress, and Drupal offers a combination of responsive themes and module-based means to bring HTML5 and CSS3 elements into Drupal 7. The new Drupal 8 due in 2016 promises to be fully HTML5 compliant.

DESIGNING PAGE LAYOUTS USING CSS

Cascading style sheets (CSS) have been the mainstream way to lay out and visually style web pages for well over a decade, and they now handle complex typography and provide the foundation for responsive web design. As we have become more and more dependent on CSS for almost every detail of page design, CSS has become

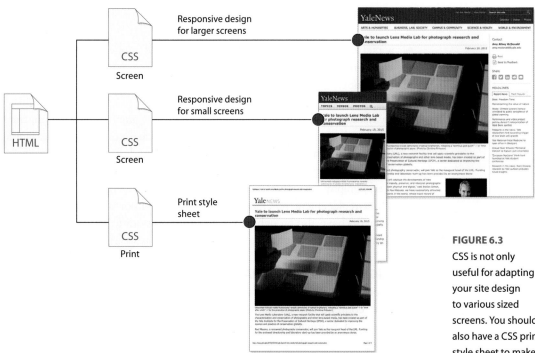

FIGURE 6.3
CSS is not only useful for adapting your site design to various sized screens. You should also have a CSS print style sheet to make pages printed from your site look more professional and useful to readers.

progressively more complex. The description for the second version of css was more than five times the length of the original css specification. The most current version of css is css3, and it is still very much a work in progress, as the specification is far more massive than that of css 2.1. The css3 project is so large that the w3c working groups have divided the css3 specification into more than fifty modules, some of which have been broadly implemented in browsers for years. But many css3 modules and specifications are still unimplemented, or only sporadically supported across desktop and mobile browsers.

Luckily, the web itself is the most up-to-date reference for the current state of web browser brands, versions, and support for the many new html5 and css3 elements and features. Here are a few reference sites that should be in your core set of web resources.

Testing for and current status of html5 and css3 elements and browser support:

- Can I Use?: caniuse.com
- css3test.com: css3test.com
- css3 Click Chart: css3clickchart.com

Current web browser statistics:

- w3schools, Web Browsers: www.w3schools.com/browsers/browsers_stats.asp
- w3counter, Browser Market Share: www.w3counter.com/globalstats.php
- Statcounter global stats: gs.statcounter.com

As always with CSS updates there are dozens of new graphics, animation, transition, and page layout features in CSS3, but two new features stand out as significant—even foundational—enhancements of web technology: the @media queries that are the basis of responsive web design, and the @font-face element that finally frees web typography from the limitations of "web safe" operating system fonts or gimcrack font-replacement schemes. A slew of more minor but useful CSS3 typographic elements have also brought real typographic options to web pages. We'll discuss web fonts and the CSS3 enhancements to typography in Chapter 9, Typography.

ENCODING PAGES FOR OPTIMAL ACCESSIBILITY AND READABILITY

HTML source order is the sequence in which elements, such as site identity, navigation, primary content, related content, and footer information, appear in the document source code. Normally a reader of a web page doesn't see the raw HTML code; he sees at least a minimally styled version of the HTML in the web browser window, and normally a web site has additional custom CSS code that creates the layout and typography we expect from finished web pages.

Proper HTML source code order matters for several reasons:

1. There are times when the normal CSS styling is not present due to a technical failure on the site, or sometimes in mobile or wireless contexts the bandwidth is so limited that the HTML shows up in the browser unstyled. If your source HTML is in a logical order (fig. 6.4) the reader should still be able to access your content and links, albeit in very plain form.
2. Source order matters for accessibility, as web browsers for blind users expect a certain logical code order, and blind users of your site will be able to quickly skip past your header and navigation areas and get to the main page content.
3. Keeping your main site navigation links and primary page content high in the source order contributes to search engine optimization. Pages with too much CSS or JavaScript in the header area may bury the main page content so deeply down in the HTML file that search engine spiders don't see it, or de-rank the page content because of excessive code.

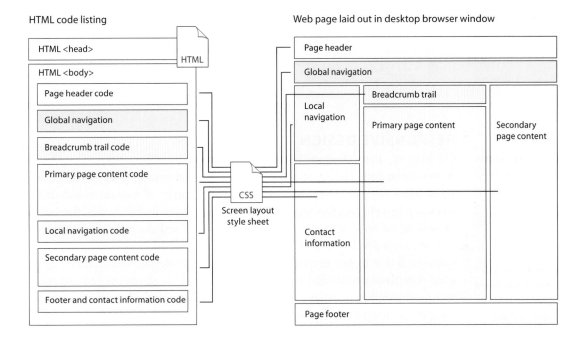

HTML code listing

Web page laid out in desktop browser window

Modern web pages use style sheets to lay out the content, graphics, and navigation elements on web pages, maintaining a clear separation of HTML content and visual styling.

Selective display of page elements

Another aspect of document design is inclusion of elements that are relevant to different contexts and coding the document to allow elements to display or not, as appropriate. For example, although they are fundamental to any screen design, navigation links are not helpful when printed on paper. With a document coded for selective display, you can use css in the print style sheet to hide header or sidebar navigation links in printed versions of the page.

In print, seeing the full link URLs may be helpful when you want to return to the page or cite the article, and this is easy to accomplish with css styling for print. Print css style sheets often hide HTML elements like navigation links, graphic page headers, and footer information. This results in a much cleaner printed version of the page, but sometimes readers are confused when what comes out of their printers looks so different from what they see on the computer screen.

See the Recommended Reading section at the end of the chapter for the best reference books on HTML5, css3, and responsive web design techniques.

FIGURE 6.4

CSS gives you tremendous flexibility in page layout, but logical HTML source order—the sequence in which you list HTML markup and content—still matters, as there are times when CSS is not operating, and CSS is largely irrelevant to browsers for the blind.

RESPONSIVE DESIGN

On May 25, 2010, designer Ethan Marcotte published "Responsive Web Design" in the magazine *A List Apart,* and the article and subsequent book of the same title changed the web design industry. With the concept of responsive web design, Marcotte brought together the new capabilities of css3 media queries, the quickly expanding universe of mobile computing hardware, and the realization among everyone creating web sites that mobile users were fast becoming the majority of web users—and that mobile users did not want a stripped-down, dumbed-down experience from their phones and tablets. Responsive web design (rwd) offered both a technical approach to making web sites more usable across the huge current range of computing viewports and an overarching philosophy that melds well with "mobile-first" design and content strategies.

Responsive web designs are built around three concepts:

- A "fluid" or flexible page layout, structured on units proportional to the size of the browser window.
- Flexible, proportionately sized images and audiovisual media.
- css3 media queries that determine the width of the browser screen and respond accordingly.

BUILDING ON LIQUID LAYOUTS AND PROPORTIONAL MEASUREMENTS

Many web designers have long advocated for "liquid" layouts—that is, web page designs that expand or contract based on the width of the browser window instead of being set to a fixed width. Fixed-width layouts were the most popular form of web design until a few years ago, and they have many virtues, particularly in complex page layouts where the gestalt visual design relationships (see Chapter 8, Graphic Design) helped make sense of the information on the page. But fixed web page layouts have many disadvantages as well: big designs (for desktop screens) or small designs (for mobile screens) are fixed, and do not easily adapt to a web world where screen sizes range from wristwatches all the way up to giant conference room monitors. Responsive design offers both a means to adapt to screens of any size and a way to recover some of that design control that was lost when we moved away from fixed layouts.

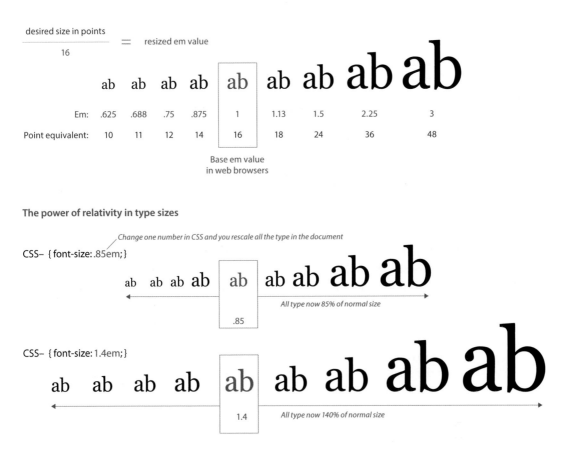

$$\frac{\text{desired size in points}}{16} = \text{resized em value}$$

Em:	.625	.688	.75	.875	1	1.13	1.5	2.25	3
Point equivalent:	10	11	12	14	16	18	24	36	48

Base em value
in web browsers

The power of relativity in type sizes

Change one number in CSS and you rescale all the type in the document

CSS– { font-size: .85em; }

.85   *All type now 85% of normal size*

CSS– { font-size: 1.4em; }

1.4   *All type now 140% of normal size*

Responsive layout designs begin with a liquid layout grid based on a proportional set of percentage measurements instead of fixed pixel widths. Columns, gutters, border areas, and other spaces (in multicolumn layouts) are specified as percentages of the width of the browser window, and the whole design expands or contracts as needed to "fluidly" adapt to the available space. More sophisticated fluid layout and css styling also makes the typography proportional to a single base type size based on em (or rem) units. However, as shown in Figure 6.3, purely proportional liquid layouts don't entirely solve the problem of many screen sizes, because on small screens a specification of width: 100% gives you absurdly squished layouts on small screens and absurdly stretched layouts on large screens.

Em-based typographic sizes (fig. 6.6) are important for two reasons:

- Users can easily and universally rescale your typography if the type is too large or small on their device—an important feature for accessibility for readers with vision impairments.

FIGURE 6.6
Em-based proportional type specifications allow page coders and designers to create complex typography systems that can be easily scaled up or down, depending on the screen size and resolution of the user's display.

FIGURE 6.7
(facing page)
Several properties
of CSS3 allow you
to rescale page
images that grow or
contract based on
the available screen
size, and never spill
beyond specified
boundaries. You
can also specify
several sizes of the
same image, so
that you don't send
huge desktop-sized
image to users with
smartphones.

• Relative type sizes can be easily scaled under css control, usually by using a font-size element on a global page scale, like the `<html>` or `<body>` tags. By scaling the value of em, you can enlarge or contract all of the typography on a page at once, a useful ability in responsive design, where you can quickly scale the typography of a page to comfortably match the overall screen size and pixel density.

Proportional images and media

Pictures and embedded videos can also be sized in proportional units, either in ems or in percentages of screen width. A handy bit of css code aids in this process. By specifying `max-width: 100%` in the css styling of a container for images or video, you can both proportionately size the container and assure that the image within the container always fills the container (100 percent of maximum width) but never exceeds the size of the container. Thus not only does page layout fluidly change to fill the browser window, but all images also fluidly change size as space dictates.

Given the wide range in screen sizes these days, how do you avoid the inefficiency of sending desktop-sized images to small-screen devices like phones and tablets? By using the HTML5 source set (`srcset`) attribute of image elements, or better yet, by using the new `<picture>` element, you can provide multiple sizes of an image, and the minimum width size appropriate for each image, so that phones get the small version and desktop screens get the large version.

So far so good, but pure liquid layouts don't fully solve the problem of many screen sizes, because a proportionately miniature layout on a smartphone isn't usable without a lot of zooming to enlarge the layout text to legible size.

Media queries

The media queries introduced with css3 form the crucial third piece of responsive design, as media queries allow you to custom-tailor your layout, typography, and embedded media to best match the available space within the user's browser window, or viewport.

Although they are primarily used to investigate the width of the web browser display width, media queries can deliver much more information on the nature of the user's display device, including:

• Orientation
• Aspect ratio
• Color or monochrome display
• Resolution in dpi
• Scan (for television monitors, progressive or interlaced scan)

```
img, embed, object, video {
    max-width: 100%;
}
```

← *CSS assures that images and other media objects fill their containers, but don't spill beyond the bounds of the container.*

Phone   Tablet   Laptop

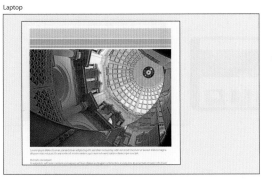

Liquid layouts that fill the available screen width

```
<img
    srcset="Tate-Britain-Lynch-S.jpg 310w, Tate-Britain-Lynch-M.jpg 620, Tate-Britain-Lynch-L.jpg 1000w"
    src="Tate-Britain-Lynch-M.jpg"
    alt="The HTML5 srcset tag allows the browser to pick the appropriate-sized image, to speed page loading."
/>
```

Small version for phones   Medium version for tablets   Large version for laptops & desktops

Tate-Britain-Lynch-S.jpg

Tate-Britain-Lynch-M.jpg

Tate-Britain-Lynch-L.jpg

Media queries offer a means to conditionally test various aspects of the user's display screen, then to selectively load style sheets that respond to those conditions and provide the most appropriate layout, typography, and graphics. These style sheets for specific ranges of screen sizes are normally triggered by css3 media queries designed to activate at certain minimum sizes, or "breakpoints." You can see the style breakpoints easily on a responsive site like the *Guardian* newspaper (theguardian.com) or the *Boston Globe* (bostonglobe.com). On your desktop or laptop computer, gradually reduce the width of your web browser window and you'll see the layout first squeeze to fit the frame, and then suddenly jump to a new layout style as you hit a "breakpoint" keyed to a minimum width of the browser window.

FIGURE 6.8

Responsive design isn't just a matter of adjusting the layout width: Notice how the top navigation bar evolves through the desktop and laptop versions, through a tablet-sized version, and finally to a trigram menu icon at the smallest smartphone width (rosenfeldmedia. com).

The following media query sets the width of the main content area (`container`) to 970 pixels when the viewport is greater than 1,200 pixels wide.

```
@media (min-width: 1200px) {
    .container {
    width: 970px;
    }
}
```

Responsive design isn't simply about stretching or miniaturizing a page layout—it's about delivering a unique layout of the content and navigation that is best optimized for a particular range of screen sizes. Most responsive designs use at least three different layout style sheets keyed to viewport width breakpoints for smartphones, tablets, and larger desktop or laptop screens. We've shown sample breakpoint measurements here (fig. 6.9), but there are no magic or universal formulas for positioning design breakpoints. The most important factor is how your layout, content, and functionality look across the likely range of devices your audience will use. Look at your unique case and needs, and set your design breakpoints accordingly.

Responsive designs often style the primary navigation links of a site differently in each responsive style sheet—for example, a compact pop-up menu for smartphones, a compact layout of links for tablet screens, and a more expansive and conventional layout for desktop screens.

Responsive designs rarely expand to fit the entire screen of large desktop monitors and laptops. An absurdly wide page design would ruin most layout schemes, and the long line lengths for text would make the content less legible.

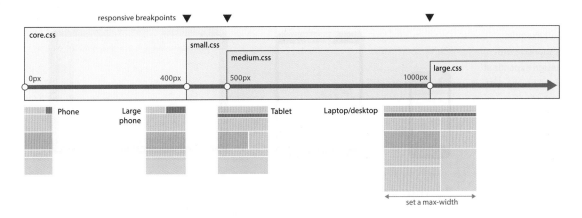

PAIRING RESPONSIVE DESIGN AND MOBILE-FIRST DESIGN

Responsive design starts from a "reference resolution" and uses media queries and customized style sheets to adapt to other screens sizes. Increasingly the reference resolution is the smartphone-sized mobile version of the site, which is then scaled up to adapt to larger viewports.

Designer Luke Wroblewski first advocated the "mobile-first" design philosophy as a response to the explosive growth of mobile computing and mobile web use. Mobile web users now outnumber desktop users, and it is no longer practical to design multiple versions of a web site to separately accommodate the needs of mobile and desktop users. Mobile users want a full web experience, not a stripped-down "mobile site" with just basic information.

RESOURCES FOR RESPONSIVE DESIGN TECHNIQUES

The coding details of responsive design are beyond the scope of this book, but we'd recommend the following references if you want to learn responsive techniques for HTML5 and CSS3. Matthew MacDonald's *HTML5: The Missing Manual* is a great place to start for a solid grounding in basic responsive design. Ethan Marcotte's *Responsive Web Design* is a more advanced look at responsive coding techniques, but Marcotte is a great explainer of the logic and philosophy behind RWD, and his book is a must-read even if you don't plan to code your own responsive pages or themes. Stephen Hay's *Responsive Design Workflow* is a great resource for examples of how to integrate responsive design philosophies and techniques into a comprehensive planning, design, and development project. See the Recommended Reading section at the end of this chapter for details.

FIGURE 6.9
Responsive breakpoints for a design that covers the range from smartphones up to desktop screens. At each minimum screen width or "breakpoint," the layout, typography, and often the basic site navigation adjust to optimize for that range of screen sizes. Once the screen width exceeds a minimum width of 1,000 pixels, the design sets a maximum width to keep the layout coherent and the text line lengths reasonably short for legibility.

FIGURE 6.10
This example
responsive site
design expands at
three breakpoints,
and sets a maximum
width of 960 pixels
for laptop and
desktop displays.

max-width: 960px

Prioritized content and functionality

Given the severe layout and bandwidth constraints of smartphones, a mobile-first design approach forces a development team to look hard at the central priorities and needs of all users, not just mobile users, and to create sites that have stripped away a lot of the graphic and textual bloat that adheres to designs that begin with a large desktop layout. On mobile screens there simply isn't room for the nice-to-have stuff—only the must-have stuff will fit.

Rather than defaulting to a desktop version of the site and then later trying to cram all the content and navigation into a small format, the mobile-first approach builds up from the most critical content and functionality and gradually adds secondary material and features as space allows. This focused mobile-first approach comports well with responsive design techniques, and agile project management that emphasizes a constant focus on high-priority goals and features.

In a common mobile layout, the material in sidebar columns tends to be pushed down below the "main" content column, resulting in a tall stack designed to fit within the tight confines of a mobile screen. However, css layouts give you complete control over where various semantic HTML containers (`<header>`, `<main>`, `<nav>`, `<article>`, `<section>`, `<aside>`) or other `<div>` containers are placed on the screen for mobile breakpoints. Carefully consider the priorities for your various page elements before burying them three screens deep in your mobile layout. For example, the content or navigation material that was at the top of your sidebar column may also belong near the top of your smartphone layout. Make your layout decisions based on content and navigation priority, not on simple layout formulas.

Universal access

Perhaps the most important benefit of a mobile-first design approach—if done properly—is that even users with older browser versions, browsers with JavaScript absent or turned off, and screen reading browsers for people with vision impairments all get a basically functional single-column site with all content and links in place. Mobile-first is an elegant example of the progressive enhancement philosophy, under which

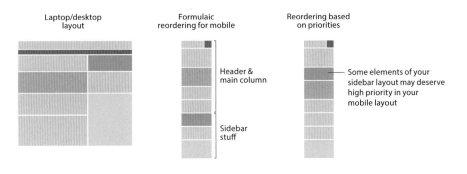

Laptop/desktop layout

Formulaic reordering for mobile

Header & main column

Sidebar stuff

Reordering based on priorities

Some elements of your sidebar layout may deserve high priority in your mobile layout

FIGURE 6.11

Avoid formulaic approaches to mobile design, where everything in the sidebar column is simply moved below the main content column. Sometimes the content at the top of the sidebar deserves special handling to keep it as visible as possible.

no user—even one with an older or otherwise limited browser—is unable to access the core content and features of the site. Users with more up-to-date browsers, better hardware, and larger screens get an enhanced and richer experience, but no one is locked out.

STARTING FROM CONTENT AND FUNCTIONALITY

As you might guess in looking at sophisticated, highly responsive sites, doing design work for such plastic and changeable responsive designs in static Photoshop comps can limit the design thinking needed to communicate the use experience across smartphones, tablets, and larger screens. The older methods of producing pixel-perfect Photoshop files that show all the visual details of template and content pages tend to push the development process in exactly the wrong direction: toward the old desktop-first, large-screen-first ways of thinking, with little feel for the subtle but important effects of interactivity, or the different possibilities of each responsive design breakpoint and layout.

Our advice is to make your "short list" of must-have items on the most minimal of mobile environments, and build up from there. On paper or whiteboards sketch out the core functional and content areas of your major screens, and translate those rough sketches into simple block diagrams that your page coders can use to create real responsive HTML and CSS mock-ups for study. While the responsive designs are built, your graphic designers can begin creating color palettes, logo graphics, example photos or artwork, typography sample sheets for each screen size, and perhaps style tiles to gradually introduce more sophisticated visuals after the functionality and content strategy of your interactive mock-ups have matured. At every step along the way your graphic designers should be involved as the designs mature, guiding their graphic and typographic evolution and gradually adding visual details that progressively enhance the mock-ups and early functional versions. Form follows function in mobile-first, browser-first development, and Photoshop becomes the last tool you use, not the first.

The point is to do as much design as possible in HTML and CSS, building from that foundational "mobile-first" simplicity and progressively enhancing the design as space and browser capabilities expand. Only when all important strategic, content, functional, and code decisions have been made should you invest in detailed Photoshop work, and then only to provide final polish to the finished graphic elements.

USING BEST PRACTICES

Responsive web design is far more than just adding media queries and a few extra style sheets to your page code; it's a new design philosophy that provides a richer, more accessible experience to all of your audience, on whatever device each may be using when she visits your site.

- Use valid, widely supported HTML5 and CSS3 to build your site.
- Take advantage of the new semantics of HTML5 and ARIA to add meaning, accessibility, and search visibility to your content.
- Use proportional measures like percentages and ems throughout your layout and typography.
- Calculate your responsive breakpoints and use of media queries based on your audience's needs, its likely range of viewing devices, and the nature of your particular content.
- Use a mobile-first approach that builds upon a minimal and foundational experience.
- Progressively enhance the mobile-first experience as screen space, bandwidth, and browser capabilities allow.
- Use a browser-first development cycle, and stay away from elaborate, desktop-oriented Photoshop comps and static graphic design. Fancy static design mock-ups are an old way of thinking, completely out of step with modern web realities.

PAGE STRUCTURE COMPONENTS

Web "sites" are complete abstractions—they don't exist, except in our heads. When we identify a site as such, what we're really describing is a collection of individual linked pages that share a common graphic and navigational look and feel. Creating the illusion of continuity across a cohesive "site" are the design features that pages share, such as their CSS and page graphics. Individual HTML pages, including how they are designed and linked, constitute the atomic unit of web sites, and everything that characterizes site structure should appear in the page templates.

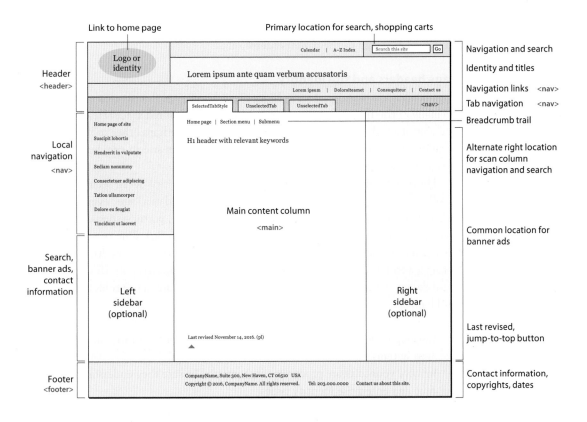

Link to home page

Primary location for search, shopping carts

Header
<header>

Local
navigation
<nav>

Search,
banner ads,
contact
information

Footer
<footer>

Logo or
identity

Calendar | A–Z Index | Search this site | Go

Lorem ipsum ante quam verbum accusatoris

Lorem ipsum | Dolorsiteamet | Consuquiteur | Contact us

SelectedTabStyle | UnselectedTab | UnselectedTab | <nav>

Home page of site
Suscipit lobortis
Hendrerit in vulputate
Sediam nonummy
Consectetuer adipiscing
Tation ullamcorper
Dolore eu feugiat
Tincidunt ut laoreet

Home page | Section menu | Submenu

H1 header with relevant keywords

Main content column
<main>

Left
sidebar
(optional)

Right
sidebar
(optional)

Last revised November 14, 2016. (pl)

CompanyName, Suite 300, New Haven, CT 06510 USA
Copyright © 2016, CompanyName. All rights reserved. Tel: 203.000.0000 Contact us about this site.

Navigation and search

Identity and titles

Navigation links   <nav>

Tab navigation   <nav>

Breadcrumb trail

Alternate right location
for scan column
navigation and search

Common location for
banner ads

Last revised,
jump-to-top button

Contact information,
copyrights, dates

STRUCTURING A PAGE

As the web has matured over the past decade, the structure of web pages in text-driven information sites has become more uniform and predictable. Although not all web pages share the exact layout and features described here, most web pages incorporate some or all of these basic components, in page locations that have become familiar to web users (fig. 6.12). Recent responsive design systems have tended to simplify header and navigational frameworks, particularly for smaller mobile screens.

If you work within a larger organization, always make your relationship to the larger enterprise a clear and meaningful part of your site design. If your institution has an identity program, use it. Adopting the design standards of the larger enterprise can save you a lot of time and money. Institutions notorious for poor governance—universities, government agencies, large nonprofit agencies—also often have chaotic web sites. Large companies sometimes have the same problems, but the standards and norms of corporate identity programs are well established in the business world, and most corporate sites start with the expectation that everyone will share a com-

FIGURE 6.12
Common elements of internal or informational web pages, along with typical HTML5 semantics and ARIA roles. It is rare for a web template to include every one of these elements. Most web pages have a simpler structure, with fewer header elements, and only a single sidebar column.

mon look and feel and user interface and that each discrete corporate site will project a clear relationship to the parent enterprise.

Page headers and site identity

Page headers are like miniature versions of the home page that sit atop each page and do many of the things that home pages do, but in a limited space. Headers provide site identity and global navigation, with search and perhaps other tools. The exact location and arrangement of the components vary from site to site, but the overall design pattern has become fairly consistent.

Headers are the most visible component of site identity. What seems real is real: a collection of pages that share headers will be perceived as a "site" even if the pages originate from various technical sources (blog software, portal systems, SharePoint, web applications, content management systems, and so on). One reason that complex enterprise sites get cluttered and confusing for users is that multiple enterprise software vendors are involved, with each vendor reluctant to do much to conform to local design standards. This is as much a software procurement problem as a design problem:

- Develop consistent enterprise identity standards for your internal and external web systems
- Involve your software procurement teams and be sure they understand the interface and enterprise identity issues
- Insist that each software vendor complies with local identity, accessibility, graphics, and user interface interoperability standards so that its products fit well within your general enterprise web experience

You'll be pleasantly surprised to see how often "our software doesn't really allow customization" becomes "of course we can do that" if you negotiate compliance with your enterprise design standards before signing a software vendor contract.

Home link

Placing your organization or site logo in the upper left corner of the page—and linking that logo to the home page—is probably the most widely used design convention on the web, and one you should always use, except in special instances like complex forms, "shopping cart" checkout processes, and other instances where you want the user's intention fully engaged on the process. If you are not using a logo or graphic in your header, at least put a "home" link near the upper left corner of the page, where 99.9 percent of users will expect to find it.

Global navigation

Headers are the most frequent location for global navigation links that span the site. The ideal arrangement is to use an HTML list of links, styled with CSS appropriately for each viewport size in your responsive page designs. This gives you:

- **Usability:** Global links are where users most expect to see them.
- **Semantic logic:** The collection of global links should be marked up as a list, because, well, it is a list.
- **Accessibility:** The list format of links appears early in the code listing, and should be contained within an HTML5 `<nav>` element.
- **Search visibility:** A collection of your major navigation keywords, linked and at the top of the code listing, is ideal for search engine optimization.

Tabs are another widely used, easily understood convention for global navigation, particularly in the desktop-sized versions of page templates. The way to implement tab-based navigation links for larger screen designs is to style an ordinary HTML list with CSS treatment to form the "tab" graphic look around each link. Be sure you get the tab graphic details right: the selected tab should be graphically unambiguous, and the remaining tabs should clearly be behind the selected tab. This type of "you are here" marker is essential in orienting users within the site. Tabs can also be used to implement a two-tiered navigation scheme, in which a secondary horizontal list of links appears under the selected tab, again as a simple HTML list with CSS styling, to keep things semantic, accessible, and search visible (see fig. 6.2).

In designs for smaller mobile viewports the common practice is to collapse the main navigation list normally within the page header into a smaller "navicon" or "trigram" symbol to save space (HTML character ☰). The trigram became a mainstream web navigation convention when high-profile responsive sites like Starbucks and Twitter Bootstrap adopted the symbol for navigation in their smaller viewport designs. The trigram is now so common that responsive sites like the *Guardian* and *Slate* magazine use the trigram for navigation even on their large "desktop" layouts.

Breadcrumb navigation

Breadcrumb navigation is a widely used, easily understood navigation device that is particularly useful in large sites with deep levels of content organization (see Chapter 7, Interface Design). Breadcrumbs integrated into the header are best at the top of the header, as in the Library of Congress site (see the black header bar, fig. 6.13). Another popular location for breadcrumb navigation is below the header navigation, just above the main page `<h1>` title and content.

FIGURE 6.13
The Library of Congress makes excellent use of "breadcrumb trail" navigation (see the black line in the header) to make navigating the large, multilevel, content-rich site easier and more intuitive.

Search

All sites with more than a few dozen pages should offer local site search. The upper right area of the header is the standard location for search boxes (fig. 6.13). Make sure your search box is not too small to accommodate long queries. One study showed that a box twenty-seven characters long would accommodate 90 percent of search queries. Amazon's search box holds more than twice that (fifty-seven characters).

Shopping cart

Long ago, Amazon put its "cart" link in the upper right of the header, and that's where virtually all other shopping sites put it now, too. Don't buck the trend; it's one of the most firmly rooted interface conventions on the web.

Advertising

Ad-supported sites often reserve a large area above other header components for banner advertising, and research shows that users commonly expect to see banner ads in this area of the page. This layout convention has important implications, even if your site does not use banner ads, because of the widely observed phenomenon of "banner blindness." Readers commonly ignore areas of the screen that usually contain advertising, especially if the graphic content looks like a banner ad. Be sure your headers and other page graphics don't use the heavily boxed and graphically loud visual vocabulary of most banner ads, or your readers may ignore important elements of your user interface.

Sidebar column

Subdividing the page field into functional regions is a fundamental characteristic of modern graphic design. Early in the web's history, designers began using narrow sidebar columns at the edge of the page to organize navigation links and other peripheral page elements, much as scan columns have been used in print publications for a century or more. Research on web user expectations now supports the common practice of locating navigational links—particularly section or navigation—in the left column. The right sidebar is often used for advertising, so be sure that any graphic content you place there doesn't look like an ad or your readers may ignore the area.

Sidebars are also useful as locations for web search boxes, mailing address and contact information, and other more minor but necessary page elements. Research shows that the left scan column under the local navigation links is the second place most users will look for search features, after they look in the right header area.

Basic "real-world" information about who the company responsible for the site is, where the company is, and how to contact the company is often hard to find on otherwise well-designed sites. If you sell a product or service, don't hide from your customers. Display your contact information in a prominent location, such as the scan column, on every page.

Main content
Web content is so multifaceted that few general rules apply, but the following common practices make content areas easier to use:

- **Page content titles:** Don't bury the lead. Every page needs a visible name near the top, tagged as an `<h1>` heading. For all kinds of logical, editorial, accessibility, search visibility, and commonsense reasons, use an `<h1>` heading at the top of the page to let users know what the page is about. Make sure your important content keywords are in that first `<h1>`.
- **Breadcrumb navigation:** The very top of the content area is a common location for breadcrumb navigation.

- **Jump-to-top links:** Jump links are a nice refinement for long pages. These links don't need to be elaborate—just a top-of-page link will do, but a small up-arrow icon offers good reinforcement.
- **Rules:** These horizontal graphic elements can easily be overused and lead to a cluttered design. Use css to keep page rules as unobtrusive as possible, very thin, in a color much lighter than the surrounding typography. A better idea: skip rules and use a little white space to create visual content groupings or separations.
- **Paging navigation:** In multipage sequences it is convenient to have simple text links at the top and bottom of the page to move the reader to the previous or next pages in the sequence. In longer sequences it is helpful to provide information describing where they are in the series, e.g., "Page 5 of 8."
- **Dates:** Publication and update dates are often essential for assessing the currency and relevance of content. In news and magazine sites the publication date should appear at the top of the page. Other sites should display a last-updated date at the bottom of the content area (see fig. 6.12).

Footer

Page footers are mostly about housekeeping and legal matters, although they can sometimes be useful for nonessential navigation as well. These elements need to be on the page, but place them somewhere out of the way:

- Page author or, in large enterprise sites, responsible party
- Copyright statement
- Contact details, especially email
- Links to related sites or to the larger enterprise
- Redundant navigation links, for long pages or as additional navigation.

Page footers can also be used for repeating global site links. An expanded footer composed of text links adds hardly any size to the page but offers an unobtrusive place to list a carefully chosen set of links. IBM's well-designed navigation footer is almost like a site map on the bottom of every page.

FIGURE 6.14

Expanded navigation footers are an excellent way to provide a site-wide set of navigation links—essentially a map of the site at the bottom of every page—without having to take up a lot of room at the tops of pages. Here the IBM site presents six navigation categories as styled HTML lists, which is the correct semantic HTML markup for sets of related links, at very little cost in page loading speed. This is ideal for user navigation, and for search engine optimization keywords.

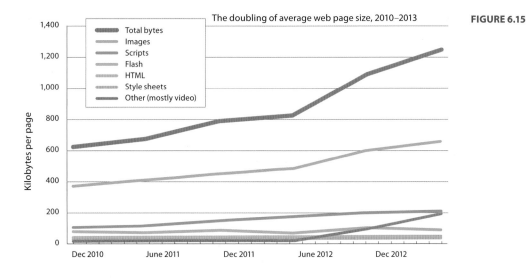

FIGURE 6.15

The doubling of average web page size, 2010–2013

Legend:
- Total bytes
- Images
- Scripts
- Flash
- HTML
- Style sheets
- Other (mostly video)

Y-axis: Kilobytes per page (0, 200, 400, 600, 800, 1,000, 1,200, 1,400)

X-axis: Dec 2010, June 2011, Dec 2011, June 2012, Dec 2012

OPTIMIZING PAGES FOR FAST DELIVERY

From about 2007 to 2010, web designers enjoyed a period during which web standards were finally coming together across the range of web browsers, the desktop view was the only consideration, and most of our audiences had enough bandwidth at home and work to enjoy web pages with lots of pictures and even video. While the picture for desktop users continues to improve every year, the rise of the mobile web has made bandwidth and constraints on web media an issue once more. Although mobile networks and wireless speeds continue to improve, mobile web computing is still quite constrained by relatively slow page load speeds. The slowness of the web on mobile devices led to the explosion of ios and Android apps to improve performance of networked services on mobile devices.

While the web publishing and design industries have long since begun to address the needs of mobile users, our addiction to big images, huge css and JavaScript payloads, and audiovisual media has continued to bloat the overall size of web pages. The average size of web pages and their associated media and css files more than doubled between 2010 and mid-2013 (fig. 6.15).

As mobile performance challenges have become more widely understood, the rate of increase in web page size has slowed, but overall web performance continues to be a balancing act between our appetite for media-rich content and our love of fast web pages. Page performance has direct and important consequences, particularly for online merchants. Walmart found that conversion rate (the rate at which shoppers become active buyers) plunges if a page takes more than four seconds to load (fig. 6.16).

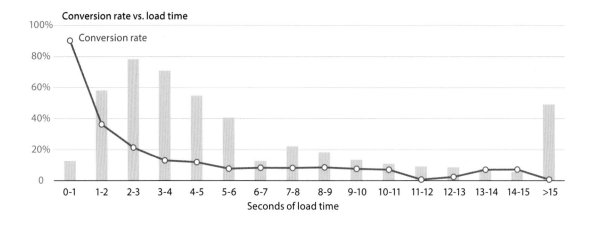

Conversion rate vs. load time

Conversion rate

Seconds of load time

FIGURE 6.16

In e-commerce, page loading speed is crucial.

This doesn't mean that you must remove all of the media from your pages, but it does mean that developers and designers need to squeeze every byte out of the overhead of pages, particularly those heavily used by mobile audiences. Techniques such as using the HTML5 srcset attribute or the <picture> element to specify several sizes of an image (think small, medium, large) to deliver the right-sized image depending on screen size, squeezing the compression rate of every image, using the GIF format for small geometric graphics and icons that would be larger in JPEG format, avoiding the use of many twenty-four-bit transparent-background PNG images, using SVG graphics wherever possible, and using compact symbol fonts to efficiently deliver icon graphics are all commonly employed to squeeze unnecessary bits out of web graphics. See Chapter 11, Images, for more information on web graphics.

DESIGNING AROUND "THE FOLD"

In 1994, the earliest days of the World Wide Web, human interface researcher Jakob Nielsen found that users of the first web browsers and web sites seemed reluctant to scroll to see portions of web pages hidden below the bottom of their display screens, and noted the importance of positioning material at the top of web pages. Three years later Nielsen retracted his finding that "web users don't scroll," because his later research showed that as users adapted to the new web medium they did indeed scroll to see content on the lower parts of web pages. Unfortunately, the "users don't scroll" dictum proved more memorable than the later retraction, and this mistaken meme has persisted in web design.

The roughly 115 square inches at the top of a home page on a standard desktop monitor constitute the most visible area of the web site. Most desktop or laptop users will be looking at your site on 19–22-inch monitors or on laptop screens, and the top 8–9 vertical inches (about 900–1,000 pixels) are all that is sure to be visible on av-

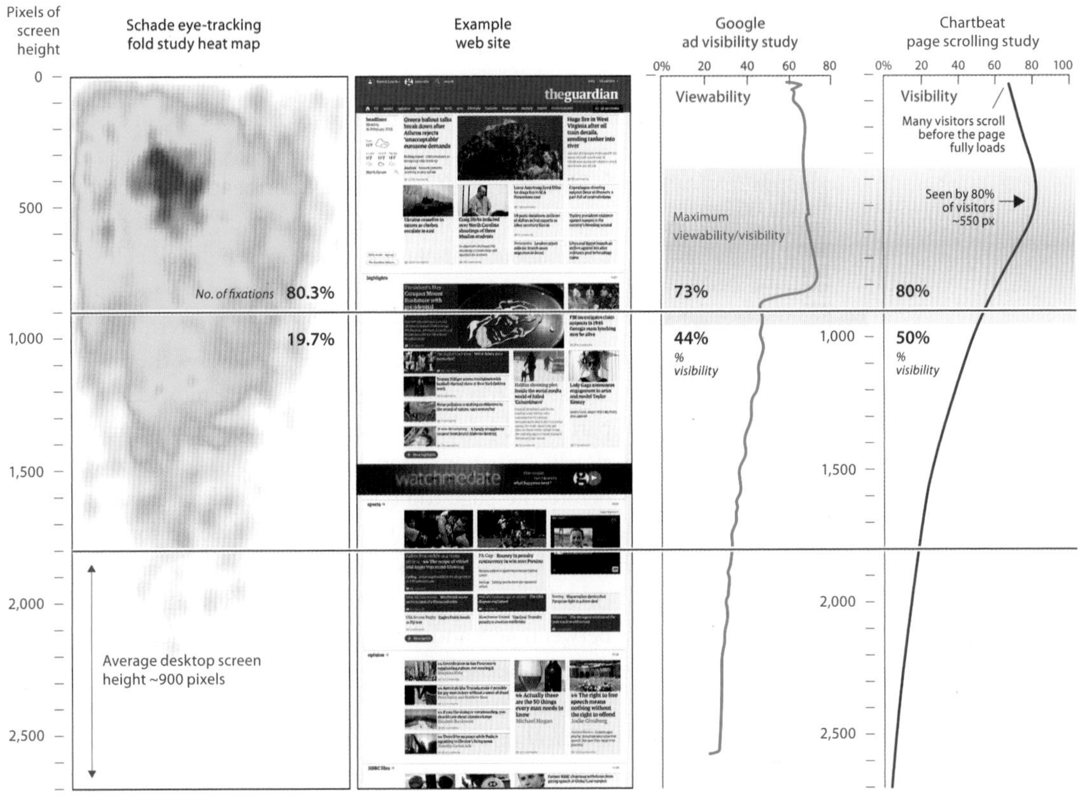
Pixels of screen height
Schade eye-tracking fold study heat map
Example web site
Google ad visibility study
Chartbeat page scrolling study
0
500
1,000
1,500
2,000
2,500
0%
20
40
60
80
100
Viewability
Visibility
Many visitors scroll before the page fully loads
Seen by 80% of visitors ~550 px
Maximum viewability/visibility
No. of fixations 80.3%
19.7%
73%
80%
44% % visibility
50% % visibility
Average desktop screen height ~900 pixels

erage screens, perhaps less on the short, wide screens of most laptops. The measures for various mobile screens differ, of course, but the basic effect is the same: the top part of the typical web page is visible, and the rest of the page is not visible unless the user scrolls. The "above the fold" metaphor refers to the middle fold in classic folded broadsheet newspapers like the *New York Times* or *Wall Street Journal*. Front-page stories "above the fold" are the most important and visible in both newspapers and web pages.

Although web users do scroll when they use the web, a number of studies have shown that there is a distinct fall-off of views in the portion of web pages that users must actively scroll to see. Eye-tracking studies done by the Nielsen-Norman Group have shown that the tops of web pages get about 80 percent of the attention (strictly speaking, eye-tracking gaze fixations on the page), with only 20 percent of fixations left for page areas "below the fold" that users must scroll to reveal. Google conducted a study on the relative visibility of web advertisements on various page locations and also found that visibility drops off sharply at the fold, as did a similar study

FIGURE 6.17
Reader behavior was analyzed with eye-tracking and other research methods to determine how often readers see content above, near, or below the bottom of display screens. It showed that content that users must scroll to reveal is much less seen and read than content "above the fold."

FIGURE 6.18

by Chartbeat (fig. 6.17). The Google study also showed a drop-off in visibility "below the fold" on smaller mobile devices, but the effect was less pronounced, especially on smaller phone screens on which users are accustomed to scrolling to see page content.

However, the Google and Chartbeat studies both showed that while attention and visibility do indeed drop at "the fold," about half of users do see material well below the fold line (roughly 900 pixels down the page). These studies also noted something that sounds a bit counterintuitive if you assume that the tops of pages are always the most visible areas: the top of the page was not the most reliably visible part of the page. Because pages are complex and often load slowly, impatient users often begin to scroll down a page before the page top has fully rendered. Users are also well aware that the page top is commonly used for advertising, and is therefore a less rewarding place to look for information. User attention and advertising visibility seem to peak between 500 and 800 pixels down the page, quite near the roughly 900-pixel fold area on most desktop and laptop screens. Chartbeat also noticed that web readers who chose to scroll down the page often spent more time there than in the "above the fold" region, suggesting that when readers found the page content compelling, they would continue to read down the page. Taken together, these studies suggest that "the fold" is not a hard-and-fast line between full attention and no attention, that the bottom visible areas above the fold get great attention, and that the dreaded "fold line" may be less important in design than previously thought. Our own conclusions are that the fold area remains a significant transition zone, and that critical material on the page is best placed no lower than 600–700 pixels down the page to guarantee visibility on desktops and laptops.

DESIGNING SCREENS OF INFORMATION

Most web page designs can be divided vertically into zones with different functions and varying levels of graphics and text complexity. As vertical scrolling progressively reveals the page, new content appears and the upper content disappears. A new graphic context is established each time the

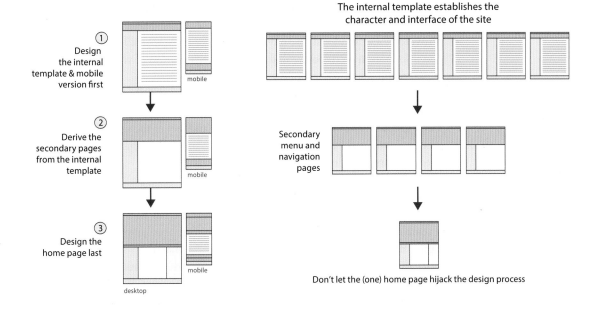

① Design the internal template & mobile version first

mobile

The internal template establishes the character and interface of the site

② Derive the secondary pages from the internal template

mobile

Secondary menu and navigation pages

③ Design the home page last

mobile

desktop

Don't let the (one) home page hijack the design process

reader scrolls down the page. Web page layouts should thus be judged not by viewing the whole page as a unit but by dividing the page into visual and functional zones and judging the suitability of each screen of information. Notice the vertical structure of the *Guardian* home page. The top screen of information is much denser with links because it is the only area all users will see (fig. 6.18).

Obviously, in responsive web design what constitutes a "screen's worth" of information will vary considerably, depending on the width of the screen in use and the CSS "breakpoint" in use. Frequently assessing the effect of various screen sizes on your evolving responsive design is yet another great reason to do as much of your design work in "live" HTML and CSS within the browser window.

PAGE TEMPLATES

Always start your page template or CMS theming work with an internal page, because the internal page template will dominate the site. The home page is important, but the home page is inherently singular and has a unique role to play. Your internal page template will be used hundreds or thousands of times across larger sites, and the navigation, user interface, mobile responsiveness, and graphic design of the internal pages will dominate the user's experience of your site. Get your internal page design and navigation right, and then derive your home and secondary page designs from the internal page template (fig. 6.19).

FIGURE 6.19
Web site production projects often become obsessed with the design and character of the site home page. The basic internal page templates will structure the vast majority of pages in your web site. We recommend concentrating on those designs first before tackling the interesting—but singular—design challenges of the home page.

Internal page templates must establish these important functions:

- **Provide global and local site navigation:** make them logically consistent with the information architecture and structural organization of your site, in both desktop and responsive mobile variants for small screens.
- **Establish a regular, repeating design framework:** this will organize content consistently throughout the site.
- **Set a graphic tone:** this establishes the look and feel of the site, ideally with a system dominated by consistent visual elements, but with enough flexibility to create distinct regions within a large site.

CREATING TEMPLATES FOR INTERNAL PAGES

In larger sites containing a variety of content, your internal page template may be a set of templates that vary in details, such as the number of columns, to accommodate the range of content and user interface needs (see fig. 6.19).

Sites that incorporate web applications, blog or wiki formats, or complex forms may need a simplified template variation that strips away some of the usual site navigation elements. Applications, complex forms, large data tables, and many kinds of highly graphic content (artwork, engineering drawings, repair manual graphics, and so on) usually require as much screen space as possible.

Secondary page templates

Most sites are organized in a multitiered hierarchy, with vertical dimensions (home, secondary pages, internal pages) and a horizontal spread of distinct content regions that graphically and organizationally help the reader navigate. Secondary page templates should be closely related to the internal page template but must accommodate these additional functions:

- Establish a tiered hierarchy of header labels that sets the relationship of the secondary page to the home page and larger enterprise site, as well as to the internal pages.
- Provide a distinct look that identifies the secondary page as a special "sub–home page" and establishes a clear content theme.

Secondary page templates help create a concrete sense of the vertical dimension of sites and may perform varied functions in the tiers between the home page and the internal content pages, such as special-purpose "landing pages" tied to advertising campaigns or publicity, where you want the readers to arrive at your site and immediately receive information relevant to the advertising that brought them to your site.

FIGURE 6.20
The home page (left) and a special program "landing page" (right, "Wild Ducks") that can act as an alternate major entry point for the IBM site, for visitors brought to the site by advertising or other links to the Wild Ducks program.

Navigation and submenu pages

Complex, multitiered sites usually need submenu pages to provide an organizing and navigational focal point for major subsections or regions of the site. These submenu pages are effectively the home page for that block of content.

Alternate "front doors" or "landing pages"

Many marketing or communications campaigns that point to web sites require a focused, immediately recognizable page to bring in visitors. These alternate entry points must bear a clear graphic and topical relation to the marketing graphics, featured product, or communications theme, but because they also function as alternate home pages, they should orient visitors to the larger site navigation as well.

Department or program home pages

Large corporate or enterprise sites require secondary or even tertiary levels of pages that act as home pages for the local department or program. In a multitiered site your template system should establish a clear hierarchy of page header labeling and titles so that readers can see the relation of a department page to the larger enterprise.

DESIGNING A TEMPLATE FOR THE HOME PAGE

Designing an effective home page can seem daunting, but if you've already thought through the fundamentals of your site navigation and have done the hard work of creating internal and secondary page templates, you have a great head start. Designing the home page layout last allows you to acknowledge the unique introductory role of the home page but places the design firmly within the larger navigational interface and graphic context of the site.

Home pages have four primary elements:

- Identity
- Navigation
- Timeliness, or content focus
- Tools (search, directories)

Good home page designs always blend these four factors. How you blend them depends on the overall goals of your site, but most good home pages do not balance all four elements equally. Home pages often have a distinctive theme in which one factor dominates. Amazon's home page is all about navigation to products. Yale University's home page projects identity. The Atlantic site is dominated by timeliness and content. Google's famously lean home page is all about tools. An effective home page can't be all things to all people. Decide what your priorities are, and build a home page that gives the user a clear sense of theme and priority.

Drop-down menus

When there is a lot of content or many merchandise categories to fit on the home page, pull-down menus can provide many choices within a small screen area. The space savings, though great, come at a cost to visibility and usability, because most choices are hidden until the user activates the menu. Careful navigation design can yield an effective hybrid strategy, in which you don't rely on drop-down menus but rather provide them as enhanced functionality for users who choose to explore them.

Drop-down menus can be implemented well using HTML, CSS, and/or a bit of JavaScript. Although a standards-based HTML/CSS drop-down menu will be somewhat accessible and visible to search engines, the full menu functionality that users expect from their Mac and Windows interfaces is not possible to reproduce using web tools alone. Web drop-downs tend to be slower and less forgiving of errors in mouse positioning than menus on Mac or Windows operating systems. Older users and users with less hand-eye coordination often dislike drop-down menus, especially if they are implemented with small font sizes and small cursor target areas.

Topical navigation versus path-splitting

Users usually arrive at a home page with specific topical or product interests or functional goals in mind. Most home pages thus feature prominent navigation lists or visual menus of topics, products, and services. Sometimes, however, users identify their interests by their identity or role. For example, it's common for university sites to "split paths" on the home page into prospective students, current students, par-

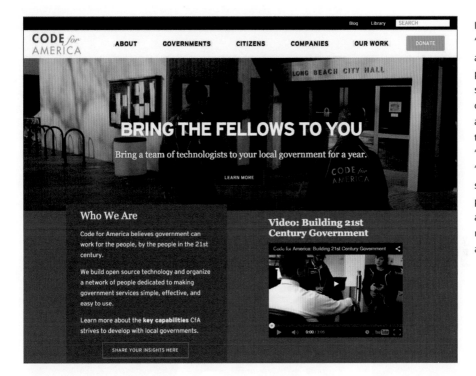

FIGURE 6.21
"Path-splitting" is a common home page navigation strategy for sites that cater to different audiences. Once the "Governments," "Companies," or "Citizens" have selected a navigation path, then other audience-specific navigation choices appear.

ents, faculty, and other groups, and then to present various submenu pages oriented to the interests and needs of each group (fig. 6.21).

RECOMMENDED READING

Cederholm, D. *CSS3 for Web Designers.* New York: A Book Apart, 2010.

Hay, S. *Responsive Web Design Workflow.* Berkeley, CA: New Riders, 2013.

Keith, J. *HTML5 for Web Designers.* New York: A Book Apart, 2010.

MacDonald, M. *HTML5: The Missing Manual,* 2nd ed. Sebastopol, CA: O'Reilly, 2013.

McFarland, D. *CSS3: The Missing Manual,* 3rd ed. Sebastopol, CA: O'Reilly, 2013.

Marcotte, E. *Responsive Web Design,* 2nd ed. New York: A Book Apart, 2014.

Wroblewski, L. *Mobile-First.* New York: A Book Apart, 2011.

Every moment we're in a web site, we're keeping a mental running tally: "Do these guys know what they're doing?"
– Steve Krug

Ask yourself: Are users trying to accomplish something when they visit my site? If the answer is "yes," then you should be concerned about usability.
– Jakob Nielsen

CHAPTER 7

Interface Design

The technology framework underlying today's web provides a platform for far more than basic link- and form-based interaction. Much of the complex behavior and functionality that has historically been the domain of native applications, including word processor, image, and video editing software, can now take place in the browser. With the added capacity for complex interfaces comes another crucial skill for web development teams—interaction design. Many web teams include visual designers and information architects but lack experience in designing user interfaces. And quality user experiences depend largely on how easy a site is to get around in while staying oriented, and how easy the features of the site are to use.

Since objects cannot speak for themselves, they need to be made to look like what they are and what they do.

—Ralph Caplan, *By Design*

DESIGNING FOR THE MEDIUM

Readers need a sense of context of their place within an organization of information. In paper documents this sense of where you are is a mixture of graphic and editorial organizational cues supplied by the design of the book, the organization of the text, and the physical sensation of the book as an object. Electronic documents provide none of the physical cues we take for granted in assessing information. When we see a web hypertext link on a page, we have few clues to where we will be led, how much information is at the other end of the link, and exactly how the linked information relates to the current page.

Even the view of individual web pages is restricted for many users. Most web pages don't fit completely on a standard office display monitor; there is usually a lower part of the page that the user cannot see. Users of small-screen mobile devices have an even more limited viewport, and a big-picture view of a web page is impossible for screen reader users, who access pages an element at a time. Web pages need to give the user explicit cues to the context and organization of the site because only a small segment of any site is available at one time.

NO DEAD-END PAGES

Web pages often appear with no preamble: users can make or follow links directly to subsection pages buried deep in the hierarchy of web sites. They may never see your home page or other introductory site information. If your subsection pages do not contain links to the home page or to local menu pages, the user will be locked out from the rest of the web site (fig. 7.1).

FIGURE 7.1

Users can enter a
site at any page and
need instant cues to
site identity and "you
are here" markers.

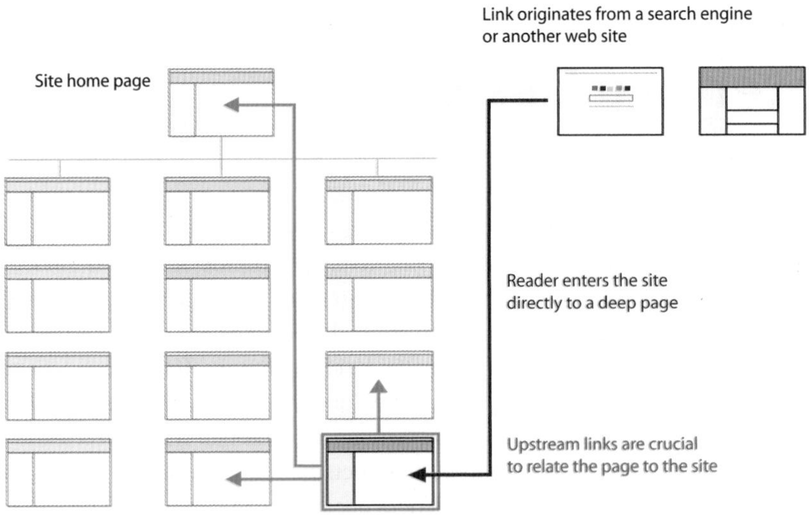

Site home page

Link originates from a search engine
or another web site

Reader enters the site
directly to a deep page

Upstream links are crucial
to relate the page to the site

Make sure all pages in your site have at minimum a link back to the home page
or, better yet, a home page link along with links to other main sections of the site.
In addition to user interface considerations, these links are crucial for search engine
visibility.

DIRECT ACCESS

Users want to get information in the fewest possible steps. This means that you must
design an efficient hierarchy of information to minimize steps through menu pages.
Studies have shown that users prefer menus that present at least five to seven links
and that they prefer a few pages of carefully organized choices over many layers of
oversimplified menu pages. Design your site hierarchy so that real content is just a
click or two away from the main menu pages of your site.

SIMPLICITY AND CONSISTENCY

Users are not impressed with complexity that seems gratuitous, especially those users who may be depending on the site for timely and accurate information. Your
interface metaphors should be simple, familiar, and logical—if you need a metaphor
for collections of information, choose a familiar genre, such as file folders. Unusual
or peculiar "creative" navigation and home page metaphors always fail because they
impose an unfamiliar, unpredictable interface burden on the user. Baffle users with
a weird home page, and they will quickly hit the "back" button and move on to the
next item on the Google results page, and you'll have lost a potential reader or customer. Let your content shine, and let the interface recede.

FIGURE 7.2

Lapham's Quarterly magazine uses classical aesthetics (centered designs, low-key but sophisticated typography, an unobtrusive interface) to produce a quiet but highly functional site identity and main header navigation. Ironically, the conservative typography and images are mounted in a highly responsive mobile-first design framework that was launched in late 2014.

The best information designs are never noticed. Once you know where the standard links are on the page header graphics, the interface becomes almost invisible. Navigation is easy and never competes with content for your attention (fig. 7.2).

For maximum functionality and legibility, your page and site design should be built on a consistent pattern of modular units that all share the same basic layout grids, graphic themes, editorial conventions, and organization hierarchies. The goal is to be consistent and predictable; your users should feel comfortable exploring your site and confident that they can find what they need. The graphic identity of a series of pages in a web site provides visual cues to the continuity of information. The header menu present on every page of the Code for America site creates a consistent user interface and strong site identity (fig. 7.3).

Even if your site design does not employ navigation graphics, a consistent approach to the layout of titles, subtitles, page footers, and navigation links to your home page or related pages will reinforce the user's sense of context within the site. To preserve the effect of a "seamless" system of pages, you may wish to bring important information into your site and adapt it to your page layout scheme rather than using links to send the reader away from your site (but be sure there are no copyright restrictions on copying the information into your site).

INTEGRITY AND STABILITY

To convince your users that what you have to offer is accurate and reliable, you will need to design your web site as carefully as you would any other type of corpo-

FIGURE 7.3
The simple but bold site headers establish both a strong site identity and a straightforward navigation system. The fully responsive site design also reduces well on mobile devices.

rate communication, using the same high editorial and design standards. A site that looks sloppily built, with poor visual design and low editorial standards, will not inspire confidence.

Functional stability in any web design means keeping the interactive elements of the site working reliably. Functional stability has two components: getting things right the first time as you design the site, and then keeping things functioning smoothly over time. Good web sites are inherently interactive, with lots of links to local pages within the site as well as links to other sites on the web. As you create your design, you will need to check frequently that all of your links work properly. Information changes quickly on the web, both on your site and on everyone else's. After the site is established, you will need to check that your links are still working properly and that the content they supply remains relevant.

FEEDBACK AND DIALOG

Your web design should offer constant visual and functional confirmation of the user's whereabouts and options, via graphic design, navigation links, and uniformly placed hypertext links. Feedback also means being prepared to respond to your users' inquiries and comments. Well-designed web sites provide direct links to the web site editor or webmaster responsible for running the site. Planning for this ongoing relationship with users of your site is vital to the long-term success of the enterprise.

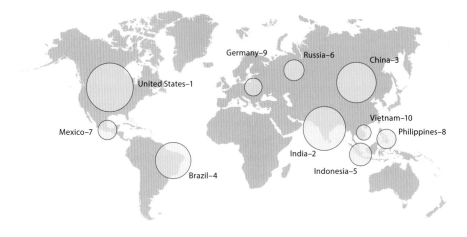

FIGURE 7.4
International users
of the web are a
huge potential
new audience, but
most of those users
are using mobile
phones with limited
bandwidth.

BANDWIDTH AND INTERACTION

Users will not tolerate long delays. Research has shown that for most computing tasks the threshold of frustration is about ten seconds. Web page designs that are not well "tuned" to the network access speed of typical users will only frustrate them. Check your web site logs to be sure that you understand your typical user's location and network connections. If you have many international users, for example, you may want to be more conservative about large graphics on your pages (fig. 7.4).

In 2013 there were more than 2.1 billion active mobile broadband subscriptions worldwide, or about 29.5 percent of the global population. In China alone there are an estimated 420 million mobile broadband users, and two-thirds of those subscriptions are for various kinds of smartphones. For many international users (and about a third of U.S. users) their smartphones are their primary computing device. All this

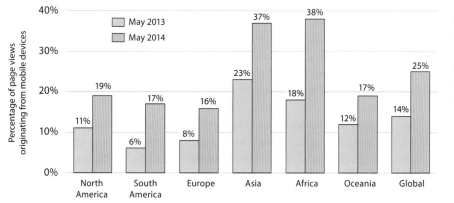

FIGURE 7.5
Mobile web users in
"third world" areas
are by far the fastest-
growing segment of
the web audience.

suggests that while high-speed Internet access has become standard in the home and office in developed countries, bandwidth is still an issue for the vast majority of the world's web users.

Beware of potentially slow dynamic content components in your site, such as excessive css or JavaScript code libraries, rss feeds, text from content management systems, or other data sources that can slow the loading of web pages.

Avoid including bandwidth-intensive videos on the main pages of your site—particularly those that are set to "autoplay." Automatically loading and playing a video has several downsides from an interaction perspective, beyond the demands it places on bandwidth usage. For example, people who use screen reader software will need to find the video controls and stop the video in order to navigate the page. Don't assume people want to load and watch videos. Instead, play videos only in response to an explicit user action, such as pressing the "Play" button.

Ideally your company webmaster should be able to supply reports and data on your typical users and their equipment. If you don't have easy access to this information from your organization's web server logs, you may be able to use a free service like Google Analytics to better understand the geography of your users.

DISPLAYS

The sheer number, variety, and orientations of modern computing screens or "viewports" pose serious challenges for the web designer. Indeed, today's dominant responsive web design methods and the css3 @media code queries that responsive design is built upon were born as an attempt to provide a reasonable user experience across the incredible spectrum of current viewports from small smartphones to giant "4k" desktop monitors.

Three intimately related—and sometimes opposing—factors govern screen graphic and user interface design in both mobile and desktop situations:

- **Screen size:** The overall physical size of the screen, as measured in inches (or centimeters). Screen size influences the visual characteristics of the display, but since mobile screens are almost always touchscreens, the physical size of the display also influences how easily users can hold the screen and manipulate touch targets within reach of their fingers and thumbs. Touch interfaces that work well on small screens may be awkward on larger tablets or phones, and vice versa.
- **Screen pixel dimensions:** The number of horizontal and vertical pixels the display contains. In general, larger viewports contain larger numbers of horizontal and vertical pixels, but the visual effect of a display is also crucially dependent on the screen resolution.

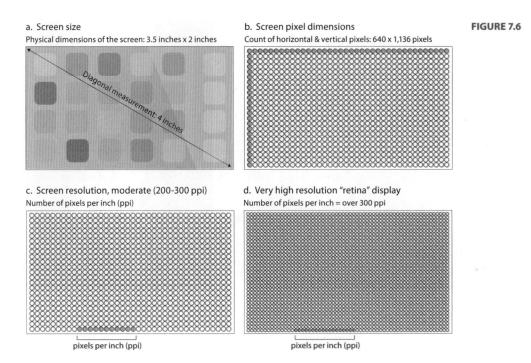

a. Screen size
Physical dimensions of the screen: 3.5 inches x 2 inches

Diagonal measurement: 4 inches

b. Screen pixel dimensions
Count of horizontal & vertical pixels: 640 x 1,136 pixels

FIGURE 7.6

c. Screen resolution, moderate (200-300 ppi)
Number of pixels per inch (ppi)

pixels per inch (ppi)

d. Very high resolution "retina" display
Number of pixels per inch = over 300 ppi

pixels per inch (ppi)

- **Screen resolution:** The number of screen pixels per linear inch (or centimeter) along each line of the display grid of pixels, a factor that combines physical screen size and screen pixel dimensions. Resolution has a major effect on the size and visual details of images and type on the screen, and recently screen resolutions have increased sharply. A similar trend is occurring in desktop and laptop displays: after nearly twenty years of computer screens with an average of 72–110 ppi of resolution, we're quickly moving to a world where all computing displays will approach the true "retina" resolution of just over 400 ppi.

To accommodate this dramatic change in resolution hardware, makers like Apple and Samsung have introduced schemes that use "rendered pixels (sometimes called "css pixels" or "virtual pixels"), in which one rendered screen pixel is actually composed of four hardware pixels. Thus an iPhone 6 screen has a physical pixel resolution of 1,080 by 1,920, but behaves for type and layout measurements as if the screen were 540 by 960. Otherwise, all web pages and typography would look miniaturized on the most recent "retina" screens of smartphones. (See fig. 11.17 for more on virtual pixels.)

FIGURE 7.7

Venice is beautiful, but it is also a confusing warren of narrow streets and canals that offer few navigation clues at street level. The churches and campaniles that tower over the city provide visual landmarks for navigation through the neighborhoods.

This need to balance the physical size of mobile viewports with the increasing resolution of display technology will be an ongoing challenge to web designers. In general this is good news: images and type look spectacular on the newer displays, and the increased legibility will bring a new world of illustration and typographic possibilities to our screens.

NAVIGATION AND WAYFINDING

In his book *The Image of the City*, Kevin Lynch coined the term "wayfinding" to describe his concept of environmental legibility—that is, the elements of the built environment that allow us to navigate successfully through complex spaces like cities and towns. The most fundamental underlying metaphor of the World Wide Web is navigation through a space populated by places we call web "sites," and thus the wayfinding metaphor is well suited to thinking about web navigation (fig. 7.7).

Wayfinding has four core components:

1. **Orientation:** Where am I am right now?
2. **Route decisions:** Can I find the way to where I want to go?
3. **Mental mapping:** Are my experiences consistent and understandable enough to know where I've been and to predict where I should go next? Can I make a coherent mental map of the spaces I have seen, and use it to predict where to go next?
4. **Closure:** Can I recognize that I have arrived in the right place?

In interviews conducted in various cities, Lynch had local residents draw maps of their cities from memory. The mental maps that residents create are crucial to wayfinding in their environment. An individual's map of the local environment is unique, but Lynch found that most people's maps were populated by five types of elements:

1. **Paths:** Familiar streets, walkways, subway routes, bus lines.
2. **Edges:** The physical barriers of walls, fences, rivers, or shorelines.
3. **Districts:** Places with distinct identities, such as, in New York, Chinatown, Wall Street, and Greenwich Village.
4. **Nodes:** Major intersections or meeting places, such as the clock in New York's Grand Central Terminal, that also present a lot of further navigational choices.
5. **Landmarks:** Tall or distinctive structures that allow you to orient over long distances.

Although you can readily see the parallels with navigation on the web, the web is a special kind of space that often doesn't provide the concrete spatial and navigational clues we take for granted in the real world of walking through a town.

- There's no sense of scale or movement in space. Web navigation has many similarities to physical movement, but actual travel on the web is magical: you just appear at the next point in your journey from page to page, and there is no experience of the landscape unfolding before you as a series of landmarks.
- There's no compass. There are no directions and often no clear sense of heading a particular direction. This lack of spatial direction is what makes links to home pages so crucial in web navigation: your orientation to home and whether you are heading away from the home page or toward the home page is the only sense of "direction" in many sites.
- You are here. All of this argues for concrete, visible, easy-to-understand navigational cues on web pages. Designers often chafe at the heavy interface framing of web pages—do we really need such a burden of headers and footers and tabs and links? Well, yes, we do. Without that navigation interface, and all the "you are here" markers it provides, we're lost in space.

SUPPORTING SEARCH AND BROWSE NAVIGATION

User interface research shows that about two-thirds of web users are browse-dominant—that is, they prefer (at least initially) to browse through menu lists of links to find information. The other third of users are search-dominant, and will go straight to the search box to enter keywords for search. However, this apparent search versus browse dichotomy is simplistic, as research also shows that most users use both browse and search, that 92 percent of users use search at some point in their online activity, and that even users who use search almost exclusively benefit from the information in the browse navigation interface of major site divisions and categories.

Jakob Nielsen has pointed to the irony that web search is used more than ever—by users who typically don't use search engines effectively. Research by usability experts consistently finds that most readers have only a vague idea how search works, do not understand how to construct efficient queries, and rarely use more advanced features such as scoped search options or "advanced search" pages. It's a testament to how good Google and Bing are that a simple search box works at all, let alone that it works most of the time for most users. Don't be misled by the fact that users these days are becoming more search-dominant. Even users who understand search well benefit from well-constructed browse interfaces.

Users often begin navigating an unfamiliar site by clicking on the persistent navigation links of the browse interface, and then shift over to search if they can't find what they need solely through clicking on links. All readers will use both the browse and search features of a complex site at some point, so supporting both navigation paradigms is important to interaction design. As the web has become larger and more complex, the dependence on search technology has become greater, both for users seeking information and for web publishers hoping users will find their content.

However, even users who depend primarily on site search for navigation also depend on the consistency of persistent site navigation to give them cues for where they are within the site, and how the site information is structured. Even if the search-oriented user never clicks on the header navigation links, that system of major content categories is still an import set of landmarks. Well-designed browse interfaces also support both findability and discoverability in web sites:

- **Findability:** Means that users can easily find content or site features that they know or assume are present in a web site—for example, finding a particular model of Nike shoes in the Zappos site.
- **Discoverability:** Means that users are routinely exposed to new content or features that they did not previously know about. For example: The "Frequently Bought Together" and "Customers Who Bought This Item Also Bought" on Amazon product pages.

Search navigation is most effective for users who already have a thorough understanding of the information space and the vocabulary needed to describe what they are looking for. Imagine word-searching for some gizmo that you don't even know the name of and you can see the problem. The persistent browse navigation of your site continually teaches search users how you describe things, and how you

FIGURE 7.8
College and university web sites have a clear target audience— prospective students. The Admissions pop-up menu on the Cornell University web site provides prospective undergraduate and continuing education students direct access to information and features that are most relevant.

categorize your information. It is often faster and easier to use a hybrid approach in large sites like Amazon, where you might start by browsing through major product categories, and then use the search box once you are pretty sure that you are in the general region of what you are looking for.

Search does not replace good browse navigation for another reason: many local search tools don't work very well, producing irrelevant results, few results, or far too many results. For example, in many local search systems (such as those built into CMS products) the query "child study center" yields all results for "child," all results for "study," and all results for "center," none of which is remotely relevant. In really poor search engines even enclosing a multiword phrase within quotes doesn't help. A good browse interface can help make up for poor local search results.

DESIGNING NAVIGATION

Most web sites are composed of pages, each with a unique URL. Navigation design is about providing a map describing the topography of the site, and systems of transport for moving from one location to another.

Menus highlight popular destinations

We tend to think of navigation primarily as a means of getting from here to there. Another key function of navigation is to show users what you are offering and what options they can pursue. In this way, your navigation system is like a feature list, and if you don't make clearly visible the options that would appeal to your target audience, they may not get past the home page. (Alan Cooper and team describe menus as a "pedagogic vector," teaching users what an application can and cannot do.)

Think of navigation as a map of your site's features and functionality. What key attributes do you need to expose to keep your target audience on your site? What are they most interested in? How can you describe and display those features so they are immediately evident and meaningful? A user-centered approach can help focus the development team's attention on including the most relevant aspects of a site from the user's perspective, and can sometimes resolve internal conflicts around what

FIGURE 7.9
An elegant
implementation of
breadcrumb trails
makes the W3C's
extensive and deeply
layered content easy
to navigate.

must be included in the main menu. Make sure your menus accurately represent the scope and primary focus of your offerings, and map to the expectations of your target audience.

Paths lead the way

In web sites, paths are the consistent, predictable navigational headers and links that appear the same way throughout the web site. Paths can be purely in the user's mind, as in your habitual navigation through a favorite newspaper site. Paths can also be explicit site navigation elements such as breadcrumb trails that show you where you are in relation to the overall site (fig. 7.9).

Create consistent, well-marked navigation paths through the use of persistent navigation built into the design of every page. Use persistent navigation elements like header links, "you are here" markers, and breadcrumb trails to establish and reinforce a sense of location and coherent movement through the information space. Clear, consistent icons, graphic identity schemes, page titles and headings, and

FIGURE 7.10
In the Rosenfeld
Media site a stable
set of section
markers (Books,
Services, Events)
gives users a firm
sense of where
they are in the
information space
and how to drive
deeper into the site
or hop directly to
another section.

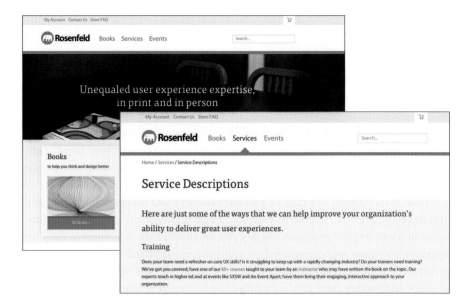

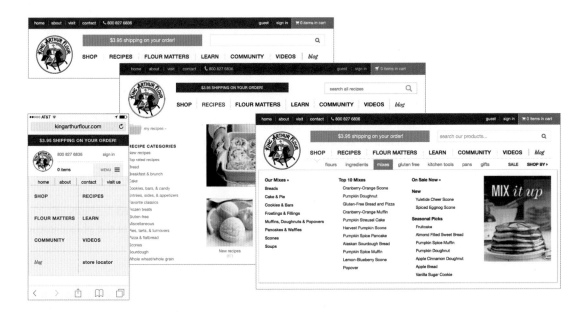

graphic- or text-based overview and summary screens can give users confidence that they can find what they are seeking without wasting time.

Users should always be able to return easily to your home page and to other major navigation points in the site. These basic links should be present and in consistent locations on every page. Headers provide basic navigation links and create an identity that tells users they are within the site domain. In the King Arthur Flour site, for example, the header appears on every page (fig. 7.11). The header is efficient (offering multiple choices in a small space) and predictable (it is always there, at the top of every page), and it provides a consistent identity throughout the site.

Links support discovery and exploration

Hyperlinks are a key component in web site navigation and wayfinding. Unlike the navigation systems of headers, menus, and breadcrumbs, links are typically embedded within the content of the page. They are invitations to explore different facets of the content on the page in more detail.

The most effective links are:

- **Distinguishable:** Many designers object to the default underlining of web links as disruptive of "type color" on the page, and restyle links to eliminate underlining and to change link colors. Underlining is critical, particularly for inline links (links that appear within the text block), since the color difference may not be distinguishable for people with color perception issues.

FIGURE 7.11

A simple, clean header system that nicely expands in the one complex area of the site ("Shop," right screen example). Note the mobile version, with large, easy-to-use touch targets and a very consistent graphic identity with the main site.

- **Self-explanatory:** Users don't derive much benefit from vague or poorly worded links, or from stock phrases like "click here" or "for more information." Links should be self-explanatory, and not require users to follow the link to determine its destination.
- **Relevant:** Users scan pages for content, and are more likely to settle in and read your page if they spot relevant keywords. Highlighting keywords is also crucial for search engine optimization (SEO), as the major search engines give extra weight to keywords within links. "Front-loading" links has accessibility benefits as well, since screen reader users tabbing through links are able to quickly understand the nature of the link without needing to listen to the entire link phrase.
- **Concise:** Long phrases of linked text emphasize the decreased legibility of underlined text, and usually overemphasize the importance of the phrase in the context of the page content.

Links are so common that we now take them for granted, but hyperlinks define the very nature of the web and are a crucial part of the web user interface. Eye-tracking research shows that readers begin scanning a page in the standard "F" pattern that emphasizes the top left portion of the page, but then quickly shift over to scanning the body of the page for major headers and scanning any linked text on the page. Thus graphic design practices such as using CSS to decrease (or even eliminate) the contrast of web links hurts the scanability of page content. Ensuring links are clearly identifiable and easy to comprehend is a key component of interaction design.

A clear "scent" makes choices easier

Coffee used to be easy: it was regular or black. Now with six kinds of mocha skim lattes on offer, coffee has become yet another potential point of stress in your day. In Western societies we equate freedom with a range of choices, but as psychologist Barry Schwartz points out in his book *The Paradox of Choice,* an excessive range of choices causes stress, slows our decision making, makes us generally less satisfied (did I make the right choice from my eighty-nine options?), and makes us more likely to walk away from making any choice at all. "Give the user choices" is a constant mantra in user interface design, but too many choices delivered simultaneously leaves most users overwhelmed and likely to abandon the path altogether (fig. 7.12).

Too many links and menu options can inhibit exploration by offering so many choices that it's difficult to choose. Work to maintain a limited set of major navigation categories (ideally seven to ten at most), and progressively disclose additional details as needed in each subsection of the site. In many sites these navigational nodes are built into the persistent browsing hierarchy of the site, with drop-down or

FIGURE 7.12
As pages get more complex, you risk overwhelming the reader with the "Times Square effect" of too many competing visual stimuli.

pop-up menus that present many secondary options within each major site navigation category.

You may find it difficult to convince others—colleagues on the development team, clients—that less is more when it comes to link and menu options. Instead, you might be encouraged to provide lots of options in order to minimize the number of times users need to click to get to their destination. Usability expert Steve Krug explores this concept in his book *Don't Make Me Think*. His second rule of usability is "It doesn't matter how many times I have to click, as long as each click is a mindless, unambiguous choice." The key is to provide a clear path, with self-explanatory labels that don't require much decoding by the user.

Boundaries and landmarks provide orientation

Consistency is the golden rule of interface design and wayfinding, but there is a paradox at the heart of consistency: if everything looks the same, there are no edges. How can you tell where you are or when you have moved from one space to another? A well-designed site navigation system is built on a consistent page grid, terminology, and navigation links, but it also incorporates the visual flexibility to create identifiable regions and edges within the larger space. In a corporate site, if you move from one region to another—say, from marketing to human resources—you ought to notice that you just passed an important regional boundary (fig. 7.13), but the two areas should be similar enough to assure you that you are still within the same company site.

"You are here" orientation cues are particularly important in the web interface, since users often arrive at a page without having followed a deliberate and repeatable path. For example, one point of web wayfinding that is quite unlike navigation

SCENT OF INFORMATION

The theory of the "scent of information" originated at Xerox PARC, where researchers theorized that people confronting a large and complex information space become "informavores," exhibiting the same information as animals hunting prey. Users pick up a scent trail that appears to map to their desired outcome. They follow the trail, becoming more confident and eager if the scent grows stronger. If they lose the scent, they backtrack and try again.

Web sites with strong scent trails are usually those that demonstrate deep insight into and understanding of the target audience for the site. Through user research and a goal-directed design process, the development team has mapped the design of the user interface to meet user goals in a way that maps to their mental models. In this way, users have confidence in working with the site, have fewer failed attempts, and are generally satisfied, happy, and successful in working with the site.

What gives a site strong scent trails? Here we summarize key principles from the section "The Tao of Scent" from "Designing for the Scent of Information," a concept report from Jared Spool, Shristine Perfetti, and David Brittan of User Interface Engineering (www.uie.com).

- Links that are easily distinguishable from other elements (for example, blue and underlined) work best.
- Links communicate scent best when they contain keywords ("trigger words") at the beginning of the link phrase, and are descriptive and clear, accurately describing the page they link to. Confidence grows when the words in the link are prominent on the destination page.
- Users do not mind clicking through multiple pages as long as the scent grows stronger with each click and they sense they are moving toward their goal.

in physical space is Search, which cuts across all the normal wayfinding boundaries to provide a view of every occurrence of a keyword or phrase across the web site. Search can deliver you directly from one point in a site to another, and that direct connection makes the user all the more dependent on "you are here" cues from the user interface of the site.

Both the browse and search aspects of navigation must support the user's sense of location and orientation to the major landmarks of a site. Core page components and interface elements are relevant to both browsing and searching; they establish

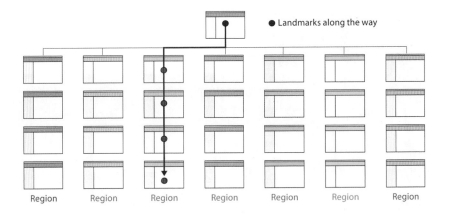

● Landmarks along the way

Region   Region   Region   Region   Region   Region   Region

FIGURE 7.13
In large sites users should be able to readily see when they have passed important organizational boundaries. If all the pages look identical, it's harder to tell where you are within a large site.

and maintain a broad sense of a web site as a navigable space and provide a "you are here" sense of local placement within the larger dimension of the site. Breadcrumb trails, tabs or links that change color to indicate the current location, and section titles all contribute to a firm sense of place within a site (fig. 7.14).

These landmark and wayfinding elements are especially important to users who navigate by searching. The browse interface allows users to move gradually through a site, seeing various landmarks as they pass through the site hierarchy (see fig. 7.13). Web search allows a user to cut directly into a site hierarchy with no preamble. Users who come to your site from a general Internet search engine like Yahoo! or Google may arrive directly at a page deep within the organization of your site. As web search becomes the way most of your audience reaches your site, the percentage of users who enter your site at the home page is decreasing all the time.

Create a unique but related identity for each site region, within a larger design system that is consistent throughout the whole enterprise. These "affiliated design systems" are common in enterprises with many divisions, and can provide unique subsection identities while reinforcing the overall enterprise identity.

FIGURE 7.14
The core components of a web page header. Every page should include persistent and consistent identity, navigation, and search features. These are what define an identifiable "site" on the web.

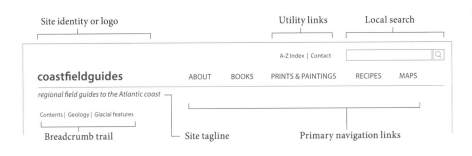

Site identity or logo   Utility links   Local search

A-Z Index | Contact

coastfieldguides   ABOUT   BOOKS   PRINTS & PAINTINGS   RECIPES   MAPS

regional field guides to the Atlantic coast

Contents | Geology | Glacial features

Breadcrumb trail   Site tagline   Primary navigation links

Home page

Landmark subsection

FIGURE 7.15

MIT's home page and its news site obviously share a close design and functional relationship. Major subsites become navigational landmarks within the larger information space, by both their distinctiveness (you are here) and their obvious relatedness (you are within MIT's core web presence).

Consistency makes navigation easier

Consistency in creating and maintaining landmarks is critical for successful way-finding, whether in the virtual "space" of a large web site or in the actual space of a large urban transportation hub. New York City's Penn Station is notorious for its poorly designed, confusing, and chaotically maintained signage. Penn Station is the nation's busiest train station, and is a meeting point for four rail systems: Amtrak, New Jersey Transit, the Long Island Railroad, and the New York City subways. Each of the rail systems maintains its own separate set of signage in the station, and Penn Station itself adds yet another layer of signage, for a total of five unrelated and competing sign sets, no two of which share any design conventions or color sets. Each railroad tries to orient its riders within the station, so many competing and overlapping signs overwhelm the user with visual noise.

The analogy to large, poorly coordinated web sites is nearly perfect. Large enterprises like companies, government agencies, and (particularly) universities often present cluttered Penn Station–like mixes of uncoordinated user interfaces and visual designs. Each area of the larger site tries to "perfect" its own little piece of the domain with locally unique designs and interfaces, and the result is often a confusing experience for readers who must constantly cross system boundaries to find what they need.

FIGURE 7.16

Five separate and competing signage systems make New York's Penn Station a notoriously confusing place to navigate. The station is a perfect analog to jumbled corporate and university sites. If every department insists on going its own way, you get user hell, and a poor reflection on the larger enterprise.

In contrast, most modern airports have solved the user experience and wayfinding issues through carefully coordinated signage systems and wayfinding designs. Guided by widely understood and consistent design conventions—arrival boards, departure boards, gate sign systems, universal icons and symbol systems—even travelers who don't speak the local language can usually find their way to the right plane at the right time.

FIGURE 7.17

Most airports have learned the lessons of coordinated design, and have comprehensive wayfinding systems that allow thousands of people to navigate a complex physical layout and get to their flights on time.

User expectations for
search location:

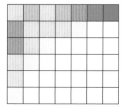

Placing a search box in the scan column ——
allows space for more options

Primary search location, but in a constricted space

| Department logo | Search this site | Go |

Section title line

Breadcrumb trail | Page name

Search this site:

| Search options ▼ |
| Go |

Copyright ©2016 Name of the company. All rights reserved.
Last revised date.   Contact us

FIGURE 7.18
Conventions are
your friends. Always
put the search box
where users expect
to find it.

Poor navigation (in train stations or web sites) can have important consequences. As users become confused, their confidence in their abilities to find the correct next step leads to a decrease in trust in the site in general, which may lead them to abandon the site, or not to buy the product they were seeking—even if they find it—because they no longer trust the site.

Most text-oriented informational web sites are converging on a relatively consistent layout of header, footer, local navigation, and content elements that together make a useful, familiar starting point for web interface designs. In general, people find the familiar easier to use and remember, and if your site follows these familiar patterns, users will quickly adapt and begin to focus on your unique content, features, or products (fig. 7.18).

As you design the interface for your site, remember that the ideal web interface should never compete with the page content for the user's attention. The interface is the frame, not the painting.

Search also needs wayfinding

The most fundamental support for users who prefer to search is to make search easily available from every page of your site. Users expect that any site of more than a few pages will have a search feature. Research shows that there are specific areas of the page where users expect to see a search box (fig. 7.19), and that most users expect a simple uncomplicated search box and don't understand or use "Advanced search" options.

Try to let users know the scope of what they are searching, but keep the search scope controls simple and low-key, as many users never use scope controls even

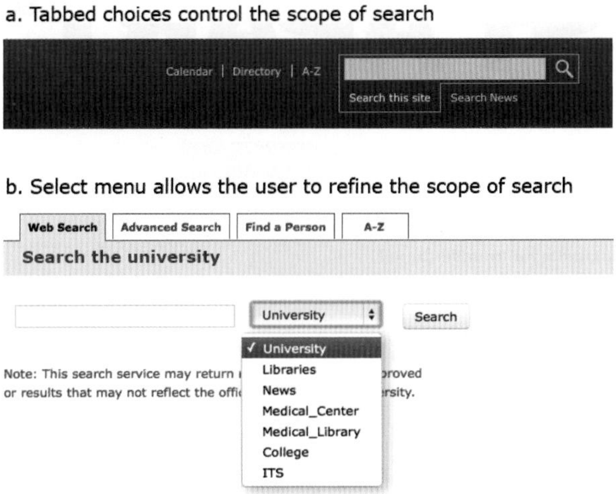

a. Tabbed choices control the scope of search

b. Select menu allows the user to refine the scope of search

FIGURE 7.19

The search options you offer may determine the practical location of your search box. Simple header search boxes work well for most situations, but if you offer scoped search or other options, you may need a bit more room for the pop-up scope menu.

when controlling scope would produce better results. It's confusing when a user enters a keyword thinking that he is searching only the current web site but then gets search results from the whole company or the whole Internet ("Results 1–100 of about 5,100,000,000 for 'Help'"). In simple search forms you can make the scope of the search clear in the field label, or in a subtle drop-down menu beside the search box. Where there is more room on the page, the search form can offer more options to control the scope of the search (fig. 7.20), but keep it simple.

To preserve a sense of place within your site, the results of a user's search query should appear on a page that looks like the rest of the web site. For large institutions, as long as the larger institutional site is well organized and graphically consistent, every small subsite does not need to have a custom search page.

Search is powerful, but web search is no substitute for a coherent site architecture, carefully expressed in your page design and navigation. Ironically, search navigation is heavily dependent on those interface elements and page design features that we think of as part of the standard browsing interface. By cutting out the intermediate steps in browsing through an information hierarchy, search can deliver the user to pages deep inside a web site, where only the "browsing" interface of site

FIGURE 7.20

FIGURE 7.21

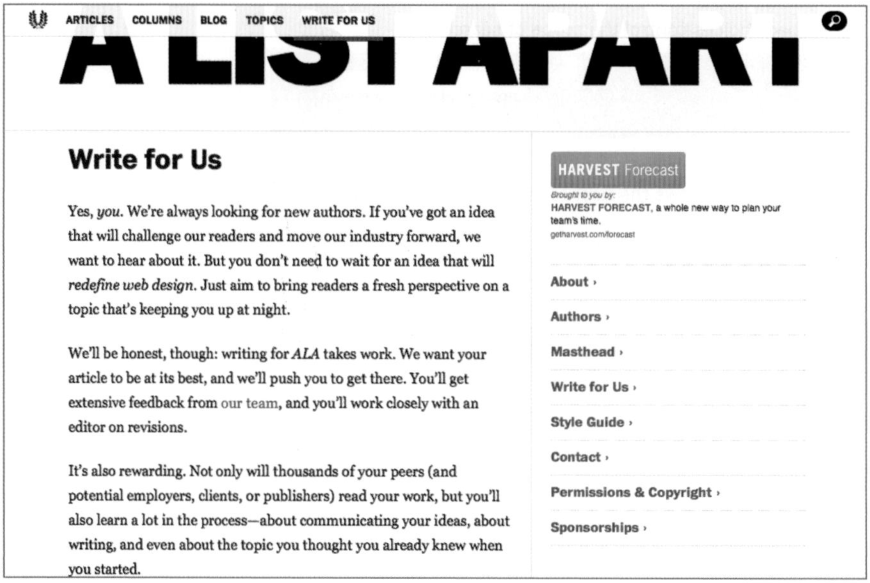

graphics, page titles, breadcrumb trails, and navigation links can supply the cues that allow users to establish their "you are here" location within the site.

PROVIDING NAVIGATION SYSTEMS

Several interaction design conventions have emerged to help users move along a path in their quest for information and functionality. Conventions aid interaction because they make use of users' existing knowledge—what Donald Norman calls "knowledge in the head." For example, in this book we use standard page numbers and running feet for orientation within the book, and we provide a table of contents and index for wayfinding. Readers generally do not need to learn how to interact with a book. When you follow design conventions for web navigation systems, users will be able to apply what they already know about exploring web sites to navigating your site.

Headers for global wayfinding

Web page headers convey the site identity, provide major navigation links, and often offer a search feature. The header is where people expect to see a consistent statement of your organizational identity, and the header graphics and text are probably the most important elements in making a collection of web pages feel like an identifiable "site" rather than a random assemblage of files. User research shows overwhelmingly that users expect that the top left area of your page header will contain both a visual indication of who you are and a link back to your site's home page.

FIGURE 7.22

Users also expect that the header will play an important role in global navigation within your site. Important navigation links are often arrayed horizontally within the page header, as links and as a menu bar with drop-down menus. For responsive sites, menu items collapse into a single drop-down menu or slide-out "drawer" on smartphones.

Menus for local wayfinding

Most web sites have too many layers of content and functionality to have everything accessible from the primary navigation, although some sites try, using "mega menus" to provide access to secondary items. These menus can be effective in providing users a more direct path to reaching their goal. However, mega menus can be difficult to implement so that they are usable with the keyboard and work on small devices. They can be disorienting for people who use screen magnification, where only a small portion of the screen is visible at one time. The user may not know the menu is expanded because the affordances—the border and drop shadow—are not visible. Complex menus also create challenges for responsive design, as there are too many options to collapse into a single menu.

More often section navigation displays on the internal pages, in a column on the left- or right-hand side of the screen. According to most user interface and eye-tracking studies, users quickly adapt to content navigation within either the left column or far right column of web pages—just be consistent in how you lay out your navigation on all pages. Left navigation columns are much more common and therefore have an edge in usability because all web users are familiar with them, but with the rise of "mobile-first" responsive sites with simpler two-column page layouts, the navigation column is often on the right side. That said, the right column is sometimes used for parenthetic "related links" or advertising. Given the user expectation that right columns contain advertising, any right-column menu you use should look very different from advertising, or many users may ignore your section navigation.

Breadcrumb trails for navigation and orientation

Breadcrumb trails are a powerful yet easy-to-understand navigation device of web pages. The name is derived from the metaphor of leaving breadcrumbs along your path to find your way back where you came from. In practice, a breadcrumb trail is a simple hierarchical list of web links showing the structure of a site, usually starting with the home page and ending with the major navigation page closest to your current location. Each step in the breadcrumb trail is a clickable web link, so that users have both a visual indication of their current location within the site and a clickable menu of major navigation sections for the site. In addition to its user interface advantages, the breadcrumb trail plays a potentially powerful role in adding major linked keywords to each web page, increasing the search visibility and keyword relevance of a page.

INTERACTION

With web interaction at its most basic, users interact with pages by clicking on links and submitting forms. This interaction initiates a dialog between the client, usually a web browser, and the server: the browser sends data and page requests to the server, and the server collects data and returns pages. Once the server delivers a page, all

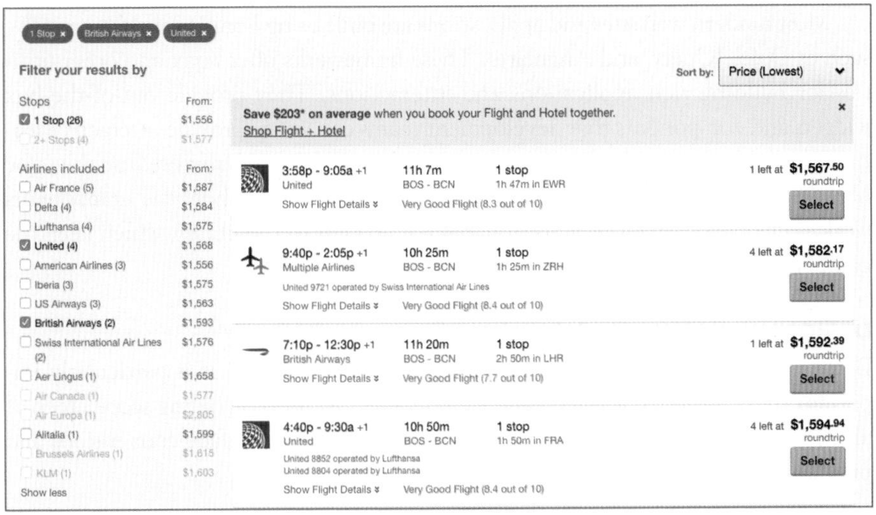

FIGURE 7.24
Expedia provides dynamic updates of flights that match the search query. Users can update the filters to show only nonstop flights, or only certain carriers, and the results update dynamically, without the user needing to resubmit the search.

dialog is suspended until the browser makes another request. What the user does with the page is immaterial, unless another link is clicked or another form submitted. This client-server model does not lend itself to the type of interaction we have come to expect when working with computer interfaces. Take required fields, for example. In a basic web environment, once the user submits the form, the server checks the data and, if fields are missed, returns the form to the user to complete. This exchange can occur repeatedly if the user does not locate all of the required fields before submitting.

A more effective approach is client-side interaction, providing feedback along the way to help avoid errors, rather than having the user correct errors after completion. With a dynamic form, the fields are validated as they are completed, and the "submit" button is active only when all the fields are complete. On the web, client-side interaction is made possible through a combination of technologies, including HTML, JavaScript, CSS, and the Document Object Model, or DOM. The elements make up Dynamic HTML, or DHTML, which is a way to dynamically update page content, structure, and styling after the page is loaded in the browser.

Ajax, which stands for asynchronous JavaScript and XML, is a technique for providing both dynamic interface elements and dynamic page content, and it is frequently used for building web applications. With Ajax, the page sends requests for small bits of data in response to user actions—for example, zooming in on a map—and the data are displayed in an area of the page without requiring the entire page to reload. Ajax has performance benefits because no individual user action requires a full page reload. Ajax also provides much more in the way of interactivity by allowing for dynamic and responsive user interfaces.

Most modern web sites and applications are built using libraries and frameworks, such as Dojo, JQuery, and Angularjs. These frameworks offer Ajax and other utilities for building rich applications and interactions. They provide out-of-the-box widgets and components that development teams can use to provide interactive features, to the benefit of development teams and users. When many sites use the same libraries, usability is improved since users are familiar with how the components work. The product team benefits from regular updates to the library, which keep the components compatible with new devices and technologies.

DESIGNING INTERACTION

Because web applications place greater demands on the user, it is particularly important to focus on what is relevant to and valued by users, avoiding scope creep at all costs. In designing your application, use recognizable interface conventions and provide guidance to help your users be successful.

Users define relevance

Good interface design arises from restraint. All too often, applications are cluttered and complicated by the enthusiasm of their developers, who add in features and functionality because they can and because they might be useful to some users. Users also often get carried away in their requests for features, thinking, Wouldn't it be great if the application did this, that, and the other thing, and not taking into account the complexity that inevitably results. In the end, users benefit more from simple designs than from a wealth of features. The cost of adding features that benefit a few users is too high to justify the negative effect on overall usability and ease of use. You are better off focusing on the most critical functions of an application and avoiding all nice-to-have or easy-to-add features. Address those critical features with a design that is uncluttered by unnecessary elements.

The 80/20 rule is helpful for efforts to address the primary needs of the target audience. Following this rule for interaction design, 20 percent of the web site features are used 80 percent of the time. The remaining 80 percent of the features that are in use or under consideration should be evaluated to determine whether they add enough value to the web site to justify their cost, both in resource allocation and in simplicity and usability of the user interface. Removing unnecessary functionality and content allows interaction designers to focus on providing exceptional experiences that appeal to the primary needs of the target audience.

Patterns improve usability

Design patterns are recognizable patterns for interaction, such as drop-down menus for accessing subsection pages and paging navigation for moving through a sequence of pages. Design patterns are designs that have been introduced and proven effective and then are widely adopted until they become conventions. After widespread adoption, the approach becomes a pattern that is readily recognizable by users, which improves usability. Users can leverage what they know and don't have to create a new mental model for interaction at each site.

Design patterns for interface elements do not have to look the same, but they do need to share the same interaction model and features. Don't employ a design pattern and change the way it works. Modifying an existing design pattern is worse than adopting a new approach because it conflicts with the users' mental model for how the pattern works, and users will have to unlearn and learn how to work with your site.

Make sure to account for diverse modes of interaction when implementing design patterns, including people who use touch and keyboard navigation. For example, the established convention for interacting with a button using the keyboard is to use the Space or Enter key to execute whatever action is associated with the button. Some developers create buttons using a link, or anchor, element rather than a native HTML button. Links activate using the Enter key, and pressing Space on a link initiates a page scroll rather than activating the custom button. For interaction, design patterns are about how things function as well as how they look, and honoring conventions is an essential part of providing enjoyable and accessible user experiences.

People use different interaction methods

Modern web sites include functionality based on three modes of interaction: menu and hyperlink selection, form fill-in, and direct manipulation.

People who work with web sites have different methods for using them. Some people use only a keyboard, even when working with touchscreen devices like smartphones. Keyboards offer benefits, such as minimizing the physical effort and fine motor skills needed to work a web site. For people who are blind and cannot see the screen, the keyboard is the way to review and operate interactive components. Alternative input devices like voice-recognition software and switch devices operate by activating keyboard-based commands. Touchscreen devices are clearly designed for pointing, but it's important to keep in mind that any interaction based on mouse-only events, such as a menu that appears on mouse hover, will not be accessible because there is no equivalent touch gesture.

Even complex direct-manipulation interactions, such as drag-and-drop, can be made to work with keyboard keys: directional arrows, the Tab key, the Enter key. Put aside your mouse and work through your interactive components using the keyboard only to make sure they can be worked using interaction methods other than a mouse.

Responsive sites must also take into account different interaction modalities on touchscreen devices. It's safe to assume that most people use gestures to interact with

CHOOSING FORM OVER FUNCTION: DISABLING PINCH ZOOM

Design has always involved a tension between form and function. The expression "form follows function" is often used as a reminder to designers to make sure that the primary driver in decision making is supporting how something works rather than how it looks. This injunction is based on the idea that success in design is defined by how well the product performs in meeting functional requirements rather than aesthetic ones. With a platform like the web, in most cases, function outweighs form in terms of meeting user needs and achieving business goals. But that does not mean that form always follows function.

Case in point: disabling pinch zoom on mobile web sites. Pinch zoom is a gesture that allows users to zoom in and out of web pages on mobile browsers. It's what allows us to zoom in to see which cousin photobombed our brother's wedding photo. It's what allows us to zoom in and tap the tiny text in the footer to call the restaurant and make a reservation. The web is full of crucial information that is difficult to see and controls that are too small to operate with a coarse pointer like a fingertip. People who have low vision require zoom to access content and functionality on mobile devices.

It's possible through code to disable the pinch zoom feature, and some responsive and mobile sites employ this strategy on the premise that since the designs are optimized for mobile, zooming should not be necessary, and the zoomed view of the layout and content is not aesthetically desirable. As a result, users who have learned to pinch and zoom will not be able to use their customary strategies, which are part of muscle memory, to consume content and access functionality. People who require zoom to access content and functionality will be locked out entirely. The cost to usability is high, merely for the sake of aesthetics.

This dynamic is common on the web—removing link underlines, for example. Graphic designers avoid underlined text because underlining interferes with letterforms. Hyperlinks were originally presented as colored and underlined in order to be readily visible, and to ensure that people who can't perceive color could distinguish links from surrounding text. When CSS provided the means to remove underlines, there was a collective sigh of relief among designers and a proliferation of color-only hyperlinks. Given the importance of links in wayfinding and interaction, the usability and accessibility costs for this principally aesthetic concern are high. All users have to seek out and maybe even hover over colored text to determine whether it's a link. Users who can't perceive colors may miss links altogether. On what is essentially a functional device, and one that is fundamental to participating in work and life, form really must follow function, to ensure that everyone can access the features of the web.

web sites on touchscreen devices, although it's possible to use a keyboard. In fact, using a Bluetooth keyboard and VoiceOver on your ios device is one of the best ways to evaluate the accessibility of your mobile web site. But in most cases, the mobile context precludes the use of a keyboard, and most people interact using touch. Touch interaction precludes the use of anything that involves a hover event, such as menus or tooltips that display on mouse hover. But mobile interaction has additional nuances because of users who use touchscreen devices using screen reader, such as VoiceOver on ios and TalkBack on Android, and also using the zoom features of the devices. These modalities have specific gestures that make mobile devices accessible to people with vision impairments.

PROVIDING INTERACTIVE COMPONENTS

The basic interactive web components are hyperlinks and form elements, including text input fields, radio buttons and checkboxes, drop-down menus, and buttons. Over time the web has evolved to support much more complex functionality, as designers and developers have engineered support for rich interactions such as drag-and-drop and group selection. There are costs to moving away from standard HTML to custom components, including compatibility and accessibility. Modern browsers and assistive technology provide fairly standard and complete support for HTML. Engineering custom components requires some wrangling to produce something that is usable on all software and devices, via a keyboard or a pointing device.

For accessibility, interactive components must meet the following success criterion from the Web Content Accessibility Guidelines (WCAG) 2.0:

• **4.1.2 Name, Role, Value:** For all user interface components (including but not limited to: form elements, links, and components generated by scripts), the name and role can be programmatically determined; states, properties, and values that can be set by the user can be programmatically set; and notification of changes to these items is available to user agents, including assistive technologies.

The guidelines note that the success criterion "is primarily for web authors who develop or script their own user interface components. For example, standard HTML controls already meet this success criterion when used according to specification." In other words, if you use standard HTML elements correctly, you are providing an accessible user experience without additional code to accommodate assistive technology. For example, the following HTML checkbox provides programmatic information about its name ("I agree to the terms and conditions"), its role ("checkbox"), and its state ("checked"). This information is encoded, which means it's available to software, such as assistive technology. When screen reader software reads information about the control, it can convey all details necessary, so that someone who can't see the control can operate it successfully. In addition, the control functions as expected using the keyboard—the Space key toggles the state between checked and unchecked.

For a custom checkbox, the name, role, and station information must be added manually to the HTML code by the web site developer, and the behavior of the checkbox must be scripted, so the checkbox functions as an actionable element and responds to the correct keyboard commands. The custom code and scripts that power the custom checkbox must be regularly revisited and validated across operating systems, browsers, and devices.

Typically it's design considerations that cause development teams to turn to building custom components. And there was a time when there were significant limitations as to what styles could be applied to interactive elements, such as buttons and checkboxes. However, modern web technologies afford a great deal of visual customization of native HTML elements. Given the overhead of managing custom code and the many nuances to providing accessible solutions across devices and means of use, we recommend favoring standard HTML components over custom controls and widgets. Choose a custom component as your last choice, having exhausted all standard options. And even then, think carefully about whether a certain visual design or distinctive behavior is worth the costs of veering off course. Users benefit from consistent and predictable user interface designs. The development team and client may feel it's worth the overhead to craft a custom widget. Do your users?

Buttons

Buttons typically appear as rounded rectangles with a single word or short phrase, an image icon, or some combination of the two. Like elevator buttons or a doorbell, they often have a visual affordance that encourages users to tap, click, or press Enter to initiate the action indicated by the button.

Since links can be styled to look like buttons, some sites use an anchor element as a link. This can cause usability issues for screen reader and keyboard users. Even if a link looks like a button, it announces and behaves like a link. For example, pressing the Spacebar key on a link scrolls the page, whereas pressing Spacebar on a button executes the action. It's important to understand the difference between buttons and hyperlinks—links enable navigation among pages, and buttons execute an action—and use the correct control for the task.

Menus

Menus are lists of options from which users select what best fits. In the context of navigation, menus are both informative, in revealing options, and functional, in providing a means to move from one area of the site to another, or to choose to access

WAI-ARIA AS A LAST RESORT

WAI-ARIA (accessible rich Internet applications suite) is a W3C specification that builds on HTML, providing additional markup that can be used by assistive technologies, such as screen reader software, to allow users to access and manipulate dynamic web interface elements developed using Ajax, JavaScript, HTML, and other technologies. For development teams, ARIA may seem like just the thing to bridge the perceived gap between what's possible with native HTML elements and what's desirable for interaction design, as a means to make complex interactions accessible for people with disabilities. But even proponents of WAI-ARIA encourage you to first exhaust options for native HTML elements. In the W3C document Using WAI-ARIA in HTML, the "first rule of ARIA use" is:

> If you can use a native HTML element or attribute with the semantics and behavior you require already built in, instead of repurposing an element and adding an ARIA role, state, or property to make it accessible, then do so.

This is due in part to the overhead that comes with creating and maintaining custom controls. The following list details all the aspects you must validate and maintain with custom controls—attributes that are available out of the box with native HTML elements. Controls that do not have these attributes will not be usable by some users.

- **Focusable:** Can you get to the control using the keyboard?
- **Operable:** Can you operate the control using the keyboard?
- **Expected operation:** Can you use standard keys to operate the control?
- **Clear indication of focus:** Can you easily see when the control has focus?
- **Label:** Does the control have a text label that is associated with the control?
- **Role:** Does the control have the correct role associated with the control?
- **States and properties:** Are all of the corresponding states and properties associated with the control?
- **Color contrast:** Are the control and its label usable for people who have low vision or issues with color perception?
- **High-contrast mode:** Is the control usable when high-contrast mode is enabled?

specific functionality. Menus use the design strategy of progressive disclosure, where only the most immediate and relevant layer displays initially, and additional options are revealed when the user selects the main menu item.

- Menu bars for interaction control have been around for a long time in graphical user interfaces, where a list of options displays horizontally across the top of the screen to provide access to available content and functionality. On web sites, menu bars typically allow users to move from one page to another. Selecting an item on the menu bar opens a drop-down menu with additional options. Keep the number of items in a drop-down menu to those that are most relevant to the target audience. Ensure that menus are operable using a pointing device, touchscreen, and keyboard, and that they follow established conventions for keyboard operation. One common mistake is to display drop-down menus on hover, making the drop-downs unusable by keyboard and touchscreen users.
- Tab panels are commonly used to navigate between different panes. This interaction device allows for related content and functionality to display on the same page. The tabs allow users to move between different panes without the change of context of loading a new page.

For form fill-in, menus are helpful for collecting information in a standard format. They work with information where the possible responses are known, such as dates. Using a menu makes for cleaner data collection since the responses can be standardized in both substance and format, whereas users can enter the wrong information, or the right information in the wrong format, in a text input field. In some cases, menus can improve usability. They provide a list of acceptable choices for inputs where the options are not known—for example, choosing shirt size and color. But they can also be tedious with familiar information, such as birth year, or home state or province, where entering the information from the keyboard would be faster than scanning through a long list of options.

- Drop-down menus have the benefit of providing many choices in a small space, but they can be hard to use. In particular, menus with many options, such as to choose your state or country, are challenging to scan. It can be easier to enter a state or country code than to choose it from a select menu, particularly on mobile devices, where scrolling through a long list of options is cumbersome.
- Radio buttons are easy to scan because the options display on the page. However, because a long list takes up screen space, and because long lists are hard for readers to parse, limit your radio button groups to four to six options.
- Checkboxes allow users to make multiple selections. Single checkboxes are also the right control for binary choices, such as yes or no, in which checked means "yes." A list box is another component that allows users to make multiple choices from a list of options.

- Always set menus to nonactionable defaults to keep users from submitting information that is incorrect simply by neglecting to choose from the menu. For example, make the checkbox default unchecked, and the first item of a select menu a null value, such as "None" or "Select an item."

Inputs

Form fill-in using input fields and scrolling text areas allows users to type information directly into a field rather than choosing from a predefined menu of choices. Fields are required when the information is open-ended and therefore cannot be represented in a menu. Fields are sometime preferable for information that is easier to enter into a field than to choose from a menu. For example, even though dates are predefined, it may be easier to enter the information into a form field than to choose it from a set of menus. "Year of birth" menus, for instance, need to be enormous and can be awkward to manipulate. A simple input field is the easier choice.

- Text inputs are open-ended text fields that allow users to enter characters. Some text inputs have auxiliary controls, such as a date input that allows users to enter the date manually or choose a date from a date-picker widget. Other auxiliary controls include steppers and sliders that can be used to increment values in a text input. A text area is best for cases where users must enter long passages of text.
- Combo boxes allow users to either enter information into an input or select a predefined value from a drop-down menu. This hybrid input/menu control provides the best of both worlds—the efficiency of text entry with the informative and functional aspects of a menu, and the text input provides information about current status by displaying the selected value.
- Autocomplete is a feature often added to text inputs. As the user types information into the field, a list of options that match the entered text displays as a drop-down menu. The list updates as the user types, narrowing down options as more text is entered. The user can choose to select an option from the drop-down menu or simply finish typing. Autosuggest is a variant on autocomplete, where the drop-down menu items do not provide a direct match but rather suggest options that might be more correct and germane—options without spelling errors, for example.

Toggles

A toggle is a control that, when activated, switches some functionality between an on and off state. Toggles are commonly used in desktop software toolbars, to apply formatting such as bold or italic to a block of text, for example. On the web, toggle controls are used for form fill-in—a single checkbox functions as a toggle control, for example, with checked meaning "yes" and unchecked meaning "no." But they are also frequently used for display-related interactions, such as showing hidden content and functionality. Toggles allow for simple user interface designs for complex functionality. The most important features are in the foreground, while features that are necessary but used infrequently are still close at hand.

- Panels and drawers are components that contain secondary content and functionality that the user can elect to show or hide as needed. The show and hide control is typically an icon, such as a "+" and "-" or an arrow that swivels to indicate the open or closed state of the panel. For example, an accordion component is a set of overlapping panels that users can expand and collapse.
- A content toggle reveals hidden content, like an FAQ, where the answer displays only when the user selects the "expand" control. Typically FAQs provide an "expand all" option, for users who want access to all of the content.
- Trees are hierarchical lists of items arrayed in outline format, with toggle controls to expand and collapse sections and subsections. Trees are sometimes used for navigation, to provide direct access to section and subsection pages.

GUIDING INTERACTION

A central goal of any design is to be self-explanatory—to tell people how to interact with functional elements. For web forms and interactions, design should guide users through the functional elements of the page and, using instructions, labels, prompts, and design patterns, explain what is expected and how the page works. The designer's role of benevolent guide is critical to user success—more important in some ways than the design of the functional elements themselves. With gentle guidance, users can recover from mishaps better than when they have to puzzle out a confusing interface on their own.

Labels

Control labels must convey enough information to users, such that they know what will happen on activating the control. A clear sign of failure is if the user must activate the control to determine its purpose—similar to needing to follow a link to ascertain its destination. Icons can be effective labels when they are easy to decipher, either because their meaning is clear or because they are familiar, such as the text formatting icons used on most text editor toolbars. When the meaning is not clear, icons are best paired with descriptive text. The icons are easy to visually scan and recognize, and the text provides additional clarity about the purpose of the control.

For form fill-in, labels are essential guides, telling us what information to provide in form fields. HTML provides a means to attach form labels to form fields, so there is never any mystery about what information is being requested. The `<label>` element associates a label with its element using the `id` attribute:

```
<label for="departdate">Departing (YY/MM/DD):</label><input
    type="text" id="departdate" />
```

When form fields are marked up with labels, the relationship of label to field is available to software. For example, screen reader users can enter a form field and hear its label, along with any instructions contained within the label. Without the label, that information must be gleaned from browsing the surrounding text.

Do not use "placeholder" text for essential information, such as the field label. Placeholder text is appealing because the text displays within an input field and can provide guidance without using precious screen space. However, default text disappears when the user activates the field to enter information, which is just when the instructions are needed most. (Was that year, month, day, or day, month, year?) Also, placeholder text typically displays as low-contrast gray text on a white background, making it difficult to distinguish. Placeholder text is intended to be an auxiliary aid, to help with data entry. If the information is essential to successful form completion, put it on the screen, alongside the corresponding form element, so that everyone can benefit from it.

Help and instructions

Contextual help offers answers and guidance within the context of the page rather than sending the user to a help section of the site. A common implementation of this is through a "?" icon next to a new or potentially confusing feature. Contextual help is often provided via a dialog, panel, or tooltip. This method allows users to get help without having to deviate from the task at hand.

A web form often needs to provide instructions beyond simple form labels. Some types of information, such as dates and credit card numbers, for example, need to share a standard format. Ideally, the user can enter the information in a variety of formats, and the system will be smart enough to reconfigure the information to the required format. In reality, however, not all our systems are that smart, in which case we need to ask the user to enter the information in the required format. A date, for example, can be entered in a variety of formats, but your back-end system architecture may require a specific format, such as year, month, and day. Provide an example in the field label, for example, "Departing (yy/mm/dd)."

- **Required fields:** Note which input fields are required, and use a universally accessible method. Don't rely on color, because not all users can distinguish colors. One convention is to use an asterisk ("*") to denote required fields. Also, ensure the field is marked as required in code, so that it is available to assistive technology.
- **Tooltips:** Tooltips are often used to provide additional information about controls and inputs. Tooltips display when the user hovers the cursor over an interactive component, providing additional context and instructions for using the component. Relying on a mouse to make your interface accessible is problematic, as discussed above in the section on supporting different interaction modes. Keyboard and touchscreen users will not benefit from the guidance provided via a tooltip.

Feedback

The best way to handle errors is to keep them from happening. For example, users unintentionally delete files. One way to prevent this is to ask users to confirm their choice every time they ask to delete a file, which can quickly turn into nagging. A better approach is to allow users to go ahead and delete but to save all deleted messages in a location where they can be readily retrieved. Google keeps deleted files for its web applications in a Trash folder. It's only when you elect to empty the trash that you are prompted to confirm your intention. Not all errors can be prevented, however, and interaction design involves responding to errors in a way that is informative and helps users get back on track.

Error handling can happen on the server, after the user submits the form, or inline on the client, as the user interacts with the form elements. Feedback in the server-side model typically takes the form of a returned page with an error message indicating that the form was not successfully received.

Inline error messages provide feedback as the user works through a form rather than after the fact, on submission—for example, a form with required fields where the fields are monitored and feedback is provided to the user during form completion, and the "submit" button is disabled until all required fields have been completed. Inline feedback is more usable than after-the-fact feedback because users can respond to errors as they work through the form rather than having to ascertain which form elements are in error, fix the error, submit the form again, and hope for the best. Instead, users can fix errors as they occur and feel confident their submission will be successful.

When an error does occur, let the user know in a way that is helpful. Provide specifics about what happened: "Your password is incorrect" rather than "Your username and password do not match." Provide the explanation adjacent to the field in question—in this case, next to the password field. Ensure the error messages are accessible to assistive technology by encoding name, role, and state information into error messages (see section on responding to errors, above).

In responding to errors, make sure your error messages are tuned to users' needs. Error messages are too often written in programmer speak, either too detailed and specific or too vague, offering little in the way of explanation and guidance on where to go next ("Operation failed: try again"). Give users just enough information about what happened. They don't need to know that the error number is 404, but they do need to know that the page they requested cannot be found on the server. Provide guidance about what to do in response to the error. If the page cannot be found, offer search and a site map to help the user find it, along with links to the main sections of your site. And a little humor is always welcome.

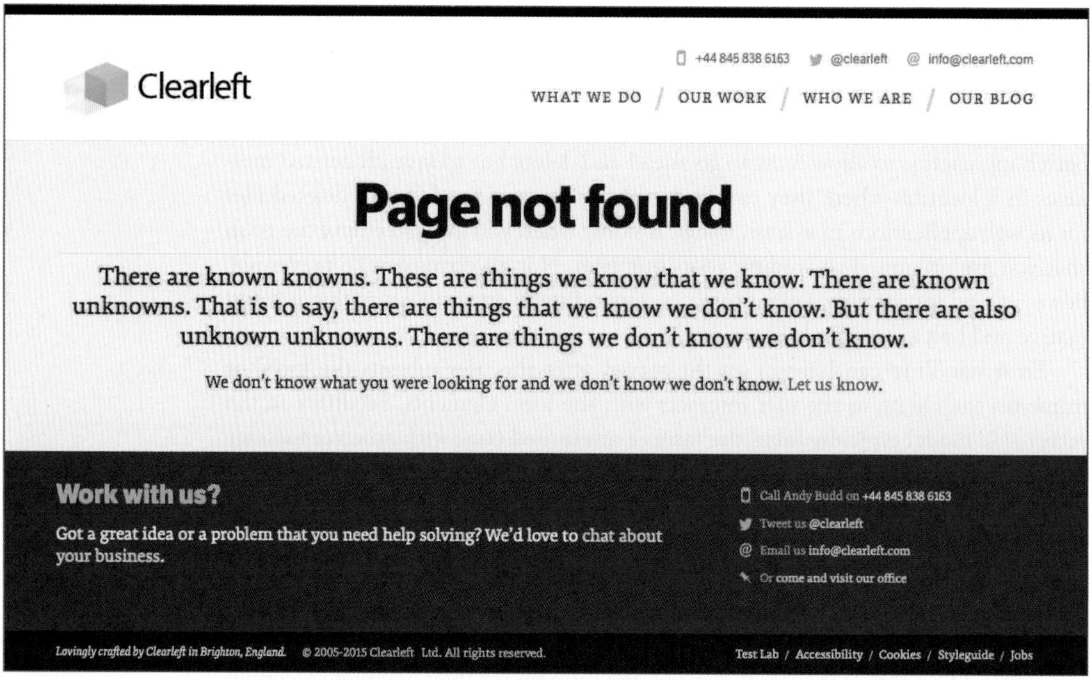

FIGURE 7.25

Typing errors, broken links, and missing pages are inevitable. Don't just point out the "Error 404." Provide as much help as you can to the user in your "error" screens, with search, navigation, and suggestions.

INFORMATION DESIGN

Concepts about structuring information today stem largely from the organization of printed books and periodicals and the library indexing and catalog systems that developed around printed information. The interface standards of books in the English-speaking world are well established and widely agreed upon, and detailed instructions for creating books may be found in such publication standards manuals as *The Chicago Manual of Style*. Every feature of the printed book, from the contents page to the index, has evolved over centuries, and readers of early books faced some of the same organizational problems that users of hypermedia documents confront today. Johannes Gutenberg's Bible of 1456 is often cited as the first mass-produced book, yet even after the explosive growth of publishing that followed Gutenberg's invention of printing with movable type, more than a century passed before page numbering, indexes, tables of contents, and even title pages became expected and necessary features of books. Web documents are undergoing a similar—albeit faster—evolution and standardization.

Although networked interactive hypermedia documents pose novel challenges to information designers, most of the guidance needed to design, create, assemble, edit, and organize multiple forms of media does not differ radically from current practice in print media. Most web documents can be designed to conform to *Chicago*

Manual of Style conventions for editorial style and text organization. Much of what an organization needs to know about creating clear, comprehensive, and consistent internal publishing standards is already available in such general publishing style guides as the *Franklin Covey Style Guide for Business and Technical Communication* and *The Gregg Reference Manual*. Don't get so lost in the novelty of web pages that basic standards of editorial consistency, business communications, and graphic design are tossed aside.

DESIGNING INFORMATION

Web pages differ from books and other documents in several crucial respects: hypertext links allow users to experience a single web page separate from its context. For this reason web pages need to be more independent than pages in a book. For example, the headers and footers of web pages should be more informative and elaborate than those on printed pages. It would be absurd to repeat the copyright information, author, and date of a book at the bottom of every printed page, but individual web pages often need to provide such information because a single web page may be the only part of a site that some users will see. This problem of making documents freestanding is not unique to web pages. Journals, magazines, and most newspapers repeat the date, volume number, and issue number at the top or bottom of each printed page because they know that readers often rip out articles or photocopy pages and will need that information to be able to trace the source of the material.

Given the difficulties inherent in creating web sites that are both easy to use and full of complex content, the best design strategy is to apply a few fundamental document design principles consistently in every web page you create. The basic elements of a document aren't complicated and have almost nothing to do with Internet technology. It's like a high school journalism class: who, what, when, and where.

Who

Who is speaking? This question is so basic, and the information is so often taken for granted, that authors frequently overlook the most fundamental piece of information a reader needs in order to assess the provenance of a web document. Whether the page originates from an individual author or an institution, always tell the reader who created it and what institution you are associated with.

What

All documents need clear titles to capture the user's attention, but for several reasons peculiar to the web, this basic editorial element is especially crucial. The page title and major headings are also crucial for search engine visibility. The page `<title>` element is the most important determinant of keyword relevance for search engines, so craft your titles carefully if you want users to find your content.

When

Timeliness is an important element in evaluating the worth of a document. We take information about the age of most paper documents for granted: newspapers, magazines, and virtually all office correspondence are dated. Date every web page, and change the date whenever the document is updated. This is especially important in long or complex online documents that are updated regularly but may not look different enough to signal a change in content to occasional readers. Corporate information, personnel manuals, product information, and other technical documents delivered as web pages should always carry version numbers or revision dates. Remember that many readers prefer to print long documents from the web. If you don't include revision dates, your reader may not be able to tell whether the version she has in hand is current.

Where

The web is an odd "place" that has huge informational dimensions but few explicit cues to the place of origin of a document. Click on a web link, and you could be connected to a web server in Sydney, Chicago, or Rome—anywhere, in fact, with an Internet connection. Unless you are well versed in parsing URLs, it can be hard to tell where a page originates. This is the World Wide Web, after all, and the question of where a document comes from is sometimes inseparable from whom the document comes from. Always tell the user where you are from, with (if relevant) your corporate or institutional affiliations.

Incorporating the "home" URL within the page footer is an easy way to maintain the connection to where a page originated. Once the user has saved the page as a text file or printed the page onto paper, this connection may be lost.

Every web page needs:

- An informative HTML page title (within the HTML `<title>` tag), which also becomes the text of any bookmark to the page
- A prominent title at the top of the local content area, identifying the primary purpose or content of the page
- The creator's identity (author or institution)
- A creation or revision date
- A copyright statement, Creative Commons statement, or other statement of ownership to protect your intellectual property rights
- A link to a local home page or menu page, in a consistent location on all pages
- A link to the local site home page
- A link to the home page of your enterprise or company

Most web pages should also incorporate these additional elements:

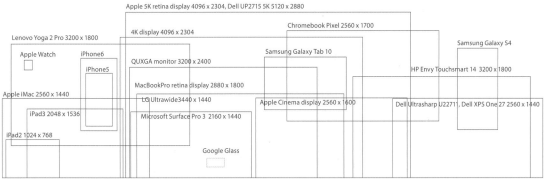

Apple 5K retina display 4096 x 2304, Dell UP2715 5K 5120 x 2880

Chromebook Pixel 2560 x 1700

Lenovo Yoga 2 Pro 3200 x 1800

4K display 4096 x 2304

Samsung Galaxy S4

Apple Watch   iPhone6

Samsung Galaxy Tab 10

QUXGA monitor 3200 x 2400

iPhone5

HP Envy Touchsmart 14 3200 x 1800

MacBookPro retina display 2880 x 1800

Apple iMac 2560 x 1440

LG Ultrawide3440 x 1440

Apple Cinema display 2560 x 1600

Dell Ultrasharp U2271, Dell XPS One 27 2560 x 1440

iPad3 2048 x 1536

Microsoft Surface Pro 3 2160 x 1440

iPad2 1024 x 768

Google Glass

Screens shown proportionally in pixel dimensions, not physical size.

- An organization logo or name near the upper left corner, with a link back to your home page
- Navigation links to other major sections of your site
- At least one heading to identify and clarify the page content
- Mailing address and contact information or a link to this information
- Alternate ("alt") text identifying any graphics on the page

FIGURE 7.26

Include these basic information elements and you will have traveled 90 percent of the way toward providing your users with an understandable web user interface.

MOBILE INTERFACE DESIGN

Mobile Internet technology is one of the fastest-growing and most exciting areas of modern computing and mass communications. In 2014, 58 percent of American adults owned a "smartphone" capable of running sophisticated applications ("apps"), and worldwide the number of Internet-connected devices exceeds the number of people; that number is expected to climb to more than 1.4 devices per capita by 2016. Although we call them "phones," our smartphones and cellular-enabled tablets are actually powerful small computers that also happen to be able to make "phone calls" (two-way radio communications, really). Although smartphones and tablets can now do things that only powerful desktop computers could do just a few years ago, there are many practical, physical, and cognitive constraints on mobile users that affect virtually every aspect of the user experience with the tiny computers most of us carry around every day.

When mobile computing and smartphones became common after the introduction of iPhones and Android phones, most web designers and interface experts advocated special mobile-only sites that were stripped-down and simplified versions of full "desktop" web sites, on the notion that the typical mobile user was a harried, distracted person "on the go," who needed just a few basic services and points of information, and that any "real" or complex interactions would get done later on a laptop or desktop computer. In fact, it quickly became apparent that most mobile users wanted a full user experience from most sites, that they were not always on the go when using their smartphones, and that for about 31 percent of web users the smartphone is the primary computing device.

Luckily this evolving sense of the mobile user coincided with two other important trends in web design: the rise of "responsive" web design using the new screen-sensing and layout capabilities of css3, and "mobile-first" content and design strategies that recognize that most of us now live in a multiscreen, multidevice world where sites should "respond" in intelligent ways to multiple sizes of displays and many kinds of usage situations. A decade ago it might have made sense to start your new site design with fixed-width sketches in Photoshop. That kind of desktop-oriented fixed-width thinking is irrelevant to current realities in a world where the average person uses many sizes and shapes of screens every day.

Today it makes far more sense to view typical use cases or "user stories" within a continuum of screen sizes or "viewports," where in a typical day a person might do a quick review of a few emails on a smartwatch while getting up in the morning, check her regular news sites on a smartphone during the morning commute, review dozens of sites in a typical workday on a desktop computer with twin large monitors, and also review yet more sites from a laptop or tablet while attending a business meeting.

DESIGNING THE MOBILE USER EXPERIENCE

Mobile user experience design is not too different from traditional forms of web design for larger screens, but almost every usage constraint and potential user experience problem is amplified by the difficulties of working in a small-screen/touchscreen environment. The increased cognitive load that small screens, mobile-use contexts, and small touch targets create is considerable, and calls for special attention to mobile design beyond just rearranging your content layout for smaller screens.

Mobile context

Although many mobile device users access their phones and tablets under quiet, controlled conditions, much of mobile computing is done in potentially distracting environments where intermittent use and disruptions are common, and even simple tasks are harder to accomplish than in the desktop world of larger screens, physical keyboards, and mouse or touchpad pointers. Aside from environmental challenges, small screens also impose more cognitive load on the mobile user because the increased scrolling needed tends to hide important navigation or content in the off-screen areas, forcing users to remember more about content or controls they have already scrolled past.

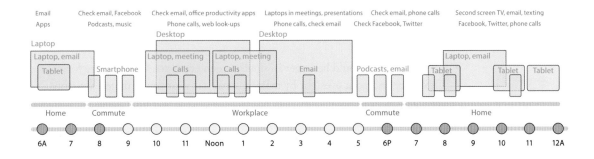

FIGURE 7.27

Make sure that information handy to mobile users is prominently displayed or easy to find in the mobile view of your site. Street addresses or store locations are important for local shoppers, and your phone number should be easy to find and click for no-dial access on a smartphone. Mobile conversion (visit and purchase) rates are about five times as high on tablets as on smartphones (5 percent versus 1 percent), suggesting that cognitive load, payment challenges, and other awkward logistics are still major issues in small-screen mobile web shopping.

Components of mobile UI

Mobile style sheets often simplify site headers and navigation for mobile displays, but navigation remains critical for mobile users. While simplification is generally a good mobile strategy, if you remove too many "you are here" cues and navigation links, the mobile user has no choice but to continually bounce between the home page—often the only available landmark in many mobile presentations—and pages deep within the mobile site. Footer-based navigation links can be a way to provide more navigation choices without cluttering the top of a mobile page.

The mixed desktop, tablet, and smartphone page-navigation metaphors define an emerging problem in mobile design. Don't mix up desktop and tablet interface metaphors: tablet users are accustomed to horizontal "swipe" gestures in mobile app content and ebooks, but desktop web and mobile phone web users are not. Most responsive sites and desktop web sites use vertical scrolling.

Desktop screens are almost always oriented horizontally, but mobile devices offer equally convenient portrait or landscape modes, particularly with tablets and very large smartphones. Portrait versus landscape usage is about evenly split among tablet users, with about 54 percent of tablet users preferring the landscape mode of viewing web content. However, mobile phones tend to be held vertically by most users—as seen in the myriad vertical videos and "selfies" on the web—and therefore mobile web layouts should assume a portrait orientation for most use cases.

True "responsiveness" in the mobile environment means a lot more than just rejiggering your content boxes for smaller screens:

- Touch targets should be larger in small-screen contexts. Compensate for poor dexterity and poor eyesight by making sure that your touch targets (buttons, navigation links, field forms) are really large enough for the user to hit without missing the target or, worse, hitting the wrong target.
- Adapt your typography for small screens and high resolution. Although smartphone screens are gradually getting larger, they are also increasing in resolution. This effectively creates opposing trends (see the longer discussion of mobile screens below), as the higher resolution of the newer "retina" screens can actually cause graphics and type to look smaller on some screens. This means that your css3 code (@media queries) needs to check for both screen size (min-width, the total number of horizontal pixels on the screen) and effective resolution (min-resolution, or pixels per inch) to judge what type sizes are most appropriate for mobile displays.
- Ensure snappy performance. Mobile responsiveness in web page code becomes a bit pointless if the mobile web browser must download large amounts of unneeded graphics and style code, particularly as most mobile users experience some intermittent (or extended) network access problems in a typical day. If your page designs require hundreds of kilobytes of css3 code, you might be better off designing a mobile app than a web-based solution.
- Make payments easy. Don't expect a mobile user to fill out a long form, complete with a sixteen-digit credit card number. Use preset systems like PayPal, Apple Pay, or Amazon Payments, or expect most prospective customers to bail out before purchasing.
- Provide accessible content and functionality. Accessibility for mobile is critical, and touchscreen devices have built-in assistive technology, including screen reader software, magnification, and inverted colors. bbc's mobile accessibility guidelines are an excellent guide to mobile-specific features that support accessibility.
- Provide access to the "desktop version." This ideally means you just provide the user with a way to switch the view to the "desktop" css styling of your site. With today's broad spectrum of mobile device screen sizes and resolutions a mobile user of a large phone or small tablet may simply prefer the "desktop" version of your site for some tasks, especially if you hide some content or features from mobile users, or require data entry forms that are not coded for responsive display. Ideally you should use a browser cookie to remember the user's preferred browsing style.

Also, you should assume that your mobile web users are competent adults who are doing exactly what they prefer to do when they look at your site in a mobile web browser. Don't constantly nag mobile web users to switch to the "app" version of your content, or pop up annoying windows that advertise your mobile app. Offer the app alternative as a lower-key link or banner ad instead.

Screen sizes and orientations

The physical size of a mobile touchscreen has important usability design implications, because although screen sizes are quite variable, our fingers and thumbs are the same size they always were, and interface layouts that work very well on a small, vertical smartphone screen might prove to be awkward on a tablet with a much larger screen. This is particularly true for users who hold their tablets in both hands and manipulate virtual keyboards or buttons with their thumbs. The larger size of recent smartphone screens is also posing a challenge to one-handed touchscreen users, whose thumbs are too short to reach across the expanded screens dimensions.

As screen sizes increase, Fitt's Law begins to operate in a more significant way in mobile interfaces. Fitt's Law describes a universal constant in graphic interfaces: the time required to acquire a target and to use the target to take action is a function of the distance to and size of the target. In other words, small distant targets take more time to find, and may not be noticed at all. Clickable targets like buttons may benefit from slightly enhanced sizes in various responsive mobile designs, to be noticed, and on small screens to provide a large enough target to touch accurately.

ENTERPRISE INTERFACE DESIGN

The web can provide a powerful framework for promoting group cohesion and identification with the large missions and goals of an enterprise, but only if the user interface, information architecture, and graphic design of the enterprise's web sites consistently promote a common purpose and shared identity across all the major elements of the public-facing web sites and the organization's internal sites and intranet. Most large corporations have well-established corporate identity programs that now include comprehensive web design and interface standards.

PROVIDING A COHESIVE EXPERIENCE

Many smaller companies, federal, state, and local government sites, college and university sites, and nonprofit institutions produce chaotic, poorly organized web sites because the institutions lack consistent, widely implemented web publishing standards. Nobody sets out to produce a chaotic enterprise web presence, but an insistence on trying to optimize each individual site within the larger organization is a guarantee of disorder and confusion for users. You can't optimize a library by writing a great book, and no single web site—no matter how well designed—will ever improve an enterprise's overall web presence.

The only long-term approach to improving an organization's web presence is a consistent approach to web interface design, one that explicitly recognizes the larger context of the enterprise and the web in general. Ideally this set of consistent standards becomes the "enterprise interface" across all forms of web information publishing and web-based access to applications. In today's large organizations, web content can flow from dozens of major information sources. A consistent, comprehensive approach to the enterprise interface is the best way to maximize the return for the enormous investments that companies make in web publishing and web applications.

A chaotic web presence sends one consistent message about an organization: contempt for the user. Users spend 99.99 percent of their time on web sites other than yours, and potential readers couldn't care less that you want your little part of the larger site to look unique. If your organization has web standards, always incorporate them into your site design and user interface. If you don't have standards, lead an effort to create them. Research on the most effective corporate intranets and portals shows that users are most productive, most efficient, and overwhelmingly more satisfied with sites that employ a consistent, comprehensive interface and design standard throughout the organization's web presence.

Coherence

A coherent interface presents the enterprise clearly and comprehensively, conveying an understandable picture of the organization's structure and functioning, products and services to clients, internal communications and management policy, and overall mission and goals. Building a legible, easily navigable corporate web structure is more than just a graphic user interface issue. A well-structured site rich with useful content directly represents the depth and breadth of an enterprise more comprehensively than any previous medium.

Symbolism

As networked work environments have become the norm and various forms of telecommuting and remote access are routine, web-based work environments are the dominant force in creating and maintaining the corporate ethos, attitudes, and values. For most employees the organizational web presence has become the most visible and functional evidence of social cohesion and common purpose across the enterprise.

Positioning

A clear and recognizable identity program helps distinguish an enterprise from peers and competitors. This is especially critical on the Internet, where everyone has a web site and all web sites appear in the same limited venue (a browser window on the user's screen). A user may visit a dozen organizational sites in a browsing session and be exposed to many graphic themes. Web users' expectations of the Internet as a communications medium are determined mainly by what they have seen in other sites, and what they've seen is mostly like confetti: weightless, colorful, and chaotic. Will users remember your pages if your site looks like nothing else they've seen in your larger enterprise?

Cohesive, comprehensive design transcends immediate commercial objectives. Enterprises need to differentiate themselves not only in the products and services they offer but also as social entities. In too many corporate, university, and government sites, the lack of a comprehensive group identity and shared sense of mission is made painfully obvious by the chaotic condition of their web sites. An effective web presence can be a powerful tool for enhancing the status and competitive positioning of an enterprise, but only if the web site effectively projects a feeling of trust in the knowledge and competence of the organization that produced it.

RECOMMENDED READING

Colborne, G. *Simple and Usable Web, Mobile, and Interaction Design*. Berkeley, CA: New Riders, 2011.

Cooper, A., R. Reimann, D. Cronin, and C. Noessel. *About Face: The Essentials of Interaction Design*. Hoboken, NJ: Wiley, 2014.

Krug, S. *Don't Make Me Think, Revisited*. Berkeley, CA: New Riders, 2014.

———. *Rocket Surgery Made Easy*. Berkeley, CA: New Riders, 2010.

Linderman, M., and J. Fried. *Defensive Design for the Web: How to Improve Error Messages, Help, Forms, and Other Crisis Points*. Berkeley, CA: New Riders, 2004.

Shneiderman, B., C. Plaisant, M. Cohen, and S. Jacobs. *Designing the User Interface: Strategies for Effective Human-Computer Interaction*. Upper Saddle River, NJ: Prentice Hall, 2009.

RELAX
Nothing is
in control

CHAPTER 8

Graphic Design

G raphic design is the artful arrangement of images and words into planned form. If the form is not carefully planned, it is not design. If the arrangement is not artful, it is not design. If the designer is involved only after all the important decisions are made, then design is mere decoration—the design is there only to make things "nice," and nice is mediocre.

USING DESIGN LOGIC

Design creates visual logic and seeks an optimal balance between visual sensation and graphic information. Without the visual impact of shape, color, and contrast, pages are graphically uninteresting and will not motivate the viewer. Dense text documents without contrast and visual relief are also hard to read, particularly on smaller or relatively low-resolution screens. But without the depth and complexity of text, highly graphic pages risk disappointing the user by offering a poor balance of visual sensation, text information, and interaction. Graphic design has its roots in language, and is still fundamentally about typography, and typography is a means to represent spoken language in print. In seeking the ideal balance, great design is about walking the tightrope between visual and intellectual stimulation, producing "differences that make a difference," in Edward Tufte's phrase, while respecting and taking advantage of the millennia-long traditions of written communications in human culture.

FLUID LOGIC

Given the myriad of current and future computing device sizes and shapes, today's extremely plastic web page designs usually begin under the surface of the visual field, with the structure of the underlying "responsive" code, and not with static visual tools like Photoshop or Illustrator. This is a deep challenge to designers educated in the traditional "canon" of print design, with its fixed visual planes and the mechanical technologies of ink on paper. When every "page" can exist in multiple forms and layouts, when style itself seems blown apart into visual confetti and fragmentary "style tiles," it can sometimes seem as if graphic design as a discipline has reached the end of history.

Not so. Web communications has never had a greater need of the visual intelligence and unifying force of graphic design. Yes, the landscape has changed in fluid

Sometimes magic is just someone spending more time on something than anyone else might reasonably expect.

—Raymond J. Teller, quoted in *Esquire*, 2012

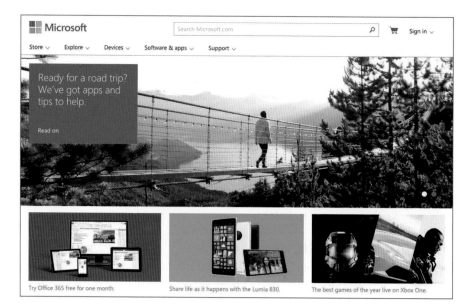

ways that can make traditional designers queasy, but the fundamentals of contrast and focus, texture and pattern, color and typography have not changed, and still operate in powerful ways to knit together the slippery digital bits of graphics and words into a meaningful whole on the display screen. In a prescient article written more than fifteen years ago, "A Dao of Web Design," designer John Allsopp wrote: "The web's greatest strength, I believe, is often seen as a limitation, as a defect. It is the nature of the web to be flexible, and it should be our role as designers and developers to embrace this flexibility, and produce pages which, by being flexible, are accessible to all."

BUSINESS LOGIC

Visual and functional continuity in your web site organization, graphic design, and typography are essential to convince your audience that your web site offers them timely, accurate, and useful information. A careful, systematic approach to page design can simplify navigation, reduce user errors, and make it easier for users to take advantage of the information and features of your site. Good web design is more important than ever. As the matrix of our online world begins to fully meld with "real life," and we begin to live fully within our mixed virtual and actual landscapes of kitchen and Twitter, Facebook and the office, Amazon and the grocery store, the elements of online design are becoming more permanent, architectural, and even environmental.

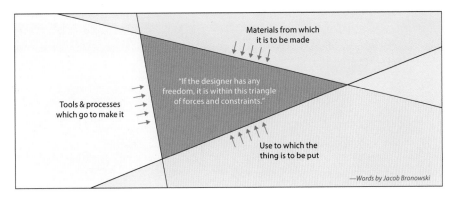

FIGURE 8.2
Every good design is
an optimal balance
of circumstances,
the available tools
and technology, and
usefulness to users.

EVOLVING A STYLE

Don't set out to develop a "style" for your site, and be careful about simply importing the graphic elements of another web site or print publication to decorate your pages. The graphic and editorial style of your web site should evolve as an organic consequence of consistent and appropriate handling of your content and page layout. Prefer the conventional over the eccentric, never let the framing overwhelm the content, and remember that the best style is one that readers never notice—where everything feels logical, comfortable—and beautiful—but where heavy-handed visual "styling" never intrudes on the experience. As Edward Tufte has said, "If you look after truth and goodness, beauty looks after herself."

It may seem that today's rapid technical changes constitute a unique challenge, but as scientist and historian Jacob Bronowski wrote many decades ago, designers have always had to reconcile rapid social, technical, and business environment changes, and while our digital tools can sometimes seem like a mixed blessing, we designers have never had more powerful, useful—and fun—tools at our fingertips. The best design aims at the balanced "sweet spot" of current thought, technical capabilities, and most of all, the needs of the audience.

DESIGN INTEGRITY

Design quality is the respect you owe to the audience, and a means to convey sincerity and trustworthiness of thought and purpose. Careful, considered, and informed craft is the respect we show to our users and readers. Design is the process of making things right, with intention, and with purpose.

APPRECIATING THE IMPACT OF ATTRACTIVENESS

Many people are skeptical about the role of visual aesthetics in the user experience—and of designers who insist that graphic emotive impact and careful attention to a site's visual framework really contribute to measurable success in usability. The

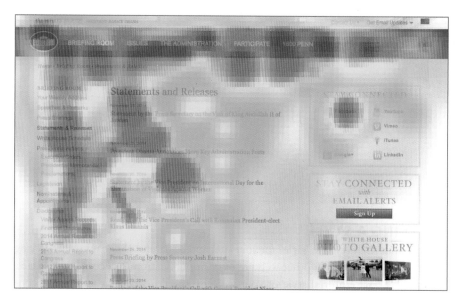

FIGURE 8.3

Eye-tracking studies produce "heat maps" that show the most intensive eye traffic (red is most; blue or clear is least). The upper left of the page (the so-called golden triangle) gets the most attention, but, as you can see, eye traffic in the left navigation and the start of content lines also attracts attention in a classic "F" pattern across the top and down the left side.

visual aesthetics that frame and define content are much more than simply a "skin" that we can apply or discard without consequence. Users react in fast, profound, and lasting ways to the aesthetics of what they see and use, and research shows that the sophisticated visual content presentation influences user perceptions of usability, trust, and confidence in the web content they view. Those judgments begin within fifty milliseconds of the user seeing the first page of your web site.

EYE-TRACKING AND AESTHETIC RESPONSE

Many eye-tracking studies show that large graphics and graphic elements attract few "gaze fixations," but can we really conclude that large, aesthetic, tone-setting graphics have no lasting effect on the user's attitudes toward a site? Another body of web user experience research shows that web site users are powerfully influenced by aesthetics, and that positive perceptions of order, beauty, novelty, and creativity increase the user's confidence in a site's trustworthiness and usability. Recent design writing and interface research illustrate how visual design and user research can work together to create better user experiences on the web: experiences that balance the practicalities of navigation with aesthetic interfaces that delight the eye and brain. In short: there's lots of evidence that beauty enhances usability.

Eye-tracking is a good method for analyzing and understanding how users see, interpret, and use information. However, on the basis of eye-tracking studies some user interface researchers assert that because study participants (apparently) pay little attention to large graphics on web pages (few eye-tracking gaze fixations), we can infer that large page graphics have little influence on users. Here we are talking

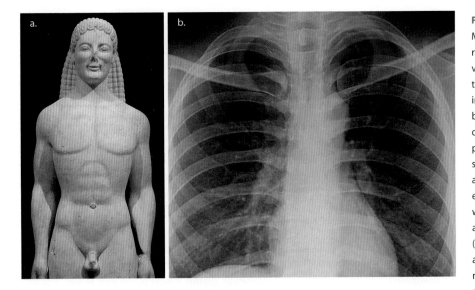

FIGURE 8.4
Many professions
rely on complex
visual judgments
that are near-
instantaneous. In
both art history and
diagnostic radiology
practitioners make
sophisticated
and considered
evaluations of
what they see, but
an authentication
(in art history) or
a diagnosis (in
radiology) more
often than not starts
with a millisecond
glance and an instant
gut feeling that
something is right or
wrong.

not about catalog images or other images closely related to merchandise or tasks but about the images and other graphic content that designers use to create a site's aesthetic ambiance. Context is important here: In such studies, participants have a set of specific tasks to accomplish, and thus their gaze tends to focus on navigation links, titles, labels, and interface controls such as buttons and form fields. Expressive or visual tone-setting graphics are rarely useful in such tasks, and it's not surprising that users performing these tasks (apparently) ignore most page graphics, as indicated by the infrequent gazes directed at large images.

To reconcile the differing views of the proper role of visual aesthetics, we need to understand how the brain processes images and responds to what we see.

"GUT" REACTIONS

Thanks to the work of the early-twentieth-century gestalt psychologists—and to many studies since—we know that the brain's response to images is extremely complex, and in many cases nearly instantaneous. The process seems semimagical and therefore untrustworthy. How could something so complex happen so fast? How can we trust the results of a process we don't thoroughly understand? Research confirms that users make aesthetic decisions about the overall visual impression of web pages in as little as fifty milliseconds (one twentieth of a second). These instant visceral reactions to web pages happen in virtually all users, are consistent over visit length, and strongly influence the user's sense of trust in the information. In short, users have made fundamental, consistent, and lasting aesthetic decisions about the credibility and authority of sites before significant eye-tracking events even begin.

FIGURE 8.5

The take-home message of our affective response system is that we make fast visceral judgments about what we see, and that those instant judgments have a profound and lasting effect on how we trust and value what we see. However, it can sometimes take many seconds to become consciously aware that we have made important visceral judgments about what we are looking at.

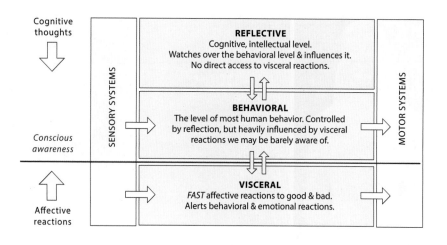

In intensely visual fields such as art history and diagnostic radiology, this kind of sophisticated, complex, nearly instantaneous gestalt visual judgment is well known and respected, although the exact neural mechanisms at work are not well understood. In his book *Blink* Malcolm Gladwell tells the story of the Getty Museum's famous kouros, a nominally ancient Greek statue now widely regarded as a modern forgery. Although the provenance and mineralogy tests seemed to provide definitive proof of the statue's age, independent art history experts were almost universally negative in their first visceral reactions to the statue. Thomas Hoving's immediate reaction to the statue's unveiling was "fresh," hardly the right word for a sculpture that had supposedly been buried for two thousand years. At first, the experts had only their gut visual reactions as proof, but their skepticism caused the Getty to reconsider, and the evidence supporting the statue's age and provenance fell apart on closer inspection.

AFFECTIVE RESPONSE AND DECISION MAKING

In psychology, emotional reactions to stimuli are called affective responses. Affective responses happen very fast, and are governed in an automatic, unconscious way by the lower centers of the brain that also govern basic instincts (food, fear, sex, breathing, blinking, and so on). Think of affective responses as the brain's bottom-up reaction to what you see and feel. Cognitive responses are your brain's slower, top-down, more considered responses. They're governed by your personal cultural views, learning, experiences, and personal preferences that you are aware of and can easily articulate. Affective reactions assign value to your experiences; cognitive reactions assign meaning to what you see and use.

Affective and cognitive responses to visual stimuli are governed by a three-stage process in the brain, at visceral, behavioral, and reflective processing levels.

	REFLECTIVE INTERPRETATION The intellectual level of seeing. Heavily dependent on your value judgments, social expectations, personal knowledge, and prior experience with the medium and types of messages. Emotional and intellectual reactions to what you see.

Conscious interpretation

	SYMBOLIC Language, typography, numbers, iconography, abstract diagrams or artwork, user interface elements. Symbolic content must be seen and decoded (read), and depends heavily on prior knowledge and experience. Slower, as decoding takes time.

	REPRESENTATIONAL Pictures, videos, and realistic artwork. Governed by prior visual experiences, so no decoding is needed. Recognition and understanding is not (usually) contingent on prior knowledge.

	VISUAL SYSTEM The neural infrastructure of vision, which is entirely within the visual cortex of the brain. Perception of light and dark, colors, patterns, shades, shapes, textures, lines and edges. Facial recognition and interpretation lie here as well.

The visceral ("gut") processing level reacts quickly to appearances. It's the visceral reaction to web pages that researchers measure when they detect reaction times as fast as fifty milliseconds. It's crucial to understand that these instant good/bad visceral-level affective responses are largely unconscious: it can take seconds or minutes to become consciously aware of your first, visceral reaction to a stimulus—particularly a stimulus as complex as a web page.

Behavioral-level processing involves the more familiar aspects of usability: it responds to the feel of using the site, the functionality, the understandability of the structure and navigation, and the overall physical performance of the site. At this level, users are consciously aware of their attitudes toward the behavior of the system, and their reactions (pleasure, for example, or frustration) play out over seconds and minutes as users interact with a site. It's at this behavioral level that techniques such as eye-tracking are most powerful and trustworthy, because they offer detailed moment-by-moment evidence of what users consciously decide to look at and do to fulfill a given task.

Visceral (affective) reactions can take a relatively long time to bubble up through layers of processing to enter conscious awareness at the behavioral or reflective level, but that doesn't mean that affective reactions don't immediately influence thought. In fact, it's the instant, preconscious pleasure of seeing a well-designed page that makes you predisposed to find a beautiful design easy to use—an effect that lingers

FIGURE 8.6

It takes time to fully process what we see, but our emotional reactions, and the more fundamental processes of our visual systems, tend to react long before we consciously make decisions about what we see.

long after the slower, conscious behavioral and reflective levels of processing kick in and make you aware of how you feel about what you see.

Reflective processing of reactions is the most complex level, and typically involves a user's personal sense of a site's beauty, meaning, cultural context, and immediate usefulness. Reflective processing often triggers memories and encourages pragmatic judgments about the overall aesthetic worth and value of what a user sees. Eye-tracking and traffic logs are irrelevant at this level, but user interviews can give you insight into your user's reflective judgments. Reflective processing of what we see also involves layers of symbols and meaning created not just by the more automatic sensory components of vision (color, pattern, shade, contrast, facial recognition), but also by our more nuanced and complex reactions to representational images (photos and realistic artwork), and to the symbolic elements of pages (typography, icons, diagrams).

VISUAL DESIGN

SHAPING THE VISUAL PLANE

At its most fundamental, graphic design is about organizing visual elements on a plane: manipulating graphics, various media, and typography to produce a visual order that reflects and enhances the messages of the content. In today's ever-expanding world of screens ranging in size from the watch on your wrist to whole walls of conference rooms, it can seem that the edges of the visual plane have become simultaneously unknowable and inescapable. Our designs are surrounded by the edges of thousands of devices, and we can only approximate how our layouts will respond to this diversity of planes.

Today's visual plane on digital devices is:

- **Variable:** We no longer know the size or even the physical characteristics of the field we design upon. We have lost control over the borders of our work, and no longer have those fundamental edges to guide our work and act as a reference frame.
- **Dynamic:** Our designs for screens are built on the fly, and we can never be entirely certain what browsers, operating systems, fonts, colors, or other foundational display technologies will be present to support the design.
- **Ubiquitous:** The good news is that our designs have never had a wider audience, and that information displays are now unbound from desks and have become truly environmental. Designers have never had a more powerful, plastic, or useful visual plane to work upon.

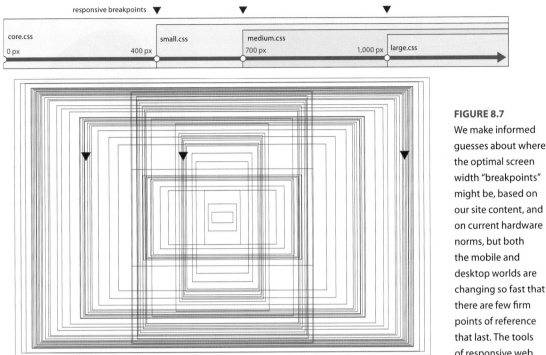

FIGURE 8.7
We make informed guesses about where the optimal screen width "breakpoints" might be, based on our site content, and on current hardware norms, but both the mobile and desktop worlds are changing so fast that there are few firm points of reference that last. The tools of responsive web design are the best tools we have to "future-proof" our designs.

- **Responsive:** The only rational way forward in this multiscreen world relies on the foundations of responsive web design: fluid page grids, responsive images, and css3 media queries that allow your designs to respond in intelligent ways to the variety of screens on which they live.

Where once designers knew the firm dimensions of the visual field and built against known borders and limits, today's web designer knows only that there is a screen of unpredictable height and width, and that the screen has a top to build down from, and a center to build out from. The good news is that all the fundamental tools of visual design still work: typography, color, contrast, size relationships, and even complex layouts work well in fully responsive designs.

The design process must also evolve to support the variability of graphic design:

- **Old design:** Define a plane with fixed edges and proportions, and a fixed grid, and populate it with content.
- **Transitional:** Define a flexible grid and populate it.
- **New:** Design from the content out, "mobile-first," starting with the most basic and important content, and building out from there.

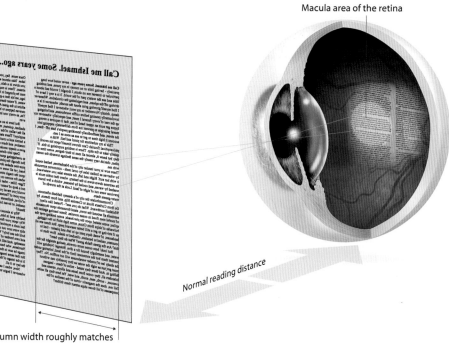

Macula area of the retina

Normal reading distance

Typical column width roughly matches
the macula, the "sharp focus"
part of the retina.

FIGURE 8.8

Columns of text work
well because they
complement aspects
of our visual system.

Line length

The ideal line length for text layout is based on the physiology of the human eye. The area of the retina used for tasks requiring high visual acuity is called the macula. The macula is small, typically less than 15 percent of the area of the retina. At normal reading distances the arc of the visual field covered by the macula is only a few inches wide—about the width of a well-designed column of text, or about twelve words per line. Research shows that reading slows as line lengths begin to exceed the ideal width, because the reader then needs to use the muscles of the eye or neck to track from the end of one line to the beginning of the next line. If the eye must traverse great distances on a page, the reader must hunt for the beginning of the next line (fig. 8.8).

Given the user-defined nature of the web and the vagaries of technology, it's impossible to control line length in all circumstances. A line that is designed to display a comfortable sixty-six characters per line of standard text will become a narrow, twenty-character line if the user enlarges the default browser text size. A multicolumn layout with fixed column widths can easily become difficult to read with enlarged text.

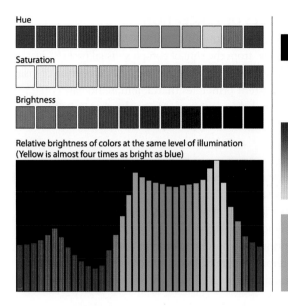

Hue

Saturation

Brightness

Relative brightness of colors at the same level of illumination
(Yellow is almost four times as bright as blue)

The optimal combination for legibility is black on white

White text on black is almost as good for legibility

Optically bright colors like yellow disappear on white

Inherently dark colors like blue or red work much better

Gradient backgrounds almost always create legibility issues because some part of the text will suffer from poor contrast and reduced legibility. If you must use a gradient, stick with black text, and avoid using dark colors in the background.

The 10 percent of males who are partially red-green color-blind would find this paragraph almost impossible to read, particularly because the green and red colors are very close in brightness level. Don't depend on color alone to produce contrast in text.

Both responsive design and universal usability principles (see Chapter 3) offer a great solution to the line-length problem by ensuring that the page design can fluidly adapt in width, so that users are not locked into a single view that may not work well for them. All current browsers also allow users to change the overall size of type in web layouts, giving users additional flexibility to adapt layouts for comfortable reading. In responsive layouts for larger screens designers can set a css "max-width" for the page to prevent a layout from expanding to absurd (and less legible) widths on larger display screens.

Color and contrast

Color and contrast are key components of universal usability. Text legibility is dependent on the reader's ability to distinguish letterforms from the background field. Color differentiation depends mostly on brightness and saturation. Black text on a white background has the highest level of contrast since black has no brightness and white is all brightness. Hue is also a factor, with complementary colors, such as blue and yellow, producing the greatest contrast. Be sure your color choices do not make it hard for users to distinguish text from background. Also, never forget that almost 8 percent of male readers have some trouble distinguishing fine shades of red from shades of green (fig. 8.9).

FIGURE 8.9

Not all colors and color combinations are created equal, especially for the 8 percent of males who have some degree of color blindness.

USING THE GESTALT PRINCIPLES OF PERCEPTION

The gestalt psychologists of the early twentieth century were fascinated with the mind's ability to see unified "wholes" from the sum of complex visual parts ("Gestalt" is German for "whole" or "whole form"). Their research into the perception of visual patterns yielded a number of consistent principles that dominate human visual reasoning and pattern recognition, and these principles form the theoretical basis for much of modern graphic design. The following principles are those most relevant to web page design:

- **Proximity:** Elements that are close to each other are perceived as more related than elements that lie farther apart (fig. 8.10a).
- **Similarity:** Viewers will associate and treat as a group elements that share consistent visual characteristics (fig. 8.10b).
- **Continuity:** We prefer continuous, unbroken contours and paths, and the vast majority of viewers will interpret Figure 8.10c as two crossed lines, not four lines meeting at a common point.

FIGURE 8.10

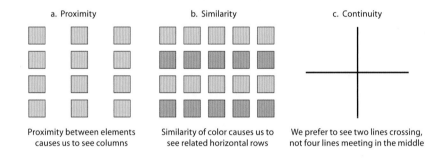

a. Proximity b. Similarity c. Continuity

Proximity between elements causes us to see columns

Similarity of color causes us to see related horizontal rows

We prefer to see two lines crossing, not four lines meeting in the middle

- **Closure:** We have a powerful bias to see completed figures, even when the contours of the figure are broken or ambiguous. We see a white square overlying four circles (fig. 8.11a), not four circles that each have a section missing.

Figure-ground relationships

In figure-ground reversal the viewer's perception alternates between two possible interpretations of the same visual field: you see either a goblet or two faces, but you cannot see both at once (fig. 8.11b). Proximity has a strong effect on figure-ground relationships: it's easier for most people to see the goblet when it's wider and the "faces" are farther apart (fig. 8.11c). Also, visual elements that are relatively small will be seen as discrete elements against a larger field. The small element will be seen as the "figure" and the larger field as the "ground" around the figure.

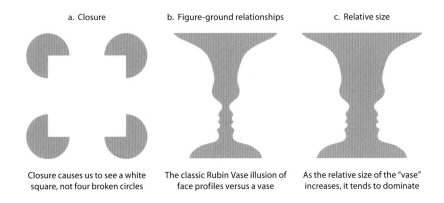

FIGURE 8.11

a. Closure

b. Figure-ground relationships

c. Relative size

Closure causes us to see a white square, not four broken circles

The classic Rubin Vase illusion of face profiles versus a vase

As the relative size of the "vase" increases, it tends to dominate

Uniform connectedness

Uniform connectedness refers to relations of elements that are defined by enclosing elements within other elements, regions, or discrete areas of the page.

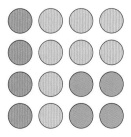

FIGURE 8.12

Uniformity allows us to see a blue column and a green group

Uniformity is a common organizing device in interfaces

Uniformity, enclosure, and proximity help to distinguish groups

1 + 1 = 3 effects

The "white space" between two visual elements forms a third visual element and becomes visually active as the elements come closer together. The well-known visual illusion below of gray "spots" appearing in the spaces between the dark squares shows the worst-case scenario for 1 + 1 = 3 effects, but this principle applies to all closely spaced elements in which the ground forms an active part of the overall design.

FIGURE 8.13

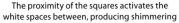

The proximity of the squares activates the white spaces between, producing shimmering

The more complex the layout, the worse the shimmering optical illusions and 1+1=3 effects

FIGURE 8.14

Even at the initial scanning stage the viewer should see an orderly and predictable pattern of contrasts, conveying a clear sense of priority (left). Pages with a more haphazard pattern make it difficult to decide what to concentrate on first (right).

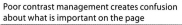
Good management and hierarchy of contrast

Poor contrast management creates confusion about what is important on the page

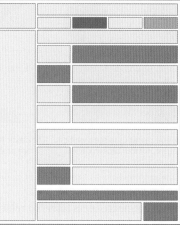

VISUAL STRUCTURE

Design creates visual pathways that highlight and reinforce content. Design elements must have meaning and never look arbitrarily "styled" simply to attract attention. Every element on the page ought to be there for a clear and identifiable purpose, in logical semantic relationships with other page elements that make content engaging and easy to read and understand.

UNDERSTANDING THE ORIGINS OF VISUAL STRUCTURE

Even in a medium that often seems to be entirely about the frenetic present and the immediate future, we are deeply influenced by the past. The proportions of your business card are based on the Parthenon's facade. Responsive sites like A List Apart use the same page layout as *The Book of Kells* (c. 795). Christophe Plantin or Aldus Manutius would recognize any story page in the New York Times site as essentially kin to his own work, however alien a computer screen might seem to these Renaissance printers.

A page is a visual architecture, full of implicit messages about the structure and relative importance of the content. Design, if it means anything, means planning. Page design requires an analysis of the project's strategy and objectives, and a thorough understanding of your audience and its needs. Developing a beautiful and functional visual structure is essential to any communications project: you must attract the reader before you can transmit a message. We normally think of content as fairly straightforward stuff—you look at a page, read the words, and get the message. But great page design has always been a subtle but profound mix of explicit and implicit messages. Explicit meaning from the words and images conveyed, and implicit

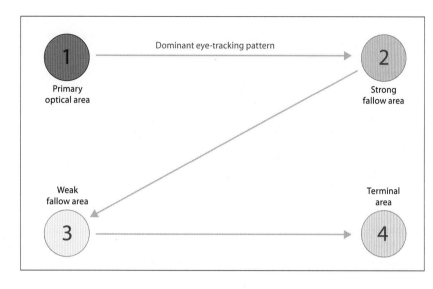

FIGURE 8.15
In European languages we read from the top left in a zigzag pattern down the page, often referred to as the "Gutenberg diagram" or the "Gutenberg Z." This basic visual scanning pattern creates a hierarchy of visual attention. Eye-tracking studies consistently show that the most noticed part of any page dominated by text is the upper left corner.

meaning from the typography, graphics, and visual hierarchy of contrast and emphasis. It is the designer's task to create a visual architecture, using implicit graphic tools that reinforce the explicit messages from content.

Design is also about the designer. Design can be approached subjectively, as an artist does his artwork, making visual decisions based primarily on personal visual tastes and preferences. Many postmodern design approaches are explicitly rejections of modernist objective design, although deeply subjective design is rarely seen outside the fine arts and fashion worlds. But art is an answer to a puzzle born within the artist, and design is the creative answer to a puzzle posed by others.

Objective design was pioneered by modernist Swiss and German designers like Herbert Matter and Josef Müller-Brockman, and expanded by later designers like Braun's Dieter Rams and Apple's Jonathan Ive. Objective design incorporates the Bauhaus philosophies of functionalism and gestalt visual psychology, with the aim of creating modular and systematic designs based on objective physical and psychological phenomena. Objective design loves modular systems, design grids, and systematic ways of investigating design problems. Within the web creation disciplines, the areas of page coding, information architecture, user interface design, and accessibility tend to be the most research-based and objective. Graphic design and marketing are inherently more subjective in their synthesis, but even design can be analyzed objectively with user testing and A/B testing of different designs.

Most contemporary web design is objectivist in philosophy, but that doesn't necessarily mean that the ideas and structures seen in today's web are all new ones. We are bound to our past even as we create our future.

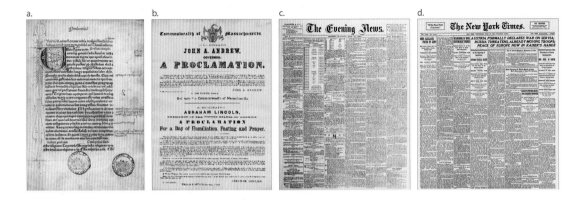

FIGURE 8.16 Before and well after the invention of movable type, page design was mostly a matter of filling one or several columns of text from top to bottom (a and b). This relatively simple page design persisted well into the nineteenth century, when a combination of the telegraph and more sophisticated printing techniques led to increasingly complex page designs in commercial documents and newspapers (c, newspaper from London, 1881). Gradually newspapers began to develop contrast and structure, with bolder headlines, subheads, and slightly more generous white space to try to direct and organize the reader's attention (d, *New York Times*, 1914).

Classical page design

The first mechanically printed pages with movable type grew out of older traditions of illuminated manuscripts and calligraphy. The fundamental design they used was so practical that most pages today use the same structure: in Western languages we read from top to bottom, scanning left to right on each line in the classic "Gutenberg Z" or "Gutenberg diagram" reading pattern. Page structure in classical layouts is based mostly on the placement of margins, within which the text and graphic content flows top to bottom in a single or sometimes a double column.

Many of the design innovations now associated with the modernist movement are actually much older. Swiss designers didn't invent "white space" in the 1950s. The best classical page design rarely used more than 50 percent of the (printed) page area, and used space wisely in support of both legibility and graphic innovation, even if the overall visual vocabulary was restrained by modern standards. "Form follows function" is a core tenet of modern design, but the saying was born in the classical era. American architect Louis Sullivan, a teacher of Frank Lloyd Wright, first used the phrase in an 1896 book on the form of early Chicago skyscrapers, but also credited the original thought to the ancient Roman architect Vitruvius (c. 70–15 BC).

Classical page design tended to use—and still uses—stately humanistic typefaces, both ancient and modern: Bembo, Caslon, Centaur, Garamond, Goudy, Jenson, and Palatino, to name a few, now thankfully all available via css3 web fonts. Mixing

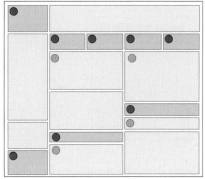

Visually monotonous, no obvious entry points; reading gravity and the "Gutenberg Z" take over

Contrast creates clear primary and secondary entry points to content

FIGURE 8.17 Monotonous gray fields of uniform text do little to organize the reader's attention, and most people will default to a simple top-to-bottom, left-to-right scanning pattern to try to make sense of the page content. Modern design techniques use various sizes of type and contrasting graphics to draw the eye to content "entry points" in the page design (the red dots).

typefaces isn't modern either—the practice was born in practicality: early printers had only so many sizes of particular typefaces, back when "having a font" meant spending a small fortune on thousands of pieces of metal type in large wooden cases.

The classical top-to-bottom linear page structure dominated most page design well into the late 1800s, when the combination of new communications media like the telegraph and early telephones and more advanced hot-metal typesetting and lithography led to increasing complexity in print publications, with much slower corresponding changes in page design and typography. A glance at a newspaper of the time shows the problem: the only notion of "design" was classic top-to-bottom layout, but with multiple columns pages had grown too complex for that approach. "All the news that's fit to print" usually meant all the news that could be crammed onto the front page, in type just barely large enough to read. Not unlike many web home pages from the 1990s.

Modern design

In the early twentieth century, page designers began to break the ancient top-to-bottom Gutenberg diagram model of the page. In newspaper and early magazine design, the page began to be treated as a unified field, where the size and contrast of page elements were used to create "entry points" for the reader's wandering eye. The aim of modern page design is to create a rational, rules-based visual architecture for the page, where the size and contrast relationships of typography and graphics create a visual hierarchy, which the reader assumes to reflect the relative importance of the content.

Contrast draws the eye. Eye-tracking studies show that even modern readers of web and print documents follow a scanning pattern based on the classic top-to-bottom, left-to-right Gutenberg diagram, but modern readers are far more likely to start reading at other points on the page besides the top left, especially in complex

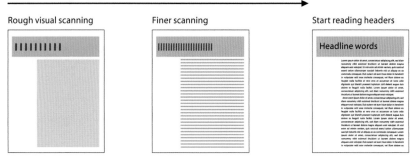

Visual scanning of page structure over time

Rough visual scanning　　　Finer scanning　　　Start reading headers

layouts that offer many topics to choose from, like the typical news or e-commerce home page.

Modern design strives—at least in theory—to be an analytically neutral mediator and transmitter of information, even if that is a goal it rarely achieves. The best modern design is quite proudly synthetic and creative, but neither of those qualities is in short supply today. The tools and products of modern design are now ubiquitous—available to anyone with even a modest computer and budget, and we live in a virtual stew of cell phone shots, selfies, web pages, Facebook posts, and Vine videos. What stands apart today is the quality of thinking and making, and the usefulness of the ideas we communicate, which have become the hallmarks of professionalism in modern design.

ESTABLISHING VISUAL HIERARCHIES

Pages that lack a clear graphic center of interest make it harder for the reader to engage, because it takes more time and effort. We begin to make sense of any visual display by doing a quick visual scan, structured by the basic conventions of Western

FIGURE 8.19
Sage magazine's simple but confident layout can be parsed in an instant, and allows the reader to settle quickly into appreciating the lead article.

FIGURE 8.20
With its wall-
to-wall content
juxtapositions and
multitude of graphic
design ticks and
tricks, the USDA
home page fails the
primary design test
for a home page:
what's important,
and where should I
focus my attention?

languages and the way web pages are normally laid out, particularly pages with significant text content (fig. 8.18).

The lessons here are simple:

- Use conventional page layouts, and avoid radical departures from normal form, as they tend to confuse the reader. This attachment to conventional form isn't some particular burden that web designers bear, as all media have their forms and conventions. That's what allows us to engage with them quickly and without a lot of cognitive load just to "get" the basic layout. Book design is an ancient and respected design craft, and yet the "rules" of book design run to several hundred pages in *The Chicago Manual of Style*. The rules don't smother book design, they enable it.
- Your priorities ought to be immediately and graphically obvious. Clear page hierarchies enable the start of reader engagement by using the basic visual tools of contrast in weight and size, color, and typography to make it obvious where to look, and ideally to supply enough narrative interest (the words) and visual clarity (images and layout) to pull the reader in from initial scanning to full engagement with your content.

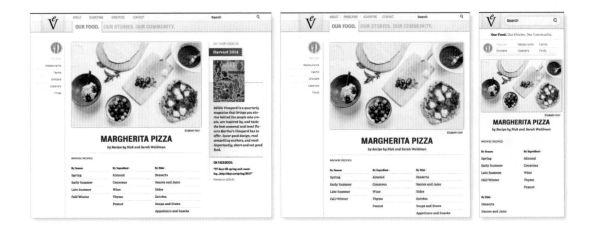

FIGURE 8.21

Edible Vineyard's beautiful and fully responsive site is continual proof that sophisticated design sensibilities and a highly usable and inviting interface are perfectly possible in responsive web design.

Visual hierarchies and negative space

Well-crafted hierarchies are about more than just graphic contrast, or all we would need to organize a page would be big heavy headlines, a picture near the top, and smaller blocks of text running down the page. Indeed, that's the basic formula for a huge percentage of web pages on the Internet—not because it's dysfunctional, but because it's straightforward and it works.

More sophisticated and complex page layouts use the gestalt visual principles discussed earlier to create meaning and order on the page, grouping related items through careful arrangements, using the tools of proximity, similarity, continuity, and closure to create visual structure.

All gestalt visual principles—indeed all of typography and graphic design—depend on negative space, or "white space," to create conceptual groups and legibility on the page. Without significant white space on the page to create ordering and groups, graphic design is not possible. All the possibilities of establishing a visual narrative, and using contrast, visual weight, tonal emphasis, and graphic narrative to guide the reader disappear when white space is squeezed out of a page and everything becomes a wall-to-wall cacophony of competing graphics.

White space is achieved through margins and padding around elements, and it's the white space that forms groups of elements, and delineates groups from one another. For example, adding more padding above a subsection heading than below tells the reader that the heading belongs to the following block of content, and that the content of the preceding section is distinct from the subsequent section.

Clarity of intent and design looks simple but requires enormous discipline, both in the messaging strategy and in the graphic design that supports it. Most organizations fail at this because the easiest way to appease competing groups of stakeholders is to parcel out pieces of the home page. When everybody gets a little slice of

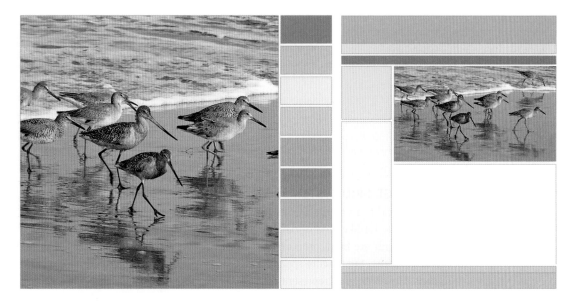

attention, what you usually get is a noisy fail that is often—ironically—an accurate reflection of the muddled thinking behind the business and communication strategy.

Unity, simplicity, and focus

Great designs create a clear center of interest to attract the reader's attention, within an overall page architecture that establishes a unified sense of order and balance. The graphic tools of contrast and weight are powerful, but can quickly become visually exhausting and distracting if you overuse them. Readers benefit from gentle but clear guidance, but resent having a bold visual constantly shoved in front of their noses. If you've got good content, trust that the quality will be obvious—you don't need to shout about it to get attention.

Effective contrast

Horizontal rules, decorative bullets, prominent icons, and other visual markers have their occasional uses, but apply each sparingly (if at all) to avoid a patchy and confusing layout. The tools of graphic emphasis are powerful and should be used only in small doses for maximum effect. Overuse of graphic emphasis leads to a "clown's pants" effect in which everything is equally garish and nothing is emphasized.

Color palettes chosen from nature are an almost infallible guide to color harmony, particularly if you are not a trained graphic designer. Subtle, desaturated colors make the best choices for backgrounds or minor elements. Avoid bold, highly saturated primary colors except in regions of maximum emphasis, and even there use them cautiously (fig. 8.22).

FIGURE 8.22
Colors drawn from nature are almost always both harmonious and subdued. Use Photoshop's eyedropper tool to explore color palettes drawn from photos of natural environments.

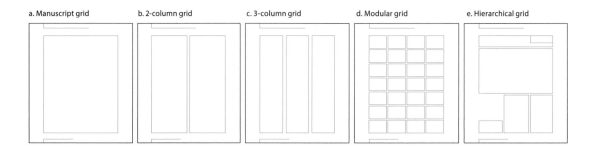

FIGURE 8.23

USING PAGE GRID SYSTEMS

The page grid is a popular means to provide a consistent, predictable structure for page layouts. Unlike traditional fixed-page grids for print, the best contemporary web page grids are fluid, proportionally spaced grids that adjust to fit the width of smaller screens, but usually specify a maximum width (css max-width) for larger screens. However, grids represent only part of the solution to efficiently constructing web pages.

Origins of grid systems

Page grids are most famously associated with the 1950s modernists of the Swiss design schools, such as Josef Müller-Brockmann, but page grids are thousands of years older. Every carefully designed page uses a grid. The oldest and most basic layout grid is the manuscript grid, widely used well before movable type was invented, and still widely used today in books, blogs, and layouts for smartphones. The classic manuscript grid (fig.8.23a) has a single dominant column, although sometimes the wide margins might be used for marginal notes or parenthetic materials. Since the rise of mechanical printing and more standardized forms for books, the manuscript grid usually incorporates simple headers or chapter titles, as well as simple footers for page numbers.

Column grids (fig. 8.23b, c) existed before Johannes Gutenberg invented movable type around 1452, and by the early 1800s became the most widely used layout for newspapers and early magazines. Column grids were particularly flexible for introducing woodcut or, later, etched graphics into periodicals, books, and early mass-circulation magazines. Most print magazines, advertising and informational print publications, brochures, and web sites today use some form of multicolumn layout.

Today the modular grids (fig. 8.23d) popularized by modernist designers in the 1950s and 1960s are the best-known layout grids in print and web design. This form of fixed-layout grid was briefly popular in web design in the 2006–2011 period, as css support in browsers became more reliable and sophisticated. Ready-made frameworks like the 960 Grid (960.gs) enjoyed brief popularity before the sharp rise in

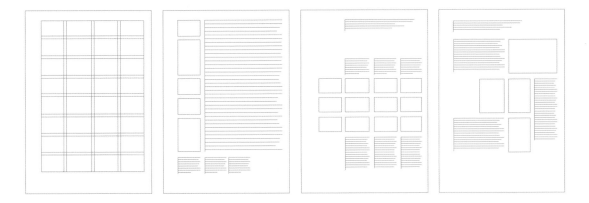

mobile computing made fixed-width web grids irrelevant for most uses. As responsive web design matures, we will probably see a return to more complex modular layout grids for at least desktop-sized page layouts.

The hierarchical grid (fig. 8.23e) is a more free-form variant of modern grid design, typically used in special situations like highly graphic print or web pages, such as magazine photography spreads or home pages on web sites. In hierarchical grids one or several dominant graphic elements anchor the page design, although text elements are typically set in conventional single- or multicolumn grids.

Modern grid systems

In the 1920s the Bauhaus school in Germany blended the theories of gestalt psychologists with modernist theories on form, color, and layout for the printed page. The early Bauhaus graphic designers were also much influenced by the Russian Constructivist artist, graphic designer, and architect El Lissitzky, whose bold geometric page designs and posters still inspire designers today. After the Bauhaus was closed by the Gestapo in 1933, many of the faculty moved to Switzerland. Swiss design was strongly influenced by the Bauhaus, but it was later Swiss designers like Jan Tschichold and Josef Müller-Brockmann who gave us modern layout grids and design modularity. In the 1950s and 1960s modernist designers like Charles and Ray Eames, Paul Rand, and Massimo Vignelli made modernist design the signature look of corporate America.

Müller-Brockmann was the most articulate of the advocates for grid-based design systems, and his book *Grid Systems in Graphic Design* is considered the definitive modernist statement on grids in print design. Modernist designers used grids across the spectrum of print graphic design projects, but grids provided a particularly powerful means of bringing consistency and rationality to complex documents like books and magazines. Grids provide a repeatable system for content presentation and placement.

FIGURE 8.24
Josef Müller-Brockmann's sketches for various page designs within a twenty-four-unit print page grid, showing the wide range of possible content and graphic treatments available within even a simple modular grid.

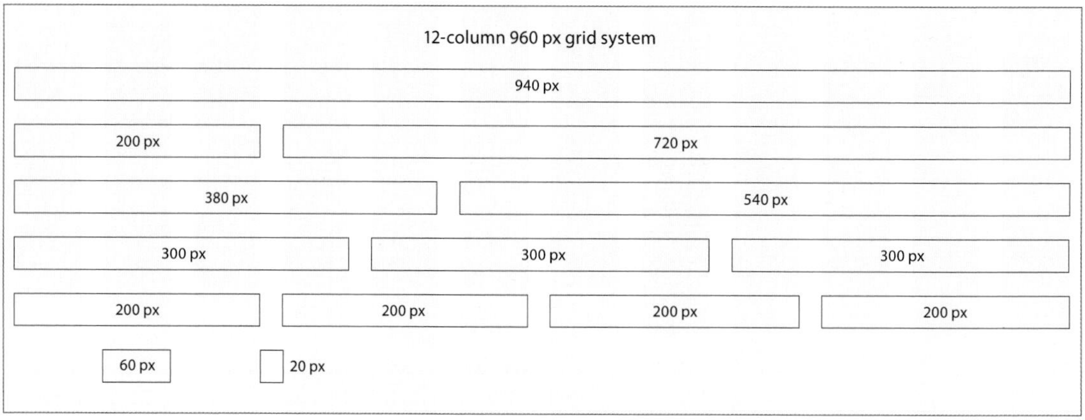

12-column 960 px grid system

940 px

200 px | 720 px

380 px | 540 px

300 px | 300 px | 300 px

200 px | 200 px | 200 px | 200 px

60 px | 20 px

FIGURE 8.25

Grid systems may seem like a hindrance to creative layout, but when used appropriately, they can bring consistent structure to layouts without producing graphic monotony (fig. 8.24).

For the first decade of the web's evolution true grid systems were not practical, as "web design" then consisted largely of hidden tables and transparent GIF graphic spacers that were required to produce anything beyond the bare minimum of a single-page column. The growth of browser support for CSS in the early 2000s was due mostly to the efforts of activist web designers like Jeffrey Zeldman and the Web Standards Project, who were vocal advocates for a "standards-based" design with consistent implementations of CSS and HTML across the major browsers. As standards-based design became practical, the increasing sophistication of web layout tools like CSS2 and XHTML led to a revival of interest in grid-based layout among web designers.

Grid-based CSS design frameworks like 960 Grid (960.gs) became popular as a means to structure fixed-width web template designs using classic modernist grid principles. With the rise of mobile computing and responsive web design, fixed-grid systems evolved to become more fluid and responsive, and the rationality and modular thinking of the classic grid systems is now adapted for more fluid designs on small screens, and classic fixed-width grid layouts where screen space allows. Former *New York Times* design director Khoi Vihn and U.K. web designer Mark Boulton have written extensively on grid systems for the web, in both fixed and responsive implementations. As the CSS3 flexible box layout ("flexbox" for short) becomes more widely and reliably supported in browsers we should see increasingly sophisticated flexible and responsive grid frameworks emerge.

For a brief time in 2005–2010 printlike fixed-width grid designs for web pages became popular. The CSS2 of the time became sophisticated enough to create print-

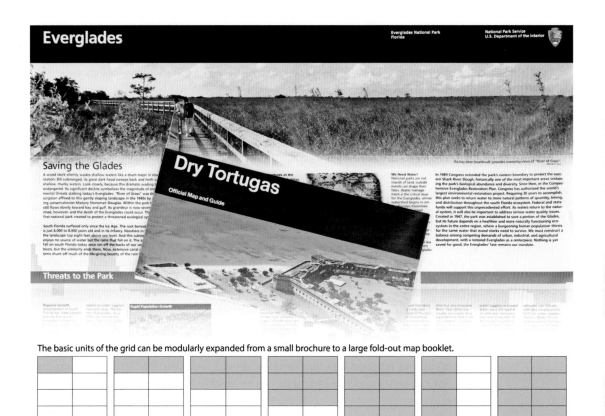

The basic units of the grid can be modularly expanded from a small brochure to a large fold-out map booklet.

like grids, and mobile users were usually relegated to highly simplified "mobile" sites with only the most basic information and interactive features. The "960" grid (www.960.gs) shown here (fig. 8.25) was one of the most popular web grid systems, and is still seen in older fixed-width site designs.

Module and program

The modern design movement of the 1950–1960s is famous for its dedication to grid layouts, but grids were only anchor points for consistent, repeatable graphic design forms, or modules, created as components of more comprehensive design programs. The module-and-program forms of modern design formed the heart of the rationalist approach to layout and typography. Repeating design modules were effectively libraries of preconceived graphics subunits, which could make even complex print design programs more efficient, cost-effective, and visually unified through carefully programmed systems of design.

FIGURE 8.26
The National Park Service design grid for print publications. Thinking in a strategic, modular way about design systems can save a fortune in the long run.

The example in Figure 8.26 shows a module-and-program design system that is still going strong almost fifty years after designer Massimo Vignelli conceived the system for the U.S. National Park Service. Vignelli's Unigrid design system for National Park maps and brochures is both beautiful and highly functional, and the consistency and predictability of the design system has saved the Park Service millions of dollars over the lifetime of the program.

Consistent layouts

Establish a layout grid and a style for handling your text and graphics, and then apply it consistently to build rhythm and unity across the pages of your site. Repetition is not boring; it gives your site a consistent graphic identity that creates and then reinforces a distinct sense of "place" and makes your site memorable. A consistent approach to layout and navigation allows users to adapt quickly to your design and to predict with confidence the location of information and navigation controls across the pages of your site.

Established patterns

Today the conceptual descendants of the modernist module-and-program designs are web "pattern libraries," which are not just static visual examples of how repeatable content and functional design modules should look, but are "live" self-contained chunks of HTML and CSS code that can be quickly reused and customized in a web site.

In web design jargon a "pattern" is a self-contained unit of HTML and CSS code that describes a common recurring object or HTML tag in your site, such as buttons, basic input forms, characteristic ways of handling pull-quotes, block quotes, and styles for even the most basic headers, lists, tables, and other standard elements of HTML. Designers have always copied-and-pasted these bits of code for convenience, and to support a consistent way of handling things throughout a web site. Pattern libraries are carefully maintained collections of these repeating building blocks of web sites. Pattern libraries are also sometimes called "style guides" or "front-end style guides," but we prefer "pattern library" because pattern libraries—based as they are on working HTML and CSS code—are much more powerful and useful than mere collected examples of visual styling.

Most entities that need a web site already have a site, and often as a web site ages and is refined over the years, it gradually accumulates CSS code from new projects. The most conservative way to add new features and styling is simply to add new CSS code to the older CSS listings. This addition method prevents older things from breaking, but as more and more styling code accretes, the CSS can become bloated to the point where the site's performance suffers. Perhaps even worse, the old code becomes so complex and tangled that nobody remembers what code is actually used

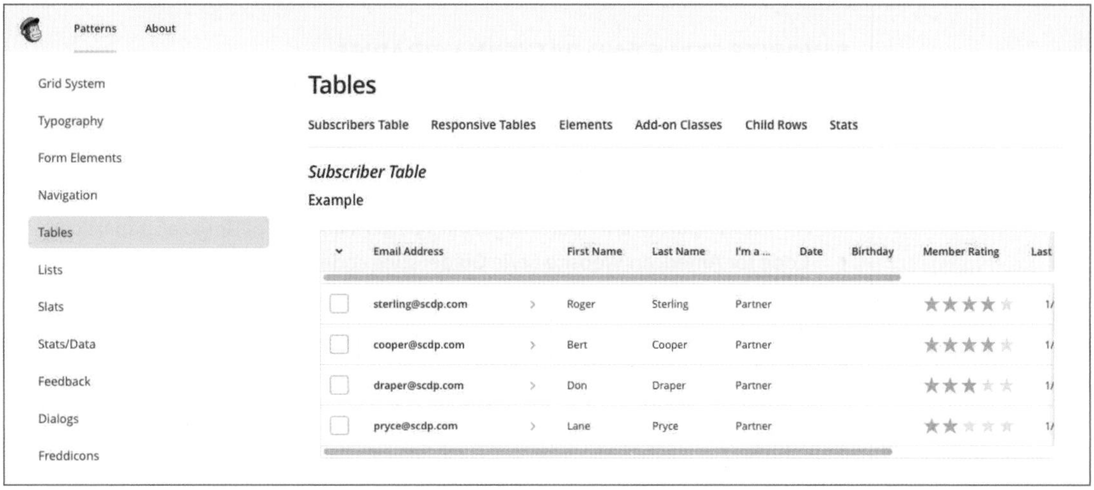

FIGURE 8.27
MailChimp's design pattern library provides a rich palette of design and interaction "patterns" for reuse, saves tremendous amounts of time in avoiding redundant coding efforts, and assures that MailChimp's site remains functionally and visually cohesive (ux.mailchimp.com/patterns).

in the "live" site and what code has long since been made redundant by newer styling projects.

Maintaining a consistent pattern library of working and tested code takes some effort but offers a number of advantages:

- A solid, reliable code library can save huge amounts of time, as new features become cut-and-paste affairs, and reduces redundancy, as nobody wastes time reinventing objects and features that already exist in your pattern library.
- A single code repository makes the HTML and CSS of your site much easier to check and maintain. This is particularly true if you keep all your pattern examples in one long web page. If you have new code to test, you can add it to the pattern library page and quickly assess whether your new code breaks any older code, or whether any of your new CSS, HTML, or JavaScript class or variable names conflict with existing site code.
- The pattern library becomes a powerful communications tool, as designers, front-end developers, and everyone else on the team have a common reference point and shared vocabulary for existing styles and features, and a quick means to check to see whether a feature already exists and can be modified from existing code.
- A thorough pattern library specifies a compatible style for all plausible HTML tags, even ones that you (currently) never plan on using. You may never have used a `<cite>` or `<abbr>` tag, but specifying a style for seldom-used HTML can prevent unpleasant surprises (ugly browser-default styling) if somebody does use those tags within your site.

FAVORITE STYLE AND PATTERN LIBRARIES

Fortunately a number of companies and organizations maintain style guides and pattern libraries that are visible to the public and can be used for inspiration and guidance. As style guide nerds, here we highlight a few of our favorites:

- A Pattern Apart (*A List Apart* magazine's pattern library): patterns.alistapart.com
- Code for American Website Style Guide: style.codeforamerica.org
- MailChimp's Pattern Library and Style Guide: ux.mailchimp.com/patterns and mailchimp.com/about/style-guide/
- Pattern Lab: Create Atomic Design systems: patternlab.io
- Starbucks responsive web pattern library: www.starbucks.com/static/reference/styleguide
- UK National Health Service, NHS Brand Guidelines: www.nhsidentity.nhs.uk
- IBM Design Language: www.ibm.com/design/language

RECOMMENDED READING

Allsopp, J. "A Dao of Web Design." *A List Apart*, April 7, 2000, alistapart.com/article/dao.

Boulton, M. *A Practical Guide to Designing for the Web*. Seattle: Amazon Digital Services, 2009.

Bradley, S. "Design Principles: Visual Perception and the Principles of Gestalt." *Smashing Magazine*, March 28, 2014, www.smashingmagazine.com/2014/03/28/design-principles-visual-perception-and-the-principles-of-gestalt.

Bringhurst, R. *The Elements of Typographic Style*, 25th ann. ed. Seattle: Hartley and Marks, 2012.

Debenham, A. *A Pocket Guide to Front-end Style Guides*. Penarth, UK: Five Simple Steps, 2013.

Lupton, E. *Type on Screen: A Guide for Designers, Developers, Writers, and Students*. New York: Princeton Architectural Press, 2014.

Müller-Brockmann, J. *Grid Systems in Graphic Design*. Fürstentum, Liechtenstein: Verlag Niggli AG, 1996.

New Perspective on Web Design: The Smashing Book #4. Freiburg, Germany: Smashing Magazine, 2013.

Warren, S. 2012. "Style Tiles and How They Work." *A List Apart*, March 27, 2012, alistapart.com/article/style-tiles-and-how-they-work.

Weinschenk, S. *100 Things Every Designer Needs to Know About People*. Berkeley, CA: New
    Riders, 2011.
West, S. *Working with Style: Traditional and Modern Approaches to Layout and Typography*.
    New York: Watson-Guptill, 1990.
Wilson, A. *The Design of Books*. San Francisco: Chronicle Books, 1993.

Typographic style is founded not on any one technology of typesetting or printing, but on the primitive yet subtle craft of writing.
– Robert Bringhurst

CHAPTER 9

Typography

Typography is the balance and interplay of letterforms on the page—a verbal and visual equation that helps the reader understand the form and absorb the substance of the page content. Typography plays a dual role as both verbal and visual communication. When readers scan a page, they are subconsciously aware of both functions: first they survey the overall graphic patterns of the page, and then they parse the language and read.

Good typography establishes a visual hierarchy for rendering prose on the page by providing visual punctuation and graphic accents that help readers understand relations between prose and pictures, headlines and subordinate blocks of text. Good web typography encodes those relationships, and adapts gracefully to different contexts of use.

> Book design is not one of those crafts that allow for infinite and unfettered creativity.
>
> —Richard Hendel, *On Book Design*

CHARACTERISTICS OF WEB TYPOGRAPHY

Web typography has several distinct differences from print typography:

- **Encoded semantics:** With web typography, hierarchy and relationships are encoded into text, such that the information is available programmatically and can be read by such tools as text-to-speech software, like screen readers, which read web pages aloud; and software that indexes documents for searching and retrieval, like search engines.
- **Adaptable display:** The visual display of text depends on many variables, such as user settings, context of use, device used, and size of the viewport. Good web typography adapts gracefully to these different contexts. In the end, the best pages are those that can be readily displayed by users, with designs that meet their needs and preferences. This is especially true for typographic design, since there is such variation in what makes for optimal readability and legibility.

SEMANTICS

It may seem counterintuitive to begin a chapter on web typography by discussing semantic markup, but typography is visual semantics—the use of visual encodings to convey structure and meaning. On the web, we can encode structure and meaning into documents. With semantic markup, we describe content structure visually and programmatically to communicate more effectively to more users. We also use

FIGURE 9.1

A menu is
semantically a list
of links, and using
HTML list elements
for marking up
menus creates a sort
of "neutral space" by
gathering the menu
items into a distinct
group.

```
<ul>
    <li><a href="/hebergement/chalet/chalet.dot">Chalet</a></li>
    <li><a href="/hebergement/chalet/chalet-nature.dot">Chalet Nature</a></li>
    <li><a href="/hebergement/chalet/chalet-exp.dot">Chalet EXP.</a></li>
    <li><a href="/hebergement/chalet/chalet-compact.dot">Chalet Compact</a></li>
    <li><a href="/hebergement/chalet/camp-rustique.dot">Camp rustique</a></li>
    <li class="active"><a href="/hebergement/chalet/yourte.dot">Yourte</a></li>
</ul>
```

semantics to provide additional layers of experience, and make connections that are not possible through visual means only. For example, we can create a table of contents by extracting headings from a document and providing a document overview in outline format.

In Chapter 5, Site Structure, we covered the basic principles of semantic content markup. Here we focus on those elements that are specific to web typography.

Neutral space

Neutral space is an attribute that we use to describe visually how elements are related and sequenced. With neutral space, such as margins, line height, indents, and blank lines, we guide readers through documents. From a semantic perspective, we can use HTML elements for a similar purpose, showing which elements are related and which are distinct. We can use semantic markup to encode the purpose of specific elements, and to describe the information hierarchy of page content. For example, sectioning markup is a way of encoding neutral space around a block of content, providing a boundary around the content and giving it a descriptive label.

TABLE 9.1

Sectioning markup
for web typography

HTML	`<body>, <fieldset>, <form>, <table>, <ul>, <ol>`
HTML5	`<article>, <aside>, <footer>, <header>, <main>, <nav>, <section>`
WAI-ARIA	`application, banner, complementary, contentinfo, form, main, navigation, search`

Information hierarchy

We use typographic conventions to convey relationships among content elements. For example, we put a bullet character in front of each item in a list of words, phrases, or paragraphs to show visually that the items are related, and typically that they are specific details related to the content preceding the list. Another common example is a heading followed by a paragraph. We signal the heading visually, using larger, bold text. As in this book, we often have a hierarchical system of headings, with page headings, section headings, and subsection headings. We convey these visually, usually through the size and position of the headings. A large heading at the top of the page is likely the heading for all the page content. Section headings are smaller, and are interspersed through the page, and subsection headings are smaller still. We can use semantic markup to encode the information relationships and hierarchy so they are available programmatically.

We also use typography to emphasize individual elements, to make them stand out as different or particularly important. One way is to set a word or phrase in boldface or italicize it to make it stand out from its surrounding context. We can use semantic markup to distinguish words or phrases from surrounding content—for example, to mark the title of a work as a citation.

Abbreviation	`<abbr>`
Acronym	`<acronym>`
Address	`<address>`
Block quotation	`<blockquote>`
Citation	`<cite>`
Computer code	`<code>`
Defined term	`<dfn>`
Emphasis	`<em>`
Headings	`<h1>, <h2>, <h3>, <h4>, <h5>, <h6>`
Lists	`<ol>, <ul>, <dl>, <menu>, <dir>`
Strong emphasis	`<strong>`

TABLE 9.2 Expanded table: Semantic HTML elements for web typography

ADAPTATION USING STYLE SHEETS

Visual typography did not have much of a role to play in the creation of the web. Tim Berners-Lee's original concept of the Internet was to create "a web of data that can be processed directly or indirectly by machines." The originators of HTML were scientists who wanted a standard means for sharing particle physics documents. They had little interest in the exact visual form of the document as seen on a particular computer screen. In fact, HTML was designed to enforce a clean separation be-

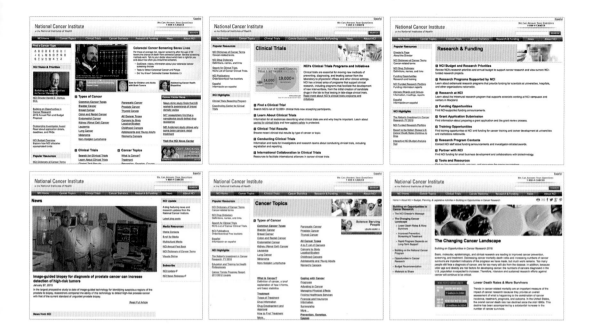

FIGURE 9.2

Multiple web page designs and typography all controlled by a single master style sheet.

tween structure and presentation, such that pages would display on every system and browser available, work with assistive technologies such as screen reader software, and be accurately interpreted by automated search and analysis software. The visual logic of the content was at best a secondary concern. In focusing solely on the structural logic of documents, they ignored the need for the visual logic of sophisticated graphic design and typography.

This division between structural logic and visual logic was reconciled through the introduction of cascading style sheets, or css. With css, web sites can contain both encoded and visual structure and meaning. Style sheets offer web designers two key advantages in managing complex web sites:

- Separation of content and design: css gives site developers the best of both worlds: content markup that reflects the logical structure of the information, and the freedom to specify exactly how each html element will look.
- Efficient control over large document sets: The most powerful implementations of css allow site designers to control the graphic look and feel of thousands of pages by modifying a single master style sheet document.

MEDIUM'S ATTENTION TO DESIGN

Designer Charles Eames said, "The details are not the details. They make the product." This attention to detail is clearly part of the success of Webby award–winning Medium, in the Best User Experience category. Medium provides a platform for publishing stories and ideas, a concept that is neither revolutionary nor particularly innovative. Where Medium leaps ahead of its competitors is in interaction and graphic design. The author experience of using Medium to publish stories is focused on enabling the activity of sharing thoughts, stories, and ideas without distraction (see Medium's streamlined editing toolbar, fig. 9.4). But most important, Medium pays close attention to ensuring that contributions display to their best effect, with lovely design and typography across devices, and even on paper (see the web site Printing Medium Stories).

In his book *The Elements of Typographic Style,* Robert Bringhurst's first principle is, "Typography exists to honor content." Medium's success is largely a function of how it has embraced this principle by honoring the contributions of its authors.

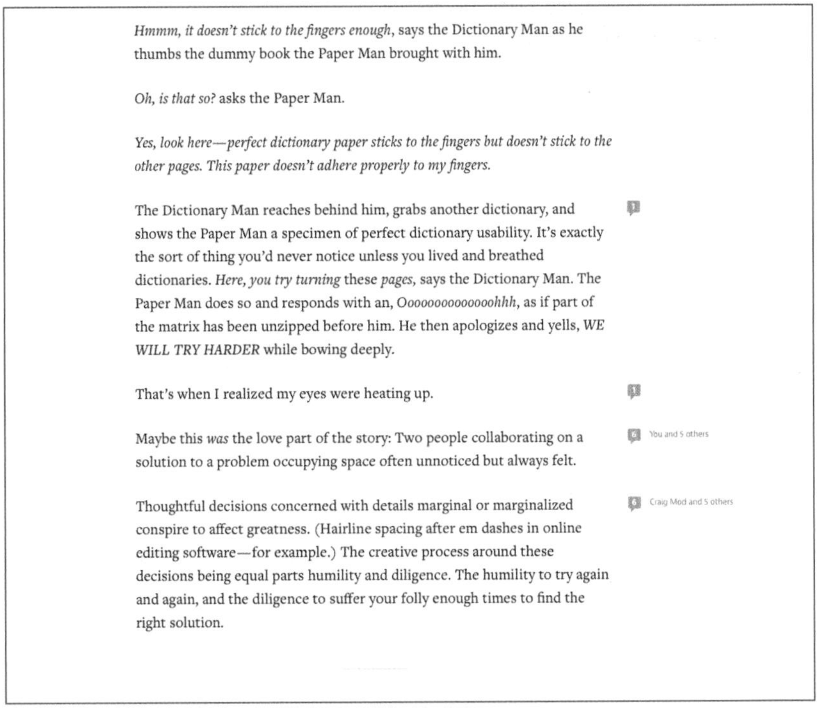

Hmmm, it doesn't stick to the fingers enough, says the Dictionary Man as he thumbs the dummy book the Paper Man brought with him.

Oh, is that so? asks the Paper Man.

Yes, look here—perfect dictionary paper sticks to the fingers but doesn't stick to the other pages. This paper doesn't adhere properly to my fingers.

The Dictionary Man reaches behind him, grabs another dictionary, and shows the Paper Man a specimen of perfect dictionary usability. It's exactly the sort of thing you'd never notice unless you lived and breathed dictionaries. *Here, you try turning* these *pages,* says the Dictionary Man. The Paper Man does so and responds with an, Oooooooooooooohhh, as if part of the matrix has been unzipped before him. He then apologizes and yells, *WE WILL TRY HARDER* while bowing deeply.

That's when I realized my eyes were heating up.

Maybe this *was* the love part of the story: Two people collaborating on a solution to a problem occupying space often unnoticed but always felt.

Thoughtful decisions concerned with details marginal or marginalized conspire to affect greatness. (Hairline spacing after em dashes in online editing software—for example.) The creative process around these decisions being equal parts humility and diligence. The humility to try again and again, and the diligence to suffer your folly enough times to find the right solution.

FIGURE 9.3

Efficiency

If you have ever used the "styles" features of a page layout or word processing program, you'll understand the basic idea behind css. The styles feature of a word processor is used to determine exactly how your titles, subheadings, and body copy will look, and then the text is formatted when you apply a style to each element. Once all the text has been styled, you can change the look of each occurrence of an element simply by changing its style information. For example, say that you set Heading 1 elements to be in Times New Roman. If you change your mind and want another font, you just change the Heading 1 style, and every Heading 1 in your document then changes to reflect the new font. css works in the same way. If you have one master style sheet controlling the visual styling of every page in your site, you can update the font property in your h1 declaration to use a new typeface and all level one headings in the site will display with the new font.

Consistency

As in traditional print publishing, high-quality web sites adhere to established type style settings consistently throughout the site. Consistency gives polish to a site and encourages visitors to stay by creating an expectation about the structure of a text. If sloppy, inconsistent formatting confounds this expectation, you will decrease your readers' confidence in your words, and they may not return. You should decide on such settings as fonts, interparagraph spacing, subhead sizes, and so on and then create a style guide to help you maintain these settings as you develop the site (see the sidebar on style guides in Chapter 10, Editorial Style). This step is especially critical for large sites that incorporate numerous pages. And with css you will have powerful tools to maintain the consistency of styles throughout your site.

User preferences

Even if you follow typography best practices and conventions, people who have visual impairments may not be able to read your text. Some people need large text due to declining eyesight, or inverted colors due to sensitivity to light. For people who have reading disorders, such as dyslexia, there is a great deal of variation with respect to which font, color, and size work best. Everyone struggles with reading under certain environmental conditions, such as glare, and because of physical issues such as stress and fatigue. Some people simply prefer a specific reading mode and welcome sites that honor their preferences.

Most browsers have a feature that allows users to override author-defined style sheets with their own style sheets. This means that a user can define a custom style sheet that meets his viewing needs. A person who has low vision might define a style sheet that renders all headings and paragraphs at 32 pixels and sets the background to black and the text to white for maximum contrast.

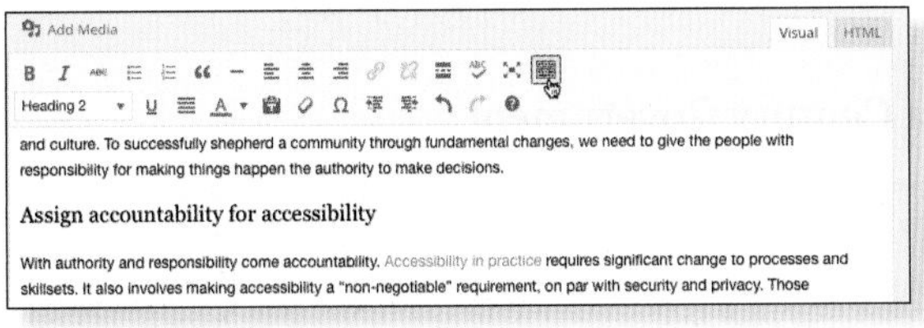

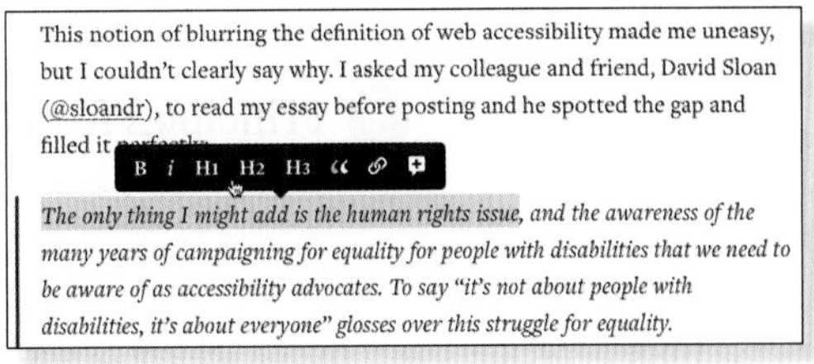

WEB TYPOGRAPHY IN PRACTICE

For most people, creating good web typography does not involve writing css rules. Most content authors work in a text editor, creating and marking up text based on the available options. The resulting text displays using whatever styling was implemented with the web site. The important thing for content editors is to utilize good text markup practices, so that the development team's carefully designed and engineered semantic and visual typography is correctly applied. This means:

- Use the semantic markup options as provided in the text editor: headings, lists, quotes, and column and row headers for tables.
- Do not use a specific element in order to achieve a visual effect. For example, don't assign a heading level based on how it displays. Instead, assign the level that corresponds to the heading's position in the information hierarchy.
- Avoid using the presentation options, such as size, font, and style (bold, italic, underlined), particularly when a semantic option exists. For example, don't set a section heading as large and bold using the font size and style settings. Instead, use the format menu to choose the appropriate heading level and let the heading display as specified in the css. Steer clear of setting color options for text. Color is tricky. It's easy to select a color that does not harmonize with the other colors on the page and, worse, one that does not provide sufficient contrast, causing issues for people with vision impairments. Let your text inherit the styling provided by the development team.
- Avoid using text characters for visual purposes, such as brackets for arrows, vertical bar or pipe for a border, asterisks for bullets. Screen reader software speaks whatever text is provided, and will speak the character (for example, "Home vertical bar About vertical bar Contact Us").
- Do not put two spaces after a period. Period.

The development team should configure the text editor to support best practices for web typography. In most cases, this means removing functionality that comes with text editors, such as underline and text color options—these options should

FIGURE 9.4
WordPress (left) has a fully featured toolbar; unfortunately, structural markup options for elements like headings are in the second level, which is hidden by default. Medium (right) has a streamlined toolbar that encourages the use of headings.

never be needed for web typography. It may also mean reordering options, putting the best options in the main toolbar and less desirable but still necessary options in a secondary drop-down menu or panel.

ELEMENTS OF TYPOGRAPHIC DESIGN

Good typography depends on the visual contrast between one typeface and another, as well as among text blocks, headlines, and the surrounding white space. Nothing attracts the eye and brain of the reader like strong contrast and distinctive patterns, and you can achieve those attributes only by carefully designing contrast and pattern into your pages. If you cram every page with dense text, readers see a wall of gray and will instinctively reject the lack of visual contrast. Just making things uniformly bigger doesn't help. Even boldface fonts quickly become monotonous: if everything is bold, then nothing stands out "boldly."

When your content is primarily text, typography is the tool you use to "paint" patterns of organization on the page. The first thing the reader sees is not the title or other details on the page but the overall pattern and contrast of the page. The regular, repeating patterns established through carefully organized pages of text and graphics help the reader to establish the location and organization of your information and increase legibility. Patchy, heterogeneous typography and text headers make it hard for the user to see repeating patterns and logical content groups. The chaos makes it difficult to predict where information is likely to be located in unfamiliar documents.

DISPLAY TYPE

A web page of solid body text is hard to scan for content structure and will not engage the eye. Many users will turn away from a "wall of words" because it's not welcoming and inviting. Some users will have a significant struggle reading long blocks of text, with unbroken paragraphs; users with dyslexia, for example, may have difficulty keeping their place without the aid of line breaks and white space. Adding display type to a document will provide landmarks to direct the reader through your content. Display type establishes an information structure and adds visual variety to draw the reader in to your material.

ALIGNMENT AND WHITE SPACE

Margins define the reading area of your page by separating the main text from the surrounding environment. Margins provide important visual relief in any document, but careful design of margins and other white space is particularly important in web page design because web content must coexist with the interface elements of the browser itself, as well as with other windows, menus, and icons of the user interface.

Margins and space can be used to delineate the main text from the other page elements. And when used consistently, margins provide unity throughout a site by creating a consistent structure and look to the site pages. They also add visual interest by contrasting the positive space of the screen (text, graphics) from the negative (white) space. If you want any understanding of graphic design or page layout, learn to see and appreciate the power and utility of "white space," the ground field behind page elements. The spaces within the ground field are as important as any other element on the page.

Justified text

Justified text is set flush with the left and right margins. Justified blocks of text create solid rectangles, and headings are normally centered for a symmetrical, formal-looking document. In print, justification is achieved by adjusting the space between words and by using word hyphenation. Page layout programs use a hyphenation dictionary to check for and apply hyphenation at each line's end and then adjust word spacing throughout the line. But even with sophisticated page layout software, justified text blocks often suffer from poor spacing and excessive hyphenation and require manual refinement to avoid "rivers" of white space that run through the text.

Modern browsers support justified text through word spacing and hyphenation, but the results are not optimal or consistent. The necessary fine spacing adjustments are not possible, and there are no options for customizing and refining hyphenation

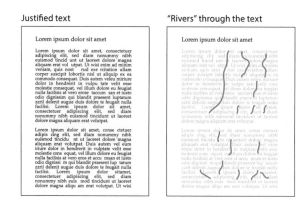

Justified text   "Rivers" through the text

options. Narrow columns can end up with large spaces between letters and words, particularly with enlarged text. For the foreseeable future, the readability of your web documents will suffer if you set your text justified.

Centered and right-aligned text

Centered and right-aligned text blocks are difficult to read. We read from left to right, anchoring our tracking across the page at the vertical line of the left margin. The ragged-left margins produced by centering or right-justifying text make that scanning much harder, because your eye needs to search for the beginning of each new line.

Left-aligned text

Left-aligned text is the most legible option for web pages because the left margin is even and predictable and the right margin is irregular. Unlike justified text, left justification requires no adjustment to word spacing; the inequities in spacing fall at the end of the lines. The resulting ragged-right margin adds variety and interest to the page without reducing legibility.

Alignment of headings

Headings over left-aligned text should also be flush left. Centered headings pair well with justified text, but justified text should not be used on web pages. Centered display type contrasts with the asymmetry of the ragged-right margin of left-justified body text and produces an unbalanced page.

LINE LENGTH

Printed magazine and book columns are narrow for physiological reasons: at normal reading distances, the eye's span of acute focus is only about three to four inches wide, so designers try to keep dense passages of text in columns not much wider than

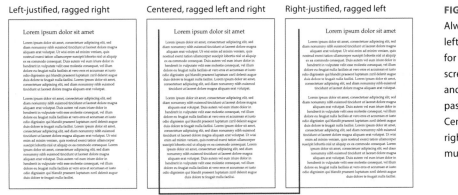

Left-justified, ragged right	Centered, ragged left and right	Right-justified, ragged left

A ragged left margin makes for difficult reading

FIGURE 9.7
Always use flush-left text alignment for web and other screen displays and for long text passages in print. Centered and flush-right designs are much harder to read.

that comfortable eye span. Wider lines of text require readers to move their heads slightly or use their eye muscles to track over the long lines of text. Readability suffers because on the long trip back to the left margin the reader may lose track of the next line.

On the web, there is no magic number representing a comfortable line length, or measure, given the variability and diversity of devices, window widths, and text size settings. The best approach is to use flexible units to specify the width of the text block and a responsive layout that will adapt to different text sizes as well as different devices (see Chapter 6, Page Structure).

LEADING

Leading is the vertical space in a text block, the distance from one baseline of text to the next. Leading strongly affects the legibility of text blocks: too much leading makes it hard for the eye to locate the start of the next line, whereas too little leading confuses the lines of type, because the ascenders of one line get jumbled with the descenders of the line above.

In print the general rule is to set the leading of text blocks at about 2 points above the size of the type: for example, 12-point type with 14 points of leading. On the web we suggest more generous leading to compensate for longer line lengths. Use relative measures, such as ems or percentages, to set leading relative to text size.

INDENTS

There are two major schools of thought on denoting paragraphs. The classic typographic method uses indentation to signal the beginning of a new paragraph (as in this book). However, many technical, reference, and trade publications use a blank line of white space to separate paragraphs. Indented paragraphs work especially well

Ideal line length for legibility is about 66 characters

Call me Ishmael. Some years ago - never mind how long precisely - having little or no money in my purse, and nothing particular to interest me on shore, I thought I would sail about a little and see the watery part of the world. It is a way I have of driving off the spleen, and regulating the circulation. Whenever I find myself growing grim about the mouth; whenever it is a damp, drizzly November in my soul; whenever I find myself involuntarily pausing before coffin warehouses, and bringing up the rear of every funeral I meet; and especially whenever my hypos get such an upper hand of me, that it requires a strong moral principle to prevent me from deliberately stepping into the street, and methodically knocking people's hats off - then, I account it high time to get to sea as soon as I can. This is my substitute for pistol and ball. With a philosophical flourish Cato throws himself upon his sword; I quietly take to the ship.

Generous leading often improves legibility

Call me Ishmael. Some years ago - never mind how long precisely - having little or no money in my purse, and nothing particular to interest me on shore, I thought I would sail about a little and see the watery part of the world. It is a way I have of driving off the spleen, and regulating the circulation. Whenever I find myself growing grim about the mouth; whenever it is a damp, drizzly November in my soul; whenever I find myself involuntarily pausing before coffin warehouses, and bringing up the rear of every funeral I meet; and especially whenever my hypos get such an upper hand of me, that it requires a strong moral principle to prevent me from deliberately stepping into the street, and methodically

Indented paragraphs are ideal for extended prose

I went to the woods because I wished to live deliberately, to front only the essential facts of life, and see if I could not learn what it had to teach, and not, when I came to die, discover that I had not lived. I did not wish to live what was not life, living is so dear; nor did I wish to practise resignation, unless it was quite necessary.

I wanted to live deep and suck out all the marrow of life, to live so sturdily and Spartan-like as to put to rout all that was not life, to cut a broad swath and shave close, to drive life into a corner, and reduce it to its lowest terms, and, if it proved to be mean, why then to get the whole and genuine meanness of it, and publish its meanness to the world; or if it were sublime, to know it by experience, and be able to give a true account of it in my next excursion.

Spaced paragraphs are often used for technical docs

I went to the woods because I wished to live deliberately, to front only the essential facts of life, and see if I could not learn what it had to teach, and not, when I came to die, discover that I had not lived. I did not wish to live what was not life, living is so dear; nor did I wish to practise resignation, unless it was quite necessary.

I wanted to live deep and suck out all the marrow of life, to live so sturdily and Spartan-like as to put to rout all that was not life, to cut a broad swath and shave close, to drive life into a corner, and reduce it to its lowest terms, and, if it proved to be mean, why then to get the whole and genuine meanness of it, and publish its meanness to the world; or if it were sublime, to know it by experience, and be able to give a true account of it in my next excursion.

FIGURE 9.8   for longer blocks of prose, where the indents signal new paragraphs with minimal disruption to the flow of text. Blank line spacing between paragraphs, in contrast, makes a page easy to scan and provides extra white space for visual relief. Either approach is valid as long as the style is implemented consistently throughout the site.

TEXT SIZE

Scalable text is essential to the goals of universal usability. To ensure scalability, use relative units to control the typography—type size, margins and indents, leading—on the page. We recommend setting the body text to the default text size defined in users' browser settings and setting all text variants (such as headings, captions, and links) using relative units, such as ems or percentages. An em in the web context is the same as the font height, which makes it a relative unit and therefore flexible. For example, if the user-set default is 16 pixels, than a two-em text indent would be double, or 32 pixels. But if the user used the text zoom feature of the browser to change the text size to 18 pixels, the indent would change to 36 pixels to reflect the larger type size. Use a responsive design approach that adjusts the layout in response to text size settings.

RESPONSIVE TYPOGRAPHY

The accessibility benefits of a responsive design approach are less touted than those for cross-device support. However, the adaptation behavior of responsive designs works well for users who have low vision and need large text to read. People with low vision can use screen magnification software to access online content and functionality. The experience of using screen magnification is like holding a magnifying glass over a portion of a page and moving the magnifier around the page to read. Only the portion of page below the magnifying glass is readable at one time.

In a responsive layout—designed using flexible units, such as percentages or ems—when the user enlarges text using the browser zoom feature, all the text, controls, and layout adjust to the larger text size. The layout will adjust at different breakpoints, as it would when viewed on a table or smartphone. And typographic devices that aid readability, such as line length and line height, adapt to the text size and layout, improving the readability at larger sizes.

FIGURE 9.9 Responsive design benefits people who need large text to read. In this example from the *Guardian*, enlarging text in the browser shifts the layout to the tablet and smartphone view, making all the content display comfortably in the browser window. On sites that don't adapt, users who need large text must often scroll horizontally to read.

EMPHASIS

There are time-honored typographical devices for adding emphasis to a block of text, but be sure to use them sparingly. If you make everything bold, then nothing will stand out and you will appear to be shouting at your readers. A good rule of thumb when working with type is to add emphasis using one parameter at a time. If you want to draw attention to the section heads in your document, don't set them large, bold, and all uppercase. If you want them to be larger, increase their size by one measure. If you prefer bold, leave the heads the same size as your body text and make them bold. You will soon discover that only a small variation is required to establish visual contrast.

Italics

Italicized text attracts the eye because it contrasts in shape from body text. Use italics for convention—for example, when listing book or magazine titles—or within text for stressed or foreign words and phrases. Avoid setting large blocks of text in italics because the readability of italicized text is much lower than in comparably sized roman ("plain") text.

Bold

Boldface text gives emphasis because it contrasts in weight from the body text. Section subheads work well set in bold. Boldface text is readable onscreen, though large blocks of text set in bold lack contrast and therefore lose effectiveness.

Underlining

Underlined text is a carryover from the days of the typewriter, when such options as italics and boldface were unavailable. In addition to its aesthetic shortcomings (too heavy, interferes with letter shapes), underlining has a special functional meaning in web documents. Most readers have their browser preferences set to underline links. This default browser setting ensures that people with monochromatic monitors or people who are color blind can identify links within text blocks. If you include underlined text on your web page, it will certainly be confused with a hypertext link.

Color

Although the use of color is another option for differentiating type, colored text, like underlining, has a special functional meaning in web documents. You should avoid putting colored text within text blocks, because readers will assume that the colored text is a hypertext link and click on it. When using color for emphasis, bear in mind that some users cannot distinguish colors. Use additional visual emphasis that is accessible without color, such as bold for headings and underlining for links.

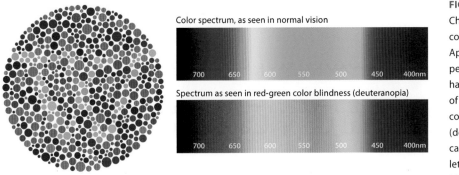

Color spectrum, as seen in normal vision

700 650 600 550 500 450 400nm

Spectrum as seen in red-green color blindness (deuteranopia)

700 650 600 550 500 450 400nm

FIGURE 9.10
Choose your type colors carefully. Approximately 9 percent of males have some degree of red-green color blindness (deuteranopia) and cannot read the letter in the circular Ishihara color test at the left. The bottom color spectrum on the right simulates the spectrum as seen by people with red-green color blindness.

Also be sure that there is sufficient contrast between the background and text on your page. Although contrast is particularly important for vision-impaired users, all users will benefit from greater readability.

Capitals

Capitalized text is one of the most common and least effective methods for adding typographical emphasis. Words set in all capitals should generally be avoided—except perhaps for short headings—because they are hard to scan. This is because we read primarily by recognizing the overall shape of words, not by parsing each letter and then assembling a recognizable word. Words formed with capital letters are monotonous rectangles that offer few distinctive shapes to catch the eye (fig. 9.11).

We recommend down-style typing (capitalize only the first word and any proper nouns) for your headlines, subheads, and text. Down style is more legible because as we read, we primarily scan the tops of words. Notice how much harder it is to read the bottom half of the same sentence. If you use initial capital letters in your headlines, you disrupt the reader's scanning of the word forms.

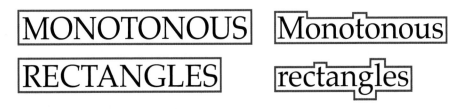

FIGURE 9.11
We read by quickly assessing the shapes of familiar words. All-caps text makes monotonous word shapes that must be read slowly, letter by letter.

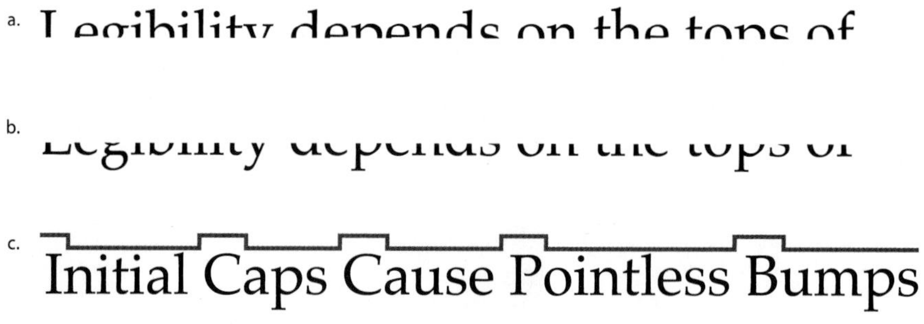

FIGURE 9.12
The tops of words
(a) are much more
important to
legibility than the
bottoms (b). Initial
caps disrupt and
slow the scanning
process (c).

a. Legibility depends on the tops of

b. Legibility depends on the tops of

c. Initial Caps Cause Pointless Bumps

To read a block of text set in all capital letters, we must read the text letter by letter, which is uncomfortable and significantly slows reading. As you read the following paragraph, notice how tiring the process is:

STRATEGIC PLANNING IS NOT A BAG OF TIPS, TRICKS, OR SPECIAL TECHNIQUES. IT'S NOT ABOUT PREDICTING THE FUTURE—WE CREATE STRATEGIES PRECISELY BECAUSE WE CAN'T PREDICT THE FUTURE. STRATEGIC PLANNING IS NOT A WAY TO ELIMINATE RISK. AT BEST STRATEGY IS AN ATTEMPT TO IDENTIFY AND TAKE THE RIGHT RISKS AT THE RIGHT TIMES.

Spacing and indentation

One of the most effective and subtle ways to vary the visual contrast and relative importance of a piece of text is to isolate or treat it differently from the surrounding text. If you want your major headings to stand out more without making them larger, add space before the heading to separate it from any previous copy. Indentation is another effective means of distinguishing bulleted lists, quotations, or example text (such as the capitalization example, above).

TYPEFACES

Each typeface has a unique tone that should produce a harmonious fit between the verbal and visual flow of your content. Most of the traditional serif typefaces we use today can trace their roots back to the typography of Imperial Rome, which you can still see today on monuments scattered throughout the Mediterranean world.

The variety of heavily used typefaces we have today originated mostly from the two centuries after Johannes Gutenberg invented movable metal type in around 1450. Printers such as Aldus Manutius (originator of italic faces), Nicholas Jenson, and Christophe Plantin designed or commissioned the early models for the Roman-derived "humanistic" or "old style" faces still in wide use today, albeit in digital form. Humanistic faces like Garamond (1532), Caslon (1725), and their more modern

Web	Web	Web	Web	Web	Web
Serif	Sans serif	Humanist or Old Style	Modern	Slab serif	Geometric sans serif
Minion Pro	Helvetica	Garamond	Bodoni	Claredon	Futura

derivatives Goudy (1916), Times New Roman (1932), and Palatino (1948) are some of the most widely used typefaces today, because of their beautiful forms and outstanding legibility. The text you are reading now is set in Goudy.

FIGURE 9.13

Fine typography has a rich history that unfortunately is beyond the scope of this book, but if you are curious about the letterforms you have used since childhood, and will use for the rest of your life, we highly recommend Robert Bringhurst's *The Elements of Typographic Style*, Ellen Lupton's *Thinking with Type*, and a more recent book dedicated to fine web typography, Jason Santa Maria's *On Web Typography*.

THE TERMINOLOGY OF TYPEFACES

Type design is an ancient and complex craft, and has its own vocabulary for describing the anatomy and details of letterforms. Figure 9.14 shows some of the more common terms for describing the details of letters.

SIZES OF TYPE

If you have any experience at all with various typefaces, you have noticed what seems like an odd discrepancy in type sizing: some typefaces are much larger than others, even when they are nominally set to the same point size. This is because our modern digital typefaces still follow forms derived from the days of metal type, when the "point size" of type was derived from the dimensions of the rectangular metal slug, or "sort," that supported the actual printing face of the letter. Within the type slug size typographers had some freedom to produce more delicate typefaces with smaller "x-heights" (fig. 9.15a and b), or larger, more robust faces that more completely filled the face of the slug. Thus the lowercase letters of Baskerville are

FIGURE 9.14

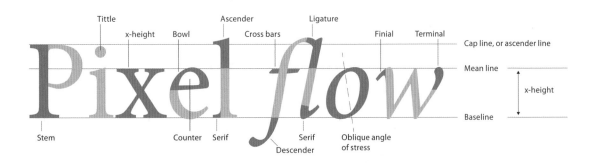

a.

Proportionately large
x-height in modern typefaces

16-point Helvetica

b.

Smaller x-height
in classic typefaces

16-point Baskerville

c.

16-point slug size

Same baseline

FIGURE 9.15

considerably smaller than the lowercase letters of Helvetica, even when both are set to a 16 point size (fig. 9.15c).

In general, typefaces with larger x-heights are considered more legible, particularly in less than ideal conditions, such as very small point sizes, or on the relatively low-resolution traditional 72–96-pixels-per-inch screens of older computers and smartphones. The well-known pair of serif and sans serif typefaces Georgia and Verdana were designed for Microsoft by famed typeface designer Matthew Carter specifically for outstanding legibility on computer screens. Carter designed both faces with relatively robust overall dimensions and large x-heights to make Georgia and Verdana easy to read from screens.

LETTERSPACING AND KERNING

Two critical skills in handling web typography are letterspacing and kerning using css. Letterspacing is most commonly used to improve the legibility of type set in all caps, where more generous spacing between letters helps the eye distinguish the relatively monotonous shapes of capital letters from one another. In general, all instances of all-caps lettering should provide some extra letterspacing using css (for example: h1 { letter-spacing: 2px; }).

Kerning is adjustment of the space between individual letterforms, and is particularly important when you use large "display" sizes of typography in your page designs. Kerning is used to improve the aesthetics of type when two adjacent letters seem too far apart, leaving an awkward gap that disturbs the smooth flow and rhythm of the line of type (fig. 9.17). You can use negative values of the css letterspacing property to pull together specific pairs of letterforms to improve the look of large, prominent display type headers.

FIGURE 9.16

Spacing between
letters helps
legibility, particularly
with all-caps
lettering.

JOHANNES GUTENBERG —— All caps without letterspacing

JOHANNES GUTENBERG —— All caps with letterspacing

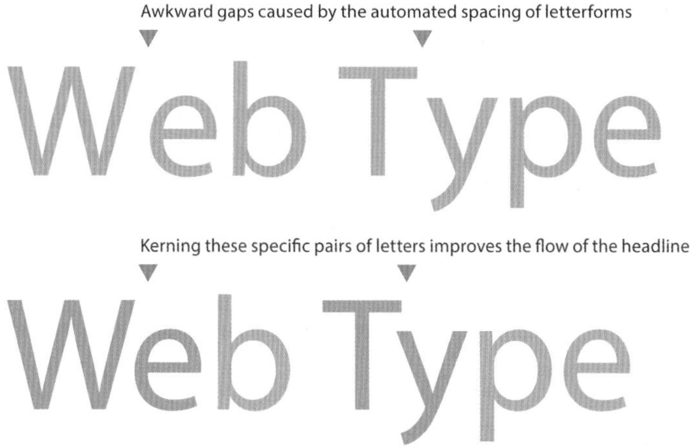

Awkward gaps caused by the automated spacing of letterforms

▼ ▼

Web Type

Example CSS:

.kern {
   letter-spacing: -0.1em;
   }

Example HTML:

<span class "kern">W</span>
<span class "kern">T</span>

Kerning these specific pairs of letters improves the flow of the headline

▼ ▼

Web Type

FIGURE 9.17
Kerning is normally used on the web only to improve large blocks of "display" type.

ADAPTED TRADITIONAL TYPEFACE

Times New Roman is a good example of a traditional typeface that has been adapted for use on computer screens. A serif typeface like Times New Roman is about average in legibility on the computer screen and has a moderate x-height. Times New Roman is a good font to use in text-heavy documents that will probably be printed by readers rather than read from the screen. The compact letter size of Times New Roman also makes it a good choice if you need to pack a lot of words into a small space.

DESIGNED FOR THE SCREEN

Typefaces such as Georgia and Verdana were designed specifically for legibility on the computer screen; they have exaggerated x-heights and are robust compared with more traditional typefaces in the same point size. These screen fonts offer excellent legibility for web pages designed to be read directly from the screen. However, the exaggerated x-heights and heavy letterforms of Georgia and Verdana sometimes look massive when transferred to the high-resolution medium of paper.

TYPEFACES FOR OTHER MEDIA

Much of our attention is focused on the screen version of our pages, but we also have control over how a page looks when printed on paper. Print offers a far richer palette of options when it comes to selecting a typeface; many more typefaces look good on paper than the relatively few that are readable and attractive onscreen. In contrast, there is no point specifying a typeface for handheld styling since most devices have only one font.

CHOOSING TYPEFACES

The most conventional scheme for using typefaces is to use a serif face such as Times New Roman or Georgia for body text and a sans serif face such as Verdana or Arial as a contrast for headlines. Various studies purport to show that serif type is more legible than sans serif type, or vice versa. You can truly judge type legibility only within context—on the screen, on paper—as users will see your web page.

You may use either a variation of the serif font or a contrasting sans serif face for the display type. It is safest to use a single typographic family and vary its weight and size for display type and emphasis. If you choose to combine serif and sans serif faces, select fonts that are compatible, and don't use more than two typefaces (one serif, one sans serif) on a page.

SPECIFYING OPERATING SYSTEM TYPEFACES

Web typography has blossomed over the past five years with the @font-face css element (see the next section) widely supported, and web fonts available (free and for fee) from many typographic suppliers. But there are still many good reasons to use the common operating system fonts like Times, Arial, Trebuchet, Georgia, and Verdana. These system fonts are highly legible—if also highly familiar—and they load fast and reliably. Unlike downloadable web fonts, system fonts don't add any bandwidth burden to your pages. This could be a crucial advantage when designing pages for mobile use, where the advantages of fast response may far outweigh the aesthetic constraints of sticking with the standard Mac os X and Windows font groups. The browser will check for the presence of each font (in the order you provide), so you can specify three or four alternates before the browser applies the default font, for example, "Times New Roman, Georgia, Times." As a fail-safe effort, you can end your font declaration with a generic font designation such as "serif." That way, if the browser cannot find any of the listed fonts, it will display the text in an available serif font:

```
p { font-family: "Times New Roman", Georgia, Times, serif }
```

Notice that multiword font names such as Times New Roman must appear within quotation marks in your specification. Also note in the font example below that although "Trebuchet" and "Trebuchet ms" are the same typeface, the exact name you specify in the font list matters. If you want both Macintosh and Windows users to see the typeface Trebuchet, then use both names in your font declaration:

```
p { font-family: "Trebuchet MS", Trebuchet, Verdana, Arial,
    sans-serif }
```

A good way to make sure that your type settings are functioning correctly is to set your browser's default proportional font setting to something that is obviously different from your intended font. For example, set your browser's default font to Courier if you are not using Courier in your document. When you view your page, anything that appears in Courier must not be marked up properly.

USING WEB-BASED FONTS WITH THE CSS @FONT-FACE ELEMENT

Wide support for the css3 @font-face has finally brought the full range of typographic possibilities to web communications. Although browser support is not perfect yet—there are still multiple font file formats to consider—web-based typographic services like Adobe Edge Fonts, Font Squirrel, Google Fonts, TypeCast, and TypeKit now make it possible to use almost any major mainstream typeface in your web work. Web fonts may be local files on your web server along with your site files or cms, or the fonts may be referenced "live" from online font sources like Google Fonts through using an @font-face tag that references Google directly:

```
<link href='fonts.googleapis.com/css?family=Open+Sans'
    rel='stylesheet' type='text/css'>

@import url(fonts.googleapis.com/css?family=Open+Sans);
    font-family: 'Open Sans', sans-serif;
```

Google, Adobe, and Font Squirrel all provide some fonts for no fees. Google's huge (and growing) web font library is entirely free for use.

The advantages of being free to use a wide range of mainstream and decorative typefaces is obvious, but there are some significant aesthetic and performance disadvantages to using too many web fonts in your web work.

Performance impact of web fonts

Most web fonts need to be referenced from sources like Google Fonts on the fly, as your page loads into the reader's browser, and standard web fonts like Google Fonts may be 30–50 Kb each, or about the size of a moderate-sized graphic in JPEG format. It does not take too many @font-face requests before your page loading will be noticeably slower. Pages that already contain many images will be particularly slow to load, and if you are also using symbol fonts to supply icon graphics for your page design the loading will slow further. This doesn't mean that you can't use multiple fonts on your design work, but if your pages are already loaded with graphic content, you might want to check continually with online speed testing like Google's PageSpeed or Pingdom (tools.pingdom.com) to be sure you understand the performance implications of your web font work.

Typographic aesthetics

If you are not a trained graphic designer or web typography expert, you can still explore web typography to improve the form and function of your pages. Web-based services like TypeCast (typecast.com) make it both easy and fun to rapidly explore many different web font options before you make a commitment to particular combinations. Here are a few basic considerations if you are not a designer used to making typographic decisions:

1. Keep it simple, and use no more than two typefaces in your site. Often this means choosing a typeface for your major headings, and a contrasting typeface for your major text blocks. Designers will often choose a sans serif font for headlines and major titles and a serif font for the primary text blocks, or sometimes vice versa. Choose one scheme or the other, and don't add more typefaces. There are several families of serif/sans serif combinations that make it especially easy to coordinate your typefaces. Adobe's Stone family of sans serif and serif faces was designed to work beautifully in combination, as were Adobe's Myriad and Minion faces.

2. Don't get caught up in the endless (and pointless) debate about whether serif or san serif fonts are more legible—there are no reliable data to support so simple a proposition. There are wonderfully legible serif and sans serif fonts, and horrible fonts in both categories.

3. Stay in the mainstream. Use fonts that are familiar and have been in wide use for decades, as they have stood the test of time and will not embarrass you. Serif font mainstays like Georgia, Times, Minion, Palatino, Goudy, and Garamond are both beautiful and highly functional. Sans serif fonts like Myriad (used throughout this book), Arial, Helvetica, and Syntax are wonderfully legible in all normal font sizes.

4. Do not use decorative, jolly, eccentric, or display typefaces. Ever. Full stop.

5. Establish a simple visual and typographic "vocabulary," and stick with it. In every serious project there will be challenges you didn't predict, and situations that might seem to call for adding new kinds of type treatments, unusually large or small type sizes, or other typographic anomalies. Every experienced designer knows that it's almost invariably best to stick with your program, and your chosen tools, and to think the problem through with those ground rules in place. That way you're not tempted to "wing it" with unique graphics or fonts every time a new challenge arises.

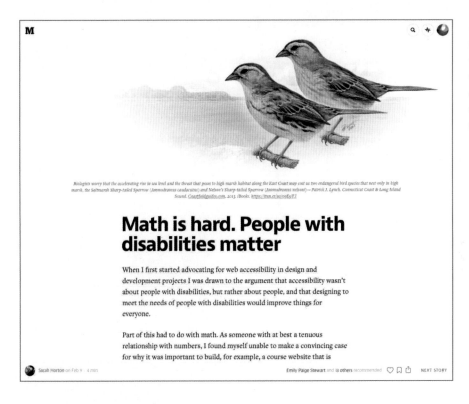

FIGURE 9.18
If you are new to typography and want to learn from one of the exemplars of web typography, study Medium.com.

RECOMMENDED READING

Bringhurst, R. *The Elements of Typographic Style*, 4th ed. Seattle: Hartley and Marks, 2012.

Lupton, E. *Thinking with Type: A Critical Guide for Designers, Writers, Editors, and Students*. New York: Princeton Architectural Press, 2010.

Santa Maria, J. *On Web Typography*. New York: A Book Apart, 2014.

Chapter 10: Editorial Style

The measure of good editorial style is whether the content is useful—whether it is real, carefully researched user needs. Too often corporate and institutional style from their goals and organization charts, forgetting that users couldn't care less what you think.

In this chapter we focus on writing style and composition best practices for channels.

Style

Online writing is best presented using short sentences that support the reading and ... to be effective ...

Simplicity isn't the goal. It is the by-product of a good idea and modest expectations.
–Paul Rand

CHAPTER 10

Editorial Style

T he measure of good editorial style is whether the content is useful—whether it meets clear user and business goals. Content should meet real, carefully researched user needs. Too often corporate and institutional web teams produce content designed primarily around internal goals and organization charts, forgetting that users couldn't care less what your mission statement is, or how you are organized.

In this chapter we focus on writing style and composition best practices specifically as they apply to the web, mobile, and social media channels.

Only connect!
—E. M. Forster,
Howards End

STYLE

Online writing is best presented using short segments of texts written in a clear, concise style and with ample use of editorial landmarks. This style supports the scanning style used by most web users. But online prose does not have to be stripped down to a few headlines and bullet points to be effective: readers will engage directly with longer written materials that are relevant, accessible, and interesting.

WRITING FOR ENGAGEMENT

Engaging content is relevant and targeted, and does not waste the users' time or demand unnecessary effort. Start with a clear content strategy, defining what you have to say, to whom, and what questions they want answered or tasks they want to achieve (see the section on "Content Strategy" in Chapter 1, Strategy.) From there, respect your users by anticipating their questions and providing answers in a way that is conversational and interesting, and that responds to diverse ways of consuming information.

Conversation

The content on your web site is most often an answer—to a question, to a need. As Ginny Redish points out in her book *Letting Go of the Words*, "Every use of your web site or mobile app is a conversation started by your site visitor." The key is to understand what the conversation is and engage with your visitors in a way that satisfies their goals. To do this, you must anticipate what questions people will have at various points as they work through your site content and features.

The first step is to make sure your information is relevant to your users. You don't want to be a bore, droning on and on about things that are deeply meaningful to your

FIGURE 10.1

The navigation links on Shining Hope for Communities anticipate questions users will arrive with and answers them directly—What is Shining Hope for Communities all about? What is effective about your work? Who is involved, and how can I get involved?

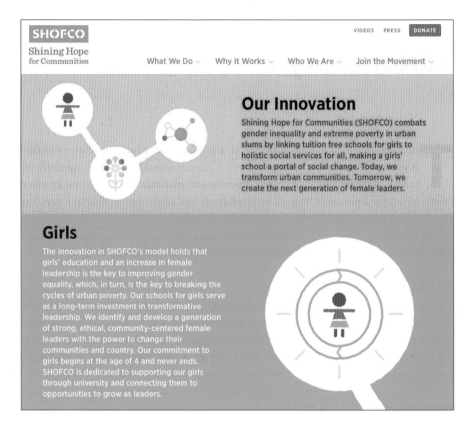

organization but that are immaterial to your web site users, who have questions and needs they have come to you to resolve. Review your content and remove anything that has questionable value to your target audience. From the content that remains, identify conversation starters to associate with the content. What questions would someone ask that would prompt you to share the content in response? Remove anything that is tangential, and revise what remains. Then identify follow-on questions and answers, and in this way construct the nodes you need to build out to support the conversation with your users.

Content chunks

In Chapter 4, Information Architecture, we discuss the concept of content chunking, and how modular content informs the architecture and structure of a site. From a stylistic perspective, good content chunks focus on purpose and audience. In most cases, users are looking for specific information, and then are looking to move on. When content is divided into chunks, it's easier to find. When chunks are the right size, users can get what they need without much effort.

DESIRE LINES

Desire lines are the pathways that arise from many people taking the same path, usually in opposition to built routes and pathways. These alternate routes typically cut across a space that was intentionally left untouched, like a protected green space, or they provide a more direct route than a corresponding sidewalk that has angles and bends. A desire line is a natural expression of impulse, visibly demonstrating how we prefer to navigate our environment when given the option, rather than following a predefined journey based on choices made by the designer. Understanding and embracing desire lines is an excellent means to designing spaces, products, and services that map to preferences, and that people want to use. In landscape design, one approach to a new space is to wait for the desire lines to emerge before marking the paths and pouring the concrete.

There are multiple methods for detecting desire lines in the digital landscape. One is through field studies, observing how people work with digital products to accomplish their goals. New projects can benefit greatly from field studies of comparable products, observing ways in which users who are familiar with the products follow the paths defined by the design and architecture, and where they veer off and create a more desirable path to achieving goals. Another approach is to track paths through web site content using techniques like eye-tracking and web analytics, and to adjust the content and architecture over time to map more closely to actual use patterns.

An understanding of desire lines is critical when working with content chunks because you must provide a path. One of the only benefits of long, complex documents is that all the required information is probably contained somewhere on the page. Even if it's difficult to find, at least it's there—somewhere. Users can make their way through the document without having their experience constrained by predefined paths and trails. But as when you wander in the woods, there's no clear path to getting where you want to go, and it's easy to get lost. Content chunks are much easier to use and navigate between, but the path from one to the next must be logical, direct, and clearly marked to help people reach their desired destination.

But what makes a right-sized chunk? You don't want to divide up content so much that users must visit multiple pages to get a complete answer and accomplish their goals. The granularity of a chunk should correspond to whatever size is required to answer the essential questions that make the content relevant to your users in the first place. Which brings us back to the conversational aspect of your content and your content strategy. Take your content strategy—defined by matching business goals with an understanding of users and their questions and "desire lines"—as a starting point. Use the content strategy as a starting point for creating coherent and comprehensive content chunks. Use the architecture of your site to create paths that map to your users' logical paths, making it easy to move from one chunk to the next in getting all questions and needs answered.

Headings are a key component in the success of a content chunking strategy. When headings are used as hyperlinks, they are signposts marking the path from one content chunk to the next. As page and section headings, they confirm users' arrival at the desired destination. Headings should be descriptive and clear. They should start with keywords (see "Keywords," below) that are familiar and quickly recognizable, and should entice users to read on by speaking to the question at hand.

Clarity

Keep the subject matter of each page focused, and express the subject using language that is clear and concise. This topical focus helps the reader evaluate the page content quickly and has many advantages for search engine visibility, where a clear and quickly identifiable content theme is important to search ranking.

Here we summarize best practices for web writing, drawing on several sources, including Ginny Redish's *Letting Go of the Words*, Strunk and White's *The Elements of Style*, and the Federal Plain Language Guidelines.

- Prefer the standard to the offbeat. With so many competing sources, a unique voice may distinguish your pages, but beware of going over the top. There is a fine line between engaging and annoying.
- Address users directly. Use "you," "I," and "we" to make the information inviting and personal, and to further reinforce the conversational nature of the discourse.
- Use active voice. Sentences that use active voice place the actor before the action, and are easier to comprehend than sentences that use passive voice. "We will mail your package on Friday," not "Your package will be mailed on Friday." (One trick for determining whether a sentence uses passive voice is whether it can accommodate a "by ____" at the end: "Your package will be mailed on Friday by us.") Also, putting the actor at the beginning of a sentence conveys energy: "We sometimes fail to deliver packages on schedule," not

"There are occasional cases in which we are unable to deliver a package on schedule."

- Keep it short. Short sentences naturally follow from using active voice. As Strunk and White point out, "Brevity is a by-product of vigor." Focusing on short sentences reinforces the best practice of cutting out unnecessary words. And short paragraphs are easier to read and understand, and also add white space to the page to make it more inviting.
- Use plain language. The objective of plain language is to write clearly so that users can "find what they need, understand what they find, and use what they find to meet their needs." Plain language does not mean dumbing down your text. It means writing clearly and conversationally so that people can

INVERTED PYRAMID

The inverted pyramid is a method for presenting information whereby the most important information, represented by the base of the pyramid, is presented first and the least important (the tip) is presented last. Information designed using this model begins with a lead that summarizes the information, followed by the body, where the information presented in the lead is elaborated on and substantiated, in descending order of importance. Thanks to its long use in journalism the inverted pyramid style has a number of well-established advantages:

- Important information comes first, where it is more likely to be seen and remembered
- This front-loading of content permits efficient scanning for information
- A content-first approach benefits anyone who is working with a small "viewport," including people using screen reader and screen magnification software and people accessing the page on a small-screen mobile device
- The initial major facts establish a context for later secondary information
- The structure places facts and keywords at the head of the page, where they carry more weight in search engine relevance analysis

understand what you are saying without needing to expend a great deal of time and energy. As Ginny Redish explains, "Write so that busy people understand what you are saying the first time they read it."

- Write for a global audience. Remember that you are designing documents for the World Wide Web and that your audience may not understand conventions specific to your corner of the world. For example, when including dates, use the international date format of day/month/year (14 March 2009). Spell out abbreviations that might not be familiar, such as state or province names. Also, consider that any metaphors, puns, or popular culture references that you use may make sense only in the context of your language and culture.

PUTTING CONTENT FIRST

Make sure the text you present is of immediate value. Avoid empty chatter such as "welcome" messages from unit managers or instructions on how to use the site. Don't use the first paragraph of each page to tell users what information they'll find on the page. Start with the information, written in a concise and engaging style. The inverted pyramid style used in journalism works well on web pages, with the conclusion appearing at the beginning of a text. Place the important facts near the top of the first paragraph, where users can find them quickly. In crowded home pages, it's often good practice to provide only the lead and perhaps a "teaser" sentence, with the body of the article available through a hyperlink.

Keywords

Keywords are the words people use when they want to find content and functionality like yours. When defining keywords for your content, use the words that your site visitors use. Positioning keywords at the beginnings of sentences, headings, and links makes scanning more effective. Initial keywords also help with link and heading lists. Applications such as screen readers give users a list of links or a list of page headings. Such features are more usable when links and headings begin with keywords than when every link or heading begins with "The."

Keywords are also important to support effective search engine results. When readers use web search engines, they generally use words or short phrases that describe what they are seeking. Along with the text of the page title, these keywords become the crucial determinants of your page's relevance rank in the search engine's indexes. For search engine optimization, a good keyword strategy is to make sure that key page elements are working in concert to portray the page content accurately. Ideally, there is one keyword or key phrase for your page, and it is mentioned in most or all of the following elements:

- Page title
- Major `<h1>`, `<h2>`, or `<h3>` headings
- First paragraph of text
- Inbound links to the page

One thing you should never do is pack in gratuitous repetitions of keywords or use sophomoric tricks like creating white text on a white background to hide keywords. All the major search engines know that even in well-written and edited text, keywords and phrases will make up only 5–8 percent of the number of words on the average page of text. Pages with a suspiciously high keyword rate will lose search engine ranking, and pages that use hidden word repetition tricks may be banned from mainstream search engines.

The best keyword advice for good search visibility is simple: write clear, well-edited, interesting prose, and check your page titles and the other elements mentioned above to make sure the key descriptive words or phrases are featured.

LINKING MEANINGFULLY

The primary design strategy in thoughtful hypertext is to use links to reinforce your message, not to distract users or send them off chasing a minor footnote in some other web site. Most links in a web site should point to other resources within your

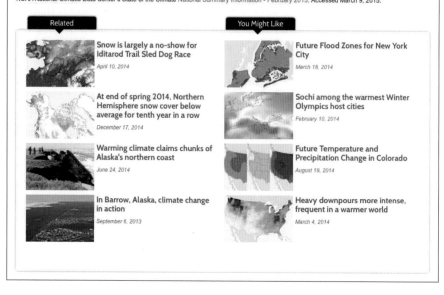

site, pages that share the same graphic design, navigational controls, and overall content theme. Whenever possible, integrate related visual or text materials into your site so that users do not have the sense that you have dumped them outside your site's framework. If you must send your reader away, make sure the material around the link makes it clear that the user will be leaving your web site and entering another site by following the link. Provide a description of the linked site along with the link so that users understand the relevance of the linked material.

Descriptive links

Most of your web visitors are passing through on their way to some other destination and will appreciate your efforts to make the trip as straightforward and predictable as possible, with few meaningless side trips or dead ends. Key to the success of any trip is the clarity of the signage along the way, which in the web context comes in the form of links.

Links are the signposts that help users know which route is most likely to get them to their destination. Good link text gives users a description of the page that will load, allowing them to make informed decisions about which path to take.

Bad link text, such as nondescriptive "click here" links or catchy but meaningless phrases, forces the user to follow the link to learn its destination. Nondescriptive links often lead to dead ends, requiring users to retrace their steps and waste time.

When writing links, never construct a sentence around a link phrase, such as "click here for more information." Write the sentence as you normally would, and place the link anchor on the keyword or phrase that best describes the additional content you are linking to. Bear in mind that hyperlinks aren't just a convenience for the user; they also add semantic meaning to the page. By choosing to link a particular word or phrase, you have signaled to both users and search engines that it is potentially important as a search keyword.

- Poor: <u>Click here</u> for more information on link underlines.
- Better: <u>Link underlines</u> help users identify links.

COMPOSITION

The look of text layout strongly affects how readers relate to written content. The contrast produced by headlines, subheads, lists, and illustrations gives users visual "entry points," drawing their eyes down the page and into the content. Although the heading and list markup might look excessive in print form, on the web this markup has two big advantages:

- Frequent headings and lists of items favor both scanning and methodical readers by adding visible structure to the online reading experience.
- The added structure of heading and list markup aids in search engine optimization and online searches for content, because the additional markup provides explicit semantic emphasis, heading keywords, and context cues that listed items are strongly related to one another.

PROVIDING VISUAL LANDMARKS

Users approach a web page with a quick skim in order to form an overview of the page and determine whether the information they are seeking is likely to be found there. Even methodical readers will appreciate your efforts to accommodate online reading patterns rather than forcing readers to slow down and pick their way through your pages in order to glean information. The following guidelines support both the skimming and reading behaviors of online readers.

Titles

Web page titles are designated in the HTML document <head> section with the <title> element. The title is crucial for several reasons. The title is the first thing users see and the first thing screen reader users hear. It is the text that displays in the browse history, and becomes the default text for any bookmarks the user makes to your pages. In addition, most search engines regard the page title as the primary descriptor of page content, so a descriptive title increases the chance that a page will appear as the result of a related search query.

The page title should:

- Contain carefully chosen keywords and themes for the page
- Form a concise, plainly worded description of the page contents
- Be unique

Some enterprises make it a policy to incorporate the company or organization name as the initial part of the page title. Although this practice is often useful, you should always consider the length of your page title. The page title also becomes the bookmark text, and many web browsers truncate long page titles (more than sixty-five characters, including spaces) in a way that makes them less legible. If your page title starts with a company name, the most relevant part of the page title may not be visible in a reader's bookmark for that page. If you plan to include your organization name, have it come last. Start with the title of the page, then the section, and then the site—for example, Graduate Programs—Volunteer Opportunities—Peace Corps.

Headings

Browsing a page is easier when the text is broken into segments topped by headings that describe the subject of each segment. This often means breaking up long paragraphs, and using more subheadings than you would for print publication. Remember that in the restricted world of a laptop, tablet, or smartphone screen, a paragraph can easily fill the screen with a visually monotonous block of text.

Such editorial landmarks as titles and headings are the fundamental human interface device in web pages, just as they are in any print publication. A consistent approach to titles, headings, and subheadings in your documents will help your users navigate through a complex set of web pages. Choose an approach and stick with it throughout your site.

Headline style is bold, capitalizing the initial letters of important words:

- Document titles
- References to other web sites
- Titles of documents mentioned in the text
- Proper names, product names, trade names

Down style is also bold, but capitalizing the first word only:

- Subheads
- References to other sections within the site
- Figure titles
- Lists

Lists

Like headings, lists aid scanning. They also group related items visually, quickly conveying a related set of concepts through a simple typographic device. It's easy to tell visually whether the list is long or short; with a numbered list, users know immediately how many items are in the list. And numbered lists are particularly helpful for presenting a sequence of instructions, such as required steps to complete a task.

When lists use parallelism, applying the same structure to sentences or phrases, the items are easier to scan and comprehend.

UNIFORM CONNECTEDNESS

We use the gestalt principles of perception to decode the structure of a document visually. One task in making sense of a document is determining which elements are related and which are not. Uniform connectedness defines groups of related information, frequently using "common regions," in which elements are grouped within a bounding box or uniform background.

Structural markup provides the means to use uniform connectedness to group elements in a nonvisual and machine-readable way. A list tag in essence draws a line around several items and asserts that they are related. The `<table>` tag connects data in rows and cells into a single expression of a concept. Even the `<cite>` tag surrounds a phrase and declares its relatedness as a book, magazine, or article title. Using uniform connectedness both on the surface in the visual design and in the structural markup in underlying page code allows both visual and nonvisual users to make sense of the structure of a document.

STRUCTURAL MARKUP

HTML is a markup language that adds a layer of structural meaning to documents. It works by wrapping elements, such as titles, headings, paragraphs, lists, tables, addresses, and citations, in defining tags. The result is a machine-friendly document that can be read and interpreted by software. Tags tell software, for example, that the text from point A to point B is a heading, and the following text block is a paragraph, and so on. For example, when a web author defines a block of text as the page title, web browser software can display the page title in the browser title bar, in the browser history, and as a bookmark.

On the surface, a structured document looks no different from one that uses font size and other visual formatting to distinguish elements such as headings. Functionally, however, structure gives power and utility to the web. Take, for example, the heading of this section. `<b>Structural markup</b>` is visually identifiable as a heading because it is bold and sits directly above plain text. But software cannot infer that it is the primary subheading of this section because `<b>` means nothing more than bold. If the chapter title is marked as `<h1>Structural markup</h1>`, software knows that the page is about structural markup, and that in turn facilitates all kinds of functions, such as returning the page on searches for structural markup or adding the page to compilations about structural markup.

When marking up text, think about what each text element is and not what it should look like. Tag each element with the appropriate HTML structural tag, and then use CSS to manage its visual properties (see "Semantic markup" in Chapter 5).

RHETORIC AND WEB DESIGN

Rhetoric is the art and technique of persuasion, through oral, written, or visual media. The contemporary World Wide Web is a unique combination of all three media, but audience reaction to your high-tech web site is still governed by aspects of rhetoric that the Greek philosopher Aristotle identified almost twenty-four hundred years ago. In *The Art of Rhetoric,* Aristotle outlined three major elements of rhetorical persuasion that can easily be understood in relation to web design.

Ethos Ethos establishes the credibility of an information source. Does the speaker have the credentials and seriousness of purpose to be believed? Many otherwise distinguished and credible institutions still present a painfully amateurish web presence—government and higher education sites being especially notorious offenders—and the credibility of the host institution suffers the consequences of that poor presentation. Even small lapses can erode the ethos of a site: broken links, missing graphics, outdated content, and misspelled words all damage the overall trustworthiness of a site. Ironically, with attention to editorial detail, ethos can also be easily spoofed on the web. Many email scams depend on carefully crafted forgeries of real sites like eBay, PayPal, and personal banking sites. Beware of cheap thieves in expensive suits.

Pathos Pathos is the art of developing a positive emotional response in the viewer. Most sites don't develop high emotional responses in users, but a well-designed home page with attractive graphics and interesting articles and links makes users more likely to explore your site. A strong appeal to pathos is central to many marketing web sites, particularly where the user's identification with an upscale brand image is crucial.

Logos Logos uses reason, logic, statistics, convincing examples, and depth of information to persuade an audience. A newspaper front page or home page isn't just about packing the maximum amount of news into a given space. Over weeks, months, and years, a news source builds credibility with an audience through the sheer depth and breadth of information, carefully presented news photography, and information graphics, now augmented on the web with audiovisual media.

Review your rhetoric Go to your home page and do your best to see the site anew, the way a stranger might, who knows you only through your web presence. Does the rhetoric of your site support or erode the user's sense of the credibility, trustworthiness, and humanity of your enterprise?

PRESENTING CLEAR LINKS

Embedded hypertext links pose two fundamental design problems. They disrupt the flow of content in your site by inviting the user to leave your site. They can also radically alter the context of information by dumping the users into unfamiliar territory without preamble or explanation when they follow the embedded links to new pages—particularly when those new pages are outside your site.

When placing links on the page, put only the most salient links within the body of your text, and group all minor, illustrative, parenthetic, or footnote links at the bottom of the document, where they are available but not distracting.

Underlining

Underlining is a carryover from the days of handwriting and the typewriter, when options such as bold and italics were not readily available as ways to distinguish elements such as headings and emphasized words or phrases. Typographically, underlining is undesirable, since it interferes with the legibility of letterforms. However, link underlines ensure that users who cannot see colors—users with color vision issues, and users who access the web on devices that do not display color—can distinguish links from other text. For universal usability, links must be visually identifiable with or without color. Links that display within a navigation column or button bar are clearly links and do not necessarily need underlining. However, links that appear within body text should be underlined to set them off from the surrounding text.

Visited and unvisited links

Most web sessions involve trial and error. For example, finding a phone number or a price or location may involve multiple rounds of searching and following unproductive paths. The process can become circuitous if there is no way to tell where you have already looked, with repeat visits to pages that did not prove fruitful. By providing different link colors for visited and unvisited links, you allow users to identify the paths they have already taken.

RECOMMENDED READING

Redish, G. *Letting Go of the Words: Writing Web Content That Works*, 2nd ed. Waltham, MA: Morgan Kaufmann, 2012.

Strunk, W., and E. B. White. *The Elements of Style*, 4th ed. New York: Longman, 1999.

Wachter-Boettcher, S. *Content Everywhere: Strategy and Structure for Future-Ready Content.* Brooklyn, NY: Rosenfeld, 2012.

Zinsser, W. *On Writing Well*, 30th ann. ed. New York: Harper Perennial, 2006.

Who are you going to believe,
me or your own eyes?
– Groucho Marx

Images

G ood diagrams and interesting illustrations are visually arresting and create documents that are distinct and memorable. Illustrations can convey
complex quantitative or spatial information quickly, transcending language
barriers, and can combine with text to complement many styles of information
gathering and learning. New tools have increased our ability to create information
graphics, and the web provides a full-color multimedia forum unbounded by the
costs of publishing and distributing paper.

Good design is
clear thinking made
visible.

—Edward Tufte

WEB IMAGING STRATEGIES

INTERFACE AND BRANDING

Consistent interface and identity graphics across a collection of web pages define the
boundaries of a web "site." Although web designers could build a site without images, most users would not readily recognize a collection of bare pages as a cohesive
"site," and such a site would seem unpleasantly odd, well outside of design norms and
user expectations. Site-defining identity graphics do not need to be elaborate, but
they do need to be consistent across the range of pages in a site for the user to establish a sense that your pages are a discrete region—related perhaps to a larger whole if
you work in a major enterprise, but in some ways distinct as a "place."

CONTENT IMAGES

Content images serve a number of purposes, complementary to text content:

- **Illustrations:** Graphics can show you things, bringing pieces of the world into
  your document.
- **Diagrams:** Quantitative graphics and process diagrams can explain concepts
  visually.
- **Quantitative data:** Numeric charts can help explain financial, scientific, or
  other data.
- **Analysis and causality:** Graphics can help take apart a topic or show what
  caused it.
- **Integration:** Graphics can combine words, numbers, and images in a
  comprehensive explanation.

FIGURE 11.1

On the web, graphics create places. Page headers and other identity graphics allow us to easily recognize collections of web pages as "sites."

A chart or diagram is an implicit promise to the user that you'll make a complex world easier to understand. Our advice on graphic communications is the same as on written communications:

- Trust the reader's intelligence. Don't dumb down your material on the supposition that web users are somehow fundamentally different kinds of people from print readers and have no interest in complexity. Regular readers of web sites may once have been distinguishable from other publishing audiences, but now everyone reads the web.

- Respect the medium. The readers are the same as in print media, but the web has a different profile of strengths and weaknesses. Take advantage of the web's enormous capabilities to communicate complex color visuals without the expense of printing and physical distribution.

- Tell the truth as you understand it. Distorting quantitative data isn't just a failure to communicate; it's a betrayal of the reader's trust.

- Don't cherry-pick your data. If you are making a case with visual evidence, don't process and edit your visuals so heavily that the audience has no choice but to accept your point of view. Trust your viewers enough to give them the data: let them look at the same higher-resolution images or ambiguous results that you saw and decide the issue for themselves.

- Be bold and substantial. A serious interest in visual communication doesn't require that you use only small, mousy graphics in pale colors. Visual evidence can't become persuasive if no one ever notices it. Just don't ever try to wow an audience with bright graphics to make up for thin content.

FIGURE 11.2
Even at 72–96 ppi, photographs on the web have always looked great on full-color screens, because of the much higher dynamic range that photos on screen have compared with print. On the screen, photos literally shine at you, producing a much richer range of lights and darks than is possible from light reflected from color printing on paper pages.

ABOUT WEB IMAGES

UNDERSTANDING IMAGE TYPES

Bitmap or raster images

Bitmap (or raster) images are composed of a fine grid of pixels (picture elements). Each pixel has a particular color, and because the pixels are small and can be any one of millions of colors, the raster image format is typically used for photographs and complex artwork.

Vector images

Vector images use mathematical descriptions of lines, polygons, points, curves, and fill effects to create an image. Vector images are typically simple and diagrammatic, like graphs, charts, and diagrams, and rarely have the depth or complexity of raster images like photographs. But vector images have some critical advantages over raster images:

- Because vector image files are just shorthand descriptions of shapes, the files are small, and can be downloaded quickly.
- Vector images can be scaled to any size without a loss of quality.
- Although vector images are mostly diagrammatic, with complex shading and colors they can be very realistic.

Scalable vector graphics—SVG

SVG images are vector graphics saved in an open-format XML file type, instead of a proprietary vector image format like Adobe Illustrator (.ai) files. Most Illustrator graphics can be saved in SVG format and used directly on web pages. As vector images, SVG graphics can be scaled to any size without a loss of quality, and they are compact in size, making them increasingly popular for creating graphics for mobile applications and responsive web sites, at least for relatively simple images and shapes.

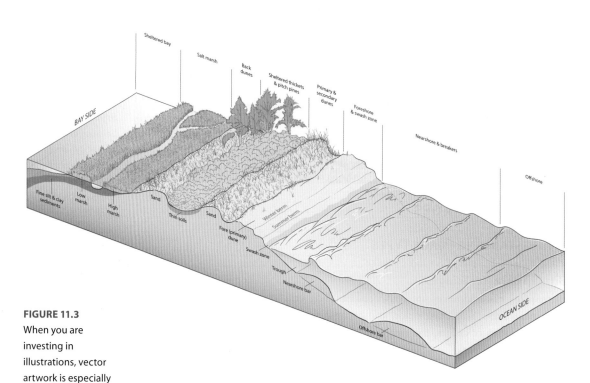

Labels on figure:
Sheltered bay
Salt marsh
Back dunes
Sheltered thickets & pitch pines
Primary & secondary dunes
Foreshore & swash zone
Nearshore & breakers
Offshore
BAY SIDE
Fine silt & clay sediments
Low marsh
High marsh
Sand
Thin soils
Sand
Fore (primary) dune
Winter berm
Summer berm
Swash zone
Trough
Nearshore bar
Offshore bar
OCEAN SIDE

FIGURE 11.3
When you are investing in illustrations, vector artwork is especially attractive because you can use it in so many different media: web, apps, ebooks, and print. Ironically, vector illustrations this complex may not save you any bandwidth as SVG graphics. You're often better off converting complex vector art to JPEGs in various resolutions for 1× and 2× displays.

CSS-based graphics

Cascading style sheet (css) visual styling has long been used to create simple—or complex—graphic effects on web pages through css code alone. Probably the most common css graphics are graphic buttons, where pure css techniques are used to transform simple HTML spans, divs, and links into graphic buttons in any color or shape, with shading, edges, drop-shadows, hover and click states, and other effects. css techniques can create complex graphic effects on web pages that actually have no embedded JPEG, GIF, or PNG graphics: just HTML elements styled with css.

Icon fonts

Icon fonts provide a convenient way to load dozens or even hundreds of vector-based symbols and icons into your web site in an extremely compact form. Instead of alphanumeric characters, an icon font is full of icons, so with a single HTTP request your web page now has hundreds of vector-based symbols available. Icon fonts allow you to easily use css to change the size, color, drop-shadow, or other graphic characteristics of the icons.

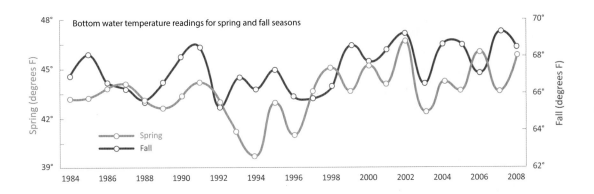

Bottom water temperature readings for spring and fall seasons

Spring (degrees F)

Fall (degrees F)

Spring
Fall

1984 1986 1988 1990 1992 1994 1996 1998 2000 2002 2004 2006 2008

UNDERSTANDING IMAGE FILE FORMATS

The primary web file formats are raster images in GIF (pronounced "jiff"), JPEG ("jay-peg"), and PNG ("ping") files. All three common web graphic formats are so-called bitmap graphics, made up of a checkerboard grid of thousands of tiny colored square picture elements, or pixels. Bitmap files are the familiar types of files produced by cell phone and digital cameras, and are easily created, edited, resized, and optimized for web use with such widely available tools as Adobe's Photoshop or Elements, Corel's Paint Shop Pro and Painter, or other photo editing programs.

For efficient delivery over the Internet, virtually all web graphics are compressed to keep file sizes as small as possible. Most web sites use both GIF and JPEG images. Choosing between these file types is largely a matter of assessing:

- The nature of the image (is the image a "photographic" collection of smooth tonal transitions or a diagrammatic image with hard edges and lines?)
- The effect of various kinds of file compression on image quality
- The efficiency of a compression technique in producing the smallest file size that looks good

GIF

The CompuServe Information Service popularized the graphic interchange format (GIF) in the 1980s as an efficient means to transmit images across data networks. In the early 1990s the original designers of the World Wide Web adopted GIF for

FIGURE 11.4
A simple chart in SVG format. If you do this kind of graphic in Adobe Illustrator, it's best to "outline" all the typography to avoid possible font problems when the SVG is displayed in some browsers.

FIGURE 11.5
The vector-based graphics in icon fonts such as Font Awesome can be scaled to any resolution and are a great solution to providing a lot of icon graphics with only a single HTTP request.

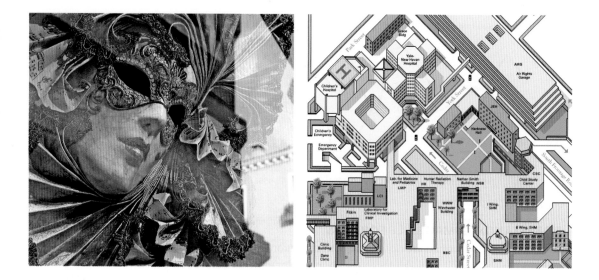

FIGURE 11.6

The Lempel Zev Welch (LZW) image compression techniques in the GIF file format are particularly efficient at compressing simple fields of color and hard-edged diagrammatic graphics (right side). Photographic images (left side) look far better in JPEG or PNG file formats.

its efficiency and widespread familiarity. Many images on the web are in GIF format, and virtually all web browsers that support graphics can display GIF files. GIF files incorporate a "lossless" compression scheme to keep file sizes at a minimum without compromising quality. However, GIF files are 8-bit graphics and thus can accommodate only 256 colors.

The GIF file format uses a relatively basic form of file compression (Lempel Zev Welch, or LZW), which squeezes out inefficiencies in data storage without losing data or distorting the image. The LZW compression scheme is best at compressing images with large fields of homogeneous color, such as logos and diagrams. It is much less efficient at compressing complicated "photographic" pictures with many colors and complex textures (fig. 11.6).

You can take advantage of the characteristics of LZW compression to improve its efficiency and thereby reduce the size of your GIF graphics. The strategy is to reduce the number of colors in your GIF image to the minimum necessary and to remove colors that are not required to represent the image. A GIF graphic cannot have more than 256 colors, but it can have fewer. Images with fewer colors will compress more efficiently under LZW compression. For example, when creating GIF graphics in Photoshop, don't save every file automatically with 256 colors. A simple GIF image may look fine at 8, 16, or 32 colors, and the file size savings can be substantial. For maximum efficiency in GIF graphics, use the minimum number of colors that gives you a good result.

The conventional (noninterlaced) GIF graphic downloads one line of pixels at a time from top to bottom, and browsers display each line of the image as it gradually builds on the screen. In interlaced GIF files the image data are stored in a format

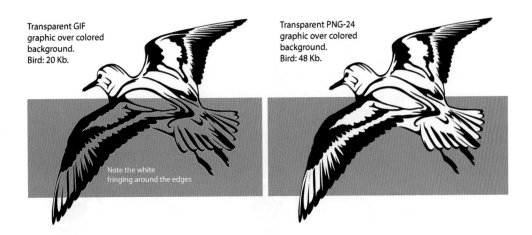

Transparent GIF
graphic over colored
background.
Bird: 20 Kb.

Transparent PNG-24
graphic over colored
background.
Bird: 48 Kb.

Note the white
fringing around the edges

that allows browsers that support this feature to build a low-resolution version of the full-sized GIF picture on the screen while the file is downloading. Some people find the "fuzzy-to-sharp" animated effect of interlacing visually appealing, but the most important benefit of interlacing is that it gives the user a preview of the full picture while the picture downloads into the browser.

Interlacing is best for larger GIF images such as illustrations of 200 × 100 pixels or greater. Interlacing is a poor choice for small GIF graphics such as navigation bars, buttons, and icons. These small graphics will load onto the screen much faster if you keep them in conventional (noninterlaced) GIF format. In general, interlacing has no significant effect on the file size of average GIF graphics.

The GIF format allows you to pick transparent colors from the color lookup table of the GIF. You can use image-editing software such as Photoshop to select a single color in a GIF graphic's color palette to become transparent. Usually the color selected for transparency is the background color in the graphic. Unfortunately, the transparent property is not selective; if you make a color transparent, every pixel in the graphic that shares that color will also become transparent, which can cause unexpected results.

JPEG

The other graphic file format commonly used on the web to minimize graphics file sizes is the Joint Photographic Experts Group (JPEG) compression scheme. Unlike GIF graphics, JPEG images are full-color images that dedicate at least 24 bits of memory to each pixel, resulting in images that can incorporate 16.8 million colors.

JPEG images are used extensively among photographers, artists, graphic designers, medical imaging specialists, art historians, and other groups for whom image quality and color fidelity is important. A form of file called "progressive JPEG" gives

FIGURE 11.7
Transparent background GIF graphics can handle only 256 colors, but transparent GIFs persist because they can be very small in file size compared with transparent background PNG-24 graphics. Unfortunately, only a single color can be specified as transparent in a GIF graphic, and this often results in visible color fringing when GIFs are placed against a contrasting background color.

FIGURE 11.8
JPEG compression
was designed to
handle the smooth,
relatively soft-edged
tonal transition seen
in photographs.
JPEG is much less
efficient with the
artificially hard edges
of graphics and
typography, where
its compression
algorithm produces
"noise" in the form
of clouds of stray
pixels near the hard
transition lines.

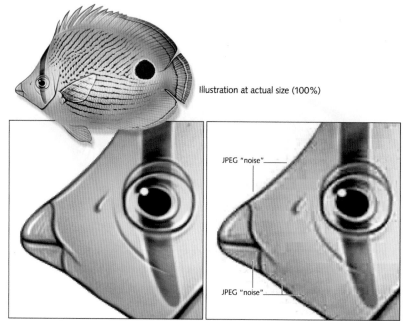

Illustration at actual size (100%)

JPEG "noise"

JPEG "noise"

Uncompressed illustration, 500% enlargement   Heavy JPEG compression, 500% enlargement

JPEG graphics the same gradually built display seen in interlaced GIFs. Like interlaced GIFs, progressive JPEG images often take longer to load onto the page than standard JPEGs, but they do offer the user a quicker preview.

JPEG compression uses a sophisticated mathematical technique called a discrete cosine transformation to produce a sliding scale of graphics compression. You can choose the degree of compression to apply to an image in JPEG format, but in doing so you also determine the image's quality. The more you squeeze a picture with JPEG compression, the more you degrade its quality. JPEG can achieve incredible compression ratios, squeezing graphics down to as much as one one-hundredth the size of the original file. This is possible because the JPEG algorithm discards "unnecessary" data as it compresses the image, and it is thus called a "lossy" compression technique. Notice in Figure 11.8 how increasing the JPEG compression progressively degrades the details of the image. The checkered pattern and the dark "noise" pixels in the compressed image are classic JPEG compression artifacts. Note the extensive compression noise and distortion present in the image at the right, particularly around the type labels.

Save your original uncompressed images! Once an image is compressed using JPEG compression, data are lost and you cannot recover them from that image file.

GIF image, **428** Kb file size
Poor image quality due to dithering

PNG image, **968** Kb file size
Excellent quality, lossless compression

JPEG image, **280** Kb (quality = high-8)
Very good quality and file size

Always save an uncompressed original file of your graphics or photographs as backup. If your digital camera produces JPEG images, set aside the "camera original" JPEG files and work with copies when you edit the files for web use. Each time you save or re-save an image in JPEG format, the image is compressed further and the artifacts and noise in the image increase.

PNG

Portable network graphics (PNG) were designed specifically for use on web pages, and they offer a range of attractive features, including a full range of color depths, support for sophisticated image transparency, better interlacing, and automatic corrections for display monitor gamma. PNG images can also hold a short text description of the image's content, which allows Internet search engines to search for images based on these embedded text descriptions.

PNG supports full-color images and can be used for photographic images. However, because it uses lossless compression, the resulting file is much larger than with lossy JPEG compression. Like GIF, PNG does best with line art, text, and logos—images that contain large areas of homogeneous color with sharp transitions between colors. Images of this type saved in the PNG format look good and have a similar or even smaller file size than when saved as GIFs. However, widespread adoption of the PNG format has been slow. This is due in part to inconsistent support in web browsers. In particular, Internet Explorer does not fully support all the features of PNG graphics. As a result, most images that would be suitable for PNG compression use the GIF format instead, which has the benefit of full and consistent browser support.

FIGURE 11.9

A comparison of GIF, JPEG, and PNG graphics and compression efficiencies. PNG graphics can be excellent in visual quality, but are always much larger than the equivalent JPEG graphic. GIF is a poor choice for photos.

GIF—Diagrams, icons, and illustrations with simple color fields and no subtle shading are ideal for the GIF file format

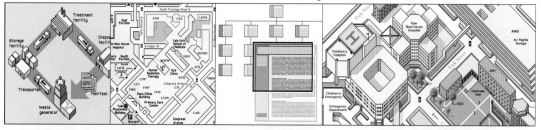

JPEG or PNG—Photographic images, complex icons, and realistic illustrations are ideal for the JPEG or PNG file formats

FIGURE 11.10
A graphic summary of typical web image types and optimal file formats.

USING WEB IMAGES

CHOOSING THE RIGHT FILE FORMAT

Having a good understanding of the strengths and weaknesses of the various graphics formats can save you a lot of "weight" on your overall web page download sizes, as well as a lot of heartache when your well-crafted graphics don't look right, or prove to be too big for your page performance budget. There are no magic formulas that say "always use JPEGs for this; always use PNGs for that." Make your best calculations about what format is likely to work well, but then test your assumptions by exporting your graphics in different formats and checking the file sizes. In larger image sizes (say, bigger than 150 × 150 pixels) the file format choices are pretty straightforward, but small graphics can fool you. A small, hard-edged icon graphic ought to work well as a GIF, but sometimes a JPEG or a PNG actually looks better and isn't much larger.

Interface elements

Small page navigation graphics, buttons, and graphic design elements such as logos and icons are often handled as noninterlaced GIF or PNG graphics. In reviewing your page comps in Photoshop, you should always be looking for opportunities to handle elements like background color fields, frames, rules, and buttons with CSS3 graphic effects rather than with graphics. Often the best, lowest-cost graphics are no graphics at all.

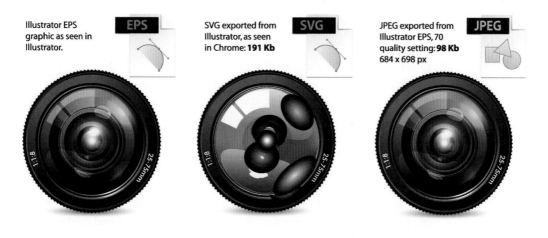

Illustrator EPS graphic as seen in Illustrator.

EPS

SVG exported from Illustrator, as seen in Chrome: **191 Kb**

SVG

JPEG exported from Illustrator EPS, 70 quality setting: **98 Kb** 684 x 698 px

JPEG

The combination of icon fonts, css sprites (graphics referenced in css code), and css graphic effects can give you a lot of visual flexibility at very low download cost, particularly if you invest in creating custom icon fonts that contain only the icons you are likely to use. Free icon fonts such as Font Awesome (originally developed for Twitter Bootstrap) are a great resource, but there is little point in downloading hundreds of icons when you are probably using only ten or fifteen of them in your site. Icon font utilities such as IcoMoon (icomoon.io) allow you to create custom icon fonts, and can also convert svg icons and symbols to font characters.

Scalable vector graphics (svg) can also be useful for simple graphic shapes, icons, and small iconic illustrations without many complex effects, such as graduated fills or transparencies. As the name suggests, svg graphics are based on mathematical description of curves, points, lines, and other shapes, and can be scaled to any size without a loss of quality. This is a powerful advantage in this transitional period in computer displays, where 72–96-ppi "conventional" or "1x" display screens are being replaced with "retina" or "2x" displays with more than 200 pixels per inch (see below for more on retina displays). Because an svg graphic can scale independent of screen resolution, an svg graphic looks good on both kinds of displays.

Sophisticated browser support for svg graphics gets better all the time, but there are drawbacks to svg as a format for more complex vector graphics such as illustrations. To display a vector svg graphic on a web page the browser must render the svg into pixels, a process that takes time and can be unpredictable for very complex illustrations, data graphics, and maps produced in vector drawing programs like Adobe Illustrator (fig. 11.11). Until browser support for complex vector graphics becomes more accurate and reliable, it's best to create the illustrations in tools like Adobe Illustrator, but then to render the final results in png or jpeg graphics that can reliably capture the subtleties of shading and transparency.

FIGURE 11.11

Complex photorealistic vector diagrams can be scaled for any print or screen use, but converting them to SVGs for direct display on web pages is not always the best strategy for image size or quality. Often the best and most reliable way to capture the subtleties of great Adobe Illustrator artwork is to convert it to a JPEG or PNG bitmap graphic.

Although there can be problems with converting complex vector graphics to the svg format, vector graphics are an excellent investment because:

1. svg support in browsers will continue to improve.
2. Vector artwork can be scaled into multiple resolutions of bitmap jpegs or pngs, with excellent quality at each size. This is useful in schemes that deliver page graphics based on screen resolution, where you create both 1x and 2x versions of illustrations to optimize for each kind of display screen.
3. Vector graphics can also be used for print.

Photographs and illustrations

jpeg is the file format most widely used for complex color illustrations and photographs. In general jpeg graphics are efficient in compression and produce excellent results on modern display screens and in print uses. On the new retina or 2x display screen a suitably sized jpeg photograph or illustration easily rivals the best print renditions of graphics and photographs.

If you use a lot of jpegs in your web work you need to be particularly careful always to preserve the camera-original photos (jpeg or Camera raw) or original Photoshop artwork at full resolution, even though such original images are rarely used at full resolution on web pages. jpeg uses a "lossy" image compression system that degrades the quality of an image when it is saved in jpeg format. Normally this trade-off of image compression versus image quality is not obvious to the casual web reader, but lossy compression has important implications if you ever need to rescale or edit your jpeg images. Thus when working in the jpeg format, it is good practice to work only on copies of the original files to avoid the quality loss of recompressing a jpeg photo.

PROVIDING ALTERNATIVES FOR IMAGES

html has built-in fallbacks designed to allow web pages to work under different conditions. One of these is the `alt` attribute of the `<img>` tag. The `alt` attribute allows you to supply an alternate text description with any images you place on your page. Users who cannot see your images will see or hear the text you supply using the `alt` attribute:

```
<img src="banner.gif" height="30" width="535" alt="Web Style
    Guide">
```

In the above example, people accessing the site using screen reader software would hear the phrase "Web Style Guide" read aloud. Google Images would use the alternate text, or alt-text, to catalog the image.

Writing good alt-text is an epigrammatic art, challenging your ability to describe the content and function of an image in just a few words. The point is not to use words to express the details and nuances of an image but rather to describe the image within the context of the page. This distinction is critical in deciding how much, or how little, to say about an image.

For functional images, such as buttons, logos, and icons, the text should say in words the same thing that the image says visually. A banner graphic that identifies the company should do the same with the text alternative: "Acme Carpet Cleaners." Interface icons should describe the functionality represented by the icon: "Play," "Pause," "Rewind," "Fast Forward."

At times alt-text is not useful—for example, for a print icon next to a "Print this page" link. In cases where an image is there for visual purposes only, and does not provide additional information, you should include an empty `alt` attribute (`alt=""`). An empty `alt` attribute hides the graphic from assistive technologies like screen reader software.

Complex content images, such as illustrations, diagrams, and charts, require more lengthy descriptions than can be included in an `alt` attribute. In many cases, the best approach is to include a caption with the image, which benefits all users in comprehending the information contained in the image. For example, for a chart that shows lifespan increase over time, include the data in an accessible table with the image. That way screen reader users have access to the same information, and people who comprehend numbers better than visualizations also benefit. HTML5 provides the `<figure>` and `<figcaption>` elements to make a programmatic connection between image and caption.

The W3C's document HTML5: Techniques for Providing Useful Text Alternatives is an excellent resource for understanding the best approach to take when describing images in different contexts (www.w3.org/TR/html-alt-techniques/).

OPTIMIZING IMAGES FOR THE SCREEN

The computing and web world is currently caught in an awkward straddle between the old 72–96-ppi (pixels per linear inch) or 1x display standard and the newer "retina" or 2x high-resolution display screens. In retrospect it's surprising how long the 72–96-ppi display resolution lasted. Virtually everything else in computing has changed enormously in the twenty-five years of the web's existence, but several factors combined to leave us stuck with the 72–96-ppi standard for so long.

We've made a major transition in display technologies, from the old huge cathode ray tube monitors to new flat screens capable of displaying very high resolutions. But flat screens were very expensive when they first appeared on the market, so the old 72–96-ppi standard hung on to keep the costs of the new screens reasonable. The combination of maturing flat screen technologies and increasing computing

COLOR TERMINOLOGY

Color is the response of our eye and brain to various wavelengths of light. Readers with normal vision can sense wavelengths of light from 400 nanometers (near ultra-violet) to 700 nm (near infrared).

Computer screens use an additive color system that combines phosphors of red, green, and blue primary colors, which, when added together in various proportions, produce the more than sixteen million colors possible on RGB screens. The maximum brightness of all three RGB primaries produces white light on the screen.

The visible light spectrum

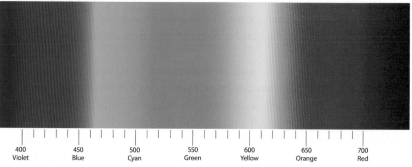

| 400 | 450 | 500 | 550 | 600 | 650 | 700 |
| Violet | Blue | Cyan | Green | Yellow | Orange | Red |

The combination of red, green, and blue light produces all other colors, and white light at the center

In computer graphics you'll see these common terms used to describe the character-istics of colors, known as the HSB color system (for hue, saturation, and brightness), commonly used in graphics programs like Adobe Photoshop.

• Hue is the wavelength of color along the spectrum of visible light. An easy way to think about hue is as a color name: "yellow," "orange," or "red."

- Saturation describes the intensity of a color, ranging from pure high-chroma colors to near-gray versions. Saturation is useful to signal depth in displays. In daily life we expect faraway objects to look desaturated and gray because of atmospheric effects (atmospheric perspective) and foreground objects to be more intensely colored. Thus in design we often use desaturated colors for backgrounds and draw attention by using full-saturated colors (sparingly!).
- Brightness is the lightness or darkness of a color or how close to either black or white a given color is.

Hue

Saturation

Brightness

Four classic formulas for combining colors, called "color harmonies," are used in all forms of design.

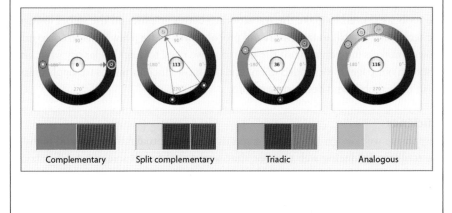

Complementary   Split complementary   Triadic   Analogous

```
<picture>
  <source media="(min-width: 64em)" src="high-rez.jpg">
  <source media="(min-width: 38em)" src="med-rez.jpg">
  <source src="low-res.jpg">
  <img src="med-rez.jpg" alt="Loads on
    non-supporting browsers.">
  <p>Accessible text.</p>
</picture>
```

high-rez.jpg

med-rez.jpg

low-rez.jpg

FIGURE 11.12
The source-set attribute (`srcset`) of the HTML picture element (`<picture>`) is a great means for automatically sending the most efficiently scaled image to screens ranging in size from smartphones to large desktop monitors.

power even on mobile devices has now made dramatically higher screen resolutions possible, and over the next few years screens of 200 ppi or more will become the new standard for all kinds of computing displays.

The rise of mobile computing and the change in display resolutions leaves web developers with two major challenges in dealing with graphics:

- **Efficiency:** How to supply the optimally sized image to the vast range of computing devices and screens sizes
- **Resolution:** How best to distinguish between older 1x screens and newer retina screens, and supply much higher quality graphics to those newer displays

The good news is that the HTML5 and CSS3 standards already give us many of the tools we'll need to make the transition to better graphics on the web. However, the technology is still in transition and probably will be for a few years to come until browser makers fully implement the new tools we need to quickly identify what kind of screen our pages have landed upon, and the most efficient means to supply graphics in both mobile and desktop situations.

Efficiency

Responsive web design (RWD) has given us the conceptual framework and many of the tools for producing web content that works well for all screen sizes. For background and core page framework graphics specified in CSS the solution to dealing with various screen resolutions is straightforward: in your various CSS "breakpoint" solutions for small, medium, and large screens, you can specify small, medium, and large versions of your bitmap graphics suitably sized for each range of screen widths. Web designers can also use vector-based graphics like icon fonts and SVG graphics

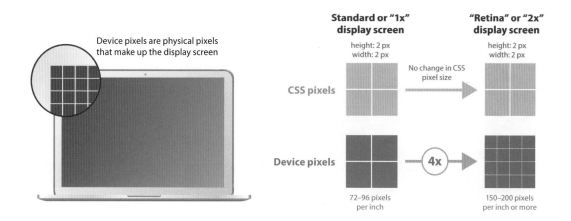

Device pixels are physical pixels that make up the display screen

Standard or "1x" display screen

"Retina" or "2x" display screen

CSS pixels

height: 2 px
width: 2 px

No change in CSS pixel size

height: 2 px
width: 2 px

Device pixels

4x

72–96 pixels per inch

150–200 pixels per inch or more

that work well at any resolution, or use CSS-based graphic effects that don't require any additional graphics files at all.

FIGURE 11.13

This leaves us with the question of how to optimize the response to HTML-based graphics placed in-line within the page content, specified with image <img> tags. Luckily, the HTML5 specification has already proposed a useful solution to this problem: a means to specify various image size alternatives within the new <picture> element, keyed to screen width (fig. 11.12). The source attribute lets us specify a set of possible images to be served, based conditionally on the minimum width of the screen (in CSS pixels). <picture> elements must always include a conventional image element <img> as well. The built-in <img> tag provides a graceful fallback for browsers that don't support the <picture> element. If the <picture> element is unsupported, the browser simply uses the built-in <img> element, so that everyone sees at least a medium-resolution image.

Resolution and pixel density

The second major challenge in our transition to high-resolution screen media is sending the right image to the right screen: serving moderate-resolution images to 1x devices (of whatever screen size) and high-resolution images to 2x or retina screens, except perhaps where such large images might affect page performance, as in mobile devices.

One immediate challenge web developers have faced and dealt with is how you describe sizes and distances when the number of physical or device pixels has more than doubled with new retina screens. In the older 1x world of 72–96-ppi screens the answer was obvious: one pixel in the image directly equated to one physical pixel on the display screen. If you suddenly doubled the density of display pixels and made no other changes, every image would have the same number of pixels, but on a 2x

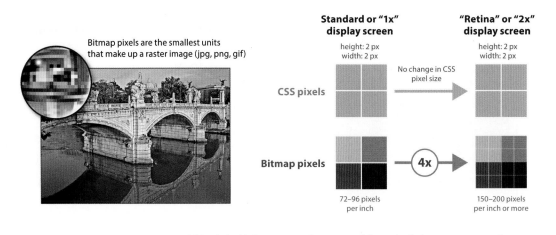

Bitmap pixels are the smallest units that make up a raster image (jpg, png, gif)

Standard or "1x"
display screen

"Retina" or "2x"
display screen

height: 2 px
width: 2 px

height: 2 px
width: 2 px

CSS pixels

No change in CSS
pixel size

Bitmap pixels

4x

72–96 pixels
per inch

150–200 pixels
per inch or more

FIGURE 11.14

screen it would look half the size, and text would similarly be miniaturized on retina screens.

The answer to this puzzle is virtual measurements, where the pixel numbers specified by HTML and CSS no longer have a 1:1 relationship to physical or device pixels. These "CSS pixels" more or less equate the measurements of older 1x screens. Instead of a one-to-one relationship of CSS pixel to screen pixel, one "CSS pixel" would actually describe the area covered by four device pixels on a 2x screen (fig. 11.13). For typography on new high-resolution screens, responsive web design already uses the relative measure of em units, where one em is roughly the equivalent of 16-point type, regardless of the screen resolution.

Similarly, bitmap image sizes specified in HTML or CSS pixels now use virtual pixels: on a conventional 1x display one image pixel equates to one screen pixel. On a retina or 2x screen, each virtual "CSS pixel" equates to about four device pixels (fig. 11.14).

The web world is in transition, and the available methods for identifying retina or 2x screens and serving up high-resolution image just to those screens is currently pretty gimcrack, with a number of JavaScript or server-size technologies vying to fill the gap between what we need and what current web browsers can reliably deliver.

Luckily, the longer-term solution is obvious and already part of or proposed HTML5 and CSS3 code standards. The @media query tag that much of responsive web design is based upon can do a lot more than just determine screen width: media queries can also determine the resolution of the display, and the resolution versus physical size of the display—at least theoretically. The HTML5 srcset attribute and <picture> element can automatically send the right-sized image for a given screen size—at least theoretically. Much will depend on how quickly web browser makers adopt these vital image-quality tools, and exactly how consistently they are implemented.

RECOMMENDED READING

Creative Suite: Web graphics optimization options. Adobe, Inc., 2015. help.adobe.com/en_US/
  creativesuite/cs/using/WSC7A1F924-DD38-49b4-B84B-EFF50416C860.html.

Optimizing Content Efficiency: Image optimization. Google Developers, 2015. developers.
  google.com/web/fundamentals/performance/optimizing-content-efficiency/image-
  optimization.

Schmitt, C. *Designing Web and Mobile Graphics: Fundamental Concepts for Web and Interactive
  Projects.* Berkeley, CA: New Riders, 2012.

————."Responsive Media." Lynda.com Course, 2014. www.lynda.com/Illustrator-tutorials/
  Responsive-Media/161465-2.html.

Willamson, J. "Creating Icon Fonts for the Web." Lynda.com Course, 2014. www.lynda.
  com/Glyphs-App-tutorials/Creating-Icon-Fonts-Web/157228-2.html.

A story should have a beginning, a middle and an end, but not necessarily in that order.
— Jean-Luc Godard

Video

Digital video and audio forms such as podcasts are widely used on all kinds of business and organizational web sites, and it has never been easier or cheaper to add short video programs, audio clips, or podcasts to your web and social media presence. The change in the video production industry has been remarkable, particularly over the past decade. With relatively modest video equipment and the average desktop computer, you can now achieve better technical quality video than a $100,000 studio could have made possible fifteen years ago.

The most honest form of filmmaking is to make a film for yourself.

—Peter Jackson

At first, online video emulated older long-format styles of movies and television, with long cinema-style opening sequences and closing credits, and story lengths of twenty minutes or more. But as YouTube, Vimeo, Facebook, and other digital media sites began to be viewed as serious media distribution channels, fundamental shifts took place in the style of video storytelling itself, and a new genre of short documentary, news, and promotional videos has emerged. These new videos are short, anywhere from fifteen seconds to ten minutes in length, averaging about three to four minutes.

This doesn't mean that the average web or communications professional can casually pick up a consumer video camera and expect to produce material equivalent to that of the best online media professionals. But the huge barrier of audiovisual equipment and software costs has dropped dramatically, and it is now possible—with training and experience—for small web and communications teams to produce useful and compelling audiovisual content without needing to hire a professional video team for every project. Just as important, YouTube, Vimeo, and social media channels like Facebook, Twitter, Tumblr, and others have made it fast and easy to distribute video productions to a potential worldwide audience.

WEB VIDEO STRATEGIES

Online video is a major communications channel, widely used in business communications, e-commerce, marketing, education, and popular programming. Online video is a distribution medium that rivals broadcast television for viewership, in number of viewers and hours watched.

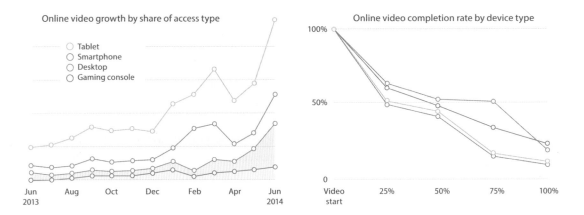

Online video growth by share of access type

○ Tablet
○ Smartphone
○ Desktop
○ Gaming console

Jun 2013   Aug   Oct   Dec   Feb   Apr   Jun 2014

Online video completion rate by device type

100%

50%

0

Video start   25%   50%   75%   100%

FIGURE 12.1

Consumption of online video is growing exponentially, particularly on mobile devices. However, mobile users don't stick around long, so make sure you grab their attention right away and give them something compelling to stay for.

PROVIDING A GOOD EXPERIENCE

The attention-grabbing power of audiovisual media demands careful user interface considerations to avoid annoying and disrupting the reader's experience with an unexpected blast of video and audio. The Golden Rule in any audiovisual experience is user control. Users should have enough information to make an informed decision about whether or not to load the video. The user should always explicitly click a "play" button to initiate video or audio content.

- Provide important details. Video content embedded on your web pages requires more time from the user, because there's no convenient way to rapidly scan the content of a video until it has fully downloaded into the browser. Try to give users the title, some caption description, and the overall length of the video.
- Do not autoplay. One obvious tenet of the Golden Rule of control is never to autoplay video content, but lately Facebook has been defaulting to autoplaying videos in its newsfeed, and raising alarm particularly from mobile users who are seeing their cell phone data rates rise sharply as a result. It seems we're doomed to repeat the same user interface mistakes with every new medium: for all kinds of practical, financial, and basic courtesy reasons, never autoplay audiovisual content.
- Keep it short. People's online video expectations and viewing circumstances are very different from conventional "long-form" television viewing, and there are substantial differences in viewing and video completion rates even between mobile and desktop viewing. Although mobile users often start videos, they are much less likely to complete a video program, particularly as program length goes beyond 3 minutes. While there is not a lot of research so far on the optimal length of informational or educational online videos, the

marketing and news worlds have settled on 3–4 minutes as the ideal length for promotional and news YouTube videos, and not coincidentally this is similar to the average length of a single story in the major network evening news programs (about 2.3 minutes).

- Get to the point. Online video viewers are not generally "settled in" like television watchers for a long viewing of video content. You need to grab the user's attention right away in short-form video with "fast-start" introductions that begin delivering real content right away, even while the title graphics are still on the screen. This means no long cinema-like introductions or corporate flying-logo sequences. Start the story immediately, and do your titles or other required information as graphics at the bottom of the screen.

PROVIDING ALTERNATIVES FOR AUDIO AND VIDEO

A text version of the audio track makes your video content more search-friendly, accessible, and discoverable. With text, every word in your video becomes a searchable item, which can be particularly useful for specialized or technical video content, where a title and a few keywords alone would not be sufficient to make the content discoverable. Text makes the information in the audio accessible to people who can't hear the audio. When the text is presented as synchronized captions, people can watch the video while reading the captions. This type of multichannel presentation is helpful for everyone, aiding in comprehension, for example, for nonnative speakers of the language of the video.

Some technologies help with creating text alternatives. For example, speech-to-text technology can help in creating a text version of spoken audio, but the accuracy is not optimal. One option for creating a text version is to use a speech-to-text tool for the first pass and then edit the transcript for accuracy, for example, using YouTube autocaptions as a starting point, editing, and uploading a revised and accurate version.

However, professional transcribers are best at creating accurate alternatives, and the best approach is to budget time and resources for creating alternatives. Like good lighting, talent, and equipment, providing video alternatives should be just another facet of producing quality video.

For audio transcription, services like SpeechPad (www.speechpad.com), Rev (www.rev.com/transcription), and Amara (amara.org) charge by the minute to create transcripts from video. The process is easy: you provide the transcript service site with a link to your video, pay online, and depending on the service level you choose, you get a transcript text file back via email in several hours or several days. Uploading the returned caption file to distribution sites like YouTube and Video is straightforward.

Video description is a method for making visual information accessible to people who can't see the video. The method uses the natural gaps in the audio track to narrate the action and information conveyed visually. Video description is also called audio description or described video, and is something of an art. WGBH's Media Access Group (www.wgbh.org) is a leader in media accessibility, providing captioning and video description services. Like audio transcription, the best way to provide quality video description is to budget time and resources and hire experts, then integrate the results into your video presentation so that everyone can access and benefit from it.

CHOOSING A DISTRIBUTION CHANNEL

There are two ways of looking at online video delivery vehicles like YouTube and Vimeo:

- As "channels" that people visit to browse and find content, either specifically through searching, or by browsing through what's current and popular on YouTube or Vimeo's home and specialty pages, and on your own YouTube or Vimeo "channel."
- As an embedded video played within your own web site, but sourced from Vimeo or YouTube.

Facebook is the other major video delivery channel for short-form videos. Facebook is not a major destination site specifically for video, but it is by far the dominant social medium, and should be a major component of a video content campaign. You can also embed Facebook videos and posts in your web site.

All three presentation forms should have a place in your video distribution strategy, as Facebook, Vimeo, and YouTube have different approaches, different strengths, and a different mix of audiences.

YouTube

YouTube is by far the dominant channel for online video distribution, and YouTube is also the second-most-used search platform on the Internet, behind only Google itself—YouTube's corporate parent. If you want your video work to be discovered and noticed, you must post it on YouTube. However, that doesn't mean YouTube is the only or even the first place to upload your video content.

Aside from being the most popular distribution channel for video, YouTube is also free. Because YouTube is funded through online advertising, it might be the best choice if you want to monetize your video content by placing advertising on it through YouTube and Google partner programs. YouTube's dominance as a search platform means that your video content is more likely to be discovered through web search, particularly if you always provide a full transcription of the video along with the video file itself (see above for more on audiovisual transcription).

The fact that YouTube is large, free, and advertiser supported is also the biggest drawback to YouTube as a distribution medium. YouTube is visually noisy, crammed with low-grade home videos, and does its best to distract your audience with enticements to view other "related" (perhaps competing) content at the end of every video. By default YouTube does not show your carefully crafted video at a high-quality setting. Yes, knowledgeable viewers can easily select higher-quality settings, but most users don't know about and don't bother with the setting.

Competition for attention is fierce in a distribution channel where one hundred hours of video are uploaded every minute, and YouTube itself works to cannibalize your audience by constantly exposing viewers to "related content." In marketing videos it's not unusual for competing companies to buy Adwords on each other's names and brands, hoping to shift audiences away from competing products and services. YouTube distribution can also be complicated for business-to-business (B2B) communications, as many corporations and large institutions block YouTube content from their internal networks.

To take maximum advantage of the YouTube site itself, develop your YouTube channel page and carefully manage and prioritize the video content you feature on your channel. Provide professional-quality cover art and assign a staffer to keep the channel up to date with your latest videos, monitor the channel for comments, and report on the traffic levels on the channel. Always title and label your videos with likely search keywords and SEO in mind, just as you would with other online content. Provide an accurate, edited transcript for each video, which you can upload along with your video.

Vimeo

Vimeo is the major alternative to YouTube for hosting and viewing online video content. While Vimeo is a much smaller company than YouTube, Vimeo has a loyal following in the video production industry for its high-quality video presentation services.

Vimeo is a much quieter online video service and distribution channel, primarily because it is a paid service that does not run advertising in or around its video content. Anyone can watch Vimeo content for free, but if you routinely produce and upload videos, you will probably opt for one of Vimeo's paid upload and presentation services. The fee-for-service nature of Vimeo cuts out almost all the junky home videos and grumpy cats of YouTube—a strong attraction for professional corporate and institutional marketing and informational videos.

Vimeo attracts communications professionals with a sophisticated media player that is graphically quieter and more controllable than YouTube's player, particularly in the ability to embed a video with higher-quality video settings so that the video looks its best by default.

Another strong attraction for media professionals is Vimeo's ability to password-protect videos, making it an ideal means to share draft versions of videos in production with clients without exposing the draft to the larger web video audience. On YouTube you can upload a video and select an option to keep the video "private" from search and channels display, but "private" YouTube videos do not have passwords and are visible to anyone who happens to discover them. With the Vimeo Pro service you can also reserve some videos for paid on-demand viewing or purchase.

On the downside, while the Vimeo audience is substantial, it is tiny compared with YouTube's gigantic worldwide audience. The chances of your video programming being discovered by a mass general audience is much lower on Vimeo, and you cannot generate advertising income the way you can with YouTube videos that attract many viewers.

Facebook

If your corporation or enterprise already has a significant following on Facebook, the primary strength of Facebook video is the ability to leverage a large social media audience. Recently many more video publishers have begun using the social power of Facebook to launch videos directly on Facebook, bypassing YouTube, or at least launching first on Facebook before posting to other video channels. Many observers of the social media marketplace have noted the videos loaded directly to Facebook receive more Facebook user engagement (as much as 40 percent more) than videos posted to YouTube and referenced only in Facebook posts.

Of course Facebook video posts largely disappear from your followers' newsfeeds in a few hours, and engagement drops to near zero within twenty-four hours (see "Social Media Strategy," in Chapter 1), so despite the major social media advantages Facebook offers, you'll need other channels to maintain a steady presence for your video content over time.

A multichannel strategy

The different strengths and features of Facebook, YouTube, and Vimeo can be a plus if you use them all as part of a general strategy to maximize the presentation quality and audience for your videos. If you have a large Facebook following, the obvious first move is to post new video content on Facebook. You might use Vimeo as a higher-quality alternative for embedding videos in your own web site, and for launching new video content as part of email marketing and web-based communications campaigns. You could then post the same videos later on YouTube to take advantage of the much larger and more varied audience of YouTube, and the search visibility of YouTube content.

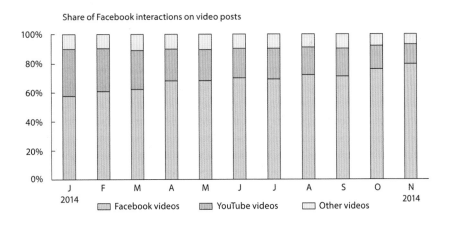

Share of Facebook interactions on video posts

Facebook videos ☐ YouTube videos ☐ Other videos

FIGURE 12.2
Facebook users engage increasingly with Facebook video more than with any other video type— even YouTube.

For Facebook, Vimeo, or YouTube always be sure to embed the URL for your web site in:

- The metainformation you supply to Vimeo or YouTube about the video (keywords, descriptions, and so on).
- In the video itself at the end: "For more information, see www.whatever.edu."

VIDEO PRODUCTION

Until the past decade you didn't see many short online videos, except those from news outlets and large corporations with media departments (and substantial media budgets), or very amateurish home-movie videos. There wasn't much content between the two extremes because small but high-quality HD video cameras were expensive, as was capable professional video-editing software.

Lightweight video production doesn't depend on simply acquiring a camera and software. Knowing what to do with either takes a bit of training and experience, but luckily the web itself offers a rich banquet of excellent video content on which to model your productions, as well as detailed and well-designed online courses on video hardware, production techniques, and video editing.

EQUIPPING FOR LIGHTWEIGHT VIDEO PRODUCTION

With lightweight video production the goal is to keep the equipment costs relatively modest and the logistics of video production manageable for a single person or a small video team of two to three people at most. Don't buy more than you or a partner can carry. This level of audiovisual equipment will get you up and running and able to produce professional online video and audio results once you've mastered the equipment itself and had some practice with editing. Of course you can spend much

MEDIA PLAYER ACCESSIBILITY

Accessibility and adaptability are key considerations when choosing a platform for your video—how to ensure that your video content plays on all devices and is accessible to everyone, including people with disabilities. It's important to evaluate the accessibility and cross-device compatibility of the media player that comes natively with the video distribution platform. Test the player in different platforms and devices to understand the user experience it provides out of the box. Also evaluate the accessibility of the player for people who use the keyboard to operate controls, and people who use assistive technology such as a screen reader. Do all the controls receive keyboard focus, and can you operate them using appropriate keyboard keys? Can you see which control has focus? Try using the media player with a screen reader. Are all the control names announced, and do they make sense? Also ensure that the media player offers captions, and that the controls to enable captions are accessible using the keyboard. (See Chapter 7, Interface Design, for more on creating accessible interaction.)

FIGURE 12.3

Sometimes you may need to look farther afield to provide an accessible and usable interface. There are several pockets of activity around creating media players that work with common platforms, such as YouTube. The following are sources of insight into what makes an accessible media player and a selection of accessible media players.

- Henny Swan's article "Accessibility Originates with UX: A BBC iPlayer Case Study," www.smashingmagazine.com/2015/02/23/bbc-iplayer-accessibility-case-study
- Vision Australia's Accessible YouTube Player, www.visionaustralia.org/digital-access-youtube
- Nomensa's open-source Accessible Media Player, github.com/nomensa/Accessible-Media-Player

more on video equipment, but our advice is to start modestly, and add more complex and capable equipment only once you thoroughly understand your needs, and have enough production experience to spend wisely on tools that will significantly upgrade your capabilities.

Video camera

If your primary goal is to produce short online videos to support your web communications, then use a video camera, not a still camera that also shoots video. Still professional cameras (digital single-lens reflex cameras, or DSLRs) shoot excellent video but typically have poor audio recording capabilities, with low-quality audio preamplifiers, and usually they offer no "audio out" or headphone jacks to monitor the audio recording along with your video. The ability to constantly monitor your audio recording is absolutely crucial to good video production technique, as most short videos are based on interviews, and good audio quality in interviews is paramount.

The best video cameras for lightweight video production are at the top of the consumer product lines—the so-called prosumer video cameras. These cameras offer a wide range of useful automatic focus, exposure, and audio recording modes, but more important, they allow manual control over the major camera functions. Manual focusing, manual control of exposure, and manual control of audio recording levels are particularly important to producing consistently professional results. Much of the time you can shoot great video in automatic modes, but if you can't shift to manual control, there are many shooting situations where you just won't get good-quality results. Most current consumer-level high-definition video cameras offer decent video and audio recording, and a headphone jack to monitor the sound you record, a critical advantage over most DSLR cameras.

If you can afford to spend a bit more on a video camera, low-end professional cameras offer two significant advantages over prosumer cameras: they have built-in connections for professional audio "XLR" connectors, and they have many more physical dials and switches for controlling camera functions. The prosumer cameras often have the same features as low-end professional cameras, but it is much slower to dig through a series of touchscreen menus than simply to flip a physical switch or to turn a control dial. Balanced-line XLR audio connectors are the professional standard for both line-level and microphone-level audio connections, and all professional cameras have built-in XLR audio connectors. This gives you access to a large selection of professional microphones and makes it easy to hook your camera to professional sound systems used in auditoriums and event venues.

However, if you have a prosumer or more modest video camera, you can get an XLR adapter that will adapt the miniplug microphone jack on your camera to the larger XLR plugs. You can also use a video adapter/recorder, which both adapts your small video camera for XLR plugs and can record an additional digital soundtrack for backup in important recording situations.

Tripod

If you haven't shot a lot of video, it might seem odd to highlight a technically modest accessory like a tripod, but for day-to-day video production work a good solid tripod specifically made for video work is as important as a good camera. Video tripods are different from still-photography tripods in two important ways: they come with "fluid heads" that allow smooth panning and tilting during video recording. Even a good-quality, well-oiled still tripod head can't match a fluid head for smoothness of movement. Video tripods also have a special central camera post that allows you to quickly level the tripod head, important for on-the-go shooting situations, and much faster leveling than the typical still-photography tripod.

Microphones

All video cameras come with built-in microphones, but unfortunately these built-in microphones are useless for most video shooting, except perhaps for capturing the ambient sounds of environments where clear speech is not crucial. The two kinds of microphones that are essential for lightweight video production are lavalier microphones for interviews and shotgun microphones for interviews and most other kinds of recording situations.

Lavalier microphones ("lav mics") are the little microphones you see clipped to the shirts or collars of people interviewed on television, or onstage at speeches and other events. The most convenient lav mics for interviews are wireless, so you don't have a dangling cord to conceal, or to run across the floor, creating a trip hazard. Shotgun microphones can be used both for interviews and for general video recording. Shotgun mics are directional, with their maximum sensitivity pointed forward along the long axis of the microphone body. When mounted on a camera, shotgun mics do a decent job with informal interviews and for capturing ambient sounds in general video clips. They are also useful for recording events and speeches where you can't get a feed directly from the "house sound" system to your camera. We prefer to use lav microphones for interviews because they do a better job of excluding environmental sound and recording a person's voice, but a shotgun mic mounted on a microphone boom and pointed directly at the subject can work almost as well.

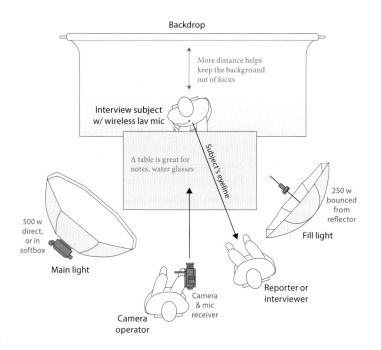

Backdrop

More distance helps
keep the background
out of focus

Interview subject
w/ wireless lav mic

A table is great for
notes, water glasses

Subject's eyeline

500 w
direct,
or in
softbox

Main light

250 w
bounced
from
reflector

Fill light

Camera
& mic
receiver

Reporter or
interviewer

Camera
operator

FIGURE 12.4
A typical
"lightweight"
lighting setup for
an interview. Not
all interviews use
a backdrop, as
often an office or
conference room
setting provides
an undistracting
background.

Lights

Modern video cameras can shoot decent video in surprisingly low light levels, but you will almost always want to supplement office-level lighting conditions with one or several small video lights, particularly for interviews. Plain office lighting usually results in dull-looking video, and the direct overhead lights are often unflattering to people's faces. We recommend at least one 500-watt light, sometimes directly pointed at the subject, but more often bounced from a small white photo lighting umbrella to soften the light. In interviews this single light is just enough to open up shadows around the eyes and under the chin, and provides just enough "sparkle" for crisp-looking video. If you have time, a second 250-watt light to fill on the side opposite the main light will open up the shadows a bit more.

PLANNING A VIDEO

Most short informational videos are built around the backbone of an interview, or perhaps interviews supplemented with narration. In the short online video genre, narration is less common than in other forms of video and television, for several reasons. Professional narrations are expensive, and even for a two-to-four-minute video it can cost several hundred dollars to hire a pro to narrate (more on narration below). These days the best online videos use only the voice of the primary interview subjects, giving the whole production an authentic first-person feel. This also explains why good audio is so important in short video: your video will mostly be built around the interview, so a clear, clean soundtrack is crucial to making a professional production.

Research

To do a good interview you'll need at least one research conversation with your subject so that you understand the point of the video and the essential stories or explanations to cover, and to get a sense for how to construct a short video that conveys the core information. People who don't do videos are used to longer television programs, and they may want to cram too much into a short video, or may panic when they hear how short the video is and think that they can't possibly cover anything useful in 3 minutes or less. The average network television news story is 2 minutes, 23 seconds. You can cover a lot of ground in 60 seconds if you plan it well.

Try to arrange to do your interviews in a space you know well—ideally your conference room or other small room temporarily converted to a studio. If you do the interview in your subject's office or work area, try to arrange a research visit to talk over the general point of the video and see the space you will be shooting in. Beware of noisy open-plan offices, or rooms with loud air handlers or air conditioning.

Bringing a small audio recorder or video camera and headphones to the research interview can be a real eye-opener. In daily life we ignore most of the subtle ambient sounds around us. We physically hear the noisy HVAC systems, hissing vents, and distant traffic, but most of the time our brains screen the sounds before they reach our conscious awareness. However, video cameras and microphones will pick up the background noise. This is another reason why monitoring your sound with headphones is mandatory—with headphones you will hear all of that background noise, and can take steps to turn off the air conditioning, or move to a quieter room.

In any planning meeting or conversation find out about the possibilities for shooting "b-roll" of your subject's work environment and plan for any footage you'll need to illustrate the major points of the video. If the main subject of the video works closely with colleagues or friends, it can be interesting to shift between the main interview and comments from colleagues you also interview. But beware of trying to add too many voices to a two-to-three-minute video, as it may be confusing to the viewer to keep all the speakers straight. Usually an interview with one main subject is more than enough to make a great short video.

Permissions

If you work in an enterprise communications department, you are already aware of any organizational polices on written permission to film subjects. Always get a signed permission form from anyone outside your organization whom you highlight in your film. Local policy may also require permission forms from staff members of your own organization. It is not generally necessary to get permission from people in public situations like streets, parks, or open campuses, but always err on the side of caution if your video appears to highlight a particular identifiable person, and get a signed release. Never film children or minors under any circumstances—public or not—without the close participation of their parents, and get signed release forms from the parents.

SHOOTING INTERVIEWS

Short informational videos typically center on first-person perspectives and insights from one person, shared through an interview. To shoot effective interviews, create a comfortable setting, and ask the questions that will get at what is interesting and engaging about the subject. Given the right context, most people are eager to talk about their work to someone who is eager to listen.

Setup

Positioning the video camera and tripod well away from your subject is useful for several reasons. At a longer distance the camera is less "in their face." If you are behind your lights, the camera is even less obvious and intrusive. The longer shooting distance also means you'll use a more telephoto lens setting, which is more flattering to the face. Set up the camera on your tripod so that the lens is no higher than the subject's eye level. A position slightly lower than eye level can also be flattering to many people.

The best situation is to have two people on the crew: one to ask questions, and another to monitor the camera and audio. That way you get a clean eyeline as well—just ask your subject to look at the interviewer and have a conversation. If you have to do everything yourself, sit just to the side of the camera, close enough to monitor the video, but slightly off the camera line. Ask the subject to look at you, not the camera lens. This slight off-axis eyeline creates the feeling that the viewer is watching a conversation from the side, just as she might if she were in the room when the conversation was recorded.

Whether you are doing the interviewing yourself from behind the camera or working with a partner, keep the following in mind:

- If you are only going to use the subject's voice in the video and will not include the interviewer's questions, remind your subject that he must incorporate the question in his answers:

  Q: Where were you born and raised?
  A: I was born in Chicago, but raised in California. My parents moved there when I was just a year old, and…

C. John Smith, M.D., FACC
Professor of Cardiology & Diagnostic Radiology

FIGURE 12.5
Start your interview with a relatively wide head-and-shoulders shot that gives you room enough to place a "lower-third" graphic on the screen without overlapping your subject's face (left). Later you can move in for tighter views (right), but for better composition try to avoid placing the subject's face directly in the middle of the video frame.

- Watch out for cross-talk in interviews. It's perfectly natural for people's sentences to slightly overlap when they are having a conversation, so ask both interviewer and subject to leave a clean pause between questions and answers, so that you can edit the audio later without hearing the questioner.
- Always provide generous glasses of water for your interview subject and interviewer. Speaking for an extended period of time is dry work, and speakers are always grateful to see the water.

Set the camera on a tripod and move it as little as possible. Always start with a relatively wide view that leaves you enough room to place an introductory "lower-third" graphic at the bottom of the screen without cutting off the speaker's chin. You can do tighter shots later for more variety of viewpoints. Generally you should frame the speaker as shown in Figure 12.5, and avoid putting the speaker's head directly in the middle of the video frame, a compositionally boring shot that is also much less flexible for any title graphics you may need to add in editing.

Interviewing

Interviews for short videos will be heavily edited, so assure your subjects that they are not "live on television" during the interview, and are free to stop, pause, and re-phrase their words at any point. Ask them to pause briefly if they stop and restart, as this makes it much easier to edit the interview later. Often you'll find that it can take several questions and a bit of time before even experienced subjects "settle down" and are their most relaxed and articulate, so try to schedule a minimum of twenty to thirty minutes with your subjects to get the best material. An easy conversational style is ideal for interviews, and helps put subjects at ease.

In informational videos based on interviews you usually have lots of opportunity to hide awkward cuts in the video caused by editing out pauses by "covering" the cuts with b-roll views that illustrate what the speaker is saying. Normally you want to avoid a "talking head" video that shows nothing but the interview subject. You'll illustrate the speaker's topics with b-roll, and occasionally come back to the "talking head" to remind viewers who is speaking. B-roll segments are a great way to hide editing cuts that remove pauses, mistakes, or other problems in the main interview.

Even if a speaker is nervous and requires a lot of editing to produce clean spoken words without a lot of pauses and "ums," and "ahs," make sure you have a clean fifteen seconds or so of speaker video that is long enough to put up a "lower-third" graphic to identify who is talking to the audience early in the video. An extended period where you're not sure who is speaking will make the viewing audience restless, so always think about getting that introductory "lower-third" sequence.

For informational videos in which the speaker must convey a lot of specific information, do not have the speaker read a document. When we read aloud our voice tone and speech cadence changes noticeably, and it always sounds artificial. Try to get your speaker to prepare and practice making the points without reading. Having notes close by is fine, as long as the subject doesn't just read the notes aloud.

Work through one sentence or thought at a time, and take out any pauses later in the editing process. Ideally you can cover the jumps in the video caused by editing out the pauses by covering the sequences with b-roll footage that illustrates each point, but be aware that you should occasionally cut back to viewing your speaker. Those sequences where you see the speaker must be "clean" run-throughs, because any pauses you cut out will cause a jump cut in the video.

Some very slow and steady camera movements may be required to keep a very active speaker properly framed, as some people move quite a bit when they speak, even when seated. Active speakers tend to repeat their movements in a pattern. If you are filming an active speaker, watch for the pattern, and frame your shot so that the whole movement sequence is within a stationary frame. Some people rock from side to side. Don't move the camera back and forth or you'll make your audience distracted and seasick. Watch for the limits of the rocking motion, and frame the shot so the speaker's head stays in the frame.

When you shoot interviews, start the camera rolling and leave it rolling throughout the interview. You can always divide up the interview sequences later in the editing process. There's nothing worse than hearing a great story only to realize that you did everything right—except hit the "record" button.

Scripts and narrators

Sometimes the best way to tell a story is to write a script and hire a professional narrator, or record your own narration. Narration is a special professional skill, with advantages and disadvantages. To some viewers the professional narration will sound too slick, particularly if you don't coach the narrator well for the right tone and pacing for your program. To most of your audience a good professional narrator will be verbally "invisible"—that is, viewers will expect professional narration that doesn't attract attention. If the video is personal reporting on a story, you might want to try recording your own narration, which you can easily do with the same equipment you use to shoot video interviews. While your personal narration will have great authenticity, you must still produce a clean, clear, and well-paced narration for it to work well. Expect to do some rehearsals and multiple takes to get it right.

- Keep it short. A script for a short video must be concise. Estimate about 125 words per minute for well-paced narration, and don't forget to figure in the timing for any interviews you'll use along with your narration. A three-minute video that also uses a few interview clips will amount to less than one double-spaced page of narration script, so "write tight."
- Front-load the script: Tell a compelling story from the first second. Front-load your main points: let the viewers know as soon as possible the main topic of the video.
- Speak to viewers. Use personal pronouns like "you" and "yours," and avoid stilted third-person language: "one" doesn't do this or that; "you and I" do things. Use as much interview footage as possible to give the video the authentic voice of first-person experts, and to vary the voicing so it's not just one voice droning on.
- Write the way you speak. Literally—speak the script as you write it. Keep the language straightforward, using short simple sentences without long clauses. If a sentence has more than one comma in it, break it up.
- Show the story, don't just tell it. Make notes on the b-roll footage you'll need for strong visual complements to the narration.

Hiring a narrator or "voice-over talent" is pretty fast and easy these days, and the whole process can be done entirely online. Research local narration talent through web searches. Often local television reporters do voice-over on the side. If your organization has a video department, it may already have a roster of local voice-over talent it uses. Ask for sample narrations. Most professionals can easily refer you to audio samples of their work on the web.

Once you have selected a narrator, share your script with him or her and discuss the tone and pacing of your video. An experienced narrator should be able to give you good advice on your script, and may ask for language changes to make the script flow more easily in spoken language. Ask for several different readings in the final recording, perhaps faster or slower, or with more or less emphasis, or a softer or more informal reading. This will give you more flexibility when you are ready to match the narration audio to your visuals. Most voice-over professionals have their own small home studios for digital recording, and can deliver an audio file of the finished narration.

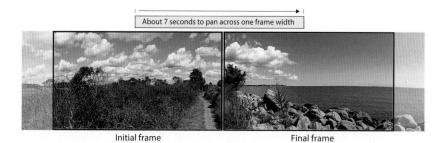

About 7 seconds to pan across one frame width

Initial frame   Final frame

FIGURE 12.6
If you pan or tilt the camera during a shot, move the camera slowly to avoid blurring the video frames. It should take about seven seconds to pan across the equivalent of one viewfinder frame.

SHOOTING B-ROLL AND OTHER SEQUENCES

The term "b-roll" is derived from the old days of twentieth-century movie editing. The backbone of a film is the visuals and spoken dialog or interviews with the main actors or documentary subjects (although you'll never hear this footage referred to as "a-roll"). B-roll is any illustrative footage or cutaway shots that help explain the main narration or interview. For example, if your subject talks about her work in a research lab, while she continues to speak you might sometimes cut away from the interview footage to show your subject working in her laboratory, talking to colleagues in the lab, and so on, as a way of making the film more visually interesting and informative. The lab footage is your b-roll, and great b-roll is essential to making a quality short video.

Techniques

Start conservatively and gradually add new tricks to your vocabulary as your skill increases. In informational and news videos—even the most stylish—the camera rarely moves, or moves so slowly you'd barely notice. Fast zooming within the shot is extremely rare, an instant mark of amateurishness. The zoom lever is there to quickly reframe shots between takes, not to use during a shot. The good news is that if your subject is somewhere in the frame, the camera is stationary on a solid tripod, and you've shot at least fifteen seconds of any b-roll scene or illustrative material, you're off to a great start.

1. Find a good viewpoint of your general subject.
2. Set up the camera on a tripod. Level the tripod. Check the level in the viewfinder or screen.
3. Carefully frame a wide shot.
4. Record at least fifteen seconds of the shot without moving the camera or zooming.
5. Choose one or several additional closer shots and detail shots, from different viewpoints, and repeat step 4 for each shot.

You need 12 seconds of video to make this work

| 3-sec. dissolve | 6-second view | 3-sec. dissolve |

Dissolve transition

Dissolve transition

FIGURE 12.7

Novice video photographers tend to underestimate how much video is required for flexibility in editing. If you have bothered to set up the camera and tripod and compose a shot, always shoot at least twenty seconds of video—thirty seconds is even better—especially of moving subjects like traffic or people. The longer shots give you many more editing options later.

The essential difference between video and still photography is time. Give yourself and your subject time. You capture still photos in a 500th of a second and quickly move on to the next shot. Good video shots take much longer, and the longer the shot is the easier the editing will be. If you've bothered to set up the camera and tripod to capture a b-roll shot, record at least fifteen to twenty seconds of video per shot, with no camera movement. If you plan to move the camera in a pan or tilt, always give yourself about seven seconds of stationary shot before you move the camera (slowly!), and at least seven seconds again once you have stopped the camera movement. Move the camera slowly. A panning shot that moves the equivalent of a full viewfinder frame should take at least seven seconds from the start of the pan to the end of the pan.

Long steady takes are especially important for editing, as they give the editor flexibility to do hard cuts or slow dissolves, or to vary the rhythm and timing of the program from long slow takes to fast cuts, depending on how the interview proceeds and what you need to show to your audience at a given moment in the program. Photographers new to video almost always shoot material that is too short in duration for editing flexibility, because they treat videography like still photography. They set up, record a few seconds of the shot, and then move on to the next thing. These very short clips leave you with virtually no editing flexibility.

Even though current video editing styles rarely leave a b-roll scene in place for more than five to seven seconds before the next shot comes on, working with at least fifteen seconds of a raw clip (twenty seconds is even better) expands your options tremendously. Consider a typical slow dissolve shot that dissolves in from the previous shot for three seconds, is on screen for six seconds, and then dissolves out for another three seconds. That's not a six-second clip; you'll need at least twelve seconds of video to get the flexibility to make the start and finish dissolves work.

Coverage

Although online videos rarely run more than five minutes, that doesn't mean you need only five minutes of b-roll material. It's not unusual for very experienced videographers to shoot raw video at a rate of 10:1 over the final edited version (not including the interview footage), and they'll often shoot even more than that for short videos. In a short video you've got a lot of storytelling to do quickly, and you want the best, most informative b-roll shots you can get. Even the best videographers don't always get the right shot on the first take. Good videographers are always looking for different, better, or more visually interesting viewpoints. In any kind of video storytelling, good b-roll "coverage" is golden, and makes the editor's job enormously easier.

COMPOSING VIDEO SHOTS

The basics of video storytelling are not rocket science: wide shots help establish a sense of place and orient the audience, medium shots bring the subjects closer, and close-ups and extreme close-ups show you the details. These basic shot types are often abbreviated as WS, MS, CU, and ECU in video editing notes. When you enter a new environment to shoot b-roll, always keep these basic storytelling views in mind. How would you explain this place to somebody who had never been here? How would you orient the viewer? What telling visual details would you pick out to give your video interest and narrative texture? Even if you are not the final editor of the story, you must always think like a storyteller when you are out shooting video. One of the oldest and truest sayings in film is "shoot like an editor."

Composing shots for video is not unlike still photography composition, or even older forms of composition for painting. You don't need to go to school for an art degree to learn the compositional basics that underlie almost all videography.

Compositional principles

In most situations an eccentric or off-center composition will look more interesting than a view of the main subject in the middle of the frame. Artists, photographers, and videographers have long used "the rule of thirds" to organize and simplify this principle, and it is remarkable how often the rule instantly improves a composition. Divide the plane into vertical and horizontal thirds, and place your main subject at one of the intersections (fig. 12.8).

Strong diagonal lines add interest and visual power to compositions, as they draw the viewer in and move her attention along the lines. This is particularly true

FIGURE 12.8

If there is a universal "secret" to great compositions in still or video photography, it is the rule of thirds. Try to place the center of your subject at one of the intersections (circles) for a strong, asymmetric composition.

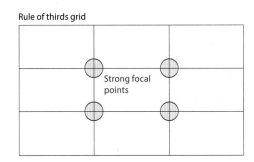

Rule of thirds grid

Strong focal points

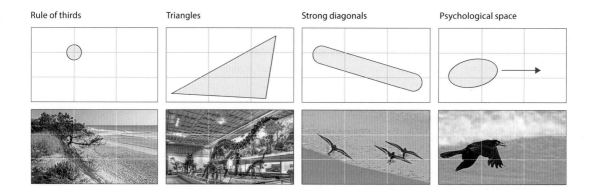

| Rule of thirds | Triangles | Strong diagonals | Psychological space |

FIGURE 12.9

Useful principles of composition.

when the diagonal lines form a triangle within the larger rectangle of the video frame. Psychological space is important when composing for people or any living thing that moves or has eyes. Organize your composition so that the subject is off-center and looking toward the larger space within a composition, not at the nearby frame edge. For moving compositions the subject should be moving into the space within the frame, not seeming to bump into the edges of the frame.

Until you have absorbed these basic rules of composition, try to always use a tripod. The steady viewpoint of a tripod allows you time to carefully consider your compositions. Many video cameras give you the option to show a visual grid in the viewfinder. This is handy for two reasons: the grid reminds you to think about composition and gives you reference lines that help you to keep the horizon level.

VIDEO EDITING

The lightweight video production revolution was not caused solely by small, inexpensive, and high-quality video cameras: nonlinear video editing software has also made it possible to edit sophisticated and polished video productions on most computers. Of course simply buying a copy of Apple's iMovie or Corel's VideoStudio Pro won't instantly make you a talented video editor. But at least now you have a choice that few people had just a decade ago: for less than $100 you can buy more flexible editing capability than $100,000 would have bought you ten years ago.

Video and film editing is a vast subject that will not fit within this chapter, but there are a few basic concepts that will help get you on your way, and some editing conventions that have emerged that are particular to the short online video format.

STRUCTURING THE STORY

Videos of any length are first and foremost stories, about interesting people and experiences. The conventional story arc of introduction, body, and conclusion is fundamental, but within this classic framework there are thousands of ways to tell a story.

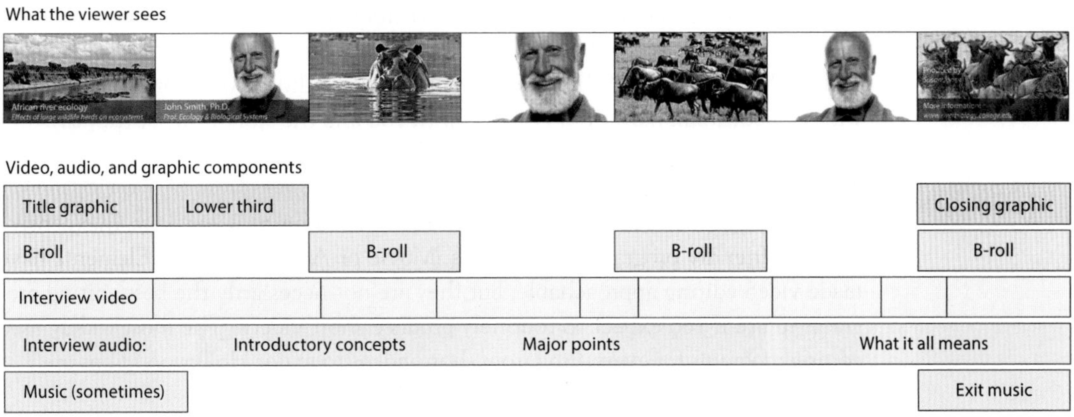

What the viewer sees

Video, audio, and graphic components

Title graphic	Lower third						Closing graphic
B-roll		B-roll		B-roll			B-roll
Interview video							
Interview audio:	Introductory concepts		Major points			What it all means	
Music (sometimes)							Exit music

After doing at least brief research, you could write out a likely script before you do any shooting or interviews, but this is exactly the opposite of the way most producers of short films work. Instead, let the story emerge out of what you see and learn as you engage your subjects, see their work and environment, and listen to them as they speak. This requires some trust and experience with the process of video storytelling, as you launch into each project not knowing exactly where the narrative will flow, and how your original notions of form and story will be bent by what you see and hear along the way.

If this discovery process sounds a bit nebulous and short on planning, it's not; it's simply realistic, and a way to remain open-minded as you gather the elements of your story. Unless you have perfect foresight, you will always be surprised as you progress in gathering the materials for a story. What you get from experience is an eye and an ear for what you need visually and verbally to tell the story, and what footage and interview questions you need. You'll develop an ear for what makes a great introduction, what sections of interview are most informative and on the central story arc. Most of all, you'll develop a gimlet eye for noise and parenthetic material that can be cut away, leaving a strong clear narrative without time-wasting clutter.

The following is a typical short video structure:

- Instant start with interesting or surprising interview audio, with strong b-roll visuals, and a title graphic
- Introduce the speaker with a "lower-third" graphic with name and title
- Set up the story context with some brief background description
- Make the major informational points, ideally no more than three
- Tell what was learned from the experiences ("what it all means")
- Fade out with "further information" web links and the company logo

FIGURE 12.10

The generalized structure of a typical short interview video of three to four minutes. Some videos use music, but most don't.

If you have never made an edited video before, start modestly. Interview interesting friends or colleagues about their work and shoot b-roll that illustrates what they said in the interviews. Whenever possible, stick to those voices and those words, without additional narration. Practice until you find the story in what they say.

EDITING VIDEO

Video editing software has become routine even for home moviemakers. Inexpensive and user-friendly programs like Apple's iMovie or Adobe Premiere Elements have made video editing approachable, but they are not necessarily the best editing programs to use if you expect to routinely produce short videos. The most widely used editing programs for everything from short videos to major Hollywood films are:

- Adobe Premiere Pro CC, www.adobe.com/products/premiere.html
- Apple Final Cut Pro X, www.apple.com/final-cut-pro
- Avid's Media Composer, www.avid.com/US/Solutions/byNeed/video-editing.html

We recommend either Premiere Pro CC or Final Cut Pro X because they are extremely capable at a moderate price. Avid's Media Composer is the most widely used editing software in Hollywood and major television studios, but Avid is considerably more expensive than its competitors, and because of the cost we would not recommend it unless your in-house video department uses Avid already and there are advantages to working with the same editing software.

We recommend the more capable midprice video editors because, for a beginner, it takes just as long to learn the basics of iMovie as it does to learn the basics of Final Cut Pro or Premiere Pro. Video editors who routinely produce short videos quickly begin hitting limitations of "friendly" consumer-level software, and then find themselves needing to learn yet another "pro" editing program to grow the quality and complexity of their editing work.

Time compression techniques

Don't use your favorite movies or television shows as models. In a three-minute video you won't have time for opening credits, lengthy expository beginnings, flying and spinning animated titles, or drawn-out endings and credit crawls. Look at the best short video work and emulate the more relevant aesthetics, graphics, and editing of the online genre.

- Start fast. The viewer should almost instantly start to see and hear interesting content in a short online video. We also begin these "fast-start" videos with a title graphic laid over the initial video, so there is no cinema-like opening sequence, just instant information.

FIGURE 12.11
All the controls and buttons of a professional video program may look intimidating at first, but it doesn't take any longer to learn basic video editing techniques with a "pro" program than it does when starting with "home" editing software like iMovie. If you have a choice, go with the more capable editing software.

- Don't bother with verbal introductions. You'll need to identify your first speaker as soon as you can, but don't bother with time-consuming verbal introductions. Just post a "lower-third" graphic with name and title as soon as you have a chance, and leave the graphic in place for at least ten seconds so viewers have a fair shot at reading it.
- Constantly trim. Assemble your initial interview and b-roll sequences, and then trim, trim, trim. You'll often find that your initial "in" and "out" edit points in both interview and b-roll clips can be trimmed down a lot. Every second counts. In a three-minute video you've got only 180 seconds, so squeeze every clip.
- Keep graphics spare and simple. No shiny animated graphics and lower thirds. In the lightweight-and-short video production world these glossy graphics take too long to produce and just look wrong in the spare aesthetic of the online video world.
- Run your last interview audio right under the final graphics screens. Push content right to the end of the video. Use lower-third graphics to post information over some of the concluding video clips. If you have a company logo screen or "for more information" screen, start posting those conclusion graphics right over your last interview audio or closing music. Squeeze every second, and make each moment do double duty when you can.
- Use video slates to fill in the gaps, or to quickly provide background material instead of using a narrator. In video parlance a "slate" is just a text slide. Sometimes you realize that you are missing some crucial points of information,

or have an awkward segue from one topic to another. Slates are a fast way to convey information or make a transition.

- Be ruthless, and don't fall in love with your first draft. Often you'll find yourself with a five-minute first draft, and further cuts just don't seem possible. Bring in colleagues to review the draft, and to help spot redundancies or off-topic sequences. If you have the time, leave the video overnight and come back to it fresh the next morning. It's surprising how often the new perspective allows you to see opportunities you didn't notice when you were tired and emotionally invested in your first decisions.

Music

You cannot use the pop, jazz, or classical music you listen to on iTunes or Spotify in your videos unless you have a legion of entertainment lawyers, and a lot of money to spend on licensing rights. If you use a popular music clip in your short video, you will probably not be able to post the video on YouTube, Vimeo, or Facebook, all of which automatically review uploaded videos for copyright violations and bounce any video that uses pop tunes in a soundtrack. However, there are inexpensive or even free sources of sound effects and music.

Occasionally you may use a properly licensed stock music piece and still get a copyright violation notice. If you quickly respond with information on the stock music agency and music selection that you have licensed, you can usually resolve the problem quickly and get your video posted.

Be very conservative when you mix background music with narration or interview audio. You should edit your videos wearing headphones, as this gives you the clearest rendition of your audio tracks, but headphones can also give you an artificially clear sense of how your audio tracks mix. When you have done the initial mix of your audio, try unplugging the headphones and listening to your soundtrack through the built-in computer speaker or external computer speakers, just as your audience is likely to do. You may find that what sounds perfect through your headphones sounds murky and distracting through speakers. Often your music mix will be too loud in the first draft, and you'll need to lower the music volume to be sure the spoken words are clear.

Stock images and video

Stock images and video clips can be incredibly useful when you are facing tight deadlines and are short of b-roll, or you don't have the budget to fly to exotic destinations to collect one or two photos to illustrate your narration.

Most stock used in low-budget short online videos is still photography, mostly for practical and economic reasons. Stock photos are much less expensive than stock video clips, and you can easily add (gentle!) panning or zooming motion to a still image with your video-editing program, so the transition from video clips to a still image is less jarring to the flow of your video.

If you are doing short videos on a regular basis, you will quickly accumulate video footage that has obvious potential for multiple future uses. Having a convenient collection of stock footage is invaluable in creating quality programming quickly, and it's the only practical way to get footage that is particular to your subject matter and your organization. If you're doing a "visit our campus" video in January in New England, you are out of luck on "campus beauty" shots unless you have access to stock video or still photography that you shot last May, when the campus looked its best. Stock reels are the easiest kind of videos to make because they are not programs. Just assemble a group of fifteen-to-twenty-second clips of your best b-roll shots, with simple hard cuts in between, in individual videos of about five to six minutes so the stock files don't get too large.

RECOMMENDED READING

Artis, A. *The Shut Up and Shoot Documentary Guide: A Down and Dirty DV Production.* Waltham, MA: Focal, 2007.

——. *The Shut Up and Shoot Freelance Video Guide: A Down and Dirty DV Production.* Waltham, MA: Focal, 2011.

Asher, S. *The Filmmaker's Handbook: A Comprehensive Guide for the Digital Age,* 2013 ed. New York: Plume, 2012.

Bass, W. *Professional Results with Canon Vixia Camcorders: A Field Guide to Canon G10 and XA10.* Boston: Course Technology-Cengage, 2013.

Lynda.com training videos for video and audiovisual software, video production, and many other audiovisual and media subjects. The best, most cost-effective training we know of for digital audiovisual professionals, beginning at $25/month.

Stockman, S. *How to Shoot Video That Doesn't Suck: Advice to Make Any Amateur Look Like a Pro.* New York: Workman, 2011.

Illustration Credits

Adobe, Adobe product screenshot reprinted with permission from Adobe Systems
Incorporated (fig. 12.11)

Adobe. *Digital Video Benchmark*. San Jose, CA: Adobe, 2013, success.adobe.com/en
/na/programs/digital-index/1304-13926-online-video-report.html (fig 12.1, adapted)

A List Apart, www.alistapart.com (fig. 7.21)

Arts and Letters Daily, www.aldaily.com (fig. 4.15)

Brand, S. *How Buildings Learn: What Happens After They're Built*. New York: Viking, 1995
(fig. 3.16, adapted)

Caterpillar, www.cat.com, reprinted courtesy of Caterpillar Inc. (fig. 11.1)

Chartbeat Blog. "Scroll Behavior Across the Web," 2013, blog.chartbeat.com/2013/08/12
/scroll-behavior-across-the-web (fig. 6.17, adapted)

Clearleft, www.clearleft.com (fig. 7.25)

Climate.gov, www.climate.gov (fig. 10.2)

Code for America, www.codeforamerica.org (figs. 6.21, 7.3, 9.5)

Cornell, www.cornell.edu (fig. 7.8)

Drupal, www.drupal.org, licensed under Creative Commons License, Attribution-
ShareAlike 2.0. Drupal is a registered trademark of Dries Buytaert (fig. 4.8, 5.9)

Edible Vineyard, www.ediblevineyard.com (fig. 8.21)

Expedia, www.expedia.com, © 2015 Expedia, Inc., reprinted with permission (fig. 7.24)

Font Awesome, fontawesome.io, Font Awesome by Dave Gandy, fontawesome.io (fig. 11.5)

Garrett, J. J. *The Elements of User Experience: User-Centered Design for the Web*. Indianapolis:
New Riders, 2003 (figs. 1, 3.20, adapted)

Google, www.google.com, Google and the Google logo are registered trademarks of Google
Inc., used with permission (figs. 2.4, 3.15)

Google. "The Importance of Being Seen," 2014, think.storage.googleapis.com/docs/the
-importance-of-being-seen_study.pdf (fig. 6.17, adapted)

Guardian, www.theguardian.com, © Guardian News and Media Ltd., 2015 (figs. 6.17, 6.18,
9.9)

Hay, S. *Responsive Web Design Workflow*. Indianapolis: New Riders, 2013 (fig. 6.9, adapted)

HootSuite, www.hootsuite.com, HootSuite Media, Inc. (fig. 1.9)

Howell, P., and P. Auster. "Phase Shift in an Estuarine Finfish Community Associated with
Warming Temperatures," *Marine and Coastal Fisheries: Dynamics, Management, and
Ecosystem Science*, 4:1, 481–495, 2012 (fig. 11.4, adapted)

IBM, www.ibm.com, reprinted courtesy of International Business Machines Corporation, © International Business Machines Corporation (figs. 6.14, 6.20)

The Internet Archive, httparchive.org/trends.php (fig. 6.15)

King Arthur Flour, www.kingarthurflour.com (figs. 4.13, 7.11)

Kiva, www.kiva.org (fig. 3.17)

Lapham's Quarterly, www.laphamsquarterly.org, the website of the literary magazine *Lapham's Quarterly* for the Fall 2014 issue, "Time." Design and development by Bluecadet (fig. 7.2)

Library of Congress, www.loc.gov (fig. 6.13)

L. L. Bean, www.llbean.com (fig. 7.20)

Louis Rosenfeld, www.rosenfeldmedia.com (figs. 6.8, 7.10)

Lupton, E. *Type on the Screen: A Critical Guide for Designers, Writers, Editors, and Students.* New York: Princeton Architectural Press, 2014 (fig. 9.17, adapted)

MailChimp, www.ux.mailchimp.com/patterns, © MailChimp, 2013 (fig. 8.27)

Massachusetts Institute of Technology, www.mit.edu (fig. 7.15)

McMullen, J. "A Rough Design Maturity Continuum," wsg4.link/rough-maturity (fig. 2, adapted)

Medium, www.medium.com (figs. 9.3, 9.4, 9.18)

Microsoft, www.microsoft.com, permission from Microsoft (fig. 4.3, 8.1)

Morville, P., and L. Rosenfeld. *Information Architecture for the World Wide Web: Designing Large-Scale Web Sites,* 3rd ed. Sebastopol, CA: O'Reilly, 2006 (figs. 4.1, 4.21, adapted)

Müller-Brockmann, J. *Grid Systems in Graphic Design: A Visual Communication Manual for Graphic Designers, Typographers, and Three Dimensional Designers.* Salenstein, Switzerland: Braun, 1996 (fig. 8.24, adapted)

Museum of Modern Art, www.moma.org (fig. 7.22)

National Cancer Institute, www.cancer.gov (fig. 9.2)

National Oceanic and Atmospheric Administration, www.noaa.gov (fig. 1.3)

National Park Service, www.nps.gov, courtesy National Park Service (fig. 8.26)

Nielsen-Norman Group, www.nngroup.com (figs. 4.7, 8.3, adapted)

OmniGraffle, www.omnigroup.com/omnigraffle (fig. 4.23)

Optimal Workshop, www.optimalworkshop.com (fig. 4.6)

O'Reilly, L. "Facebook Video Is Driving YouTube Off Facebook." *Business Insider,* December 9, 2014, www.businessinsider.com/facebook-video-v-youtube-market-share-data-2014-12 (fig. 12.2, adapted)

Sage, www.sagemagazine.org, Yale School of Forestry & Environmental Studies (fig. 8.19)

Schade, A. "The Fold Manifesto: Why the Page Fold Still Matters," 2015, www.nngroup.com/articles/page-fold-manifesto (fig. 6.17, adapted)

Shining Hope for Communities, www.shofco.com (fig. 10.1)

Sims, C., and H. L. Johnson, *The Elements of Scrum* (Foster City, CA: Dymaxicon, 2011) (fig 3.12, adapted)

Sloan, D. "An Accessible Design Maturity Continuum," wsg4.link/mature-access (fig. 2, adapted)

SocialBakers. "Understanding and Increasing Facebook EdgeRank," 2013, www .socialbakers.com/blog/1304-understanding-increasing-facebook-edgerank (fig. 1.7, adapted)

Société des établissements de plein air du Québec (Sépaq), www.sepaq.com (fig. 9.1)

Sonderman, J. "Bitly Data Shows the Best Times to Post Links to Facebook, Twitter and Tumblr," 2012, www.poynter.org/latest-news/mediawire/173308/bitly-data-shows -the-best-times-to-post-links-to-facebook-twitter-and-tumblr (fig. 1.8, adapted)

Standish Group. Standish CHAOS Manifesto, 2013, www.versionone.com/assets/img/files /chaosmanifesto2013.pdf and Standish CHAOS Manifesto, 2011, www.versionone .com/assets/img/files/ChaosManifest_2011.pdf (fig. 3.9, adapted)

Travelocity, www.travelocity.com, © 2015 Travelocity, Inc., reprinted with permission (fig. 2.3)

Twitter, twitter.com (fig. 1.10)

U.S. Department of Agriculture, www.usda.gov (fig. 8.20)

Vimeo, vimeo.com (fig. 12.3)

White House, www.whitehouse.gov (fig. 8.3)

WordPress, wordpress.org, licensed under the GNU General Public License, www.gnu.org /copyleft/gpl.html (figs. 5.11, 9.4)

W3C, www.w3.org/standards/webarch/considerations (fig. 7.9)

Yahoo!, www.yahoo.com, reproduced with permission of Yahoo. © 2015 Yahoo. YAHOO! and the YAHOO! logo are registered trademarks of Yahoo (fig. 7.23)

YaleNews, news.yale.edu (fig. 6.3)

YouTube, www.youtube.com (fig. 12.3)

Index

principles in visual perception,
266–267

uniform connectedness, 267, 320

goal analysis, in user research, 45

golden triangle, in page design, 126–127,
258

Google, 99, 174, 199, 243

Google Analytics, 53, 92, 144

Google Android operating system, 144

Google PageSpeed Insights, 169

Google search, 62, 159

graphic design, 255–283

affective responses to design, 259–260

attractiveness, 257–258

classical page design, 270–271

color and contrast, 265

consistency and, 280

contrast, 268, 271, 275

decision-making and design, 260–262

design logic, 255–257

design patterns, 232–233, 241

design thinking, 38, 44

Profile of a design thinker, 44

eye-tracking, 258–259

Gestalt principles and design,
266–267

gut reactions to design, 259–260

line length and legibility, 264–265

modern page design, 271–272

modular design, 269, 279–280

negative space in design, 274–275

newspapers, 270

objective design, 269

patterns, pattern libraries in web
design, 280–282

reading patterns and design, 268–269

simplicity and focus, 275

strategic value of, xiii

visual hierarchies, 273

visual plane, on current electronic
devices, 262–264

white space and, 274

graphics,

for social media,

Facebook, 30

Twitter, 33, 34

See also images, 325–343

grids, in graphic design, 277–280

960 grid, 278

in web page design, 278

Guardian newspaper, theguardian.com,
185

Gutenberg diagram, also called the
"Gutenberg Z," 195, 271

diagrammed, 269

gut reactions to visual design, 259–260

half-life, of a social media posting, 25

hashtags, 32, 34

Hay, Stephen, 187

`header` (HTML5 element), 175

Hear-Create-Deliver design framework, 38

help instructions, in interface design, 242

hierarchies, in information architecture,
105, 109

home page

design, 201–202, 203–205

home page links, 192

Hootsuite, social media publishing
software, 28, 33, 34

horizon effect, in project management, 83

HTML, hypertext markup language,
135–139

consistent class names in HTML5, 174

document structure in, 137–138

semantic markup, in HTML, 136–137,
174–178

viewports, web display, 173, 193

Vignelli, Massimo, graphic designer, 277, 279

Vihn, Khoi, web designer, on web page grids, 278

Vimeo web site, 23, 345

visceral reaction to design, 260–261

Visio, graphics software, 48, 130

visual
    branding, in social media, 23
    hierarchy, in page design, 269, 272
    plane, in graphic design, 262
    scanning, 272
    structure, of pages and displays, 268

voice and tone (of content style), 19
    in social media, 23

WAI-ARIA (Accessible Rich Internet Applications), 190–191, 237, 241

Wall Street Journal, web site, 199

Walmart, research on page file sizes, 197–198

waterfall project management method, 73, 74, 76, 89
    hybrid waterfall/agile project management, 84

wayfinding, 214–215, 224–225, 229–230
    See also navigation

web
    analytics, 51–53, 92
    applications, 144
    browsers
        usage statistics for, 180
        variation in, 143–144
    hosting, 67
    metrics (analytics), 51–53, 92
    pages
        accessibility for, 180
        source code order, 180

servers, 67
    web development team, 56, 64

Web Accessibility Initiative, 11

Web Content Accessibility Guidelines (WCAG) 2.0, 51, 66–67, 235–236

Welchman, Lisa, 6
    Managing Chaos book, 6

White, E. B., author, "A list of reminders," 26

white space, and design, 274

wireframes, 48, 91, 128, 130–133
    in information architecture, 130–133
    page, 59
    in user research, 48

WordPress content management software, 132–133, 145
    content management, 147, 150–153
    HTML5, 178
    and style sheets, 141
    typography editing in, 291
    Ultimate CMS plugin, 153
    White Label CMS plugin, 153

World Wide Web Consortium (W3C), 11, 173

Wroblewski, Luke, 187

XHTML, 138, 173

XML, for search engine site maps, 170–171

xSort, software for card sorting, 115–116

Yale University, multiple social media accounts, 23

YouTube, 23, 345, 348

Zipf distribution, 98, 160